T0074745

Cybersecurity and High-Performance Computing Environments

Cybersecurity and High-Performance Computing Environments

Integrated Innovations, Practices, and Applications

Edited by
Kuan-Ching Li
Nitin Sukhija
Elizabeth Bautista
Jean-Luc Gaudiot

CRC Press
Taylor & Francis Group
Boca Raton London New York

CRC Press is an imprint of the
Taylor & Francis Group, an **informa** business

A CHAPMAN & HALL BOOK

First Edition published 2022
by CRC Press
6000 Broken Sound Parkway NW, Suite 300, Boca Raton, FL 33487-2742

and by CRC Press
4 Park Square, Milton Park, Abingdon, Oxon, OX14 4RN

CRC Press is an imprint of Taylor & Francis Group, LLC

Library of Congress Cataloging-in-Publication Data
Names: Li, Kuan-Ching, editor. | Sukhija, Nitin, editor. |
Bautista, Elizabeth (Computer scientist), editor. | Gaudiot, Jean-Luc, editor.
Title: Cybersecurity and high-performance computing environments :
integrated innovations, practices, and applications / edited by
Kuan-Ching Li, Nitin Sukhija, Elizabeth Bautista, Jean-Luc Gaudiot.
Description: First edition. | Boca Raton, FL : CRC Press, 2022. |
Includes bibliographical references and index.
Identifiers: LCCN 2021049599 | ISBN 9780367711504 (hbk) |
ISBN 9780367740368 (pbk) | ISBN 9781003155799 (ebk)
Subjects: LCSH: High performance computing. | Computer security–Data
processing. | High performance computing–Security measures.
Classification: LCC QA76.88 .C93 2022 | DDC 004.1/1–dc23/eng/20211213
LC record available at https://lccn.loc.gov/2021049599

ISBN: 978-0-367-71150-4 (hbk)
ISBN: 978-0-367-74036-8 (pbk)
ISBN: 978-1-003-15579-9 (ebk)

DOI: 10.1201/9781003155799

Typeset in Minion
by codeMantra

Contents

Preface

In this fast-paced global economy, academia and industry must innovate to evolve and succeed. Today's researchers and industry experts are seeking transformative technologies to meet the challenges of tomorrow. The cutting-edge technological advances in cybersecurity solutions aid in enabling the security of complex heterogeneous high-performance computing environments. On the other hand, high-performance computing power facilitates powerful and intelligent innovative models for reducing time to response to identify and resolve a multitude of potential, newly emerging cyberattacks.

This book provides a collection of the current and emergent research innovations, practices, and applications focusing on the interdependence of cybersecurity and high-performance computing domains for discovering and resolving new emerging cyber-threats.

In the following, we will describe the chapters contained in the book.

Chapter 1, "Cybersecurity and High-Performance Computing Ecosystems: Opportunities and Challenges," by Sukhija et al., focuses on effective cybersecurity solutions to protect current and emergent high-performance computing (HPC) ecosystems comprising users, data, infrastructure, and applications supporting scientific research. Although, as we move toward the exascale future and beyond, the emerging superfacility frameworks are combining the experimental and observational facilities with high-performance computing centers, the new convergent computing platforms, along with a paradigm shift in programming applications leveraging these platforms, increasingly open the HPC ecosystems to a myriad of security risks. Intending to reduce the downtime of HPC ecosystems in the presence of unpredictable loads and malicious attacks, this chapter covers cybersecurity challenges and solutions, which, when combined effectively, will aid in proactively rearchitecting the current and emergent HPC ecosystems comprising users, data, infrastructure, and applications to delay or counteract the scale of malicious attacks and to reduce their impacts and consequences.

Chapter 2, "Approaches to Working with Large-Scale Graphs for CyberSecurity Applications," by Hawrylak et al., covers the graph techniques useful for compliance violation and cybersecurity attack prediction in the lens of high-performance computing. Graphs are a standard tool in cybersecurity evaluation and analytics. First, the authors discuss the attack graphs and dependency graphs, which are two common approaches in cybersecurity where the analysis of the attack and dependency graphs describes the system's security posture, including the system's attack surface. Next, the authors explain the potential attack scenarios that can be extracted from attack graphs. This chapter concludes with a survey of techniques useful for handling large-scale graphs, methodologies, and strategies for increasing the performance and ends with insights into future needs and directions in this area.

Chapter 3, "OMNI at the Edge," by Bautista et al., discusses the high-availability Operations Monitoring and Notification Infrastructure (OMNI) hosted at the Department of Energy's (DOE) National Energy Research Scientific Computing Center (NERSC) and its use of the state-of-the-art edge computing technologies for collecting, analyzing, and securing extremely high-volume, continuous 24×7 data in near-real-time. The authors then detail how data security is achieved not only from each staff who owns the data, but also through various devices and networks. Then, the chapter highlights the internal and external access policies and the plan to make these data available to the public for crowdsourcing analysis. Furthermore, the authors provide use cases that demonstrate how the availability of OMNI data has benefited the overall NERSC data center from facilities & machine perspective as well as from a cybersecurity standpoint. Finally, an outline of ongoing and future work is given, including upgrades being made to the data warehouse for the upcoming Perlmutter supercomputer – a system that will be 3–$4\times$ the size of ours.

Chapter 4, "Optimized Voronoi-Based Algorithms for Parallel Shortest Vector Computation," by Gabriel Falcão et al., addresses Voronoi cell-based algorithms, solving the shortest vector problem, a fundamental challenge in lattice-based cryptanalysis. First, the chapter introduces several optimizations based on pruning to reduce the original algorithm's execution time. Then, the authors illustrate the algorithm's suitability for parallel execution on both CPUs and GPUs, where speeds up to $69\times$ are observed. The authors then demonstrate using a pre-process sorting step, which requires storing the norm ordered target vectors and significantly more memory, where speedup increases to 77×. Finally, the chapter concludes by optimizing the algorithm that exhibits linear scalability on a CPU with up to 28 threads and keeps scaling, at a lower rate, with simultaneous multithreading up to 56 threads.

Chapter 5, "Attribute-Based Secure Keyword Search for Cloud Computing," by Hui Yin et al., presents the attribute-based keyword search (ABKS) that provides the feasibility to simultaneously achieve data searching and fine-grained access control over encrypted data, which is applied to the cloud computing environment characterized by data storage and sharing. In this chapter, the authors first introduce the fundamental techniques for achieving the ABKS scheme, such as the necessary components used in the attributed-based encryption. Then, by several existing ABKS schemes, the authors describe how to design a practical and efficient ABKS construction in the cloud computing environment. Further, the authors show some interesting experimental results to explain the key factors affecting the search complexity in ABKS schemes and present some ideas to design an efficient and high-performance ABKS scheme.

Chapter 6, "Understanding Cybersecurity Risk in FMI Using HPC," by Gurdip Kaur et al., examines the importance of the financial market infrastructure and elaborates its essential components used to handle financial transactions and their security. The chapter explores high-performance computing (HPC) and its integration to FMIs to transform the financial industry by speeding up financial activities in the business and reducing fraudulent transactions. Moreover, the authors provide a descriptive and visual mapping of financial risks with identified cybersecurity issues. The chapter concludes by detailing the cybersecurity risks faced by FMIs with comprehensive details on risk assessment, analysis, monitoring, reporting, and mitigation.

Chapter 7, "Live Migration in HPC," by Anil Kumar Gupta et al., presents the basics of live migration and its needs, applications, security aspects, and role in HPC (high-performance computing) and then proceeds with discussing two of the live migration approaches – live virtual machine (VM) migration and live container migration. Next, the authors discuss the challenges in this approach and then review the security aspects. The authors detail the second approach, live container migration, followed by understanding the performance measures and issues and comparative analysis of the two methods.

Moreover, the authors cover two case studies, checkpointing and restoring in "CRIU" and "OpenVZ" for container live migration. Finally, the authors compare live migration in virtual machines with live container migration concerning various attributes such as performance, challenges, and security. The chapter underlines the role of live migration in high-performance computing, discusses security breaches and possible threats, and concludes by suggesting various approaches to overcoming the same.

Chapter 8, "Security-Aware Real-Time Transmission for Automotive CAN-FD Networks," by Ruiqi Lu et al., covers high-performance embedded computing systems that are widely used in intelligent vehicles, providing the possibility of secure and real-time communication for automotive networks. The chapter first provides the preliminaries of automotive CAN-FD networks, including the differences between CAN-FD and CAN, their security vulnerabilities, and the corresponding classification of cyberattacks. Then, security-aware real-time CAN-FD transmission methods are summarized based on the three elements of security, such as confidentiality-aware real-time transmission, integrity-aware real-time transmission, and availability-aware real-time transmission. Finally, this chapter discusses the future trends of security-aware real-time CAN-FD transmission methods, including intrusion detection accuracy and response time, attack analysis and cybersecurity evaluation, and security-aware methods and resource consumption.

Chapter 9, "OntoEnricher: A Deep Learning Approach for Ontology Enrichment from Unstructured Text," by Lalit Mohan S. et al., introduces the need for sequential deep learning architectures that traverse through dependency paths in text and extract embedded vulnerabilities, threats, controls, products, and other security-related concepts and instances from learned path representations. The authors then detail the proposed approach, OntoEnricher, a supervised sequential deep learning model that factors context from grammatical and linguistic information encoded in the dependency paths of a sentence and then utilizes sequential neural networks, such as bidirectional long short-term memory (LSTM), to traverse (forward and backward directions) dependency paths and learn relevant path representations that constitute relations. Then the authors explain the implementation of the proposed OntoEnricher, where the bidirectional LSTMs are trained on a large DBpedia dataset and Wikipedia corpus of 2.8 GB along with Universal Sentence Encoder, which is deployed to enrich ISO 2700-based information security ontology. The chapter then describes training the model and testing a high-performance computing (HPC) environment to handle Wiki text dimensionality. Finally, the chapter concludes by detailing the experimental results and the test accuracy of the approach when tested with knocked-out concepts from ontology and web page instances to validate the robustness.

Chapter 10, "Intelligent Connected Vehicles," by Wufei Wu et al., presents the characteristics of intelligent connected vehicles and current in-vehicle network architecture. The authors start by showing the attack model and vulnerabilities of the existing in-vehicle network (IVN). Then the state-of-the-art countermeasures of cybersecurity enhancement for IVNs are introduced. Finally, at the end of the chapter, a discussion is given based on next-generation in-vehicle network architecture with security mechanisms and future research directions.

Chapter 11, "Toward Robust Deep Learning Systems against Deepfake for Digital Forensics," by Hongmei Chi and Mingming Peng, investigates the interactions between the development of deepfake techniques and detection of them in digital forensics. The authors first describe the structure and the associated software pertinent to the generative adversarial network (GAN) algorithms. The authors then discuss how to train fairness in deep learning (DL) algorithms to identify the typical features of all the popular GAN algorithms and how smartphones app can help in deepfake detection. Finally, the chapter concludes by detailing an innovative application tool that any digital professional can learn to adopt techniques to detect deepfake development.

Chapter 12, "Monitoring HPC Systems against Compromised SSH," by Lev Lafayette, focuses on compromising Secure Shell, which is a very well-established and well-developed cryptographic network protocol and a suite of utilities in the world of high-performance computing. The chapter starts with the description of the security breach in European HPC centers in 2020 that led the authors to exploring the possibilities of how to engage in policies, user education, and developing monitoring systems to protect against a similar instance in their environment with the knowledge that is transferable to others. Next, the authors detail a two-stage approach adopted by the HPC team at the University of Melbourne for dealing with the potential of compromised SSH keys, consisting of policy-based user education and monitoring. Finally, the chapter concludes by discussing the possibility for further and broader use of key-based SSH for enhanced security.

Overall, this book represents a substantial research contribution to the state-of-the-art solutions for addressing the threats to confidentiality, integrity, and availability (CIA triad) in high-performance computing (HPC) environments. Moreover, in addition to focusing on securing HPC environments, this book covers the groundbreaking and emergent solutions that utilize the power of the HPC environments to study and understand the emergent, multifaceted, anomalous, and malicious characteristics. As a result, the editors are confident that this book will help university students, researchers, and professionals understand how high-performance computing research fits broader cybersecurity objectives and vice versa.

Editors

Kuan-Ching Li is a Distinguished Professor in the Department of Computer Science and Information Engineering at Providence University, Taiwan, where he also serves as the Director of the High-Performance Computing and Networking Center. He has published more than 320 scientific papers and articles and is a co-author or co-editor of more than 30 books published by leading publishers. In addition, he is the Editor-in-Chief of *Connection Science* (Taylor & Francis) and serves as an associate editor for several leading journals, and is also actively involved in various capacities in the organization of several national and international conferences in several countries. He is a Fellow of IET and a Senior Member of the IEEE. Professor Li's research interests include parallel and distributed computing, big data, and emerging technologies.

Nitin Sukhija is an associate professor in the Department of Computer Science and the Director of Center for Cybersecurity and Advanced Computing (C2AC) at SRU. He received his doctorate in Computer Science from Mississippi State University majoring in High Performance Computing in 2015. His areas of expertise are high-performance computing, dynamic load balancing, performance modeling, prediction and evaluation, robustness and resilience analysis, cybersecurity, and big data analytics. Dr. Sukhija received his MBA degree in Information Systems from San Diego State University (2009) and MS degree in Computer Science majoring in Computing from National University, San Diego (2010). Dr. Sukhija has been involved in the research and management of various projects pertaining to the HPC and cybersecurity challenges in industry and academia for over two decades. Dr. Sukhija's research is recognized by publications in high-impact peer-reviewed IEEE and ACM conferences, journals, and book chapters. Dr. Sukhija is a recipient of research, career awards and fellowships. He is currently serving as an organizing committee member and reviewer for many esteemed conferences. He is currently serving as the co-chair for the ACM SIGHPC Education Chapter workshop committee and has been active in the planning and participation in Workshops series at the SC, ISC, and other conferences.

Elizabeth Bautista is the manager for the Operations Technology Group (OTG) at Lawrence Berkeley National Lab's National Energy Research Scientific Computing (NERSC) Center (http://www.nersc. gov). The group of Site Reliability Engineers ensures 24×7 accessibility, reliability, and security of NERSC's high-performance systems, data storage systems, and the facility environment. Bautista's Data Team manages a 125 TB Elastic/VictoriaMetrics-based data warehouse infrastructure that collects at a rate of 25,000–400,000 data points/second depending on the source. The types of datasets range from the facility environment (power, temperature, and humidity) to storage I/O to system logs of the HPC systems and support services. The analysis of the real-time data provides alerts to manage the facility, and the archived data are correlated to provide business decisions and future trends. Bautista supports programs that seek to involve minorities and women in STEM and advocates that the next generation of professionals has practical hands-on training as part of their education. In her career, she has served as a member of the Lab's Computing Science Diversity Group, is a member of Women Scientists and Engineers, was a delegate in the Council of University of California Staff Assemblies (CUCSA), a staff advocate group, she champions issues of retention and diversity, and is the founder of Filipinas in Computing, a community in the Grace Hopper Conference. Bautista was named one of the 100 most influential Filipina Women Globally in 2015. She has a BS in Computer Information Systems and an MBA. in Technical Management, both from Golden Gate University.

Jean-Luc Gaudiot received the Diplôme d'Ingénieur from the École Supérieure d'Ingénieurs en Electronique et Electrotechnique, Paris, France, in 1976, and the M.S. and Ph.D. degrees in Computer Science from UCLA in 1977 and 1982, respectively. He is currently a Distinguished Professor in the Department of Electrical Engineering and Computer Science at UC Irvine. Prior to joining UCI in 2002, he was Professor of Electrical Engineering at the University of Southern California since 1982. His research interests include multithreaded architectures, fault-tolerant multiprocessors, and the implementation of reconfigurable architectures. He has published over 250 journal and conference papers. His research has been sponsored by NSF, DoE, and DARPA, as well as a number of industrial companies. He has served the community in various positions and was the President of the IEEE Computer Society in 2017.

Contributors

Filipe Cabeleira
Department of Electrical and
  Computer Engineering
University of Coimbra & Instituto de
  Telecomunicações
Coimbra, Portugal

Kunj Champaneri
Department of Computer Science
Slippery Rock University of
  Pennsylvania
Slippery Rock, Pennsylvania

Hongmei Chi
Florida A&M University
Tallahassee, Florida

Narendra Chinnam
University of Melbourne
Melbourne, Australia

Thomas Davis
National Energy Research Scientific
  Computing Center
Lawrence Berkeley National
  Laboratory
Berkeley, California

Gabriel Falcão
Department of Electrical and
  Computer Engineering
University of Coimbra & Instituto de
  Telecomunicações
Coimbra, Portugal

Anil Kumar Gupta
Centre for Development of Advanced
  Computing (CDAC)
Pune, India

John Hale
Tandy School of Computer Science
The University of Tulsa
Tulsa, USA

Peter J. Hawrylak
Tandy School of Computer Science
The University of Tulsa
Tulsa, USA

Vivek Iyer
Software Engineering Research
  Centre
IIIT Hyderabad
Hyderabad, India

Junqiang Jiang
School of Information Science and
  Engineering
Hunan Institute of Science and
  Technology
Yueyang, China

Gurdip Kaur
Canadian Institute for Cybersecurity
  (CIC)
University of New Brunswick (UNB)
Fredericton, Canada

Ryo Kurachi
Graduate School of Informatics
Nagoya University
Nagoya, Japan

Lev Lafayette
University of Melbourne
Melbourne, Australia

Arash Habibi Lashkari
Canadian Institute for Cybersecurity
(CIC)
University of New Brunswick (UNB)
Fredericton, Canada

Ziba Habibi Lashkari
School of Computer Engineering
Universidad Politécnica de Madrid
Madrid, Spain

Fangmin Li
College of Computer Engineering
and Applied Mathematics
Changsha University
Changsha, China

Keqin Li
Department of Computer Science
State University of New York
New York, USA

Ming Li
Tandy School of Computer Science
The University of Tulsa
Tulsa, USA

Renfa Li
College of Computer Science and
Electronic Engineering
Hunan University
Changsha, China

Ruiqi Lu
College of Computer Science and
Electronic Engineering
Hunan University
Changsha, China

Artur Mariano
Department of Informatics
INESC TEC & Universidade do
Minho
Braga, Portugal

Aditi Pandey
MIT Academy of Engineering
Pune, India

Kaustubh Patil
MIT Academy of Engineering
Pune, India

Mingming Peng
Florida A&M University
Tallahassee, Florida

Y. Raghu Reddy
Software Engineering Research
Centre
IIIT Hyderabad
Hyderabad, India

Timothy Rice
University of Melbourne
Melbourne, Australia

Melissa Romanus
National Energy Research Scientific
Computing Center
Lawrence Berkeley National
Laboratory
Berkeley, California

Lalit Mohan Sanagavarapu
Software Engineering Research
    Centre
IIIT Hyderabad
Hyderabad, India

Luís Paulo Santos
Department of Informatics
INESC TEC & Universidade do
    Minho
Braga, Portugal

Noah L. Schrick
Tandy School of Computer Science
The University of Tulsa
Tulsa, USA

Amarjeet Sharma
Centre for Development of Advanced
    Computing (CDAC)
Pune, India

Sanskar Sharma
MIT Academy of Engineering
Pune, India

Hiroaki Takada
Graduate School of Informatics
Nagoya University
Nagoya, Japan

Yuhao Wang
School of Information Engineering
Nanchang University
Nanchang, China

Cary Whitney
National Energy Research Scientific
    Computing Center
Lawrence Berkeley National
    Laboratory
Berkeley, California

Wufei Wu
School of Information Engineering
Nanchang University
Nanchang, China

Guoqi Xie
College of Computer Science and
    Electronic Engineering
Hunan University
Changsha, China

Hui Yin
College of Computer Engineering
    and Applied Mathematics
Changsha University
Changsha, China

Gang Zeng
Graduate School of Engineering
Nagoya University
Nagoya, Japan

Yu Zhang
College of Computer Engineering
    and Applied Mathematics
Changsha University
Changsha, China

Cybersecurity and High-Performance Computing Ecosystems

Opportunities and Challenges

Nitin Sukhija

Slippery Rock University of Pennsylvania

Elizabeth Bautista

Lawrence Berkeley National Laboratory

Kunj Champaneri

Slippery Rock University of Pennsylvania

CONTENTS

DOI: 10.1201/9781003155799-1

1.1 INTRODUCTION

Today, high-performance computing (HPC) ecosystems have become central in bolstering research and innovation in diverse domains and in reinforcing world economies on the competitive international arena. In the past decade, the rapid proliferation of processing technologies for HPC has facilitated the convergence of artificial intelligence, machine learning, data analytics, big data and the HPC domain platforms to solve complex computationally intensive and data-intensive applications in various scientific and non-scientific fields. The technologies combined with the workforce facilitating complex computational competences formulate an HPC ecosystem [1].

The complex infrastructure comprising increasingly evolving and highly unpredictable heterogeneous computing systems (currently operating at petaflop capacity and planned for exaflop performance by year 2021) forms the most important and fundamental component of the HPC ecosystem [2]. The main challenge here is not only to acquire these high-end computing infrastructures, but also to retain the cutting edge by continuously updating the existing infrastructures with newer hardware and software to realize the increasing needs of solving complex problems in diverse disciplines. The applications representing simulations of complex systems behavior or software enabling system operations are another key component of HPC ecosystem [3]. Scientists, researchers and users are interested in scientific fidelity, in insight analyses and in visualizations of the simulations of the implementation of various numerical models corresponding to numerous complex phenomena pertaining to various scientific fields. Another important element of the HPC ecosystem is data. With information growth exceeding Moore's law, the traditional data processing applications and platforms are inadequate to handle the increasing amounts of generated data. The data storage, curation, sharing, analysis, visualization and privacy along with scalability of computing performance are some of the significant challenges witnessed in the era of big data. Lastly, the workforce highly trained and experienced in HPC skills is the crucial part of the HPC ecosystem [4]. As we move toward exascale future and beyond, the emerging superfacility frameworks combining the experimental and observational facilities with HPC centers, and the new convergent computing platforms along with a paradigm shift in programming applications leveraging these platforms increasingly open the HPC ecosystems to a myriad of security risks [5].

This book chapter covers significant cybersecurity solutions for protecting the current and emergent HPC ecosystems comprising users, data, infrastructure and applications supporting scientific research.

1.2   THE VITAL IMPORTANCE OF SECURING HIGH-PERFORMANCE COMPUTING (HPC) ECOSYSTEMS

As high-performance computing (HPC) ecosystems have evolved to become more and more powerful, so has their potential to do harm. Couple the advancement in cyberinfrastructures with the increasing number of domains in which HPC systems are used in that involve sensitive data and you have a recipe for disaster if one of these systems is compromised [6]. So not only would an attacker be able to harness the computational power of the machines to perform malicious activities, but also be able to have access to potentially confidential data. In today's age, data mean power, and so even non-confidential could hold some value to an attacker. Researchers working on a compromised system could have their research stolen or tampered with, causing them to lose potentially years worth of work. It is therefore imperative that HPC systems, and the application code running on them, be built with security in mind. Security is an oft overlooked component of building scientific code for a variety of reasons [7]. Many researchers simply do not have awareness of the potential risks of building an insecure system or assume that the system they are using is secure enough and they therefore do not need to worry about securing their applications. Other times, security is ignored for the sake of speed or convenience, since baking in security to their application code introduces some amount of overhead and requires extra planning and code [8]. None of these are valid reasons in today's world; threats are everywhere, and HPC systems are a major target of bad actors. There needs to be a continuing focus on training researchers in providing security measures within their application code, rather than depending upon infrastructure security.

One such thing HPC users have to be aware of when building their applications is communication within the cluster with respect to their application, and communication with the outside world. Generally, users have access to unprivileged ports on the system, to do things like interacting with streaming data that may be on an outside network. If an application does not ensure that these communications are secure and encrypted, it opens the door to attacks. Such attacks on HPC applications and computing systems could not only damage the system and application performance, but also lead to the damage in the reputation of the resource and the reputation of the security providers or data centers, which could lead to financial and more productivity losses in the long run [9]. The attacks can lead to the leakage of data from a HPC system or from user account to another, which could be devastating as it contains a lot of sensitive scientific data and results. Moreover, attacks such as distributed denial-of-service (DDoS) attacks [10] send out a large volume of packets, which if successfully delivered could make the HPC systems unavailable and impact the performance of the entire network. It could take down the system until the attack is completed, which could disrupt all the jobs executing on the computing systems [11]. Improper access control or some other security failure may allow some users to gain undesired access to sensitive information or give them the ability to execute or alter someone's code, which could lead to loss of information or a full system shutdown. Having access to sensitive data could also lead to gaining access to different systems using social engineering techniques or leakage of protected data [12]. There exist many mechanisms to avoid data leaks. One mechanism to avoid the leaks in sensitive data is DLP (data loss prevention/data leakage prevention) that aids in checking and controlling the flow of sensitive data and in reporting the leakage when detected. Moreover, more stringent access controls employing the use of encryption and decryption for data transfer and storage can be deployed in addition to other security mechanisms [13].

One of the recent data breaches was encountered by Facebook, where the personal data of 533 million Facebook users were compromised due to a bug in Facebook systems [14,15]. Moreover, recently attackers have been successful in attacking many supercomputing facilities, which include ARCHER, TAURUS and Hawk, due to which the attacked facilities went off-line [16]. One of the factors leading to the attack was compromised credentials, such as username and passwords for accessing these resources. Many attackers try to acquire sensitive information such as username and passwords of the employees working at these facilities through social engineering as around two-third of people use the same password across multiple accounts. One other type of attack that is becoming more common during COVID-19 pandemic is the ransomware attacks, which are mainly carried out by a phishing attack in the form of an e-mail with a malicious attachment [17]. Once the user/staff of the HPC facility clicks on the attachment, it allows the ransomware to execute on the user's system or user's network. Once the ransomware is in the network or in the system, it might attack the main database files (MDF), secondary database files (NDF), transaction log files (LDF) and the backup files (BAK and TRN). This would lead the data servers toward an inoperable state because the SQL server service cannot open the master.mdf files.

Due to the increase in the cryptocurrency prices, adversaries are attacking HPC systems and trying to compromise the systems in order to gain remote access and use machines' resources and processing power to perform cryptomining [18]. Once the attackers gain access, they perform malicious cryptomining by installing software, also known as cryptojacking, in which they use the system's resources to mine for cryptocurrency or steal from crypto wallets. Many national laboratories have also been working on mechanisms to defend their HPC systems against misuse of computing cycles for cryptomining [19]. The Idaho National Laboratory have designed and implemented a machine translation-based cryptocurrency mining malware detector, which uses deep learning mechanism to accurately analyze and detect such malicious mining activities [20].

With the emergence in the complexity of the HPC ecosystems, there is a need for researching, developing, analyzing, adapting and integrating cutting-edge cybersecurity solutions, thus enabling security, privacy and performance of applications and workflows executing in HPC ecosystems.

1.3 SECURITY FOR SUPERCOMPUTING INFRASTRUCTURE

The HPC ecosystem is a complex network of interconnected systems. Supercomputing systems promising to deliver exascale computing performance formulate the central pillar of the HPC ecosystem. The HPC ecosystem comprises of various supercomputers with different tiers of computing power, and each of the tiers is designed and modified based on the complexity and type of applications that will be executed on these supercomputers. For so many years, the performance efficiency and effectiveness of supercomputers have been some of the most important aspects studied and researched for a supercomputer. However, recently, with increases in malicious actors, the robustness and security of the supercomputers against the unintended events and targeted attack has become an extremely important aspect. Supercomputing infrastructures are considered critical infrastructures as they have a direct impact on research and an indirect impact on the economy if they are compromised. In May 2020, when most of the supercomputers in the Europe were expected to execute the HPC workloads that gave us a hope in finding a cure in the fight against the Coronavirus (COVID-19) research and other important researches, the computing systems were forced to shut down in order to investigate a cryptocurrency mining hack on them [16], thus necessitating the vital role of security in supercomputing environments. The following sections investigate some of the in-built security features provided by HPC vendors such as Cray and Intel, which help the computing systems to defend themselves from security attacks.

1.3.1 Software Security

Most of the modern supercomputers in the TOP500 list use Linux operating system, given its open-source system and high customizability. Each vendor that manufactures its own supercomputers has made its own specific changes to the Linux derivative they employ with no industry standards in place as each hardware design requires changes to optimize the operating system due to differences in hardware architectures [21]. The Linux open-source operating system accounts for the largest share of the supercomputer's operating systems. Due to the increased demand for supercomputers, the Linux operating system capabilities and vulnerabilities are on sharp increase. In year 2018, Red Hat, Inc. products reported more vulnerabilities than the Microsoft products [22]. In 2020, the Red Hat Enterprise Linux (RHEL) became the operating system backbone of the four world's top 10 fastest supercomputers and of top three supercomputers [23,24]. Some of the built-in security capabilities enabled by RHEL are as follows [25]:

1. Security-Enhanced Linux (SELinux): a Linux kernel security module comprising a set of kernel modifications and user

space tools supporting access control security policies, such as mandatory access control (MAC). The MAC controls enable the confinement of user programs and system services and lead to the privilege limitations, thus aiding in reducing or eliminating the ability of these programs and daemons to be compromised in case of security breach.

2. System Security Services Daemon (SSSD): implements a set of services for central management of identity and authentication and allows users to still identify when there is interruption in connecting with the server.

3. Backup Passphrases for Encrypted Storage Devices: aids in avoiding unauthorized access of data by encrypting the data on the storage devices.

4. SVirt: improves hypervisor security by controlled sharing and virtual machine isolation and thus aids in preventing unauthorized access in a virtualized environment.

5. Enterprise Security Client (ESC): provides management of smart cards by facilitating connections between users (and their tokens), the Token Processing System and certificate authority. The smart cards or security tokens store user certificates that are employed by the client authentication and single sign-on access applications [26].

1.3.2 Hardware Security

Hardware security is a vital part in fully securing your HPC environment. Like software, there are several hardware attacks that need to be defended to maintain the full efficiency of the system. As each vendor that manufactures its own supercomputer has made its own specific changes in terms of the software they use, it's the same in terms of hardware. We'll take example of two of the top known vendors manufacturing supercomputers, which are CRAY and IBM, and discuss some of their in-built hardware security features [27]. Cray uses Intel Xeon Processors that have the following built-in security features:

1. Intel Trusted Execution Technology: a set of hardware-based extensions that enable the security capabilities such as protection

environment aiding in the execution of applications with their own space shielding data and processes.

2. Intel Run Sure Technology: a resilient technology that encompasses processor, firmware and software layers to facilitate detection and recovery in state of faults with minimum interruption, thus maximizing resiliency and uptime of servers, especially while executing mission-critical workloads.

3. Mode-Based Execution Control (MBE): enables reliable verification and integrity of kernel-level code by the hypervisor and thus acts as a mechanism for shielding against malware attacks in a virtualized environment [28].

Some of the other Intel security features also include: Integrated Cray Hardware Supervisory System (HSS) and full ECC protection of all packet traffic in the Aries network. In comparison, IBM uses POWER9 processors that are designed to facilitate defense-in-depth security approach and provide layers of security protection, including hardware security, firmware security, hypervisor security and operating system security [29]. Moreover, POWER9 systems also employ a suite of cybersecurity tools for IBM Power Systems, IBM PowerSC. The POWER9 systems enable two key security features: Secure Boot and Trusted Boot, which aid in ensuring the integrity of server and in mitigating the boot code cyberattack: 1) Secure Boot, also known as Verified Boot, checks the integrity of OS kernels and performance verification and halts the boot in the event of validation failure. There are a series of kernel verification keys which are provided by the OS provider so that the system administrator can check the kernel against the original kernel signature. This helps in preventing unvetted kernels or modified kernel images from booting. 2) Trusted Boot creates a cryptographic hash of a kernel image that encompasses the recording of executable code as the system boots and thus can be used to retrieve the recordings via remote attestation and to aid in the assessment and verification of firmware and target operating system [30].

In addition to in-built hardware and software security for HPC infrastructures, there have been extensive efforts in the development of defensive technologies, such as smarter intrusion detection devices, and sensors to achieve robustness and security against the unintended events and targeted attacks. The research in the domain of intrusion detection and identification is significant, while the research in intrusion response system is still progressing. For example, the multi-agent intrusion detection system (MAIDS) utilizes colored Petri nets and comprises three components: (1) data collection agents for gathering and converting logs and system events data; (2) agents for monitoring and classifying real-time system events; and (3) the machine learning agents for providing predictive rules that are learned by processing data from logs and system events. Herein, the machine learning agents enable adjusting the underlying Petri nets to reflect the evolution of the system [31,32].

Many different cybersecurity applications also employ hidden Markov chains. A model for detecting brute-force SSH attacks by analyzing network flow data was implemented and developed by Sperotto et al. [33]. Herein, the developed model illustrated how hidden Markov chains could be utilized to model the network flow and be integrated with an intrusion detection system (IDS).

The Zeek, formerly known as Bro, is an open-source software framework and one of the most popular network intrusion detection systems (IDSs). Zeek utilizes passive monitoring of the network links where the intruder's traffic transits to detect network intruders in real time, thus aiding in detecting behavioral anomalies for achieving cybersecurity. Zeek IDS performs two tasks for real-time network traffic analysis: (1) converting network data into high-level events and (2) utilizing a script interpreter which is a programming language that interacts with the high-level events and aids in the translation of events in terms of network security [34]. Snort is a traditional open-source intrusion detection/prevention tool for performing real-time network analysis of the system. Snort facilitates sniffer mode, packet logger mode and full network intrusion detection system mode as user options; however, it lacks the capability of scripts such as Zeek that allows for highly automated workflows [35].

The intrusion response systems (IRSs) are systems that are developed for selecting an appropriate response to detected intrusion and can be divided into two broad categories: (1) static system that focuses on mapping a response to a specific type of attack and (2) dynamic system that enables the selection of the most effective countermeasure among the multiple countermeasures depending on multiple criteria.

The authors in Ref. [36] introduce a network model for choosing the response action with the ability to avert certain threats and to minimize the overall impact on the system and users, whereas the ADEPTS [37] maximizes the availability of the system at the expense of the features compromised by the attack that are isolated from the rest of the system, thus aiding in restricting the effect of the intrusion to a subset of the services. The authors in Ref. [38] propose an IRS that utilizes the stochastic nature of the detections conducted by the IDS and triggers the response action when the confidence level of the detected attack reaches a specified threshold.

1.4 APPLICATIONS SECURITY

Traditionally, HPC systems were deployed and employed for dedicated users to conduct research and development in specific domains with security being not a significant issue. However, with the advent of the shared HPC systems and emerging HPC-as-a-service concept, where the system is shared among multiple users, the security of HPC systems and applications executing on the systems has evolved as a challenging problem [39].

Even though the shared HPC systems are lucrative due to accessibility and cost-effectiveness, the shared nature of these HPC systems renders extreme difficulty in enforcing security requirements for application execution and data processing on these shared systems. Sandboxing and discretionary access control [40] are used for controlling remote connections and for protecting shared clusters against malicious activities [41]. The authors in [42] present two solutions based on National Security Agency's (NSA) Security-Enhanced Linux (SELinux) to enable security in a shared HPC cluster. The first solution employs chroot to confine the user [43]. However, the first approach prevents the user from easily sharing data. The second solution relies on two SSH server ports and facilitates user to share data.

Traditionally, virtualization technologies have been employed to fulfill the goal of protecting applications and their data from other users and potentially malicious adversaries. However, Linux cgroups followed by Linux container technology has gained momentum for usage in HPC environments. Given the container technology's ability to partition computing system resources with practically no overhead, the container technology has emerged as a dominant solution for deploying and executing distributed applications and is being adopted by data centers ranging from small to large scale and to public clouds where attaining maximum system utilization is the objective [44,45]. The container enables microservice architecture and the seamless deployment of an application across various computing environments by bundling the application's code with dependencies, configuration files and other libraries required for the application to execute. Even though container technology was not initially used with HPC, the emergence of enterprise HPC workloads and open-source projects such as Singularity [46], Charliecloud [47], Shifter [48] and Podman [49] has catalyzed the adoption of container technologies in HPC environments. Moreover, the recent Kubernetes technology aids in container orchestration, resource utilization, load balancing, automated operation tasks and application deployments, scalability of services, applications and clusters, self-healing, auto-replication and auto-placement, declarative configuration, and abstraction of infrastructure, thus enabling dynamic orchestration, portability and scalability for rapidly allocating and deallocating computational resources to HPC workloads [50].

The co-integration of containers with HPC not only facilitates the scalability, portability and reproducibility to scientific community, but also results in a myriad of the security and usability challenges. The containerized applications are distributed in nature; thus, investigating the vulnerabilities, misconfiguration or risk impact in containers becomes extremely difficult. Thus, containerization of HPC requires new approaches to compliance and security over traditional security model. One of the major security concerns is that the containers are inherently lacking isolation from the host operating system and thus depend significantly on their underlying host OS kernel for: (1) security policies; (2) resource isolation; (3) provisioning control; and (4) user communications. Therefore, any vulnerability involving host OS kernel can lead to severe security risks to all containers. Moreover, given that containers are also not isolated from one another, a security flaw in one single container can potentially lead to compromising all other containers. Furthermore, container configuration, flawed base images and their short life cycles can lead to increase in vulnerabilities and in monitoring challenges. The authors in Ref. [44] list various vulnerabilities and solutions that can aid in achieving container security. Lastly, increasing security in container can lead to performance degradation and comes at the cost of increased deployment time and decreased application performance.

Monitoring the system for abnormal user behavior is a key component in securing HPC systems. The most common attack vector is the insider attack, where either a user goes rogue or an attacker steals an authentic user's log-in information. Some of the main challenges when designing an HPC-specific monitoring are scalability, overhead and extensibility [51]. These are important features to consider when using or designing HPC system monitoring software. Scalability is necessary to expand the monitoring system as the system evolves, gaining new nodes. Overhead needs to be kept to a minimum; otherwise, the system performance is impacted, decreasing the amount of work that can be performed. Without the ability to be extensible, a system cannot incorporate new forms of monitoring as they are developed. Also, as the system evolves, there may be new and different types of actions and data that need to be monitored.

One of the most essential parts of running an HPC system is monitoring its nodes, network and overall system so that the system administrator can make informed decisions. Some tools are preferred over others. When it comes to network monitoring, some of the preferred tools are Munin [52], which mainly intensifies on plug-and-play capability, and Zabbix [53], which is mainly preferred due to its very interactive graphical user interface. There are also other tools such as collectd [54], which is preferred for reviewing performance analysis and capacity planning, and tools such as Nagios XI [55] and Grafana, which have a user-friendly and easily customizable dashboard for easy review of the monitoring statistics by the team. Other tools used include Ganglia [56], which among all of the other tools is mostly used by HPC institutions due to its large community support, and XALT [57], which is preferred due to its usefulness and compatibility to other system logs. The following section discusses some of the notable HPC monitoring tools.

XALT tool is employed by supercomputing staff for managing Linux-based clusters and supercomputers at many institutions including TACC (Texas Advanced Computing center) for job monitoring and collecting accurate and continuous job level and link time data about the libraries and executables. XALT is mainly used for collecting link time and run time data using the LD_PRELOAD environment variable. It determines the details of each parallel job which includes all information from dependencies to MPI tasks to the environment in which the job executes. XALT is extremely effective because of its usefulness and compatibility to other system logs. Ganglia is another tool employed for monitoring scalable clusters and grids in real time. This tool was an open source and started at University of California, Berkeley. Ganglia works by providing performance metrics of large supercomputers which have hundreds of nodes and helps them to monitor each of them. It uses Gmond and Gmetad, of which Gmetad is ran only on the main node and Gmond is ran on all the other compute nodes, which then collect all the node-specific data about performance, CPU, memory, network traffic and other processes. Later, the data are used for monitoring the system, which also aids in security. Some of the reasons why Ganglia is preferred over other monitoring tools for HPC systems are its ability to scale and its flexible design which helps in preventing node failure on very large systems. collectd is a Unix-based tool for collecting, storing and transferring the performance metrics of various systems and applications running on HPC systems. collectd monitors the whole system and collects data about the CPU, external devices and log files, which are made available to the system administrator for analyzing the data and detecting any bottlenecks. Some of the reasons why collectd is preferred over other tools are its large number of available plug-ins, portability and performance. The National Energy Research Scientific Computing Center (NERSC) at Lawrence Berkeley National Laboratory uses collectd for data collection process. Another open-source monitoring tool used by many HPC systems to monitor their overall system is Zabbix. Zabbix utilizes both agent-based and agentless monitoring and aids in monitoring the network utilization of the system, its CPU load and memory consumption. Once all the data are collected, Zabbix sends out all the information over the network or it could also be displayed on the Zabbix graphical user interface (GUI). One of the main features of Zabbix is that the rules could be modified and its flexible e-mail mechanism could be used to notify about any event that is considered essential by the system administrator. Zabbix is preferred over other tools due to its powerful API, which is used for data extraction, user-friendly GUI and its flexible, yet powerful alerting mechanism for sending out alerts. Munin is also an open-source client/server architecture tool used for monitoring, which focuses mainly on monitoring the network and its infrastructure of large HPC systems. Munin tool facilitates a unique way of displaying all the information about the systems using graphs through a web-based graphical user interface and has a large number of plug-ins available to use. nVision developed by Axence facilitates features such as failure detection, port mapping and network analyses and is used for the management of entire IT infrastructure. Nagios XI is another tool mainly used for monitoring large HPC systems which have hundreds of compute nodes in place. Some of the features that Nagios XI facilitates are its ability to integrate with many applications through API which could be both in-house and external, its alerting mechanism and its user-friendly dashboard. Grafana is a data analytic and monitoring tool used for monitoring and displaying interactive visualization of the collected data through a user-friendly dashboard. Grafana works by developing a connection with the data source that enables analyzing everything including the network and system performance, and displaying monitored information in the form of graphs. Some of the main reasons why Grafana is preferred over other tools are its unique approach of unifying existing data, its powerful alerting mechanism which could also be customized and its flexible and versatile dashboard which can be designed according to the teams.

1.5   DATA SECURITY IN HPC ECOSYSTEMS

In the 21st century, data security is a very vital part of HPC ecosystems as sensitive data should be protected at all times from falling into the wrong hands. In recent years, companies have been focusing more on securing data to ensure data privacy and making sure that companies don't lose their value over data breaches to ensure that they still hold reputation in the global competitive market. If data are not protected, then it could lead to social, legal or employability risks for the person. Moreover, misuse, modification or deletion of sensitive data by any unauthorized user can permanently damage business or in extreme cases affect the security. Data security is responsible for protecting sensitive information, which includes all data such as personal information, protected health information (PHI), education records, customer information and other confidential information.

There exist several frameworks for enabling the security of sensitive data processing on shared HPC systems. The services for sensitive data (TSD) from the University of Oslo are an integrated platform for collecting, storing, analyzing and sharing sensitive data, where access to the project-dedicated resources is provided via remote connection to virtual machines [58]. While working with traditional high-performance clusters, we only have two protection states when encryption tools are applied for protecting data, which are as follows: The data are encrypted or not usable by the user, or the data are decrypted that are usable by the end user. However, employing this traditional approach does not really help us now, and using encryption now in HPC settings requires serious changes to the HPC operational and execution environment.

Recently, Lawrence Livermore National Laboratory (LLNL) has developed a new cybersecurity tool called HPCrypt data protection system for secure data processing on high-end computing systems and is used to implement data encryption in HPC environments. The tool developed was designed in a way to have negligible effect on the traditional high-performance operation and execution environment and can be managed locally [59]. Furthermore, the HPCrypt system protects against information domain leaks, scales well with large data and enables simultaneous execution of both encrypted and unencrypted jobs on the cluster. The most important feature which attracted the use of this tool is that there is no need to make any changes for the tool to be used with the traditional HPC environment. The secure data processing tool has some of the following features:

1. The tool does not only protect the system against information breach between information domains, but is also scalable to sizable datasets.

2. If any user with authorized access reads or writes any sensitive or protected data, then the data are logged and auditable. Moreover, the logs also illustrate the source on all produced output.

3. All the trusted components are always identified and are also tracked on their authentication on what information they are accessing.

4. Any request is explicitly verified to ensure that it is not accessed by any unauthorized users.

5. Users owning the data and users who would like to use data are explicitly identified with clear set enforceable policy with revoke or access at any time in the future.

Industries such as banking, finance, government, education and insurance would extremely benefit from the HPCrypt software. The software does not only protect and log storage, but can also be used by the HPC cluster to transport and process sensitive data, including HIPAA, critical infrastructure information and FISMA. One other solution that also does not require modification to the existing HPC infrastructure and aids in enabling security for data processing on shared HPC systems is a platform as a service, the ODISSEI Secure Supercomputer (OSSC). The OSSC is a customizable virtualized solution that employs Private Cloud on a Compute Cluster (PCOCC) for automated provisioning and SLURM to insure strict security requirements [58]. The OSSC platform encompasses work, data, management and compute environments where each research project executes in an isolated virtual environment.

The cluster interconnects are devices which are used to connect two nodes together, so that they can communicate with each other. Two of the most commonly used network connections that are used in the TOP500 supercomputers are Ethernet and InfiniBand [60]. One of the main reasons for choosing InfiniBand over any other cluster interconnect is because the architecture of InfiniBand has features that allow better isolation and security for the system.

As per recent trends, Mellanox's InfiniBand is preferred over Ethernet in many industries and is growing rapidly. Much like the Ethernet, InfiniBand is also a layer 2 protocol and has all the security mechanisms facilitated by the Ethernet [61]. For example, if we choose to run SSH over InfiniBand rather than Ethernet, we would have all the inherent security capabilities such as protection against MITM and high-grade encryption that SSH would have on Ethernet. Mellanox Technologies have few security-related features, which are common and could be found in all kinds of devices made by Mellanox Technologies. Some of the important security features that are inbuilt in Mellanox Technologies director-grade switches are RADIUS authentication, SSH support, ability to administratively turn off ports, and more. If a node is compromised, then it won't be able to break in and affect other nodes as InfiniBand switch ports are not addressable. One of the major flaws in using Ethernet is that it gets affected if there is a standard layer 2 attack like the SYN flood denial-of-service attacks, but InfiniBand won't be affected by these kinds of attacks because it has a different handshaking process and the hardware on the receiver side would auto-discard SYN flood packets. The partitioning mechanism is used by InfiniBand for achieving security and better isolation of the system. The reason why partitioning is so much effective is because it's well defined and a part of fabric management called Subnet Management controls it centrally, and no single node has the ability to determine its own partition. Due to this feature, organizations which use InfiniBand eliminate potential hacking and security holes which could be possible in standard networks via compromised servers.

One of the other features in InfiniBand that aids in eliminating the necessity for encryption mechanism within the fabric is unicast and multicast forwarding. (If the traffic is not destined to the host, then the host can't listen to it.) The two transport mechanism types which are defined by InfiniBand to secure against unauthorized access and session hijacking are Reliable Transport (RC, RD) and Unreliable Transport (UD). The other mechanism that InfiniBand implements for avoiding unnecessary copies and reducing latency is remote direct memory access (RDMA). There are many layer 2 attacks and holes that InfiniBand handles better than Ethernet [62]. Some of them are as follows citemellano:

1. MAC Flooding Attack: A switch is sent an enormous amount of frames which contain different MAC addresses with an intention to consume all the memory space. This denial-of-service attack does not affect InfiniBand as the tables are defined explicitly, and there is no learn process like Ethernet and there is a linear forwarding table.

2. VLAN Hopping: The attack is done by using Spanning Tree Protocol; thus, this attack cannot affect InfiniBand as there is no Spanning Tree Protocol.

Given the static forwarding tables are employed in InfiniBand switches, the famous Kevin Mitnick Attack requiring LID impersonation would not be possible in InfiniBand.

1.6   USER-SPECIFIC CYBERSECURITY

Securing an HPC system is both similar to and different from securing other systems due to the nature of the system. HPC systems typically have many users, some of which may not actually be a part of the organization that maintains the systems. While it is not a wholly different challenge than securing other large systems, HPC systems need unique methods of user access control. However, since HPC systems are made up of an interconnected set of nodes, there have to be methods for authenticating and allowing users access to the other nodes securely. Another challenge with securing HPC systems is communicating between nodes securely [63]. If a malicious user gains access to the system, it might become possible for them to peer into other users' tasks and steal valuable information. While there is a fair amount of research into securing HPC systems, there are still many challenges that have yet to be overcome.

One aspect to consider when discussing HPC security is user access. User access control is an important security feature of any system, including HPC systems [1]. The goals of user access control are twofold in an HPC system: to control access to system resources (CPU time, RAM, etc.) and to control access to data stored within the system. Both of these aspects are vital considering that HPC system resources are finite and that applications running on the system may involve sensitive, possibly confidential, data. HPC systems are gaining traction in the health domain field being used to analyze large datasets and have a need to secure data access [64]. There exist many different forms of authentication for validating a user's right to access a particular system or resource. Kerberos and munge are popular protocols used to authenticate users on a network and HPC systems [65]. Munge [66] is an authentication system that came about from the need to authenticate users on HPC clusters. Munge allows for jobs to be forwarded to compute on a cluster by ensuring the validity of local UIDs and GIDs. Kerberos provides a robust security mechanism for authenticating users on a network by making a client prove to a verifier server that the client is indeed the declared user through the use of shared encryption keys. The caveat with these methods is that users have to keep their log-in information secure, meaning that they must have secure passwords and that they have to keep them secret.

There exist many more advanced methods of authentication that need to be incorporated into the system. Biometrics and smart cards are examples that are often implemented in order to provide a more secure access method [67]. Biometrics have the advantage of being both physically secure and unique from person to person. Since biometrics use a physical part of a person's body, it cannot easily be replicated or stolen, whereas smart cards can be stolen or lent out by other people. Combining the traditional username–password log-in scheme with biometrics and/or smart cards adds an extra level of security to the system. The most important thing to consider when using biometrics and smart cards as an authentication method is that the storage and transmission of the data must be secured; otherwise, the system is open to attack.

Every organization today is connected to the Internet to leverage a level of competitive advantage. As such, it is standard best practice to have a cybersecurity policy in place. They can be as simple as a set of rules governing behaviors such as how employees log in, what they are allowed to do, which sites they can access or how they store data. For a data center, are these rules any different? We will examine some best practices that include physical redundancy as well as software strategies that can be used as a basis for a cybersecurity policy [68–70].

1.6.1 Policies

At a minimum, the following policies should be documented and understood by all users of the facilities:

1. Acceptable Use: how the access and data are appropriately used, including awareness training to all users.

2. A Password Policy: how long, how complicated, lockouts and how often to change.

3. Backups: who is responsible, the user, the organization, how often and long the data are kept.

4. Network Access: who can access, how the users are vetted.

5. Remote Access: through secure shell or through VPN.

6. Guest Access: who, how to access, how users are vetted, who is users sponsor.

7. Physical Security: minimum policy on securing hardware such as screen lockouts, physical locks on desks and server room access.

Additional policies that should be considered should involve the following:

1. Confidentiality of data.

2. How the different types of data are classified.

3. Data retention.

4. Methods of implementation – policy acknowledgement forms, security incident reports and account setup requests.

5. User training.

Regardless of what policies are in place, they should be a reflection of the organization's security strategy whose goals are realistic and attainable. They should be a living document and constantly consulted through management decisions, creating new regulations and reducing various risks. Further, the policies should not inhibit the mission of the organization; rather, it should allow the organization to meet their required regulations.

Beyond policies, the best practices that are recommended to implement are mentioned below:

1. Physical Security: If you cannot touch it, then you cannot hack it. Access to the data center needs constant auditing. Expired access should be eliminated as soon as possible. The devices themselves should have some redundancy or have a hardware spare policy that can immediately replace a compromised hardware.

2. Patching and antivirus are a must and have to be kept up to date; this includes updating obsolete hardware, or hardware whose drivers are no longer secure.

3. Firewalls and monitoring traffic are a mandate.

4. Configuration File Protocols: backups, who can edit, how are they installed (configuration manager, Ansible).

5. Encryption, secure file transfers through e-mail, storage or transport.

6. Disaster recovery process is also required.

There are countless other policies and implementations that should be considered; however, the best cybersecurity policy is the one that does not hinder the mission of the organization or the work of the user.

1.7 DISCUSSION AND SUMMARY

The recently changing landscape of scientific workflows in HPC ecosystems has led to the increasing volumes of datasets that are surpassing local and network capabilities, especially those coming from experimental facilities. The analysis and computation of these data becomes a challenge due to the inability to install a capable HPC system in every facility that produces these data; thus, a new model for data generation, data transfer and data computation is needed for the next-generation paradigm. The vision is to have a networked series of facilities consisting of the experimental facility, a computational facility, a data storage facility and the software and application expertise to enable this new paradigm and new modes of exploration. Just as an HPC computational facility like National Energy Research Scientific Computing Center (NERSC) computing facility at Lawrence Berkeley National Laboratory transforms and accelerates science, so shall a superfacility enable more advanced scientific discoveries through sharing of the datasets and through correlation of the data [71,72]. There is need for the integration of multiple types of facilities through a wide area network with the speeds necessary to perform this process in near-real time. The new model/paradigm of superfacility involves generation of data from sensors in real time, with local data processing or filtering, movement of data to a storage facility, analysis and modeling to a computational facility, availability of data in real time for access and visualization for on-site researchers and remote users. To successfully execute this model, there needs to be a unified computational architecture throughout the workflow, predictable and programmable wide area network, and workflow for seamless data movement and analysis to provide a productive environment for the researchers.

One of the major challenges for the superfacility paradigm is to deploy a computational architecture that is applicable to multiple disciplines, where some codes use GPU and some employ CPU, and more importantly, this computing ecosystem can be unified across disciplines with a security model that works for all. Given the hardware and software needs are different between computation and a data-intensive workload, multiple types of systems are deployed for different uses such as simulation, data analysis, computation and visualization. For instance, NERSC computing facility has employed various computing systems over the years, such as Hopper and Edison Computing systems for computation, simulation and modeling and Carver along with Genepool and PDSF systems for data analysis. Second, for a superfacility, the deployment of a predictable and programmable network environment to support scientific applications and workflows is extremely difficult. The Science DMZ [73] creates a latency-free network path between experimental facilities and the computation and storage facilities across a wide area network. Moreover, there is a requirement of dedicated high-performance data transfer nodes (DTNs), which cost $80M+ funding to implement this design pattern in universities, and the network speeds are not as predictable. However, a superfacility workflow requires a predictable data movement. Moreover, research is being conducted to transition from control from hardware specs, such as routers and switches across the WAN, to using software-defined networking (SDN) [74]. However, this limits how applications and networks interact, thus creating challenges for automation, orchestration and optimization. There is also a need for the support of workflows that allow seamless data movement from experiment to analysis and data storage/curation. However, this requires authentication services that are standard across the workflow and through multiple facilities, and user access to all areas of the workflow. Furthermore, the capabilities may not be the same across facilities such that if one facility employs burst buffer that allows data movement and management through memory and storage, hierarchy does not assure that other facilities deploy the same, nor is user access the same in all facilities such that if one facility uses multi-factor authentication (MFA), then others use the same.

The rapid advancement and introduction of new processing technologies for HPC ecosystem has facilitated the convergence of artificial intelligence (AI) and machine learning (ML), data analytics and big data, and the high-performance computing (HPC) domain platforms and has led to a myriad of security risks. There have been a significant research and research efforts over the last few decades in developing and implementing solutions to achieving cyber-resilience in HPC environments. However, in addition to the current state-of-the-art security solutions for developing cyberattack-tolerant and survivable systems, there still exist significant challenges in protecting the HPC ecosystems comprising user, data, applications and cyberinfrastructure. With the goal of reducing the downtime of HPC ecosystems in the presence of unpredictable loads and malicious attacks, this chapter covers cybersecurity challenges and solutions, which when combined effectively will aid in proactively rearchitecting the current and emergent HPC ecosystems comprising users, data, infrastructure and applications to delay or counteract scale of malicious attacks and to reduce their impacts and consequences.

REFERENCES

[1] Ramesh Bulusu, Pallav Jain, Pravin Pawar, Mohammed Afzal, and Sanjay Wandhekar. Addressing security aspects for HPC infrastructure. In *2018 International Conference on Information and Computer Technologies (ICICT)*, DeKalb, IL, pp. 27–30. IEEE, 2018.

[2] Paul Messina. The exascale computing project. *Computing in Science & Engineering*, 19(3):63–67, 2017.

[3] Lucio Grandinetti, Seyedeh Leili Mirtaheri, and Reza Shahbazian. *Big Data and HPC: Ecosystem and Convergence*, volume 33. IOS Press, 2018.

[4] Giovanni Ponti, Filippo Palombi, Dante Abate, Fiorenzo Ambrosino, Giuseppe Aprea, Tiziano Bastianelli, Francesco Beone, Riccardo Bertini, Giovanni Bracco, Marco Caporicci, et al. The role of medium size facilities in the HPC ecosystem: the case of the new CRESCO4 cluster integrated in the ENEAGRID infrastructure. In *2014 International Conference on High Performance Computing & Simulation (HPCS)*, Bologna, Italy, pp. 1030–1033. IEEE, 2014.

[5] Alejandro Rico, José A. Joao, Chris Adeniyi-Jones, and Eric Van Hensbergen. Arm HPC ecosystem and the reemergence of vectors. In *Proceedings of the Computing Frontiers Conference*, Siena, Italy, pp. 329–334, 2017.

[6] Sean Peisert. Security in high-performance computing environments. *Communications of the ACM*, 60(9):72–80, 2017.

[7] Andrew Prout, William Arcand, David Bestor, Bill Bergeron, Chansup Byun, Vijay Gadepally, Matthew Hubbell, Michael Houle, Michael Jones, Peter Michaleas, et al. Enhancing HPC security with a user-based firewall. In *2016 IEEE High Performance Extreme Computing Conference (HPEC)*, Waltham, MA, pp. 1–4. IEEE, 2016.

[8] Geng Hong, Zhemin Yang, Sen Yang, Lei Zhang, Yuhong Nan, Zhibo Zhang, Min Yang, Yuan Zhang, Zhiyun Qian, and Haixin Duan. How you get shot in the back: A systematical study about cryptojacking in the real world. In *Proceedings of the 2018 ACM SIGSAC Conference on Computer and Communications Security*, Toronto, ON, pp. 1701–1713, 2018.

[9] Dejan Jelovac, Čedomir Ljubojević, and Ljubomir Ljubojević. HPC in business: The impact of corporate digital responsibility on building digital trust and responsible corporate digital governance. *Digital Policy, Regulation and Governance*, 2021.

[10] Vinayaka Jyothi, Xueyang Wang, Sateesh K. Addepalli, and Ramesh Karri. Brain: Behavior based adaptive intrusion detection in networks: Using hardware performance counters to detect ddos attacks. In *2016 29th International Conference on VLSI Design and 2016 15th International Conference on Embedded Systems (VLSID)*, Kolkata, India, pp. 587–588. IEEE, 2016.

[11] Alex Malin and Graham Van Heule. Continuous monitoring and cyber security for high performance computing. In *Proceedings of the First Workshop on Changing Landscapes in HPC Security*, New York, pp. 9–14, 2013.

[12] Mathieu Blanc and Jean-Franc Lalande. Improving mandatory access control for HPC clusters. *Future Generation Computer Systems*, 29(3):876–885, 2013.

[13] Pengfei Zou, Ang Li, Kevin Barker, and Rong Ge. Detecting anomalous computation with RNNs on GPU-accelerated HPC machines. In *49th International Conference on Parallel Processing-ICPP*, pp. 1–11, 2020.

[14] What really caused Facebook's 500m-user data leak? https://www.wired.com/story/facebook-data-leak-500-million-users-phone-numbers.

[15] Liyuan Liu, Meng Han, Yan Wang, and Yiyun Zhou. Understanding data breach: A visualization aspect. In *International Conference on Wireless Algorithms, Systems, and Applications*, pp. 883–892. Springer, 2018.

[16] Attacks knock supercomputing sites offline. https://duo.com/decipher/attacks-knock-supercomputing-sites-offline.

[17] Bander Ali Saleh Al-rimy, Mohd Aizaini Maarof, and Syed Zain-udeen Mohd Shaid. Ransomware threat success factors, taxonomy, and countermeasures: A survey and research directions. *Computers & Security*, 74:144–166, 2018.

[18] Fending off bitcoin mining HPC thieves. https://insidehpc.com/2021/02/fending-off-bitcoin-mining-hpc-thieves-idaho-national-labs-cryptojacking-detector/.

[19] Lexie J. Byrd, Curtis Smith, Ross Kunz, Nancy Lybeck, Ronald Boring, Humberto Garcia, Victor Walker, Katya LeBlanc, Vivek Agarwal, Ahmad Al Rashdan, et al. Big data, machine learning, artificial intelligence [powerpoint]. Technical report, Idaho National Lab.(INL), Idaho Falls, ID (United States), 2020.

[20] Doe idaho national lab creates technology to detect cryptocurrency mining malware. https://etc.g2xchange.com/statics/doe-idaho-national-lab-creates-technology-to-detect-cryptocurrency-mining-malware/.

[21] Jaehyun Song, Minwoo Ahn, Gyusun Lee, Euiseong Seo, and Jinkyu Jeong. A performance-stable NUMA management scheme for Linux-based HPC systems. *IEEE Access*, 9:52987–53002, 2021.

[22] Petra Rebrošová. Gathering vulnerability information published by software manufacturers.

[23] Open source and collaboration propel RHEL to the top of the top500, 2018. https://www.redhat.com/en/blog/year-review-2018-product-security-risk-report.

[24] A year in review: 2018 product security risk report. https://www.redhat.com/en/blog/year-review-2018-product-security-risk-report.

[25] Product documentation for Red Hat Enterprise Linux 7. https://access.redhat.com/documentation/en-us/red_hat_enterprise_linux/7.

[26] Edita Bajramovic and Andreas Lainer. Forensic-related application security controls for RHEL in critical infrastructure. In: M. Eibl & M. Gaedke (eds.) *INFORMATIK 2017*, Gesellschaft fur Informatik: Bonn, 2017.

[27] Hari Tadepalli. Intel® QuickAssist technology with Intel® key protection technology in Intel server platforms based on Intel® Xeon® processor scalable family, 2017.

[28] Data center security technology. https://www.intel.com/content/www/us/en/architecture-and-technology/trusted-infrastructure-overview.html.

[29] Nicole Schwartz Nett, Ronald X. Arroyo, Thoi Nguyen, Benjamin W. Mashak, Ruby M. Zgabay, Hoa Nguyen, Christopher W. Mann,

Erich J. Hauptli, Stephen P. Mroz, and William J. Anderl. IBM power9 systems designed for commercial, cognitive, and cloud. *IBM Journal of Research and Development*, 62(4/5):7–1, 2018.

[30] Robert Willburn. Remote memory monitoring for malware in a Talos II architecture. In *International Conference on Cyber Warfare and Security*, pp. 486–XV. Academic Conferences International Limited, 2021.

[31] Guy Helmer, Johnny S.K. Wong, Vasant Honavar, and Les Miller. Automated discovery of concise predictive rules for intrusion detection. *Journal of Systems and Software*, 60(3):165–175, 2002.

[32] Guy Helmer, Johnny S.K. Wong, Vasant Honavar, Les Miller, and Yanxin Wang. Lightweight agents for intrusion detection. *Journal of systems and Software*, 67(2):109–122, 2003.

[33] Anna Sperotto, Ramin Sadre, Pieter-Tjerk de Boer, and Aiko Pras. Hidden Markov model modeling of ssh brute-force attacks. In *International Workshop on Distributed Systems: Operations and Management*, pp. 164–176. Springer, 2009.

[34] Vern Paxson, Scott Campbell, Jason Lee, et al. Bro intrusion detection system. Technical report, Lawrence Berkeley National Laboratory, 2006.

[35] Martin Roesch et al. Snort: Lightweight intrusion detection for networks. *Lisa*, 99:229–238, 1999.

[36] Thomas Toth and Christopher Kruegel. Evaluating the impact of automated intrusion response mechanisms. In *Proceedings of 18th Annual Computer Security Applications Conference, 2002*, Las Vegas, NV, pages 301–310. IEEE, 2002.

[37] Bingrui Foo, Yu-Sung Wu, Yu-Chun Mao, Saurabh Bagchi, and Eugene Spafford. ADEPTS: adaptive intrusion response using attack graphs in an e-commerce environment. In *Proceedings of International Conference on Dependable Systems and Networks, 2005 (DSN 2005)*, Yokohama, Japan, pp. 508–517. IEEE, 2005.

[38] Natalia Stakhanova, Samik Basu, and Johnny Wong. A cost-sensitive model for preemptive intrusion response systems. In *AINA*, vol. 7, pp. 428–435, 2007.

[39] Mathieu Blanc, Jeremy Briffaut, Thibault Coullet, Maxime Fonda, and Christian Toinard. Protection of a shared HPC cluster. In *2010 Fourth International Conference on Emerging Security Information, Systems and Technologies*, Venice, Italy, pp 273–279. IEEE, 2010.

[40] Poul-Henning Kamp and Robert NM Watson. Jails: Confining the omnipotent root. In *Proceedings of the 2nd International SANE Conference*, 43:116, 2000.

[41] Mathieu Blanc, Jeremy Briffaut, Damien Gros, and Christian Toinard. Piga-hips: Protection of a shared HPC cluster. *International Journal on Advances in Security*, 4:44–53, 2011.

[42] Z Cliffe Schreuders, Tanya McGill, and Christian Payne. Empowering end users to confine their own applications: The results of a usability study comparing SELinux, AppArmor, and FBAC-LSM. *ACM Transactions on Information and System Security (TISSEC)*, 14(2):1–28, 2011.

[43] Stephen Smalley, Chris Vance, and Wayne Salamon. Implementing selinux as a linux security module. *NAI Labs Report*, 1(43):139, 2001.

[44] Sari Sultan, Imtiaz Ahmad, and Tassos Dimitriou. Container security: Issues, challenges, and the road ahead. *IEEE Access*, 7:52976–52996, 2019.

[45] Nitin Sukhija and Elizabeth Bautista. Towards a framework for monitoring and analyzing high performance computing environments using kubernetes and prometheus. In *2019 IEEE Smart-World, Ubiquitous Intelligence & Computing, Advanced & Trusted Computing, Scalable Computing & Communications, Cloud & Big Data Computing, Internet of People and Smart City Innovation (SmartWorld/SCALCOM/UIC/ATC/CBDCom/IOP/SCI)*, pp. 257–262. IEEE, 2019.

[46] Gregory M. Kurtzer, Vanessa Sochat, and Michael W. Bauer. Singularity: Scientific containers for mobility of compute. *PLoS One*, 12(5):e0177459, 2017.

[47] Reid Priedhorsky and Tim Randles. Charliecloud: Unprivileged containers for user-defined software stacks in HPC. In *Proceedings of the International Conference for High Performance Computing, Networking, Storage and Analysis*, pp. 1–10, 2017.

[48] Lisa Gerhardt, Wahid Bhimji, Shane Canon, Markus Fasel, Doug Jacobsen, Mustafa Mustafa, Jeff Porter, and Vakho Tsulaia. Shifter: Containers for HPC. In *Journal of physics: Conference Series*, vol. 898, pp. 082021. IOP Publishing, 2017.

[49] Holger Gantikow, Steffen Walter, and Christoph Reich. Rootless containers with podman for HPC. In *International Conference on High Performance Computing*, pp. 343–354. Springer, 2020.

[50] Md Shazibul Islam Shamim, Farzana Ahamed Bhuiyan, and Akond Rahman. Xi commandments of kubernetes security: A systematization of knowledge related to kubernetes security practices. In *2020 IEEE Secure Development (SecDev)*, pp. 58–64. IEEE, 2020.

[51] Nitin Sukhija, Elizabeth Bautista, Owen James, Daniel Gens, Siqi Deng, Yulok Lam, Tony Quan, and Basil Lalli. Event management

and monitoring framework for HPC environments using servicenow and prometheus. In *Proceedings of the 12th International Conference on Management of Digital EcoSystems*, pp. 149–156, 2020.

[52] Munin monitoring. https://munin-monitoring.org/.

[53] Zabbix monitoring. https://www.zabbix.com/.

[54] The system statistics collection daemon. https://collectd.org/.

[55] Nagios-network, server, and log monitoring software. https://www.nagios.com/.

[56] Ganglia monitoring system. http://ganglia.sourceforge.net/.

[57] Xalt monitoring system. https://xalt.readthedocs.io/.

[58] Michel Scheerman, Narges Zarrabi, Martijn Kruiten, Maxime Mogé, Lykle Voort, Annette Langedijk, Ruurd Schoonhoven, and Tom Emery. Secure platform for processing sensitive data on shared HPC systems. *arXiv preprint arXiv:2103.14679*, 2021.

[59] Hpcrypt data protection system. https://ipo.llnl.gov/technologies/it-and-communications/processing-protected-data-high-performance-computing-clusters.

[60] Brett M. Bode, Jason J. Hill, and Troy R. Benjegerdes. Cluster interconnect overview. In *Proceedings of USENIX 2004 Annual Technical Conference, FREENIX Track*, pp. 217–223, 2004.

[61] Daryl Schmitt, Scott Graham, Patrick Sweeney, and Robert Mills. Vulnerability assessment of infiniband networking. In *International Conference on Critical Infrastructure Protection*, pp. 179–205. Springer, 2019.

[62] Kyle D. Hintze. Infiniband network monitoring: Challenges and possibilities. 2021.

[63] Zhengping Luo, Zhe Qu, Tung Nguyen, Hui Zeng, and Zhuo Lu. Security of HPC systems: From a log-analyzing perspective. *EAI Endorsed Transactions on Security and Safety*, 6(21):e5, 2019.

[64] Khalil Alsulbi, Maher Khemakhem, Abdullah Basuhail, Fathy Eassa, Kamal Mansur Jambi, and Khalid Almarhabi. Big data security and privacy: A taxonomy with some HPC and blockchain perspectives. *International Journal of Computer Science & Network Security*, 21(7):43–55, 2021.

[65] Steven P. Miller, B Clifford Neuman, Jeffrey I. Schiller, and Jermoe H. Saltzer. Kerberos authentication and authorization system. In *In Project Athena Technical Plan*. Citeseer: Princeton, NJ, 1988.

[66] Chris Dunlap. Munge uid n grid emporium. Technical report, Lawrence Livermore National Lab.(LLNL), Livermore, CA (United States), 2004.

[67] Yanrong Lu, Lixiang Li, Haipeng Peng, and Yixian Yang. A biometrics and smart cards-based authentication scheme for multi-server environments. *Security and Communication Networks*, 8(17):3219–3228, 2015.

[68] Rudi Eigenmann and Barry I. Schneider. National strategic computing initiative. *Computing in Science & Engineering*, 20(5):5–7, 2018.

[69] Per Öster. The European Grid Initiative and the HPC ecosystem. *High Speed and Large Scale Scientific Computing*, 18:451, 2009.

[70] Arun Kumar Singh and Samidha Dwivedi Sharma. High performance computing (HPC) data center for information as a service (IAAS) security checklist: Cloud data governance. *Webology*, 16(2):83–96, 2019.

[71] Bjoern Enders, Debbie Bard, Cory Snavely, Lisa Gerhardt, Jason Lee, Becci Totzke, Katie Antypas, Suren Byna, Ravi Cheema, Shreyas Cholia, et al. Cross-facility science with the superfacility project at lbnl. In *2020 IEEE/ACM 2nd Annual Workshop on Extreme-scale Experiment-in-the-Loop Computing (XLOOP)*, pp. 1–7. IEEE, 2020.

[72] Katie Antypas, Shane Canon, Eli Dart, Kjiersten Fagnan, Lisa Gerhardt, Doug Jacobsen, Glenn K Lockwood, Inder Monga, Peter Nugent, Lavanya Ramakrishnan, et al. Superfacility: The convergence of data, compute, networking, analytics and software. In Surya Kalidindi, Sergei V Kalinin, Turab Lookman (eds.) *Handbook on Big Data and Machine Learning in the Physical Sciences: Volume 2. Advanced Analysis Solutions for Leading Experimental Techniques*, pp. 361–386. World Scientific: Singapore, 2020.

[73] Eli Dart, Lauren Rotman, Brian Tierney, Mary Hester, and Jason Zurawski. The science dmz: A network design pattern for data-intensive science. *Scientific Programming*, 22(2):173–185, 2014.

[74] Keith Kirkpatrick. Software-defined networking. *Communications of the ACM*, 56(9):16–19, 2013.

CHAPTER 2

Approaches to Working with Large-Scale Graphs for Cybersecurity Applications

Noah L. Schrick, Ming Li, John Hale, and Peter J. Hawrylak

The University of Tulsa

CONTENTS

DOI: 10.1201/9781003155799-2

2.1 INTRODUCTION

The cybersecurity landscape is ever-evolving, with no dull moments. The authors of [1] discuss that difficulties lie in the fact that both diversity and intensity of new cybersecurity threats require quick and effective countermeasure implementations. As the authors of [2] further describe, the number of exposed records in the first half of 2019 alone reached 4.1 billion, with reported breaches up by 54% compared to the year prior. The continuous increase in cybersecurity risks necessitates the need for countermeasures that eliminate and prevent threats from occurring, rather than solely focusing on detection. To add to the difficulties, as the authors of [3–5] discuss, the rise of Internet of things (IoT) and cyber-physical systems adds to the complexity of a system. Not only do cybersecurity considerations need to be made, but safety regulation compliance, maintenance compliance, and other regulatory compliance need to be ensured.

To approach a solution to determining countermeasures, modeling systems with graphs can yield promising results. When representing a system through graphs, an exhaustive approach can be taken. Beginning with all initial system qualities present, cybersecurity attacks (such as those found in the National Vulnerability Database, for example) can be tested against the system. If an attack is able to be used against a system, the system qualities will change and be captured in a new graph node. This type of graphical approach is now commonly called an attack graph [6–8]. Likewise, representing all of a system's initial qualities and examining the ways it is or can fall out of compliance is called a compliance graph [3]. Using this approach, a system can be rigorously examined to determine all ways that attacks or compliance violations can exist in a system, both in present time and in the future. This will allow cybersecurity professionals to correct the weak spots in systems, eliminate attack vectors, and identify ways to avoid falling out of compliance. However, there are a few drawbacks to this approach. With the number of items in the National Vulnerability Database, the amount of custom zero-day checking, along with the number of assets (access points, firewalls, printers, workstations, etc.), exhaustively representing all possible states of a system leads to incredibly large graphs [8]. These large-scale graphs are a common issue for other problem spaces as well. Social networks, bioinformatics, and neural networks can produce graphs with millions of vertices and billions of edges [9]. Due to the incredibly large size of these graphs, they can seldom be contained within a single system's memory. In addition, the computation power required to generate and analyze these graphs in a reasonable time makes sequential and single-system approaches infeasible. With the cybersecurity landscape constantly changing, these graphs will need to be regenerated and reanalyzed to stay current and correct. New vulnerabilities, new assets in a system, or new countermeasures render a previously generated graph outdated, and a new one will need to be procured.

Targeting high-performance computing (HPC) resources is a necessity for approaching this problem. Leveraging the increased amount of memory and the greater computing power is invaluable for reducing the time required to generate and analyze these graphs. This chapter will present graph techniques useful for compliance violation and cybersecurity attack prediction in the lens of HPC. This chapter presents a survey of techniques that are useful for handling large-scale graphs, methodologies, and techniques for increasing performance, and concludes with insights into future needs and directions in this area.

2.2 GENERATION

2.2.1 Generation Introduction

In practice, graph computations and generations do not reach full theoretical computing performance; they often achieve only a very low percentage [10]. Graph processing performance relies less on processor speed, and more on the computer's ability to access memory in a timely fashion, the complexity of data dependency, and the coarseness of parallelism [9–11]. Typically, graphs have relatively poor efficiency in terms of memory. The most apparent inefficiency is due to their large memory footprints [9]. Not only does the number of nodes and edges in a graph consume memory, but considering the data stored at each node is important to visualize the constraints on low-memory systems [10]. In addition, as opposed to data structures such as arrays, which can be optimized to better utilize spatial locality for increased cache performance, the underlying graph data structures can contain additional challenges in terms of locality [11]. These issues are exacerbated from the memory latency evident in the processor–memory gap [10,11]. This section will focus on the techniques leveraged by HPC clusters to increase the performance of graph generation.

2.2.2 Algorithm Walk-Throughs

2.2.2.1 Introduction

Beginning in 1998, researchers and cybersecurity experts began on a means to model a network of systems to perform vulnerability analysis. This initial work later became known as an early-day attack graph in the form of an attack tree. In comparison with today's representation of attack graphs, there were a few differences. As suggested by the name, these initial models were similar to trees, rather than graphs [6–8]. There were a few hindrances in these early models that led to the expansion of the representation of modern attack graphs. These hindrances were primarily in that the attack trees' sole focus was for analyzing individual vulnerabilities on single machines; they did not allow for modeling of interconnected systems that is widespread today. As a result, later work was conducted that led to the current interpretation of attack graphs to allow modeling of entire networks comprised of interconnected systems.

Attack graphs have a few different models. The authors in [12] and [13] utilize a model where the nodes represent attacks and the edges represent the conditional relationship between two attacks [14]. Another model presented in [15] and [16] utilizes a modeling system based on Bayesian networks, with each node representing a host in the network and edges representing vulnerabilities that can be used to reach other hosts in the network. This allows the visualization of both reachability and vulnerabilities' conditional relationships [14]. Each model has its unique advantages and disadvantages, and each shifts its focus to emphasize different areas of the network's security. Irrespective of the model's intricacies, attack graphs' primary focus is for modeling a network to identify vulnerable positions. As a result of increased system connectivity, the state space modeled by attack graphs grows at a rapid rate, leading to massive generation processes that can no longer be feasibly run on single systems or with serial implementations on very high performance single-computer systems [8,14,17,18]. Thus, a parallel or distributed approach to generation of these structures is required. The following subsections focus on the algorithmic approaches to working with attack graphs on a small scale, followed by the approaches necessary for working with larger systems that can be done on HPC clusters.

2.2.2.2 Attack Graphs

There are two key components when considering attack graph generation. The first is ensuring that the resulting attack graph is exhaustive – that all attack possibilities and appropriate states are properly represented and accounted for, including any permutations. The second is that it is succinct – that the model only includes states that an attacker can use to reach a goal state [12]. Later work, such as that seen in Ref. [8], indicates that using the formal logic approach to generation seen in Ref. [12] can aid in ensuring correctness by using a model checker against the resulting attack graph model [8]. Using the formal logic generation method typically results in less errors that can occur in complex network environments, and can lead to easier analysis [8]. However, the authors in Ref. [8] do draw concerns with the exhaustiveness of the tool, in that because of the duplication and permutation checking, a network with ten hosts and five vulnerabilities resulted in a graph with 10 million edges. While such an analysis provides a complete picture of the overall security posture, the huge number of edges is a scalability problem as the system size increases. Typical systems often have dozens or hundreds of hosts/nodes. However, the generation of attack vectors that map to the system is straightforward and can be generated by walking the attack graph for this representation.

The original algorithm presented by Ref. [12] proceeds by first checking a set of states deemed unsafe that put the network in a compromised or unsafe position. This is conducted in the model checking by using a set of states, a transition relation between states, the initial network states, state labeling, and a safety property. After the model checking, the transition relation is limited to only states in the unsafe set of states. Using Boolean representation and formal logic, resulting unsafe states and their transitions from initial states can be generated. As Ref. [8] states, encoding the entire network state leads to an exponential number of possible states during the model checking phase, even though not all states are reachable.

As a means of improving scalability, Ref. [8] presents an alternative representation called a logical attack graph. Due to the aforementioned reasons, namely the state space explosion, their representation desired to stay with a logical approach to generation. Rather than each statement encoding the entire network, each node would be a portion of the network represented as a logical statement. This approach was able to reduce the generation to quadratic time. Further, the number of nodes in the resulting logical attack graph is $O(N^2)$, where N is the number of nodes in the system [8]. This addressed the state space problem; however, it requires more analysis to identify actionable attack vectors for the particular system compared to the attack graph representation.

Later work, such as that presented in Ref. [18], represents nodes as network states – a description of assets (network systems) and the facts that describe them. Facts can either be qualities (such as firmware or OS versions), or topologies (relational information to other assets). The algorithms for such a representation work by expanding each unexplored node. The initial network states are added into a queue, with each state from the queue being checked against an exploit list to see if factual information in a network state can be altered.

If so, a new network state is created and added to the unexplored queue. This process is continued until no further unexplored states exist in the queue. Similar work shown in Ref. [14] illustrates the algorithm using a hash table. For determining the time complexity of this generation algorithm, $|Q_d|$ represents the total number of states and N_e represents the number of exploits. In this implementation of attack graph generation, each state must be checked against the number of applicable exploits and their facts. As a result, the time complexity is:

$$O\left(|Q_d| N_e\right) \tag{2.1}$$

Summarizing the performances of these approaches, the original algorithm presented in Ref. [12] with exponential time, the algorithm presented in Ref. [8] with quadratic time, and the serial algorithm present in Ref. [14], illustrates that efficiency improvements can be obtained by refining the information one is interested in. However, as Refs. [14,17,18] state, these improvements, while important, still do not sufficiently allow for an efficient or scalable representation of enterprise networks consisting of thousands of hosts. As Ref. [17] describes, this is even more evident when considering the size of the National Vulnerability Database, Common Weakness Enumeration database, and the number of ports a system could have opened. Thus, the resulting graphs will be very large for the typical system and both the time to generate the graph and its resulting size are important considerations. Both aspects make this a good problem for HPC systems.

2.2.2.3 *Attack Dependency Graphs*

Attack graphs are a useful tool in demonstrating possible attack vectors that can put a network in a compromised position. However, there are instances where their capabilities fall short. For example, vulnerabilities can oftentimes rely upon the presence of other vulnerabilities, or even have an increase in criticality or importance based on the combination of multiple vulnerabilities that have been exploited at the same time [19,20]. With attack graphs, one vulnerability may rank low on criticality: It may exist and is seemingly non-threatening, but another vulnerability may capitalize on the first vulnerability to pose a much larger threat. Attack dependency graphs aim to identify these exploit and vulnerability dependencies in a network.

When considering the dependencies in a network, it is useful to distinguish between the types of dependence. The authors in Ref. [21] present and define three types: redundancy dependence, graceful degradation dependency, and strict dependence. Redundancy refers to an asset that depends on multiple other resources that have redundancy. Graceful degradation dependency is a dependence where an asset can continue its operation if its dependence fails, but at limited performance or security. Strict dependence is a dependency where if an asset's dependence fails, then so does the asset.

Original attack graph models tended to revolve around the concept of state transition graphs. Each node in this model represented a possible attack state, comprised of propagated attack events from parent nodes, system qualities, and related network qualities. The edges connecting the nodes represented the probabilities of a successful attack [22]. Recent models have shifted their focus to revolve around the concept of these attack dependency graphs. In this model, nodes are expanded into two categories – nodes consisting of preconditions or postconditions ("condition nodes"), and nodes consisting of attacks ("attack nodes"). The attack nodes are equivalent to the edge representation of the original model. Edges for the attack dependency graph represent the dependency of nodes [14,22]. Using the attack dependency graphs eliminates the redundancy of the stateful model, which allows the graphs to be generated more efficiently and results in graphs of smaller size.

In addition to just checking exploit or vulnerability dependence, attack dependency graphs can be extended to also consider dependencies in services and applications [21]. Due to the rapid growth of networks, the amount of applications or services being ran or hosted in a network has also increased. As a result, attackers have new attack vectors they can attempt to capitalize on by exploiting vulnerabilities in the application dependencies, where threats can more easily propagate throughout the network. A tool called NSDMiner presented in Ref. [23] attempts to automatically discover these dependencies in a way that is simplified, is less cluttered, and reports less false negatives.

Prior to attack dependency graphs, analysts had to either manually check for dependencies, or specify automated operations to check [19]. By using an attack dependency graph, not only is the resulting graph of smaller size, but tools such as those presented in Refs.

[19,20,23] can perform the visualizations and dependency checking automatically.

2.2.2.4 Combination of Attack Graphs and Attack Dependency Graphs

The representation of the state transition graphs in attack graphs and the representation of dependencies between nodes in attack dependency graphs are both popular models with active work being pursued in both areas. In Ref. [21], the authors suggest a new approach – combining the two representations to make a unified framework.

A shortcoming of analyzing attack graphs on their own is that oftentimes, it is hard to identify how widespread an attack may be. While an attack graph can identify the ways a system can be put in a compromised position, or the criticality of affecting a singular asset, it may not illustrate the effect of the system in its entirety [21]. For instance, if an attack can cause a system component with a strict dependence to fail, the attack graph may not be able to identify the resulting asset that will also fail.

On the other hand, attack dependency graphs on their own can lead to the prioritization of remediation procedures in a way that is not optimal. For example, Vulnerabilities A and B could be present in a network, and Vulnerability B depends on Vulnerability A being exploited. Using an attack dependency graph analysis, it may suggest prioritizing Vulnerability B remediation, since that has a greater interdependence with Vulnerability A. However, from an attack graph perspective, there is a different state transition from the state containing Vulnerability A that leads to more system compromises, and with larger impacts than the transition to a state containing Vulnerability B [21].

To combine the two graph approaches together, the authors of Ref. [21] suggest an impact assessment graph, which considers the analysis of both graphs and weights their decision processes in a way that balances immediate or ongoing attacks with future attacks.

2.2.2.5 Compliance Graphs

Attack graphs and attack dependency graphs are useful tools to determine the ways in which a system is in, or may be put into, a vulnerable state. Another useful tool that can be utilized is compliance graphs.

As opposed to looking through the broader lens of cybersecurity as a whole, compliance graphs can be used for determining the compliance status of cyber-physical systems [3]. Instead of processing through the system state space by determining applicable exploits or vulnerabilities, compliance graphs determine applicable compliance violations. These compliance requirements have a broad range and can include safety regulations, maintenance compliance, or other regulatory compliance. By setting the compliance parameters to check for, compliance graphs can be used in a similar fashion to attack and attack dependency graphs. Not only can the current state of the system be checked, but possible future system states can be analyzed to determine appropriate steps that need to be taken for preventative measures [3].

As the authors of [3–5] discuss, the rise of cyber-physical systems in areas such as critical infrastructure and IoT brings new difficulties to consider for protecting systems. Not only are there the typical cybersecurity considerations, but these systems also have to be concerned with compliance regulations to ensure that the equipment is safe, is undamaged and remains undamaged, and is stable. In addition, the place of operation and whom the equipment is used for may bring about additional compliance guidelines that may need to be followed, such as SOX, HIPAA, the European Union's GDPR, and/or OECD for international usage [4,5]. Managing all aspects of compliance regulation can be time-consuming and complex, but the fines, legal sanctions, mandatory shutdowns, and other costs of compliance violation are compelling reasons to mitigate or prevent the risk of a system falling out of compliance.

The compliance graphs can be described similarly to that of the more recent attack graph representations. Nodes represent the system state, and edges represent changes to a state through an insertion, modification, or deletion of a quality or topology. Like attack graphs, qualities in the scope of compliance graphs describe an asset through facts. Topologies are slightly different; instead of showing a connection of assets through their digital means like that of attack graphs, topologies in compliance graphs need to be expanded because of the cyber-physical nature of the systems. As a result, topologies not only include the network connections of components, but also include connections of sensors or other equipment [3].

Like attack and attack dependency graphs, compliance graphs also suffer from state space explosion. The number of compliance regulations that can or need to be checked can get large very quickly. In critical infrastructure areas, the number of assets that need to be checked can also be very large, leading to the same challenge of handling these large-scale graphs that cannot be effectively managed on serial workstations. This is another challenge that has appealing solutions in the HPC space.

2.2.3 Parallel Generation Algorithms

Regardless of attack graph model, a main challenge of attack graph generation is in the state space explosion [14]. In other words, when generating an attack graph consisting of a large number of nodes and with a high depth (the number of exploits executed or changes to the system state carried out), the number of states drastically increases [14,18]. An approach to parallelizing the generation is described in Ref. [14]. A first-in–first-out (FIFO) queue is utilized to store the initial state as a frontier, and a hash table is utilized to hold the exploits and relevant network information. Using OpenMP parallel for loops and a dynamic schedule, each thread can work on a local frontier. The local frontier is a subset of the global frontier. Each thread will take portions of the global frontier and work on that subset called a local frontier. When an applicable exploit is identified, a new state is needed to be created and added to the frontier. To accomplish this, an OpenMP critical section is used. Using a critical section allows for an atomic write to the global frontier, so there is no risk of collisions, race conditions, or stale data being used. Using this parallelized approach, a new runtime complexity can be identified as:

$$O\left(|Q_d|\,N_e/n + k_1|Q_d|\right) \tag{2.2}$$

where $|Q_d|$ represents the total number of states, N_e represents the number of exploits, n is the number of threads, and k_1 is a constant. Running in an equal environment with N_e set to 7, Q_d to 25,354, and n to 24 hardware threads, the parallel attack graph generation presented in Ref. [14] provides a 10× speedup over the serial algorithm discussed in a previous section.

2.2.4 Additional Architectural and Hardware Techniques

2.2.4.1 Prefetching

Analyzing the cache miss rates on graph generation illustrates a miss rate that is higher in comparison with other workloads, due to the aforementioned memory inefficiencies. Utilizing hardware or software prefetching so that the system can better predict future memory accesses typically yields better performance for common use cases. For graphs, however, using prefetching still results in high miss rates. Since the underlying graph structures and algorithmic approaches are traditionally non-sequential, and access patterns are data dependent, the prefetcher is not able to adequately gain sufficient information to have an increased prediction rate [11].

To combat this performance difficulty, the authors of Ref. [11] continue to state that programmers can explicitly tune prefetching to have better results. In most cases, the graph generation algorithm is known in advance. By knowing the graph generation algorithm, programmers can configure the hardware prefetcher to follow the traversal order pattern. For instance, for breadth-first search (BFS), the traversal order pattern is typically the same: Process each node at level order. Configuring the prefetcher to access future items in the breadth traversal path leads to increased performance of over 2× for BFS by reducing the number of cache misses and thereby limiting the time stalled while waiting for main memory access [11].

2.2.4.2 Accelerators

While the graph generation process may be parallelized, the underlying atomic functions are largely serial [24]. When it comes to shared vertices and data conflicts, there can be slowdowns while waiting for the atomic functions to process [21,24]. This can be incredibly problematic for graphs with many high-degree vertices. To alleviate these slowdowns, techniques exist for using an accelerator that capitalizes on the incremental patterns of atomic functions and merges the results in parallel rather than computing them all atomically [24]. The parallel implementation presented in [24] continues by utilizing this merging strategy so that the accelerator can then utilize pipeline stages where the vertex updates can be processed in parallel dynamically.

Due to the memory difficulties, additional work has been done to leverage field-programmable gate arrays (FPGAs) for graph generation in the HPC space [9,25]. Coupled with their flexibility and energy efficiency, FPGAs have many potential benefits. To reduce memory strain, the traditional FPGA approach utilizes the on-chip block RAM (BRAM) to store graph information [9,25]. Depending on the size of the graph, the BRAM can store various portions of attack graph information to enhance performance. Depending on the size of the exploit list, the list can be stored here to avoid pulling it from main memory, or from taking cache space that could be better used for explicit prefetching. If a parallel approach is used that targets the FPGA, the local frontier could also possibly be stored in the BRAM depending on its size. This approach, however, is limited in its usability. For small graphs, the performance is magnitudes better. But this performance increase is not scalable, as the BRAM available on-chip is relatively small compared to typical graph sizes and is thus unable to hold the large graphs that are typically required to address problems that require HPC clusters [9].

An alternative to the BRAM approach is through leveraging the stacked DRAM technology of hybrid memory cubes (HMCs) [9]. An HMC is optimized for parallel access (more ranks; smaller page size) and has full-duplex links at speeds of almost 20× that of DDR4. The authors in Ref. [9] drew comparisons of an FPGA-HMC approach versus a Xeon E5 CPU. Both used parallelization, but since the FPGA-HMC approach had a substantially lower memory access time, the results obtained showed that this approach yielded a 3x performance improvement over the Xeon E5 CPU.

2.2.4.3 Better Data Structures

Defining and generating graphs revolve around the underlying data structure representation. Most commonly, graph data are represented in the form of an edge list, with each edge symbolizing a connection between nodes [26]. However, as the authors of [26] discuss, many of the typical graph algorithms process graphs through neighboring nodes. For instance, breadth-first and depth-first searches, as well as shortest-path algorithms process graphs through neighboring nodes. As a method to improve the performance of node exploration algorithms, adjacency lists can be used. Adjacency lists are per node and list the nodes that are neighbors. Node exploration algorithms can then use adjacency lists to quickly identify neighboring nodes, rather than computing nodes through an edge list. Historically, adjacency matrices have been used, as seen in works such as [27,28]. The authors of [26] describe that this is infeasible for today's large graphs, since the space requirement for representing all nodes in a matrix will be cumbersome and the processing time is slower. Property maps have also been used for graph representation. Property maps are defined as objects with keys and values that are mapped together. These can be used to map vertices that allow for simplistic lookups [29].

With large graphs and the need for parallelization, there has been a push for higher-performing graph algorithms. With some graphs having upward of billions of edges and billions of vertices, it is not possible to contain all of a graph's representation in a system's memory [30]. Due to this increased requirement, it is preferable to distribute a graph representation among systems [26,30,31]. Partitioning a graph representation has various approaches. As the authors of [31] discuss, partitioning can be conducted by assigning vertices to workers where each contains its own copy of lists. This is defined as a distributed adjacency list [32]. Distributed property maps can also be used, with the mapped values distributed across systems or nodes. Synchronization and communication can be used for value retrievals and updates [33].

Using distributed data structures does not come without a cost. As the authors of [30,31,34,35] discuss, communication costs begin bringing in additional overheads that damper performance. To account for communication costs, previous works have presented compression techniques. However, the authors of [31] and [35] describe that compression for large graphs has additional penalties, as now decompression and compression costs are incurred, and compression ratios may be low. Both [31] and [35] present techniques for achieving high compression ratios and low costs. Other works present alternative solutions for increasing distributed structure performance.

Regardless of costs, sequential data structures or data structures typically used for small graphs are not advisable. They are not scalable and leave performance gains unrealized for large-scale graph processing. For handling large graphs, better data structures are a necessity. Graph type plays a role in what data structures should be used; there is no data structure that will have optimal performance for every graph. Analyzing graph processing and tailoring their representations will yield far better results than taking naive approaches.

2.2.4.4 Useful Libraries

A number of libraries exist with routines for processing and analyzing graphs. These include Boost, Parallel Boost, and ParMETIS.

2.2.4.4.1 Boost Graph Library Boost Graph Library (BGL) is aimed as a "generic interface", utilizing generic underlying algorithms that provide abstraction from the graph's structure. BGL is intended to work with any other graph library or graph algorithm. Through BGL's generic programming, graph components such as edges or vertices can quickly and easily be represented by abstract classes, such as an adjacency_list class, which implements iterator functions for accessing or updating class members. Rather than individually creating all of the classes and functions, and tailoring them to each graph structure and implementation, Boost can provide all of the necessary information while remaining abstract, making it flexible to support a number of different types of graphs [36]. Boost also contains generic interfaces for representations such as property maps [29]. Instead of manually creating the mapping for vertices or edges, it can be implemented through Boost. The same exists for graph algorithms such as breadth-first or depth-first searches: Boost has these readily available to allow for simplistic incorporation into any graph structure. None of these classes or methods are strict on the underlying graph representation. These will be able to function properly for all representations, allowing for highly specific or customized graphs to benefit from typical algorithms without the need to recreate them all [37].

A notable feature of BGL is that custom graphs relying on novel or nontraditional data structures can be converted to work with BGL to take advantage of generic template functions such as breadth-first searches. This is a documented feature of BGL with a dedicated support page to assist in the conversion. The conversion avoids the overhead of new class creation or data copying by providing a wrapper to overload global functions [38]. When working with large attack graphs, keeping generation and analysis time at a minimum is ideal due to the state space explosion. For custom graphs that do not use BGL, classes would need to be created that handle all basic functions. For generation, these functions could be for creating new nodes or adding edges, which would be called a very high number of times. For analysis, these functions could be for performing searches or identifying the shortest paths. Creating extra custom classes for each of these can create overhead that slows the generation process. By using BGL to abstract the custom graph and provide generic functions with fast runtimes, the generation process can be sped up.

2.2.4.4.2   Parallel Boost Graph Library   The Parallel Boost Graph Library (Parallel BGL) is an extension of the BGL. This library is intended to provide the benefits of BGL for parallel and distributed computing and to leverage both coarse-grained and fine-grained parallelism on graph structures while remaining generic. Coarse-grained parallelism refers to conducting parallelism on large chunks of data, whereas fine-grained parallelism refers to conducting parallelism on small pieces of data. As mentioned in previous subsections, generating graphs is difficult due to the irregularity involved. As a result, leveraging coarse-grained parallelism during the generation process is difficult, since predicting patterns or exploiting locality is extremely unlikely. However, it can be useful during the analysis process. Following procedures similar to that done by the authors in Refs. [39–41], sections of the generated graph can be grouped together, and coarse-grained parallelism can be conducted on the larger sections. Due to the unpredictable nature of the generation process, fine-grained parallelism must be used. This typically suffers from a larger overhead in comparison with coarse-grained parallelism, since atomicity must be present at each vertex. Leveraging Parallel BGL's capabilities, both of these parallel techniques can be used relatively easily and relatively quickly due to their generic nature. Parallel BGL also includes data structures such as distributed adjacency lists, distributed queues, and distributed property maps. These distributed data structures allow for simple implementations on HPC systems. Other notable features of Parallel BGL are its interoperability with MPI, Graphviz, and METIS [37].

2.2.4.4.3   ParMETIS   ParMETIS is the parallelized library of METIS. METIS is a library aimed to assist with partitioning, repartitioning, and refining graph-related problem spaces. ParMETIS functions in the same manner, but is parallelized and based on MPI. It includes additional functionality for assisting with sparse matrices by computing fill-reducing orderings. One main appealing feature of ParMETIS is in its partitioning. Partitioning the graph is useful, as it will reveal concurrency, help identify proper load balancing, and allow for an efficient way to map computation to a parallel platform [42]. While this does not help with the generation process, partitioning the graph prior to analysis and then feeding the partitioned graph into an analysis tool can aid in reducing the analysis runtime. In addition, since ParMETIS is based on MPI, it is able to be performed on a HPC cluster to partition very large graphs as a preprocessing step. ParMETIS has benefits in that its processing time for its tasks is extraordinarily low, reordering million-row matrices in seconds and bisection of circuits with 100,000 vertices in minutes on Pentium processors. hMETIS is an extension library that allows compatibility for hypergraphs [43].

2.2.5 Deploying to High-Performance Computing Clusters

The previous subsections laid the groundwork for presenting the algorithms and showing general speedup techniques. This subsection focuses on appealing methods for deploying the generation process, specifically to HPC clusters.

2.2.5.1 Base Approach: General Parallelized Programming

One approach to handling the high generation time required for large attack graphs is to parallelize the generation across all or some of a HPC cluster. As opposed to traditional workstations which may have a limited number of cores, a well-designed parallel approach would be able to leverage the high number of cores and high amounts of RAM in a HPC cluster [44]. This is the approach seen by the authors of [14], as described in Section 2.2.3. Because of the increase in the popularity of distributed and heterogeneous clusters, message-passing interface (MPI) is a good candidate as a basis for parallelization [44]. To handle the distributed memory design of these systems, MPI is able to utilize its messaging technique to instruct the dispersed nodes on their tasks.

At a high level, there are some difficulties with using MPI alone. As the authors of [45] discuss, MPI can oftentimes result in a large restructuring of source code. This is because the data distribution and process synchronization need to be explicitly controlled by the programmer and cannot be done automatically. When wanting to target a wide variety of clusters for benchmarking, testing, or implementation, or if updates to a code base were conducted, restructuring the code repeatedly could be time-consuming. As a result, combining MPI with another API such as OpenMP or OpenCL could utilize the strengths of MPI, while allowing an abstracted form of parallelism at the node level through the API [45]. On the other hand, as the authors of [45] continue, using an API such as OpenMP on its own will not suffice for distributed systems. OpenMP is targeted more so for shared memory systems, and fine-tuning the parallelism is difficult. As the authors of [46] describe, properly partitioning data has additional difficulties of its own, since it is an NP-complete problem. Coordinating data distribution through MPI messages can alleviate this, as it can periodically synchronize nodes and attempt to balance the load.

2.2.5.2 Programming Model Optimizations

2.2.5.2.1 Vertex Centric   To approach the aforementioned challenges of processing large-scale graphs, the authors in Ref. [47] present a programming model called Pregel, a vertex-centric paradigm. At the time of writing of [48], this was one of the most popular programming models, and as the authors of [49] show, the vertex-centric model is used in systems such as Giraph, GraphLab, MapReduce, and Blogel.

The premise of the vertex-centric model is to use a vertex as the unit of parallelization to leverage fine-grained parallelism. During periods between global synchronization points (called supersteps), vertices are able to alter their local state, modify their edges, send messages, or change the graph topology. For the messaging, each vertex utilizes message passing to communicate with other vertices in regard to its updates, where the message is received at the beginning of the next superstep. The vertex-centric algorithm continues until no vertex changes [47].

Pregel contains optimization techniques that can be implemented on a per-problem basis. These include optimizations that can alleviate messaging overhead. The communication overhead of vertex-centric systems can be quite large and is a main disadvantage of this programming model. The amount of communication required for many vertices to effectively message all appropriate vertices, along with the synchronization, can be substantial [47,50]. Other vertex-centric systems also have their own sets of optimizations. An early disadvantage of Pregel, especially in the context of large-scale graphs, is that the computation state resides in RAM. However, later updates to Pregel have worked to push data to disks [47]. Using this on a HPC resource generally provides more available RAM for holding the computation state, but holding the entirety of large graphs is unlikely.

Attack graphs are most useful when they are exhaustive. As a result, the overall topology of the attack graph will not change during generation, nor will subsections of the graph be combined. Using a vertex-centric programming model in terms of leveraging the topology mutate function may not be beneficial from a performance standpoint, due to the frequent interactions between subgraphs resulting from expansion of each vertex and the associated messages that must be passed as a result.

2.2.5.2.2 Subgraph Centric To mitigate the high communication overhead of the vertex-centric programming model, a subgraph-centric programming model can be used [48,50]. In this model, subgraphs are used as the unit of parallelization, rather than vertices. This reduces the level of fine-grained parallelism in the problem space and is able to limit the amount of communication overhead [48]. Rather than messages being passed between all vertices, messages are passed between subgraphs. Boundary points within the attack graph can be identified and used as places to break off a subgraph and hopefully reduce the number of messages sent between subgraphs. In the subgraph-centric model, two distinct subcategories are derived: partition centric and neighborhood centric [48].

For the partition-centric model, partitions are the unit of parel-lelization [48]. As the authors of [48] state, the subgraph has vertices of two types: internal and boundary. Boundary vertices must have a transfer to communicate messages, whereas internal vertices are imme-diately able to exchange information. Due to the immediate exchange of information in the internal vertices, the communication overhead can be reduced. For the neighborhood-centric model, subgraphs are able to be customized [48]. Rather than partitions being the default unit of parallelization, the subgraphs can be explicitly configured.

2.3 ANALYSIS

2.3.1 Introduction

Analyses of attack graphs, compliance graphs, and attack dependency graphs are important to resolve potential issues in a network. However, quantifying probabilities of compliance violations or attacks, as well as damages from their occurrences is a challenge for accurate analysis [51–53]. In terms of quantifying compliance violations, damages can be identified in regulatory penalties, legal sanctions, and removal of systems from an active network [3]. Damages from attacks can be identified in terms of direct losses (data theft and damage) and indirect losses (other losses and opportunity costs). The next difficulty for analysis is the technique used. This section will focus on the methods and quantification schemes used for the analysis of the generated graphs.

2.3.2 Markov Process Model

After the generation of an attack graph, it is desirable to model an attacker's standpoint to analyze strategies or approaches that may be taken to put the network in a vulnerable state. Likewise for compliance graphs, it is desirable to model probable ways for a system to fall out of compliance. By understanding the common or likely violations that can occur, a team can work on building countermeasures. The goal of a Markov process model is to convert the generated graph into a Markov process, to use as the baseline for probabilistic predictions. The computation has been shown to be parallelizable and can be performed with a CPU and an Intel Phi Coprocessor simultaneously [51]. The work in Ref. [51] leveraged the Intel Phi's ability to perform matrix multiplication more efficiently than a standard CPU. The additional capabilities of the Intel Phi with respect to decisions and branches support the inclusion of more robust analysis and decisions about future courses of action natively on the Intel Phi compared to a standard graphics processing unit (GPU).

Leveraging the Markov process model as a defender can yield beneficial results. First, it can raise awareness to weak points in the system, which can then be flagged for additional monitoring, strengthened, or hardened against attacks. Second, it can illustrate methods for implementing a trapping state or regression state to thwart potential attackers. Identity of such states in the system is important because the number which can be effectively deployed may be limited. Third, by computing the total expected reward, it is possible to quantify the security measures in place and the potential difficulties of putting the network in a compromised position [51,54].

2.3.3   Shortest Path

When quantifying the possibility of a system compromise, there are a few considerations to take into account. Namely, these are the degree of harm that can be caused by a vulnerability, the presence and effectiveness of intrusion detection systems, the capability of an attacker, and the attack path. One method of analysis is focusing on the attack path [12]. While being a less sophisticated approach when compared to the Markov process model, determining the shortest path to an attacker's potential goal state can reveal different stances an attacker may take [55]. The shortest path also identifies the fewest actions that must occur to compromise the system, each of which could be caused by a single attacker or by a combination of attackers, each leaving the system in a more compromised state than it was previously. This type of analysis can be useful for revealing pass-the-hash attacks [56]. As the authors of [57] describe, pass-the-hash attacks steal hashed credentials, rather than the plaintext. The hashed credentials can then be passed to single sign-on services to attempt to comprise the system. If the compromise was successful, an attacker could then attempt to escalate privileges by capturing a more privileged user within the shared infrastructure environment. If an attacker was able to capture a user with enough privileges, the attacker could then commit more dangerous attacks on critical systems. Three common shortest-path algorithms are discussed below.

2.3.3.1   Dijkstra's Algorithm

Dijkstra's algorithm works by starting at a given node and works through a given graph, keeping record of known shortest distances from each node to the start node. However, since the shortest distance is calculated by adding the path from each node, the weights on the graph edges must be positive. Advantages of Dijkstra's algorithm lie in its ease of use and execution [58]. Disadvantages lie in its time complexity of $O(n^2)$, where n is the number of vertices, inefficiencies, and restriction to positive edge weights [59]. Inefficiencies in Dijkstra's algorithm are in its memory consumption. For the algorithm, the entire graph is used as an input. In the case of these large-scale graphs that can be terabytes in size, memory cannot hold the entirety of the graph [50]. As a result, it is unlikely that Dijkstra's algorithm can be used for analyzing these graphs in their entirety.

2.3.3.2 Bellman–Ford Algorithm

An alternate approach to computing the shortest path from a given node to all other nodes in the graph is the Bellman–Ford algorithm. This is a bottom-up approach, retrieving the shortest paths of nodes with lower degree first. As opposed to Dijkstra's algorithm, Bellman–Ford is able to function with negative edge weights. However, the Bellman–Ford algorithm runs at a much higher time complexity of $O(nm)$, where n is the number of vertices and m is the number of edges. In practice, the number of edges is much larger than the number of vertices [59].

2.3.3.3 Parallel APSP

As a result of the disadvantages and costs incurred by Dijkstra's and Bellman–Ford algorithms, further research has been conducted to identify better shortest-path techniques [59]. Parallelizing all-pairs shortest paths (APSP) has been performed at various degrees. The more promising trend revolves around a bucket sort approach, where a number of buckets are initialized, with their bucket number representing the number of degrees a vertex has [58]. The problem is then parallelized by having threads fill buckets accordingly. Race conditions from simultaneous bucket updates are avoided by the use of locks. Improvements to this approach are described in [58] through the use of intelligent ordering mechanisms.

2.3.4 Minimization

After the generation of attack graphs, it is possible to visualize possible attack vectors an adversary could take. Using Markov process models, it is also possible to decide upon optimal trapping states or regression states to increase a defensive position. However, there is a gap in knowing how an adversary could attack a system, and the ideal way to thwart the said attack. One analysis technique is through using minimization. Using minimization can aid in attack prevention in the two ways discussed below.

Minimization can be employed to determine if a given security countermeasure increases the security of a network [53]. Given a security countermeasure and the generated attack graph, if it prevents a transition from one graph state to another, remove the connecting edge. After repeating for all possible edge removals, if the number of attacker goal states has decreased, then the security countermeasure does increase the security of a network. If the number of goal states remains the same, then the security countermeasure is not sufficient enough to increase the security of the network. This process can be repeated with a set of countermeasures, to determine if sets of countermeasures will remove attacker goal states.

Another technique for minimization analysis is finding the smallest subset of security countermeasures that produces a desired network security threshold [53]. To do so, the minimum set of attacks that can be prevented to make the network secure must be determined. However, the authors of [53] discuss that determining this is an NP-complete problem. This becomes incredibly infeasible especially with large graphs with high numbers of possible attack vectors. But, if the minimum set of attacks was known, then a set of countermeasures could be looped through to identify the smallest number that would prevent all of the attacks in the minimum set.

2.3.5 Criticality

Determining a compliance violation or attack vector possibility is useful, but often it does not differentiate between the types of threats. There are a lot of factors to consider when handling possible threats, such as the possibility of occurrence, the attacker's competency, and the repercussions from a successful attack. As an alternative (or additional) approach to Markov process models, the authors of [60] present a seven-stage security evaluation. This evaluation will result in security levels of green, yellow, orange, or red to indicate the severity or criticality of an event.

The authors in Ref. [60] describe the seven stages as a qualitative means of describing the network security level. Stage 1 is for determining the criticality level of hosts. This is conducted by processing through all of the hosts and assigning a level in terms of high, medium, or low criticality. Stage 2 describes the severity of attacks using the Common Vulnerability Scoring System. Stage 3 makes use of the first two stages to determine the damage level of an attack. Stage 4 determines the damage level of threats. Stage 5 determines the access complexity for threats and attacks. Stage 6 utilizes the previous stage's access complexity to determine the likelihood of a threat realization. Lastly, stage 7 evaluates the network security from the likelihood of an attack and the damages caused. Using such a system can identify areas that require higher prioritization over others, as well as provide a demonstrative means to aid in pushing for appropriate countermeasures.

2.3.6   Semi-Metricity

One way to enhance the performance of graph analysis is to utilize what is known as the metric backbone [48,61]. The metric backbone, as the authors of [61] go on to discuss, is the minimum subgraph of a larger graph, which also still maintains the shortest paths. The metric backbone is used for weighted graphs, so incorporating this in conjunction with Markov process model and shortest-path analysis techniques could prove promising for handling the large-scale graphs. By using the metric backbone rather than the entire generated graph, other analysis techniques could be leveraged. The advantage of this is that the analysis conducted on the metric backbone will be exact, or be a good approximation of the analysis that would be conducted on the entirety of the original graph [48,61].

For obtaining the metric backbone, the all-pairs shortest paths problem must first be solved [61]. As discussed in a previous section, there has been promising work in parallelizing this problem [59]. Typically, as the authors of [59] state, computing the all-pairs shortest paths problem can incur high runtimes of its own. However, by using the approach presented by the authors of [59], and leveraging a HPC cluster for the parallelization, the metric backbone can potentially be obtained in a very reasonable amount of time.

2.4 CONCLUSIONS AND FUTURE WORK

Utilizing graphs is a promising method for approaching cybersecurity problems. The usage of attack graphs and attack dependency graphs can illustrate potential system vulnerabilities and the ways an adversary can compromise a system. Both of these graph techniques can display different types of information, allowing for cybersecurity professionals to tailor which data to examine and identify countermeasures most suitable for systems. Combining both attack graphs and attack dependency graphs can prove even more beneficial, allowing for more data to be examined simultaneously. Compliance graphs are another useful technique that is particularly helpful for industries needing to conform to multiple standards or compliance regulations. Compliance graphs are also worthwhile for examining cyber-physical systems that are increasingly more common.

However, processing and analyzing these graphs is a problem that sequential or single-system machines are unable to handle. With billions of vertices and edges needing more system resources, along with high computation time, high-performance computing systems are valuable candidates to utilize these graphs. Combined with parallelism, hardware techniques, better data structures, tailoring programming models, using libraries, or limiting the analysis scope, these graph techniques are more accessible, as is analysis of these graphs.

The landscape for future work in this area is plentiful. Improvements to graph representation have fertile ground, where various authors have laid the groundwork for a multitude of new techniques. Implementations and improvements of a unified attack and attack dependency graphs could prove to have promising results as well. Analysis techniques are broad, and all have potential areas of improvement. Markov process models are difficult to solve, but can lead to key insight into system countermeasures. In addition to HPC clusters, utilizing accelerators or learning techniques can simplify solutions. Minimization analysis is highly useful for cybersecurity professionals, since budgetary limits, time constraints, and inter-system compatibility prevent the implementation of all possible countermeasures. This is an NP-complete problem, so solution approaches or new estimation algorithms can provide many benefits for professionals to incorporate this type of analysis in their defense arsenal. Examining the usage and performance of a metric backbone for analysis technique is also likely promising.

Overall, graph techniques are extraordinarily useful for cybersecurity purposes. While difficult due to scalability and long computation times, high-performance computing and innovative processing techniques can reduce the typical overhead that is associated with these tools on single-system machines.

REFERENCES

[1] Y. Yanakiev and T. Tagarev, "Governance model of a cybersecurity network: Best practices in the academic literature," in *CompSysTech '20: Proceedings of the 21st International Conference on Computer Systems and Technologies '20*, June 2020, pp. 27–34, doi: 10.1145/3407982.3407992.

[2] O. B. Fredj, A. Mihoub, M. Krichen, O. Cheikhrouhou, and A. Derhab, "Cyber security attack prediction: A deep learning approach," in *SIN 2020: 13th International Conference on Security of Information and Networks*, November 2020, pp. 1–6, doi: 10.1145/3433174.3433614.

[3] J. Hale, P. Hawrylak, and M. Papa, "Compliance method for a cyberphysical system." U.S. Patent Number 9,471,789, Oct. 18, 2016.

[4] N. Baloyi and P. Kotzé, "Guidelines for data privacy compliance: A focus on cyberphysical systems and internet of things," *Presented at the SAICSIT,* Skukuza South Africa, 2019, doi: 10.1145/3351108.3351143.

[5] E. Allman, "Complying with compliance: Blowing it off is not an option," *ACM Queue*, vol. 4, no. 7, pp. 18–21, 2006.

[6] C. Phillips and L. P. Swiler, "A graph-based system for network-vulnerability analysis," *Proceedings of the New Security Paradigms Workshop*, vol. Part F1292, pp. 71–79, 1998, doi: 10.1145/310889.310919.

[7] B. Schneier, "Modeling security threats," *Dr. Dobb's Journal*, vol. 24, no. 12, 1999.

[8] X. Ou, W. F. Boyer, and M. A. Mcqueen, "A scalable approach to attack graph generation," pp. 336–345, 2006.

[9] J. Zhang, S. Khoram, and J. Li, "Boosting the performance of FPGA-based graph processor using hybrid memory cube: A case for breadth first search," *FPGA 2017- Proceedings of 2017 ACMSIGDA International Symposium of Field-Program. Gate Arrays*, pp. 207–216, 2017, doi: 10.1145/3020078.3021737.

[10] J. Berry and B. Hendrickson, "Graph analysis with high performance computing," *Computing in Science & Engineering*, 2007, doi: 10.1109/MCSE.2008.56.

[11] S. Ainsworth and T. M. Jones, "Graph prefetching using data structure knowledge," *Proceedings of International Conference on Supercomputer*, vol. 01–03-June, 2016, doi: 10.1145/2925426.2926254.

[12] O. Sheyner, J. Haines, S. Jha, R. Lippmann, and J. Wing, "Automated generation and analysis of attack graphs," *Proceeding 2002 IEEE Symposium on Security and Privacy*, Berkeley, CA, pp. 254–265, 2002.

[13] N. Ghosh and S. K. Ghosh, "A planner-based approach to generate and analyze minimal attack graph," *Applied Intelligence*, vol. 36, no. 2, pp. 369–390, 2012, doi: 10.1007/s10489-010-0266-8.

[14] M. Li, P. Hawrylak, and J. Hale, "Concurrency strategies for attack graph generation," *Proceedings of 2019 2nd International Conference on Conference on Data Intelligence and Security, ICDIS 2019*, pp. 174–179, 2019, doi: 10.1109/ICDIS.2019.00033.

[15] N. Poolsappasit, R. Dewri, and I. Ray, "Dynamic security risk management using Bayesian attack graphs," *IEEE Transactions on Dependable and Secure Computing*, vol. 9, no. 1, pp. 61–74, 2012, doi: 10.1109/TDSC.2011.34.

[16] L. Muñoz-González, D. Sgandurra, A. Paudice, and E. C. Lupu, "Efficient attack graph analysis through approximate inference," *ACM Transactions on Privacy and Security*, vol. 20, no. 3, 2017, doi: 10.1145/3105760.

[17] K. Kaynar and F. Sivrikaya, "Distributed attack graph generation," *IEEE Transactions on Dependable and Secure Computing*, vol. 13, no. 5, pp. 519–532, 2016, doi: 10.1109/TDSC.2015.2423682.

[18] K. Cook, T. Shaw, J. Hale, and P. Hawrylak, "Scalable attack graph generation," *Proceedings of 11th Annual Cyber and Information Security Research Conference, CISRC 2016*, 2016, doi: 10.1145/2897795.2897821.

[19] S. Jajodia, S. Noel, and B. O'Berry, *Topological Analysis of Network Attack Vulnerability*, vol. 5. New York: Springer-Verlag, 2005.

[20] S. Noel and S. Jajodia, "Managing attack graph complexity through visual hierarchical aggregation," in *Proceedings of the 2004 ACM Workshop on Visualization and Data Mining for Computer Security - VizSEC/DMSEC '04*, New York, 2004, pp. 109–109, doi: 10.1145/1029208.1029225.

[21] M. Albanese and S. Jajodia, "A graphical model to assess the impact of multi-step attacks," *The Journal of Defense Modeling and Simulation*, vol. 15, no. 1, pp. 79–93, 2018, doi: 10.1177/1548512917706043.

[22] G. Louthan, P. Hardwicke, P. Hawrylak, and J. Hale, "Toward hybrid attack dependency graphs," *International Conference Proceedings Series - ACM*, 2011, doi: 10.1145/2179298.2179368.

[23] A. Natarajan, Peng Ning, Yao Liu, S. Jajodia, and S. E. Hutchinson, "NSDMiner: Automated discovery of network service dependencies," in *2012 Proceedings IEEE INFOCOM*, March 2012, pp. 2507–2515, doi: 10.1109/INFCOM.2012.6195642.

[24] P. Yao, L. Zheng, X. Liao, H. Jin, and B. He, "An efficient graph accelerator with parallel data conflict management," *PACT '10: International Conference on Parallel Architectures and Compilation Techniques*, 2018, doi: 10.1145/3243176.3243201.

[25] G. Dai, Y. Chi, Y. Wang, and H. Yang, "FPGP: Graph processing framework on FPGA: A case study of breadth-first search," *FPGA 2016- Proceedings of 2016 ACMSIGDA International Symposium on Field- Program. Gate Arrays*, pp. 105–110, 2016, doi: 10.1145/2847263.2847339.

[26] S. Arifuzzaman and M. Khan, "Fast parallel conversion of edge list to adjacency list for large-scale graphs," in *HPC '15: Proceedings of the Symposium on High Performance Computing*, San Diego, CA, April 2015, pp. 17–24.

[27] N. Alon, R. Yuster, and U. Zwick, "Finding and counting given length cycles," *Algorithmica*, vol. 17, pp. 209–223, 1997.

[28] D. Coppersmith and S. Winograd, "Matrix multiplication via arithmetic progressions," in *Proceedings of the 19th Annual ACM Symposium on Theory of Computing*, New York, NY, 1987, pp. 1–6.

[29] "Property Maps | The Boost Graph Library | InformIT." https://www.informit.com/articles/article.aspx?p=25777&seqNum=6 (accessed Apr. 11, 2021).

[30] X. Yu et al., "The construction of large graph data structures in a scalable distributed message system," in *HPCCT 2018: Proceedings of the 2018 2nd High Performance Computing and Cluster Technologies Conference*, June 2018, pp. 6–10, doi: 10.1145/3234664.3234682.

[31] P. Liakos, K. Papakonstantinopoulou, and A. Delis, "Memory-optimized distributed graph processing through novel compression techniques," in *CIKM '16: Proceedings of the 25th ACM International Conference on Information and Knowledge Management*, October 2016, pp. 2317–2322, doi: 10.1145/2983323.2983687.

[32] "Parallel BGL Distributed Adjacency List -1.73.0." https://www.boost.org/doc/libs/1_73_0/libs/graph_parallel/doc/html/distributed_adjacency_list.html (accessed April 11, 2021).

[33] "Parallel BGL Distributed Property Map -1.64.0." https://www.boost. org/doc/libs/1_64_0/libs/graph_parallel/doc/html/distributed_ property_map.html (accessed April 11, 2021).

[34] M. Besta, D. Stanojevic, T. Zivic, J. Singh, M. Hoerold, and T. Hoefler, "Log(graph): A near-optimal high-performance graph representation," in *PACT '18: Proceedings of the 27th International Conference on Parallel Architectures and Compilation Techniques*, New York, NY, November 2018, pp. 1–13.

[35] J. Balaji and R. Sunderraman, "Graph topology abstraction for distributed path queries," in *HPGP '16: Proceedings of the ACM Workshop on High Performance Graph Processing*, May 2016, pp. 27–34, doi: 10.1145/2915516.2915520.

[36] "An Overview of the Parallel Boost Graph Library -1.75.0."

[37] "The Boost Graph Library -1.75.0."

[38] "Boost Graph Library: Converting Existing Graphs to BGL -1.75.0."

[39] J. Yan, G. Tan, and N. Sun, "Exploiting fine-grained parallelism in graph traversal algorithms via lock virtualization on multi-core architecture," *The Journal of Supercomputing*, vol. 69, no. 3, pp. 1462–1490, September 2014, doi: 10.1007/s11227-014-1239-1.

[40] N. Edmonds, J. Willcock, A. Lumsdaine, and T. Hoefler, "Design of a large-scale hybrid-parallel graph library," *International Conference on High Performance Computing Symposium*, Goa, 2010.

[41] N. Edmonds, "Active messages as a spanning model for parallel graph computation," 2013.

[42] "Graph Partitioning | Our Pattern Language."

[43] "ParMETIS - Parallel Graph Partitioning and Fill-reducing Matrix Ordering | Karypis Lab."

[44] P. Pacheco, *An Introduction to Parallel Programming*, Amsterdam, Netherlands: Elsevier, 2011.

[45] G. Jost and H. Jin, "Comparing the OpenMP, MPI, and Hybrid Programming Paradigms on an SMP Cluster," p. 10.

[46] N. Doekemeijer, "A survey of parallel graph processing frameworks," p. 30.

[47] G. Malewicz et al., "Pregel: A system for large-scale graph processing," June 2010, p. 11, doi: 10.1145/1807167.1807184.

[48] V. Kalavri, "Performance optimization techniques and tools for distributed graph processing," PhD, KTH Royal Institute of Technology, Stockholm, Sweden, 2016.

[49] K. Ammar and T. Ozsu, "Experimental analysis of distributed graph systems," *Proceedings of VLDB Endowment*, vol. 11, no. 10, June 2018, doi: 10.14778/3231751.3231764.

[50] R. McCune, T. Weninger, and G. Madey, "Thinking like a vertex: A survey of vertex-centric frameworks for large-scale distributed graph processing," *ACM Computing Surveys*, vol. 48, no. 2, 2015, doi: 10.1145/2818185.

[51] K. Zeng, "Cyber attack analysis based on Markov process model," 2017.

[52] S. Abraham and S. Nair, "Predictive cyber security analytics framework: A non-homogenous Markov model for security quantification," pp. 195–209, January 2014, doi: 10.5121/csit.2014.41316.

[53] S. Jha, O. Sheyner, and J. Wing, "Two formal analyses of attack graphs," *Proceedings of Computer Security Foundations Workshop*, vol. 2002-January, pp. 49–63, 2002, doi: 10.1109/CSFW.2002.1021806.

[54] B. Chen, Y. Liu, S. Li, and X. Gao, "Attack intent analysis method based on attack path graph," *The ACM International Conference Proceeding Series*, pp. 97–102, 2019, doi: 10.1145/3371676.3371680.

[55] L. P. Swiler, C. Phillips, D. Ellis, and S. Chakerian, "Computer-attack graph generation tool," in *Proceedings DARPA Information Survivability Conference and Exposition II. DISCEX'01*, Anaheim, CA, 2001, vol. 2, pp. 307–321, doi: 10.1109/DISCEX.2001.932182.

[56] E. Hogan, J. R. Johnson, and M. Halappanavar, "Graph coarsening for path finding in cybersecurity graphs," *The ACM International Conference Proceeding Series*, 2013, doi: 10.1145/2459976.2459984.

[57] D. Dimov and Y. Tzonev, "Pass-the-hash: One of the most prevalent yet underrated attacks for credentials theft and reuse," in *18th International Conference on Computer Systems and Technologies*, 2017, pp. 149–154, doi: 10.1145/3134302.3134338.

[58] Z. Ruifang, J. Tianyi, and Z. Haitao, "Application of improved Dijkstra algorithm in two-dimensional path planning problem," *The ACM International Conference Proceeding Series*, pp. 211–215, 2019, doi: 10.1145/3378065.3378106.

[59] J. W. Kim, H. Choi, and S. H. Bae, "Efficient parallel all-pairs shortest paths algorithm for complex graph analysis," *The ACM International Conference Proceeding Series*, 2018, doi: 10.1145/3229710.3229730.

[60] I. Kotenko and M. Stepashkin, "Attack graph based evaluation of network security," *Lecture Notes in Computer Science Subseries Lecture Notes in Artificial Intelligence and Lecture Notes in Bioinformatics*, vol. 4237 LNCS, pp. 216–227, 2006, doi: 10.1007/11909033_20.

[61] V. Kalavri, T. Simas, and D. Logothetis, "The shortest path is not always a straight line: Leveraging semi-metricity in graph analysis," *Proceedings of VLDB Endowment*, vol. 9, no. 9, 2016, doi: 10.14778/2947618.2947623.

CHAPTER 3

OMNI at the Edge

Elizabeth Bautista

Lawrence Berkeley National Laboratory

Nitin Sukhija

Slippery Rock University of Pennsylvania

Melissa Romanus, Thomas Davis, and Cary Whitney

Lawrence Berkeley National Laboratory

CONTENTS

DOI: 10.1201/9781003155799-3

3.1 INTRODUCTION

The growing scale of high-performance computing (HPC) systems and their support infrastructure coupled with the proliferation of sensors and system monitoring software has led to a deluge of operational data in modern HPC data centers [1]. At NERSC, these operational data are collected from thousands of sources in the data center ranging from environmental control systems to single-node memory usage and stored into a single data warehouse, the Operations Monitoring and Notification Infrastructure (OMNI). Storing these data into OMNI allows us to analyze and correlate for systems monitoring and research purposes in a more efficient way; however, there are many challenges associated with gathering complex time series data from so many heterogeneous sources in near-real time, such as latency, bandwidth, privacy, infrastructure, or availability. Further, we need to ensure the security of the data between internal staff: Groups should not be able to access data of other groups and provide a secure framework to those who are from external sources and want to perform research on our data.

Within the OMNI system, challenges associated with aggregating all data sources into a standalone data warehouse are mitigated using edge computing technologies. For example, data preparation of high-volume, high-velocity metrics from HPC systems is performed at containerized gateway nodes at the local edge before being forwarded to OMNI. These nodes also offer local buffering of data in the event that data transfer to OMNI is unavailable due to network outages or if the data warehouse has been compromised by hardware failure or cyberthreat. We also have to ensure that from a cybersecurity aspect, that data that go through one device to another or move from one internal network to another are securely transported to OMNI.

In this chapter, we will discuss the NERSC high-performance computing data center and using edge computing services to securely send data to OMNI from heterogeneous sources. We will then detail the high-availability OMNI infrastructure and its use of state-of-the-art edge computing technologies for collecting, analyzing, and securing extremely high-volume, continuous 24×7 data in near-real time. We will also discuss the cybersecurity aspects of how we keep these data secure not only from each staff who owns the data, but also through various devices and networks. We will discuss internal and external access policies put in place and the plan to make these data available for the public for crowdsourcing analysis. We will then provide use cases that demonstrate how the availability of OMNI data has benefited the overall NERSC data center, from a facilities and machine perspective as well as from a cybersecurity standpoint. Finally, we will outline the ongoing and future work, including upgrades being made to the data warehouse for the upcoming Perlmutter supercomputer – a system that will be 3–4× the size of our current HPE/Cray Cori system.

3.2 BACKGROUND

NERSC is the mission scientific computational facility for the Office of Science in the U.S. Department of Energy (DOE) and has operated many HPC systems since its inception at Lawrence Livermore National Laboratory in 1974. Sixteen NERSC systems have appeared on the TOP500 [2] list of fastest computing systems in the world. NERSC's mission is to provide HPC and compute resources to science users at high availability with high utilization of the machines in order to further the scientific research supported by the DOE Office of Science. The current NERSC HPC data center is located at Shyh Wang Hall.

The building is a 140,000-gross-square-foot (GSF) facility that houses both the data center and office spaces for Berkeley Lab Computing Sciences division employees spanning NERSC, the Scientific Computing Division who manages the Energy Sciences Network (ESnet), and the Computational Research Division (CRD). Shyh Wang Hall comprises four floors – two office floors (28,000 square feet each), one machine room floor (20,000 square feet with room to expand up to 28,000 square feet), and one mechanical level. It is outfitted with a seismic subfloor and is a LEED®-certified Gold facility, averaging a monthly Level 2 Power Usage Effectiveness (PUE) ratio of 1.07 over the past year. A Level 2 PUE is defined to be measured from the power distribution unit (PDU) outputs in terms of equipment and utility inputs in terms of facility and is collected at an interval of hourly and daily. Shyh Wang Hall has recently completed upgrading its power capacity and facility capabilities from 12.5 to 25 MW (megawatts) to prepare for the installation of the next HPC system, Perlmutter [10,11].

The challenges of properly managing the operational data at the scale of HPC data centers are complex given their distributed nature and, when considering latency, cybersecurity, workflows, and volume requirements, can compound existing issues. Changes in the compute environment can occur at nano- and microsecond scales. Therefore, we have to consider how to transmit and store data, at what point should the data be processed or encrypted, and how workflows should be coordinated as data are transferred across devices and networks. Further, from a business perspective, how much time in terms of staffing will this take and at what costs?

What types of data are considered operational data? Examples include time series data from the environment (e.g., temperature, power, humidity levels, and particle levels), monitoring data (e.g., network speeds, latency, packet loss, utilization, or those that monitor the filesystem for disk write speeds, I/O, and CRC errors), and event data (e.g., system logs, console logs, hardware failure events, and power events, essentially anything that has a start and end time). The reporting rate of these data often depends on several factors, including individual properties of the sensor or machine, the size of the data, whether or not continuous monitoring is necessary, and how quickly it is needed for analysis. Some systems do not report data by default and must be instrumented by system administrators.

In designing OMNI, we wanted the computation to occur as close to the source as possible. This minimizes overall latency for real-time analysis and archiving results. Figure 3.1 illustrates the overall data pipeline of the OMNI system for the Perlmutter HPC system; data from the HPC system along with multiple other sources provide data from Prometheus end points or a telemetry API. Data are transformed at this edge and can either go to Elasticsearch or VictoriaMetrics where they can be queried by Grafana or Kibana, two visualization tools, or can go to vmagent that handles sending the information to various areas for alerting. In this case, data are ready to be analyzed in real time by operations staff who manage the data center and need to know the immediate health of every system within their responsibilities. At the same time, a second stream of these data is sent directly to Elasticsearch and VictoriaMetrics for online archiving.

OMNI's overall design also considers where we will implement the appropriate cybersecurity practices. Within the OMNI network, operations staff have control over the types of protocols implemented. Outside of OMNI, however, protocols may change without their knowledge or control; therefore, it is policy to require anyone wanting

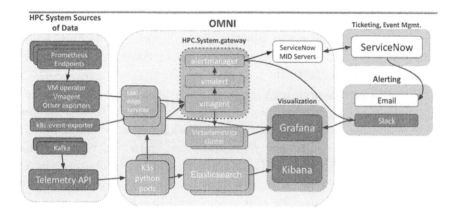

Figure 3.1 Monitoring data pipeline for the Perlmutter HPC system to OMNI.

to transmit data to OMNI to use the proper security protocols such as transport layer security (TLS) and anyone logging into the infrastructure to use a modified version of secure sockets shell (SSH) that allows the NERSC cybersecurity team to record and analyze the content of interactive SSH sessions. A multi-factor authentication (MFA) token is also required for logging in externally through a gateway. Further, non-secure protocols have been isolated externally and from each other. For example, the onewire devices (measures temperature and humidity on racks) are on a different network than the power distribution units (PDUs) or the Modbus protocol-based devices.

For daily operational considerations, such as when a user needs to see their data, or how workflows are coordinated, being highly available is crucial. When the team designed OMNI, it was meant for the system to continue collecting data as long as the facility has power. It is the first system to come up after stable power is confirmed and the last system to be turned off during a facility power maintenance. However, OMNI's main purpose was to be a data archiver and a real-time data provider. Operations staff would need an immediate analysis of the data in real time to monitor the health of the facility and its assets. OMNI is also the mechanism to store data in one location to correlate multiple data sources for decision making. As such, the data have been separated so that the source and types of data are processed differently and more efficiently. For example, slower and older data sources such as Modbus or onewire are processed and routed to Elasticsearch. Any data that have enhancements attached to them such as IP address and hostname or are text based also go to Elasticsearch. Newer, faster, and denser data sources, as well as any data that cannot be converted are ingested and routed to VictoriaMetrics.

Data in Elasticsearch or VictoriaMetrics are stored for immediate online access and queried through Grafana and Kibana. Datasets have different lifetimes within the immediate storage areas. VictoriaMetrics has more efficient compression rates so that data can be accessible online for a longer time frame. OMNI is configured with separate virtual machine (VM) clusters that hold different datasets. For example, node performance metrics may be online for 6 months, but power data can be kept for 5 years depending on the user's required indexing rate. Determining how long a user needs to have immediate access to their data helps to streamline their workflow. In the above examples, the user of power data wants to analyze multiple years of data; however, he does not need them to be that dense. Power data are currently collected one data point per 5 to 30 seconds, depending on the device. These are very dense data and immediately stored in archival storage, the high-performance storage system (HPSS), so that the team can continue to have access to the original raw data. However, for the user's needs and immediate analysis, the data are first processed by indexing different datasets that have data points every hour for one user and every 30 minutes for another user. With the new indexes, each user can immediately analyze historical data based on his needs without processing the dataset first or waiting for the processing to occur before visualizing them in Grafana or Kibana.

In designing OMNI, a big consideration is cost and where to invest our yearly budget. As such, the decision made is to use open-source software, a 3-year cycle of hardware refresh, and in-house staff who can manage the cluster. In terms of storage, the team leveraged HPSS as their archival needs. This helps mitigate costs for online, immediate storage that is kept on fast disks, while the older or raw data can be stored in the long-term storage.

3.3 OMNI ARCHITECTURE AND TECHNOLOGIES

OMNI is a flexible big data solution to collect, manage, and analyze data related to monitoring of extreme-scale computing systems [5].

This infrastructure facilitates a single location for storing the heterogeneous datasets and is comprised of two highly scalable, fast, and efficient time series databases: Elasticsearch [6] for logs, data requiring strings, and small, low-volume metric sets and VictoriaMetrics [4] for capturing high-volume metric sets from Prometheus [7]. Examples of operational data include time series data from the environment (e.g., temperature, power, humidity levels, and particle levels), monitoring data (e.g., network speeds, latency, packet loss, utilization, or those that monitor the filesystem for disk write speeds, I/O, and CRC errors), and event data (e.g., system logs, console logs, hardware failure events, and power events, essentially anything that has a start and end time). The network backbone of OMNI has recently been upgraded from a static network to a software-defined, reconfigurable network with spine–leaf topology.

3.3.1 OMNI k3s Architecture

The primary architecture of the newly upgraded OMNI system is built on k3s, a lightweight Kubernetes distribution [3]. As shown in Figure 3.2, OMNI consists of multiple k3s clusters, each of which is self-contained with master and worker nodes and its own control plane. In OMNI, a k3s cluster can consist of several different types of bare-metal hardware as well as virtual machines. Virtual machines are utilized for etcd/master/control plane pods. Every cluster consists of the same monitoring infrastructure; this monitoring infrastructure consists of a VictoriaMetrics operator (vm-operator); kube-event; kube-state-metrics; Loki/Promtail; Prometheus node exporter; for nodes with IPMI, a Prometheus IPMI exporter; and for nodes with SATA/NVME drives, a Prometheus smartctl exporter. In addition, OMNI utilizes kubernetes-mixin, a set of Grafana dashboards and Prometheus alerts for Kubernetes, in order to oversee the cluster visually using our on-prem Grafana deployment.

The vm-operator is used to manage a VictoriaMetrics agent (vmagent) instance on each k3s cluster. The vmagent, a core component of VictoriaMetrics, is used to quickly and efficiently scrape metrics from Prometheus-compatible exporters in VictoriaMetrics. It can perform operations such as reading Prometheus configurations and relabeling of data before writing into the VictoriaMetrics backend.

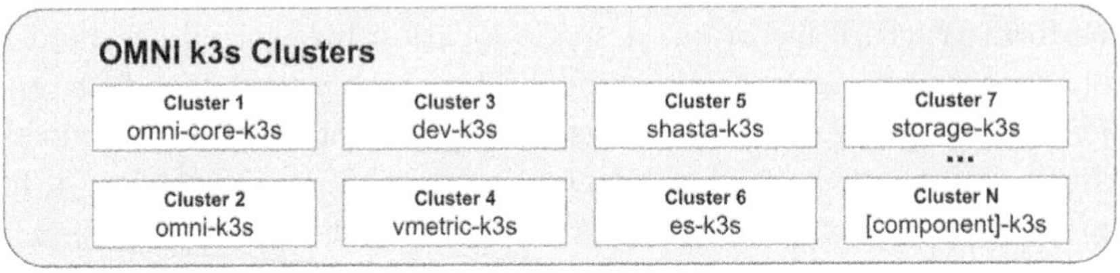

Figure 3.2 OMNI k3s self-contained clusters.

In the event that the remote VictoriaMetrics backend is unreachable, it can buffer collected metrics at the source and then send them when the backend can be reached again.

The omni-core-k3s cluster in Figure 3.2 is used to manage the core services of the OMNI nodes and switches, while omni-k3s handles all of the Modbus and Rancher gateway nodes. In the future, the Redis database as well as the core Grafana services will be managed from this cluster. Vmetric-k3s is a cluster dedicated to VictoriaMetrics, running several separate VictoriaMetrics clusters within it (vmclusters), as follows: (1) omni-vmetric for Prometheus metrics; (2) cori-sedc-vmetric for collecting Cray HPC System Environmental Data metrics from the NERSC Cori machine; (3) cori-vmetric for collecting Prometheus node exporter information, data from the lightweight distributed management system (LDMS), and snmp data from nodes on Cori; and (4) crt-vmetric for collecting facilities information about building power, temperatures, and BACnet data – BAC: Building Automation and Control.

A core tenet of the OMNI system is to be highly available and accessible 24 × 7. The use of multiple small clusters via Kubernetes gives greater flexibility and stability to the system; i.e., you can take down a small cluster, work on it, and bring it back without impacting the rest of OMNI. It also helps to focus and distribute the workloads, allowing for less bottlenecks and finer-grained tuning of Kubernetes infrastructures to meet the specific demands of the workloads it is servicing. This is especially important with the upcoming Perlmutter supercomputer, as the volume and velocity of metrics will be exponentially greater than those of the current NERSC system, Cori. Using Ansible to map a k3s cluster to an oVirt data center/cluster allows for easy creation and deployment of new clusters to the system, as OMNI continues to grow and expand.

Another important aspect of separating workloads across multiple clusters is that it lends itself to an additional layer of cybersecurity via access control. First, user access to each cluster can be granted on an individual or group level. Clusters involved in backend services have no need to be accessed by end users, and thus, restricting them from even accessing that cluster makes it less likely that they are able to compromise the system. Even *within* a k3s cluster, user access may be further restricted; i.e., the cluster administrator can control what users may access which parts of the cluster. In addition to user access control, each cluster may have a unique set of hosts (bare metal or virtual) and sensors that are allowed to access it or that are contained within it. If a host machine becomes compromised, it would potentially only affect the specific k3s clusters that it is interacting with. If for any reason the master node of one the k3s clusters were to be compromised due to a cyberattack, the attacker would not be able to access and do harm to all of the OMNI system; instead, it would be contained to the services and virtual hosts within that specific cluster as well as the hosts or sensors that it communicates with.

3.3.2 Use of Edge Computing in OMNI

The deployment of gateway and other "local edge" nodes as container- ized k3s pods allows us to monitor all computing nodes, services, and applications related to the OMNI architecture. In OMNI, data from sensors and metrics from machines can be considered the extreme edge of the network. Data from the HPC systems – containing thousands of metrics per second – are prepared and sent to OMNI via containerized gateway nodes located at the local edge. These gateway nodes utilize k3s, a lightweight Kubernetes distribution [3] , and agents of Victoria- Metrics [4]. Deployment via k3s allows OMNI to scale and reconfigure itself to meet the increased demands or in the events of faults or failures. It also provides a means of monitoring the health of the OMNI network.

Other uses of edge computing in OMNI include performing data processing at the edge, e.g., on an unused compute node where it is generated or at the gateway node where it is prepped, and then storing the computational results into OMNI. Oftentimes, this allows high-volume metrics to be flattened or downsampled, resulting in less network traffic as well as lower latency queries when querying OMNI data for monitoring purposes on the other end. In some instances, the nature of the data sent to OMNI is sensitive, e.g., system log (syslog) information from the HPC systems, and requires scrubbing and encryption before they can be sent across the network and stored into the more widely available data warehouse. Pre-processing sensitive data where they are generated and encrypting them for transfer over the network provides an important level of cybersecurity that ensures non-privileged users do not have access to passwords or information that could reveal vendor-specific details of the HPC machines or make them vulnerable to cyberattacks.

3.3.3 Securing Small Devices at the Edge

From a cybersecurity point of view, edge computing can be more vulnerable depending on its location in the infrastructure. In OMNI's case, there are small sensors such as onewire devices or older devices that use Modbus that collect and process data such as temperatures, humidity, and power, from UPS, various panels, and substations. These devices can be very small and unable to hold the software required to secure the device using current security policies. They can also be limited in protocols, so it can be a challenge to monitor traffic through them. Further, communicating with these devices can be slow and use older protocols. In designing where in the infrastructure these type of devices should be placed, there are two situations to consider.

The first scenario to consider is should these devices be placed in a wired or wireless network? The wireless infrastructure is controlled by the Lab, and the process automatically chooses an access point that is the strongest and closest to the device attempting to get an Internet Protocol (IP) address. Placing any of these devices on a wireless network has a risk that the strongest access point could be the public one. This particular network is usually hazardous and prone to attacks, the type of attacks that can potentially render a small device useless. As a result, the devices are installed via a wired, internal, isolated network. Nothing from the outside can reach them, and data can only be transmitted to the edge service and then to OMNI.

A second scenario is that these devices may not have the most up-to-date transmission speeds. In one situation, a series of sensors did not have the technology to support a virtual machine or the speed of the network card. It isn't that it was an old device. In standard construction of a building, while these devices are available, the industry just found no need to have them be up to date. They used protocols that were available many years ago, and it continued to work in many instances. However, in a state-of-the-art data center, it was inadequate and there are no replacements in existence. As much as the team wanted to secure these devices in a VM and make them useful, it was not possible, so instead, they used a small node, added it to the network, and installed the Modbus collectors on the node. The device connected to the node took advantage of the more up-to-date hardware and was able to transmit its data at the speed of the existing network.

3.3.4   Function as a Service at the Edge

To provide smaller devices with an edge computing service and security, the team implemented Function as a Service (FaaS) offered on a virtual machine (VM) after the device(s) and is the first spot accessed by the data before OMNI. On this VM, a user can authenticate and query what the data are (which are read from the OMNI backend like elastic) without letting them actually perform operations on the elastic cluster itself. While most users of OMNI are NERSC staff, there are users who are vetted, are collaborators, are affiliates, etc. These special users are not necessarily external staff, but they are outside the NERSC organization. The team has provided another layer of security for these users, especially if they are accessing data from the small devices.

Once authenticated, users are able to perform calculations, run applications, and view the devices without additional infrastructure using FaaS. The software we used can be downloaded from https://fnproject.io. It provides users simpler access to these data because the API is defined with data specifications, not just access specifications. For the user, it means the data sources can change, but the software to process the data does not. For the administrators, they do not need to define how the data are stored in OMNI, as they are already processed prior to writing to OMNI. They can also add devices as needed and still route the data through FaaS. Having this static software insulates users from change.

FaaS was originally implemented for a group of users in the Energy Technologies Division (ETD), to aggregate and compute the

Figure 3.3 Graph samples produced by Grafana to calculate power utilization efficiency with different requirements. The top graph shows a moving average in 5-minute intervals with 30-minute samples. The second graph shows a PUE calculation of 5-minute intervals.

power utilization efficiency of the facility (Figure 3.3). In 2018, ETD transitioned to software called SkySpark [9] from SkyFoundry [8]. No longer needed for analysis or the calculation of PUE, FaaS was still needed to aggregate data from multiple sources in the building into a platform that automates the calculation and data analysis. Data included those from facilities, the HPC systems, rack-level IT systems, and cooling and performance data from the building management system (BMS). SkySpark also detects anomalies in the operation and allows ETD to optimize controls of the facility directly via the BMS (Figure 3.4). For the preparation of Perlmutter, SkySpark will use the data to predict and optimize control sequences prior to its installation and even through additional power expansion of the facility [13].

Water usage efficiency (WUE) monitoring has also leveraged FaaS. As with the calculation of PUE, FaaS aggregates data from various sources, with the bulk of additional data from the Building Automation and Control Network (BACnet), devices that feed data into the BMS system (Figure 3.5). Developed under the auspices of the American Society of Heating, Refrigerating and Air-Conditioning

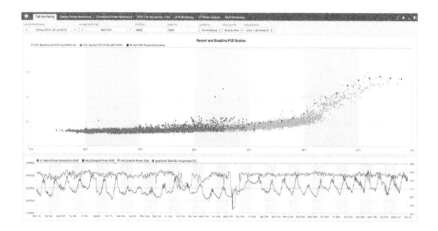

Figure 3.4 PUE monitoring scatter plot produced by SkySpark. Each dot is a 15-minute calculated event. Light Grey is the baseline period, and Dark Grey the selected monitoring period. Black is the 95th percentile indicator for the baseline scatter. The x-axis is the overall average wet-bulb temperature. The wet-bulb temperature is the lowest temperature to which air can be cooled by the evaporation of water into the air at a constant pressure. This graph is telling us that during March 2021, our PUE compared with baseline, with only 30 or so 15-minute periods above the target PUE of 1.1.

Engineers (ASHRAE), this is another standard protocol whose data are transformed and aggregated through FaaS to create various reports like the one above. Prior to feeding these data into SkySpark, an edge service processes all the data by converting them to a standard format, or by performing calculations to clean up the data that could be in different metrics, or by performing some analysis should some of the data not be in the same time frame. For example, various devices on the BACnet may not be able to transmit at the same speeds as all the other devices; therefore, data reach the edge service at different times. The process ensures that all the data for a time space are available. If OMNI expects 15 minutes of data, the edge service waits until all of the data are within the same 15-minute time stamp before processing and sending along to OMNI or SkySpark.

The edge service provided by FaaS has been advantageous in being able to calculate PUE and WUE in smaller increments. For PUE, most

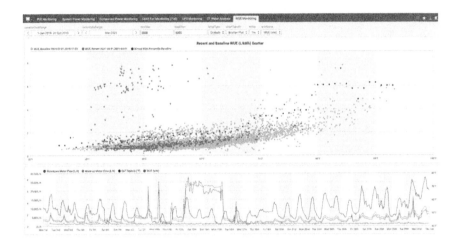

Figure 3.5 Water usage efficiency graph produced by SkySpark. Each dot is a 15-minute calculated event. Light Grey is the baseline period, and Dark Grey the selected monitoring period. Black is the 95th percentile indicator for the baseline scatter. WUE measures the rate of water evaporation versus electrical energy consumed, resulting in a measure of L/kWh. Regional weather heavily determines WUE results, so each location will have a different good versus wasteful performance threshold. NERSC is still in the phase of gathering data to determine a stable baseline and performance target. In the future, NERSC would like to be able to calculate this as efficiently as PUE.

facilities calculate it as an annual average. NERSC is able to confidently calculate PUE in 15-minute increments when needed. Although calculation of WUE is fairly new, results are promising and will help in managing the cooling system even more to create additional efficiencies.

3.3.5 Analysis at the Edge for Diagnostic and Troubleshooting Issues

While most of the data in OMNI are considered non-critical, that is, once they are gone beyond real time, they are considered archived and access to the data is not immediately available. Most teams either use data in real time, or can wait for archived data to be accessible, usually on a business day.

However, there is a class of data used by the NERSC networking team that is considered critical data; when they need access to the data,

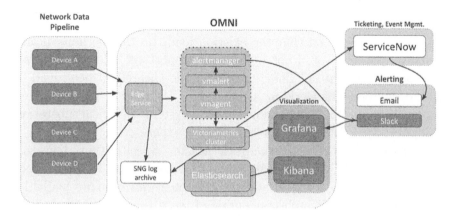

Figure 3.6 24 × 7 Pipeline of networking services at the edge and flow into OMNI.

it is critical that they do so immediately. Although these situations are rare, the design of OMNI has taken this requirement into account prior to accepting the archiving of these data. The team has leveraged the capability of sending multiple streams of data into different storage areas and provided a means of access and analysis on a 24 × 7 basis regardless of interruption in the facility. Using another edge service, as long as these devices are up and running, the critical data are collected and are accessible even if the OMNI itself becomes unavailable.

To mitigate the networking team's workflow, an edge service to function as an archiver and a point of analysis for troubleshooting is placed outside of the OMNI to process all the data coming from various devices. In addition, a separate log archiver is outside the OMNI network and has a service-level agreement with another group backup service. The network team can always access the data through the edge service; however, if the facility and OMNI become unavailable, they can also access the interface on the log archiver (Figure 3.6).

3.4   CASE STUDY OF BENEFITS OF OMNI DATA TO NERSC DATA CENTER

3.4.1 $2M Mechanical Substation Cost Savings

In preparation for the delivery of Perlmutter, NERSC leveraged the operational data analytics capabilities of OMNI to make the business decisions around the expansion of the electrical supply needs. The Lab facilities expected that the existing loads on the mechanical and electrical systems would not be able to support the additional power capacity of Perlmutter. They calculated the theoretical peak load of all the components working at full load. Using this method, they recommended adding a second mechanical systems electrical substation to support Perlmutter and its associated systems.

A caveat to the Lab Facilities Master Specification, however, permits a secondary calculation method for mechanical load planning, if at least one full year of operational power metering data are available. At this point, OMNI archives contained more than the needed data; however, analysis needed to be completed quickly, within a few days; otherwise, the project plan was to move on to purchase an electrical substation which had a 120-day lead time. There was no time to restore the very dense multiple year data from the archives and also analyze them.

OMNI online data for power consumption were re-indexed for several users, and one dataset satisfied the requirements of the Lab Facilities Master Specification for calculation. Since more than 1 year of data are accessible online, they were able to use this dataset. Its subsequent analysis demonstrated that the current operational power draw did not exceed 60% of the total power rating of the existing substation. Incorporating the expected power draw of Perlmutter, there is more than enough power in the existing substation to support the addition of the new system. See Figure 3.7, top grey line.

Before making a decision, a further study analyzed the number of expected peak cooling hours under warm conditions and how much cooling needs to happen during warmer days. The concern was how much cooling would push the mechanical power demand above the 1 MW maximum rating of the current substation. The data showed that in the mild Berkeley climate, there were very few days annually where the maximum substation rating would be stressed, and certainly not reach its full capacity. See Figure 3.7, bottom grey line.

The elimination of an electrical substation is a bold step for the large Perlmutter project planning in terms of power capacity and cost. Ultimately, this process demonstrated the usefulness of operational data analytics (ODA) and enabled the Lab facilities and NERSC management to confidently decide to forego a new mechanical substation, thereby saving the project $2 million.

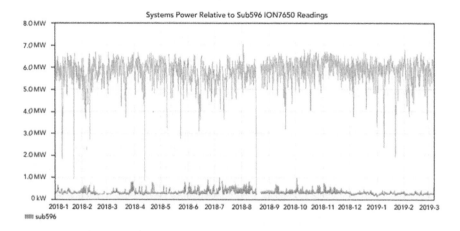

Figure 3.7 The total power load from the compute substations, (illustrated by top grey line ranging from 0 MW to 7 MW), is mostly stable relative to the mechanical substation, (illustrated by bottom grey line ranging from 0 MW to 1 MW).

3.4.2 Perlmutter Power Upgrade from 12.5 to 25.0 MW

When NERSC moved to Shyh Wang Hall in 2015, the construction of the building was supervised by the Lab's facilities. Soon after the first HPC system was installed and ran the first large job, there were power issues that shut down the system. It was fortunate that OMNI was up and running for several months and an early edge service correlated data from PDUs, power breakers, the UPS, and the system itself. The analysis determined that the power panels themselves were not configured to the needs of an HPC system.

As with a standard building, facilities configured the panels to the specifications of what normal equipment would be used in a building, not a data center. Normal office systems, even a cluster, have known power requirements and documented fluctuations. An HPC system has very high and very low fluctuations, the power draw being very high when a job runs and uses up to 99% of the system or very low if it is running only small jobs on single nodes. In this case, the system completed a very large job, drawing very high power, and when the job was completed and exited the nodes, the power dropped to a very low level for a few seconds as the system prepared the nodes to accept the next set of jobs. This huge power drop caused the power panel to trip, thus shutting down the system. The subsequent correction to replace the power panels and configure them correctly took ˜6 weeks.

The 100% power upgrade to the NERSC Shyh Wang Hall facility has presented a number of challenges in scaling to a more powerful system. The new HPE/Cray Perlmutter system will deliver 3–4× the performance of the current NERSC Cori system. However, the HPC footprint for the incoming system is actually smaller than that for Cori. Previously, next-generation systems would have an HPC footprint that was roughly equal to or slightly larger than their predecessors, which made it relatively straightforward to add larger wire feeds during a facility upgrade. Perlmutter and other emerging HPC systems in the USA are starting to exhibit the opposite behavior; that is, they have a smaller HPC footprint than their predecessors. In the case of NERSC, the smaller footprint has been leveraged to gain a much more powerful system to fit the larger space it would have previously taken [12].

With the smaller HPC footprint, the power feeds and panels are still of the same size and require more of it. Understanding the lessons learned from when the facility ran its first job, NERSC needed to ensure that future systems will not have the same power issues. As new panels are installed during the power upgrade, it was a requirement to test its power output such that it can withstand the fluctuations of usage from larger to smaller jobs.

Collecting fine-grained power data and being able to test and validate new panel configurations is paramount to both ensuring that there will be no surges or unsafe anomalies present when the new machine is installed, and providing key insights and lessons learned for future upgrades and new HPC systems.

As the upgrade progressed, engineers were able to test each panel that was configured and brought online. FaaS was able to calculate and show power fluctuations as small as seconds. Incorrect variances, faulty equipment, or data transfer speeds were able to be analyzed in real time as each panel was commissioned and marked ready. By testing the panels now, NERSC can predict the type of system they can purchase in the future and provide any power limitations to the vendor. They can also be confident that the facility can safely run the future systems.

3.4.3 Edge Service to Mitigate California's Public Safety Power Shutdown (PSPS)

In November 2018, NERSC and the Bay Area were affected by smoke that drifted to the area from the Camp Fire wildfire in Butte County, more than 90 miles away. The resulting air quality was very unhealthy for more than 2 weeks in Berkeley. To prepare for the 2019 California fire season, the primary power supplier, Pacific Gas & Electric (PG&E), decided to implement power shutdowns during occurrences of hot and windy weather to help prevent wildfires. PG&E shut down power to areas that were dry and mountainous or areas with many power cables. Because power is on a grid, large areas can be impacted, and the Lab would be impacted.

The Lab experienced its first mandatory shutdown in October 2019. Management was provided with at least a 24-hour notice of an impending shutdown, but only a 6-hour notice of PG&E turning off power at the substation. The 6-hour window is barely enough to cleanly shut down a facility as complex as NERSC. In spite of this situation, NERSC attempted to continue to provide services to their users. At minimum, management wanted to provide the users a way to log on and submit their jobs.

Edge services were key to ensuring there was enough power to keep the facility's infrastructure and key services running: active disk, log-in nodes, network switches, the cybersecurity infrastructure, OMNI, and minimal cooling even though HPC systems were powered off; it was still necessary to monitor the facility. As previously stated, the facility ecosystem is dependent on external cooling; air from outside is brought into the facility to help keep it cool. The key to maintaining the facility is cooling, not power. If the climate outside is warmer than usual, warmer air is brought into the facility, which will impact the systems.

During this type of an event, specific edge services were used to filter out any HPC system-related data that will most likely be an error because the system will be down and to process data only related to cooling power, network and everything related to facility, such as the UPS and generator. With temperatures possibly rising one degree each minute in racks or the particle count increasing rapidly if there is a fire, it is important to have enough time and warning for systems to be shut down as cleanly as possible (Figure 3.8).

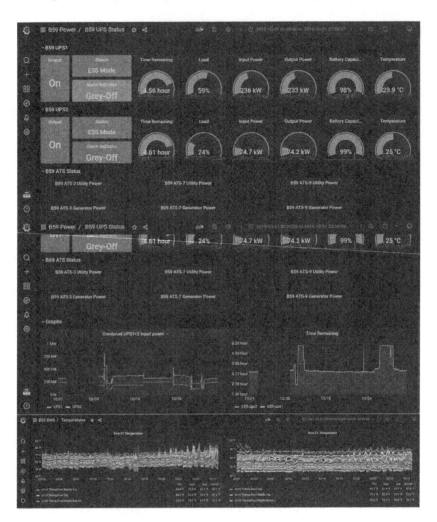

Figure 3.8 The three panels above show data points being monitored during PSPS. Panels 1 and 2 show the load on the UPS at that moment, and since the generator is not active, it has no load. Panel 3 shows the row and rack temperature fluctuations for Row C1 and Row D1.

3.5 ONGOING AND FUTURE WORK

Ongoing upgrades to the OMNI infrastructure include support for the increased size and scale of metrics that will be coming from the new Perlmutter system. This involves working with our existing metric sets on Cori and on the early-stage Perlmutter test system to understand key characteristics of the in-transit data. At this point, staff calculate that the additional data coming in from Perlmutter could be as much as 400 g/day per index and the current online storage needs to grow to accommodate this. Depending on the type of data received, more edge services can be installed to assist in the processing or analysis of data for real-time analysis.

OMNI's hardware replacement strategy is to upgrade one-third of the existing hardware each year. With the supply chain challenges resulting from the pandemic, parts may not be as available and can impact the timing of when upgrades need to be done or when new services can be installed.

Future work involves investigating a framework for alerting at the edge, allowing machines to self-alert and take mitigative actions based on their localized data in the event of loss of connectivity to or reliability of OMNI.

Additional future work makes OMNI available to external to DOE collaboration users. The team is investigating using blockchain to secure a front-end graphical interface to allow users to request a dataset for analysis.

REFERENCES

[1] M. Ott, et al., "Global experiences with HPC operational data measurement, collection and analysis," in *2020 IEEE International Conference on Cluster Computing (CLUSTER)*, Kobe, Japan, 2020, pp. 499–508. doi: 10.1109/CLUSTER49012.2020.00071.

[2] TOP500. https://www.top500.org/. Accessed 10 March 2021.

[3] k3s. "Lightweight Kubernetes", https://k3s.io/. Accessed 10 Mar. 2021.

[4] Victoria Metrics. https://victoriametrics.com/. Accessed 10 Mar. 2021.

[5] Bautista, E., Romanus, M., Davis, T., Whitney, C., & Kubaska, T. (August 2019). Collecting, monitoring, and analyzing facility and systems data at the national energy research scientific computing center. In *Proceedings of the 48th International Conference on Parallel Processing: Workshops*, Kyoto, Japan, (pp. 1–9).

[6] Elastic. https://www.elastic.co/. Accessed 10 March 2021.

[7] Prometheus: Monitoring System and Time Series Database. https://prometheus.io/. Accessed 10 March 2021.

[8] SkyFoundry. https://skyfoundry.com/. Accessed 25 March 2021.

[9] SkySpark. http://energy.ubc.ca/projects/skyspark/. Accessed 28 April 2021.

[10] Bautista, E., Davis, T., Whitney, C., Big data behind big data, Chapter 8, in: *Conquering Big Data with High Performance Computing*, R. Arora (Ed.), 1st Edition. Berlin, Heidelberg: Springer, 2018.

[11] https://cs.lbl.gov/news-media/news/2020/less-is-more-lbnl-breaks-new-ground-in-data-center-optimization/.

[12] https://www.nersc.gov/assets/Uploads/2018NERSCAnnualReport.pdf.

[13] https://www.kw-engineering.com/portfolio_page/data-center-energy-efficiency-nersc-lbl-supercomputer/.

Optimized Voronoi-Based Algorithms for Parallel Shortest Vector Computation

Artur Mariano
INESC TEC & Universidade do Minho

Filipe Cabeleira.
University of Coimbra & Instituto de Telecomunicações

Luís Paulo Santos
INESC TEC & Universidade do Minho

Gabriel Falcão
University of Coimbra & Instituto de Telecomunicações

CONTENTS

4.1   Introduction 86
4.2   SVP-Solvers Based on Voronoi Cells 90
    4.2.1   Voronoi Cell-Based Algorithm by
           Micciancio et al. 91
    4.2.2   Relevant Vectors by Agrell et al. 92
4.3   Experimental Setup 94
4.4   Algorithm Analysis 96
    4.4.1   Correlation between the Norm of Target Vectors
           and Solution Vectors 96

DOI: 10.1201/9781003155799-4

4.1 INTRODUCTION

Since the mid-1990s, the cryptography community has been studying alternatives to classical cryptosystems such as RSA and ElGamal, as these were shown to be vulnerable in the presence of quantum computers. These cryptosystems were based on the premise that the factorization of large numbers exhibits an exponential time complexity. Shor's algorithm [1–3] has shown that this class of problems can be solved in polynomial time on a quantum machine. Therefore, eavesdroppers with access to a sufficiently large quantum machine can hack the systems and access communications.

Many cryptosystems have been proposed since the rise of this so-called post-quantum era. Most of these cryptosystems are designed under the premise (or belief, in most cases) that even if adversaries had access to large-scale quantum computers, they cannot be broken. Lattice-based cryptosystems are a very prominent type of post-quantum cryptosystems. They support advanced cryptographic primitives such as fully homomorphic encryption,[1] and they are relatively efficient in practice, easy to implement and, of course, believed to be safe against quantum adversaries [3,5].

Cryptosystems base their security on hard math problems, which are typically easy to solve for the users of the system, but hard to solve for external entities. The underlying idea is that the fundamental problems underpinning the security of lattice-based cryptosystems, such as the shortest vector problem (SVP), the closest vector problem (CVP) and derivatives of these, cannot be solved (exponentially) faster with quantum computers, when compared to conventional computers. Due to the connection between the problems and the security of the corresponding cryptosystems, the algorithms that solve these problems are commonly referred to as attacks.

Lattices are discrete subgroups of the n-dimensional Euclidean space $\mathbb{R}^n$, with a strong periodicity property.[2] A lattice $\mathcal{L}$ generated by a basis $\mathbf{B}$, a set of linearly independent vectors $\mathbf{b}_1, ..., \mathbf{b}_m$ in $\mathbb{R}^n$, is denoted by:

$$\mathcal{L}(\mathbf{B}) = \left\{ \mathbf{x} \in \mathbb{R}^n : \mathbf{x} = \sum_{i=1}^{m} \mathbf{u}_i \mathbf{b}_i, \ \mathbf{u} \in \mathbb{Z}^m \right\}, \qquad (4.1)$$

where $m \leq n$ is the *rank* of the lattice. When $m = n$, the lattice is said to be of *full rank*. When n is at least 2, each lattice has infinitely many different bases.

Note that, although there are non-integer lattices, lattice-based cryptography commonly uses integer lattices in practice: Solving lattice problems on integer lattices is still hard, and integer lattices are easier to handle computationally (e.g., there are no precision/numerical problems). As an example, Figure 4.1 shows a lattice in $\mathbb{R}^2$, where the basis is $\mathbf{B} = \{\mathbf{b}_1, \mathbf{b}_2\}$. The vector $\mathbf{b}_3$ shown in the picture is a linear combination of the basis vectors. This linear combination also shows that $\mathbf{b}_1$ can be made shorter (in terms of Euclidean norm, which is the default meaning of shortness in the context of this book chapter) at the cost of $\mathbf{b}_2$, given that $\mathbf{b}_3$ is smaller than $\mathbf{b}_1$. This process, of making lattice vectors (bases) shorter by adding/subtracting other lattice vectors, is often referred to as vector (basis) reduction and is widely used in various lattice algorithms.

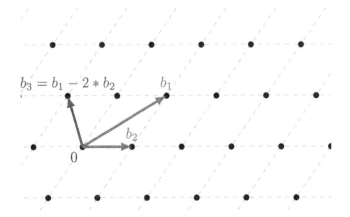

Figure 4.1 Example of a lattice in R^2 and its basis $(\mathbf{b}_1,\mathbf{b}_2)$.

Given that the security of lattice-based cryptosystems is based on problems such as the SVP, CVP and approximated versions of these, they have been widely studied over the last decade. In particular, many parallel, highly efficient versions of algorithms that solve these problems have been devised and put to the test, to assess their real hardness. Also, cryptosystems have certain parameters, such as the key size, that have to be determined based on the algorithms' practical potential/performance. Setting these parameters too high would lead to inefficient/slow cryptosystems, but setting them too low leads to insecure systems. As such, a "sweet spot" has to be found in this trade-off, so that systems are simultaneously efficient and secure. This can only happen when the best attacks are implemented on the highest-end computer architectures. This is also part of the work that we conduct and analyze in this very same manuscript.

The SVP has extensively been studied during the last decades, and two main families of SVP-solvers have emerged. As this research progressed, they evolved to become the standard algorithms in this context. The first family is the set of sieving algorithms, which repeatedly sieve a list of vectors until the shortest vector is very likely to be arrived at. The second most relevant family of algorithms is the family of enumeration algorithms. These enumerate all the possible vectors within a given search radius around the origin, and therefore, the shortest vector of the lattice is the shortest in that set of enumerated vectors. Other than these two SVP algorithm families, many are often mentioned and studied, but to a much smaller extent. Some of those families include random sampling and Voronoi cell-based SVP-solvers. The span of research around SVP algorithms is quite extensive and impractical to cover in this manuscript. To better grasp the history and evolution of this field, we refer the reader to [4,5,8–10].

In this text, we select one type of attack – SVP algorithms based on the Voronoi cell of a lattice – that has often been mentioned in the literature [11–13], but rarely studied or published about. In fact, it is often said that this algorithm becomes impractical (mainly due to memory issues) somewhere in dimensions 14–20, but this support was never evidently backed up by tests. Plus, other classes of SVP-solvers, such as enumeration and sieving, have been the subject of intense and ongoing investigation and optimization through the past decade (e.g., [14–17]). But Voronoi cell-based SVP-solvers, to the best of our knowledge, have not been optimized since their first publication [13], back in 2002. Voronoi cell-based algorithms are, however, of interest to study. First, they are asymptotically very appealing, which means that if the lattice dimension is high enough, they should be competitive with other classes of SVP-solvers. Second, there is a big room for practical improvement in Voronoi cell-based algorithms, which could perhaps lead to tractable implementations for high-dimensional lattices. In Ref. [18], we presented parallel versions, including a heterogeneous CPU+GPU implementation, of the original algorithm. In this work, we take a first step toward optimizing the original algorithm, thereby reducing the associated computational workload, and further propose parallel implementations of the optimized algorithm.

Contributions. In this manuscript, we propose various improvements for Voronoi cell-based algorithms, in the context of the SVP, and we show that the improved algorithm is still suitable for parallel execution.

We have been able to show that this algorithm can be optimized by using several norm-based optimizations. In particular, we show that computations that are, with high probability, irrelevant in the context of the SVP can be pruned. By considering previous states of the algorithm, namely the norm of the shortest known solution vector, the algorithm's workload can be dramatically reduced. Further workload reduction can be achieved if the target vectors are sorted according to their Euclidean norm prior to the evaluation of the solution vector.

We present a parallel version of the optimized Voronoi cell-based algorithm for the SVP. It is optimized to achieve the shortest vector faster and performs very well on architectures with multiple cores. This version was able to attain linear speedups on CPUs, in our experiments, compared to the baseline, original Voronoi cell-based SVP-solver. Due to the lack of support for efficient global synchronization among threads on GPUs, we cannot present a scalable implementation of the optimized algorithm in these devices. Similar to [18], we show that the non-optimized algorithm is highly suited for these architectures and competitive with the non-optimized multi-core CPU version.

The meaning of our work is twofold: First, we show that Voronoi cell-based algorithms can be made more practical than previously reported. Such practicality is achieved by introducing the above-mentioned norm-based optimizations, which are possible given that the goal is to solve the SVP. This should help to shed further light on this class of algorithms. Second, we show that the optimized algorithm is suited for parallelization, which makes it appealing for parameter selection in lattice-based cryptosystems.

Roadmap. The remainder of this chapter is organized as follows: Section 4.2 presents Voronoi cell-based algorithms including the algorithm exploited in the context of this text. Section 4.3 introduces the experimental setup. Section 4.4 presents an analysis performed on the algorithm, which serves as the motivation for our optimizations, presented in Section 4.5. Section 4.6 describes our parallel implementations, both on CPUs and GPUs, as well as their performance results. Section 4.8 concludes the chapter and points out future lines of work.

4.2 SVP-SOLVERS BASED ON VORONOI CELLS

In this section, we briefly explain a Voronoi cell-based algorithm by [11], which can be used to solve the SVP, and the algorithm we used in this work, called "Relevant Vectors", presented by [13].

4.2.1 Voronoi Cell-Based Algorithm by Micciancio et al.

This algorithm, presented in Ref. [11], describes a deterministic approach to solving the SVP (and other related problems), using the Voronoi cell $\mathcal{V}$ of a lattice as a way to arrive at the shortest vector of the lattice.

The algorithm works by rank reduction; i.e., the solution in a given dimension k requires the computation of some procedures in dimension $k-1$. Micciancio et al. show that the computation of the n-dimensional Voronoi cell of the lattice can be done by a series of CVP calls for the n-dimensional lattice, $\mathcal{V}(\mathcal{L}_n) = k \cdot \text{CVP}(\mathcal{L}_n)$, for a given number k of calls (for more details we refer the reader to [11]). Furthermore, they also show that the CVP solution of an n-dimensional lattice can be obtained by a series of CVP computations on the associated $(n-1)$-dimensional lattice, i.e., $\text{CVP}(\mathcal{L}_n) = k \cdot \text{CVP}(\mathcal{L}_{n-1})$.

Therefore, the Voronoi cell of a lattice in dimension n can be computed iteratively, starting on dimension 1 and working up toward dimension n. The solution of the SVP is the shortest non-zero vector $\mathbf{s} \in \mathcal{L}$, which, within the Voronoi cell context, is given by its shortest vector. More precisely, the solution for the SVP in this case is given by the double of the shortest vector of the Voronoi cell, as the frontier of the latter is, by definition, the midpoint between 0 and the vectors that are closest to 0.

As for the implementation of this algorithm, we start with reducing the basis and initializing the list of Voronoi relevant vectors with the first vector of the reduced basis. With this lower-dimension list, we iterate upward to dimension n, by generating a list of the so-called target vectors. For each of these, a CVP function is computed, so that we end up with the Voronoi cell vectors, which is refined so that it only contains the relevant vectors. The relevant vectors, which form the minimum set of vectors that describe the Voronoi cell of a lattice, are shown in Figure 4.2, for a given two-dimensional lattice.

The algorithm's time asymptotic complexity is $\mathcal{O}(2^{2n})$, while its space complexity is $\mathcal{O}(2^n)$, n being the lattice dimension. To fully comprehend this algorithm and its nuances, we refer the reader to [11], as we do not describe it with full details given that this algorithm is not used in this work.

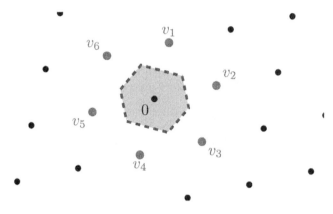

Figure 4.2 Example of a Voronoi cell in R^2 and its relevant vectors (v_1 to v_6).

4.2.2 Relevant Vectors by Agrell et al.

The algorithm used (a Voronoi cell-based algorithm called "Relevant vectors") was presented in Ref. [13]. That paper also described several algorithms to determine the solution to the SVP, CVP, and other related problems, and the algorithm used is shown in Algorithm 4.1.

Function AllClosestPoints

Input: Matrix $\mathbf{M}$, matrix $\mathbf{H}$, matrix $\mathbf{Q}$, vector $\mathbf{s}$

Output: List of vectors $\mathbf{X}$

Compute $\mathbf{x} = \mathbf{sQ}^T$;
$\mathbf{U} = \text{Decode}(\mathbf{H}, \mathbf{x})$;
Compute γ as the lowest value $||\mathbf{uM} - \mathbf{s}||$ for all $\mathbf{u} \in \mathbf{U}$;
Compute $\mathbf{X}$ as all $\{\mathbf{uM} : \mathbf{u} \in \mathbf{U}, ||\mathbf{uM} - \mathbf{s}|| = \gamma\}$
return $\mathbf{X}$

Algorithmically, "Relevant vectors" can be described by four distinct steps. First, it starts by generating the needed target vectors, that are later on used by a CVP-solver, in order to compute the Voronoi relevant vectors of the lattice. Second, the coordinate system of the data that feeds the CVP-solver is modified (i.e., the lattice basis and the target vectors). Details on the rationale behind these steps can be found in Ref. [13]. The third step is then to run an enumeration

---

Algorithm 4.1: RelevantVectors

Input: Basis matrix $\mathbf{B}$
Output: Relevant Vectors $\mathbf{N}$

$\mathbf{M}$ = Reduce($\mathbf{B}$);   /* for example, using the LLL algorithm */
$[\mathbf{Q}, \mathbf{R}]$ = QR decomposition of $\mathbf{M}$;
$\mathbf{G} = \mathbf{R}^T$;
$\mathbf{H} = \mathbf{G}^{-1}$;
$\mathbf{N} = \varnothing$;
forall *vectors* $\mathbf{s} \in \mathcal{M}$ **do**
  $\mathbf{X}$ = AllClosestPoints($\mathbf{M}, \mathbf{H}, \mathbf{Q}, \mathbf{s}$);
  if $|\mathbf{X}| = 2$ **then**
    $\mathbf{N} = \mathbf{N} \bigcup \{2\mathbf{x} - 2\mathbf{s} : \mathbf{x} \in \mathbf{X}\}$;

return $\mathbf{N}$

CVP-solver on each of the generated target vectors, a process we refer to as "decoding". This solver computes a set of vectors, which are then converted to the original coordinate system, thus resulting in the final list of candidate Voronoi relevant vectors. From these, only the valid vectors (in fact, Voronoi relevant vectors) are kept.

In terms of implementation, the CVP-solver that "decodes" target vectors is based on the Schnorr–Euchner method [19], which is an enumeration method to compute the SVP and the CVP. This is called "enumeration" because the algorithm enumerates all the possible solutions within a given radius. For more details on this algorithm, we refer the reader to papers on enumeration algorithms [13,17,19].

To increase performance, it is desirable to reduce the input lattice basis. This can be achieved, e.g., using the LLL algorithm (cf. [20]). Additionally, this enumeration-based CVP-solver function requires the input lattice basis to be in a lower-triangular form. When this is not the case, we must transform the basis to this form, while also transforming the input (target) vector(s) as well. This can be done with, e.g., a QR decomposition, in the form $\boldsymbol{M} = \boldsymbol{QR}$, where $\boldsymbol{R}$ is an $n \times n$ upper-triangular matrix and $\boldsymbol{Q}$ is an $m \times n$ orthonormal matrix. As we deal with full-rank lattices, effectively we end up with $\boldsymbol{R}_{n \times n}$ and $\boldsymbol{Q}_{n \times n}$, as $m = n$ and n is the lattice dimension. We call the QR method on the lattice basis ($\mathbf{M}$ in the decomposition), yielding $\mathbf{R}$, which we must transpose, i.e., $\mathbf{R}^T$, to obtain the desired lower-triangular matrix.[3]

The other resulting matrix ($\mathbf{Q}$) is used to transform the target vector into the coordinate system of the lattice basis when in the lower-triangular form. Note that when the QR decomposition is used, it is also needed to transform the output of the decode function back into the original form (i.e., the original coordinate system).

Once the basis is in the desired format, we generate the list $\mathcal{M}$ that contains each of the $\mathbf{s}_i$ target vectors, $i = 1, ..., (2^n - 1)$ (in practice, Steps 1 and 2 of the mathematical description above can be done together), as shown in Equation 4.2, iteratively.

$$\mathcal{M}(\mathbf{M}) \stackrel{\text{def}}{=} \left\{ \mathbf{s} = \mathbf{zM} : \mathbf{z} \in \{0, 1/2\}^n - \{\mathbf{0}\} \right\} \tag{4.2}$$

Afterward, the CVP-solver is executed on these inputs, yielding a list of vectors $\mathbf{U}$, that are processed according to Equation 4.3, resulting in the list of vectors $\mathbf{X}$.

$$\begin{aligned} \gamma &= \min \left\{ ||\mathbf{uM} - \mathbf{s}|| \text{ for all } \mathbf{u} \in \mathbf{U} \right\} \\ \mathbf{X} &= \left\{ \mathbf{uM} : \mathbf{u} \in \mathbf{U}, ||\mathbf{uM} - \mathbf{s}|| = \gamma \right\} \end{aligned} \tag{4.3}$$

The computation of list $\mathbf{X}$ does not always result in a valid output. This only happens when the list contains 2 vectors and 2 vectors only (they are symmetric to each other, thus having the same norm), which are added to the list of Voronoi relevant vectors $\mathbf{N}$. Similar to the algorithm in 4.2.1, the solution to the SVP is given by the shortest of the Voronoi relevant vectors.

4.3 EXPERIMENTAL SETUP

Table 4.1 presents the details of the CPU-based computing system used to assess the proposed parallel algorithm. The clock frequency in parentheses shown in the table pertains to the maximum frequency of the CPU, which is achieved using the Turbo Boost Technology. L1 cache values are split between instruction cache (i) and data cache (d). System A runs CentOS x86_64 with kernel version 2.6. The code has been compiled with g++ 7.2.0 with the -O3 optimization flag, as it delivered the best throughput performance.

TABLE 4.1   CPU-Based Computing System

System	A
Sockets	2
CPU	Intel Xeon E5-2660v4
Clock frequency	2.0 GHz (3.2 GHz)
Cores per socket	14
SMT	Yes (w/ HT, 28 threads)
L1 Cache	448 kB i + 448 kB d
L2 Cache	3.5 MB
L3 Cache	35 MB
RAM	128 GB

SMT stands for simultaneous multithreading and HT
stands for hyper-threading.

TABLE 4.2   Machine for GPU Tests Performed in This Work

System	B
CPU	Intel core i3 6100
Clock frequency	3.70 GHz
Cores	2
SMT	Yes (w/ HT, 4 threads)
L1 Cache	32 kB i + 32 kB d
L2 Cache	256 kB
L3 Cache	3 MB
RAM	8 GB
GPU	NVIDIA GeForce 1060 GTX
GPU Clock rate	1,759 MHz
GPU RAM	6 GB

SMT stands for simultaneous multithreading and HT stands
for hyper-threading.

The tests conducted in a GPU used System B, specified in Table 4.2, which runs Ubuntu 16.04 x86_64 with kernel version 4.13. CUDA code was compiled with NVIDIA CUDA Compiler 9.1 using the -O3 optimization flag and the -arch=sm_61 -lcudadevrt -rdc=true flags. The GPUs have compute capability 6.1 and allow for dynamic parallelism (a kernel launch within another kernel). The CPU code on this machine was compiled with g++ 5.4.0.

The lattice bases used in all tests were generated with the SVP challenge[4] generator software, compiled using NTL, version 9.3. The lattice bases generated using this tool are random (Goldstein–Mayer) lattices, which have no specific characteristic to be exploited [21]. Additionally, these lattice bases are reduced using the LLL algorithm before the main loop of the algorithm (cf. Algorithm 4.1). Unless specified otherwise, the tests presented in this work are conducted with seeds 0 through 999. They represent a total of 1,000 bases, up until dimension 10; 100 bases for dimensions 11–15; and 10 bases for dimension 16 or higher. We present the arithmetic average of all tested bases (with different seeds). We have turned off Turbo Boost, in order to have a better sense of the scalability of the algorithm, and the results obtained were fairly consistent. Executing the algorithm for more seeds would not impact the average execution time. In this context, we refer to "a test" as the execution of the program across all the seeds. Also, our tests were only conducted in these (small) dimensions, as the memory requirements of the algorithm grow exponentially. While individually they run relatively fast, performing 1000 runs per dimension would be impractical.

4.4 ALGORITHM ANALYSIS

From Equation 4.2 (cf. Section 4.2.2), we see that the computation of the Voronoi cell of a lattice involves the execution of the *AllClosestPoints* function, for each of the $(2^n - 1)$ vectors that make up the set $\mathcal{M}$. However, in practice, most of these calculations are unnecessary if our purpose is to find the solution to the SVP. As such, we describe a series of tests that we conducted, which lay the foundation of the proposed optimizations. For these tests, we used Machine A.

4.4.1 Correlation between the Norm of Target Vectors and Solution Vectors

We posed the hypothesis of a possible correlation between the norm of the target vectors and the norm of their respective solution vector, a test we started out with. The motivation to test out this possible correlation stems from the fact that, intuitively, the computation of a target vector with smaller Euclidean norm (i.e., shorter) would also result in a shorter solution vector. If this correlation held, then we could potentially exclude several target vectors, by only decoding a few small subset of these vectors, given that our purpose is to arrive at the shortest vector.

We investigated this (possibly strong) correlation by testing out several lattice bases, for dimensions 4–8, using different seeds. To this end, we sampled some lattice bases in certain lattice dimensions and studied the correlation, generalizing it to higher dimensions (note that the correlation cannot be known as target vectors are generated). Due to the impossibility of presenting all the data, we showed three different correlations, for dimension 4 (seed 960), dimension 5 (seed 0) and dimension 8 (seed 456). These are representative of the full spectrum of the obtained results.

The scatter plots in Figure 4.3 show that our thesis holds true, as we can observe a moderately strong correlation in the terms we pointed out. The actual correlation depends upon the used lattice basis (i.e., dimension and seed). For instance, some bases showed an almost perfect/linear correlation (such as in dimension 4, seed 960), while others continued to show a correlation, although not as evident as the remaining lattices. These results show the best (Figure 4.3(a)), average (Figure 4.3(b)) and worst (Figure 4.3(c)) scenarios for all the lattices we tested out, thus giving us the confidence to affirm that a correlation holds.

Note that when the correlation is not as strong (for instance, in Figure 4.3(c)), it does continue to hold for the shorter target vectors. In other words, although there are large target vectors that result in large solution vectors, it generally holds true that many small target vectors result in small solution vectors, thus supporting the proposed thesis.

Given these data, we can conclude that, in general, as a correlation applies, meaning that a shorter target vector yields a shorter solution vector, then the shortest of the target vectors should, in general, result in the solution to the SVP. The correlation may become looser as we increase the lattice dimension, but it seems to continue to hold for the smaller target vectors (cf. the leftmost vectors in Figure 4.3(c)), and we take advantage of that fact, as we show in the next section. This correlation is actually the basis of some of the algorithmic improvements we show in Section 4.5.

4.4.2 Percentage of Target Vectors That Generate the Shortest Vector

From the previous results, we posed the hypothesis of whether we should only decode a small percentage of target vectors; these would

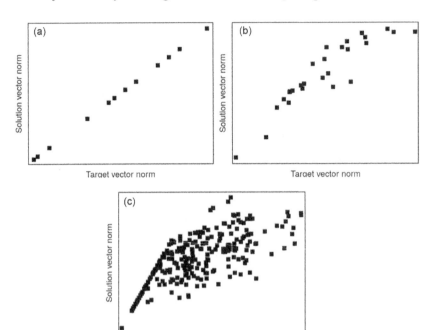

Figure 4.3 (a) Correlation for the basis in dimension 4 (seed 960). (b) Correlation for the basis in dimension 5 (seed 0). (c) Correlation for the basis in dimension 8 (seed 456). Correlation between the norm of the target vectors and the norm of their respective solution vector, for three dimensions and seeds. We omitted both axes values as they are irrelevant for correlation purposes and added considerable complexity to the figures, thus making it difficult to read them.

necessarily contain the shortest solution vector (and, as a result, the solution for the SVP). However, note that this is only true when the target vectors are sorted by increasing norm.

Also, in general, the percentage of these target vectors should be larger as the correlation gets weaker (i.e., we would need to pick more target vectors as the correlation gets weaker for that specific basis). However, note that even if the correlation for a specific basis is off in general, but holds true for the first shortest target vectors, then we would also need to decode a very small percentage of target vectors. In fact, as shown in Figure 4.3, even in the worst case of our tests,

TABLE 4.3   Position of the Target Vectors That Originate the Shortest Vector for the Bases That Failed

Dimension	#Incorrect Solutions	Position(s)	%
4	0	—	—
5	0	—	—
6	1	21	33.33
7	0	—	—
8	1	77	30.2
9	3	146, 260, 92	50.88
10	3	204, 200, 85	19.94
11	0	—	—
12	0	—	—
13	1	252	3.08
14	2	1246, 12865	78.53
15	5	4228, 911, 14181, 3495, 13599	43.28
16	1	2205	3.36
17	0	—	—
18	0	—	—
19	1	3010	0.57
20	2	11328, 856105	81.64

there is a correlation for the shortest target vectors, which supports our rationale.

To test this second hypothesis, we generated all target vectors, chose the smallest, and decoded it (i.e., computed its solution vector). We observed that the solution vector of the first target vector was always also the solution to the SVP, except for a handful of bases, which are shown in Table 4.3 (check the position column, which shows the position of the shortest vector when the first vector is not the shortest). This means that the shortest target vector does not yield the shortest solution vector (and the shortest vector of the lattice) in $<0.27\%$ of the bases we tested.

The percentage shown in the table regards the worst verified case of target vectors that need to be decoded so that we arrive at the optimal solution. However, note that these percentages may seem very high as we are testing very low dimensions. Moreover, the maximum percentage of target vectors we need to decode is highly dependent on the lattice basis we test. For instance, decoding 0.57% of the target vectors in dimension 19 would suffice to arrive at the shortest vector, while in dimension 20, one specific basis required as much as 81.64% of the target vectors. That said, there should be no clear trend in this regard.

As a result, we can affirm that, in general, sorting the target vectors by increasing norm will, very likely, lead us to find the shortest vector faster than randomly decoding target vectors as we generate them. This motivates a series of optimizations, which we explore in Section 4.5.

4.5 ALGORITHMIC OPTIMIZATIONS

In the following, we show a series of optimizations that are based on the previous analysis of the algorithm. In order to test lattices with such an execution time that allowed us to see the effects of the optimizations we implemented, we decided to use Machine A, as specified in Section 4.3, and g++ with the O0 optimization flag. If we were to use Machine B and the O3 optimization flag, some tests would run too fast, thus making it impossible to infer proper conclusions (increasing the lattice dimension would quickly lead us to hit the memory wall and impede proper testing).

4.5.1 Pruned Decoding

Many of our optimizations stem from the fact that there is a relatively strong correlation between the norm of the target vectors and the solution yielded by the decoding process, as shown in Section 4.4. Therefore, we employ a key idea: We can filter out (or "prune") some of the target vectors, along with the decoding process, if their norm "is big". In particular, we should – with some confidence degree – be able to prune out target vectors that have a norm larger than the shortest norm (for any target vector) found at any given instant. In theory, we could also use the norm of the solution vectors (and, in particular, the norm of the shortest solution vectors found up until a certain execution point of the algorithm) to prune out some of the target vectors. Note, however, that this may introduce some uncertainty as a bigger target vector than the shortest (*solution*) vector found at any point of the algorithm may actually generate an even shorter solution vector. This is because target vectors may yield, throughout the decoding process, shorter solution vectors. Note that we have not studied this angle in our correlation analysis, presented in Section 4.4; this is merely an intuitive hypothetical relation that should work well in practice.

In fact, in our experiments, this has proven to be a very effective optimization, almost without compromising the solution. In other words, even with this optimization – which we generally call pruning as we prune the set of target vectors to test – we achieved the shortest vector of the lattice in almost 99.999% of the experiments we carried out in this section.

If we regard the target vectors – which are to be decoded – as a set, we can employ our optimization in the form of pruning. This may have several variants, but during our experiments, we found out that two forms are particularly effective.

4.5.1.1 Simple Pruning

The first – and simplest – form of pruning we have employed is based on discarding target vectors whose norm is larger than the norm of the shortest (*solution*) vector found so far. We call this optimization "simple pruning". We do this by keeping a record of the shortest (*solution*) vector found throughout the execution. This optimization has resulted in significant speedups, as shown in Figure 4.4(a). The speedup of simple pruning also increased with the lattice dimension.

We note that although, in theory, this optimization may result in a compromised solution (because we may filter out the target vector that results in the shortest vector, as mentioned before), in practice, it barely happens (in our experiments, it failed for 11 bases out of 7550). We tested this optimization for one thousand seeds of each dimension. The result was always coherent with that of a deterministic SVP-solver, thereby showing that simple pruning did not compromise the result in practice. We also expect this to be the case for the vast majority of lattices in higher dimensions.

4.5.1.2 Gaussian Pruning

The Gaussian heuristic, presented in Equation 4.4, is a popular heuristic in the context of SVP-solvers. This heuristic estimates the length of the shortest vector of the lattice. It serves as the reference in the SVP challenge,[5] which accepts entries of vectors whose norm is

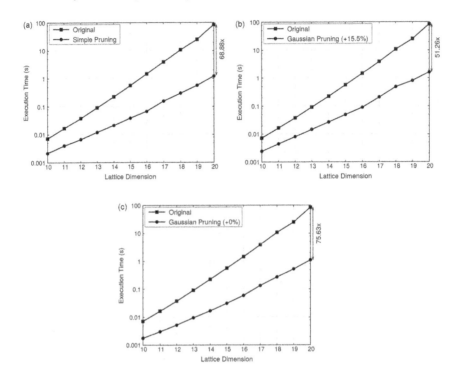

Figure 4.4 Original algorithm and pruned versions, from lattice dimension 10 to lattice dimension 20, on Machine A. (a) Original algorithm and the simple pruning version. (b) Original algorithm and the Gaussian pruning version (added margin of 15.5%). (c) Original algorithm and the Gaussian pruning version (added margin of 0.0%).

at most 5% larger than the Gaussian heuristic. In this work, we refer to this delta, i.e., the amount added to the Gaussian heuristic, as the "added margin", in Equation 4.4 as α.

$$\alpha \cdot \frac{\Gamma(n/2 + 1)^{1/n}}{\sqrt{\pi}} \cdot (\det \mathcal{L})^{1/n} \tag{4.4}$$

$$\Gamma(x) = (x - 1)!, \ x \in \mathbb{Z}^+ \tag{4.5}$$

As we observed a relatively strong correlation between the norm of the target vectors and the resulting solution vectors, together with the good results of simple pruning, we decided to test a pruned version based on the Gaussian heuristic (which we call Gaussian pruning). This reasoning is based on the fact that, in theory, if simple pruning works well, a pruning based on the Gaussian heuristic should also work well. This is due to two main ideas. First, there is a connection (although obviously not linear; otherwise, the shortest target vector would always result in the shortest solution vector) between the norms of the target vector and the solution vector, as we can infer from the results in Section 4.4.2. Second, given this connection, applying the Gaussian pruning to the target vectors would indirectly allow us to reduce the set of target vectors that are likely to generate the shorter solution vectors. Given that these connections are not linear, although improbable, the algorithm may fail to find the shortest vector if Gaussian pruning is applied. In fact, following the same rationale, we can say that this is true for both simple and Gaussian pruning.

We tested Gaussian pruning with several error margins, for lattices in dimensions 10–20, testing 500 seeds from dimensions 11–15 and 50 seeds for dimensions 16–20 (due to time constraints). As Figure 4.4(b) shows, Gaussian pruning also works very well in practice, achieving speedup factors of as much as 51.26×. Again, we also expect the trend to continue as we increase the lattice dimension.

In our experiments, Gaussian pruning only yields an invalid solution, with an added margin of 15.5%, in 11 bases out of 7550. That is, in 7539 lattice instances, the algorithm always found the shortest vector.

We tested the added margin of the Gaussian pruning extensively. We started by using an added margin of 0% and the algorithm only failed to find the shortest vectors in 24 lattice bases (out of 7550). Therefore, in the vast majority of the lattice bases, the Gaussian pruning without an added margin works very well. However, to be comparable with the baseline – the reference algorithm – we needed to include an added margin that ensures the shortest vector is found.

We selected an added margin of 15.5% for the experiments which output the same number of wrong results (11 out of 7550) as the simple pruning, thus allowing us to compare both versions in terms of execution time. We note that although this added margin always resulted in an optimal solution, that may not be the case for all lattices in all dimensions, in which case we need to update the added margin accordingly.

Yet, we tested the performance of the Gaussian heuristic for various added margins. Not surprisingly, no added margin (i.e., Gaussian

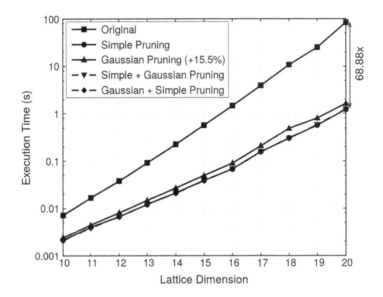

Figure 4.5 Original algorithm and the Gaussian (added margin of 15.5%), by both orders, combined and isolated, from lattice dimension 10 to lattice dimension 20, on Machine A.

pruning with no added margin) showed to attain the best performance, which we depict in Figure 4.4(c). Note that running Gaussian pruning without any added margin only failed in 24 out of 7550 lattice bases.

This indicates that there may be potential on a Gaussian pruned version which works without added margin but resorts to another mechanism to detect over-pruning, i.e., discarding the target vectors that would lead to better solution vectors. Due to time limitations, we pushed this problem to future work.

4.5.1.3 Combined Pruning

Given the results of the two previous forms of pruning, we decided to combine them, i.e., executing them one after the other. Figure 4.5 shows the performance of a combination of simple and Gaussian pruning, in both orders, against the performance of the individual pruning optimizations and the baseline.

As the figure shows, the combination of simple pruning with Gaussian pruning (with an added margin of 15.5%) does not deliver a speedup. Nevertheless, we were able to obtain a performance improvement in a large number of cases we conducted when refining some parameters (as these setups were overall less efficient than those in the figure and thus not very relevant, we refrained from showing them). We obtain a speedup of as much as $68.88\times$ when compared to the baseline. This version also fails in only 12 bases (one more than simple or Gaussian pruning) out of all the 7550 instances tested.

4.5.2   Increasing Norm Sort

Given the effectiveness of the pruning optimizations, we decided to design a way so that shorter target vectors are executed first. To this end, we sort all target vectors by increasing norm before the actual execution of the algorithm, a process we refer to as "pre-sorting". This is also motivated by the results we arrived at in Section 4.4.2. From those results, we can conclude that executing the shorter target vectors first will lead us to shorter solutions first, thus increasing the pruning extent. Furthermore, as we will show throughout this text, memory usage is a problem in Voronoi cell algorithms, and this optimization can theoretically improve this, as there is a much smaller set of target vectors to be decoded.

In theory, this enhances pruning as the number of pruned target vectors will be larger – with simple pruning or combined pruning (but not with Gaussian pruning) – if they are sorted (it does nothing if no pruning is applied, as all target vectors are executed either way). In particular, we know for a fact that the additional pruning is "safe" in the sense that it does not decrease the likelihood of solving the SVP.

We call this "safety" as, by pre-sorting the target vectors, we are prioritizing shorter target vectors that, as we see in Figure 4.3, lead to shorter solution vectors in general. As such, we are effectively pruning out larger target vectors that would not lead to the solution to the SVP either way (with a high probability). In fact, they could have been decoded if pre-sorting was not used and they were some of the first target vectors in line of execution. Therefore, the solution provided by these larger target vectors would eventually be superseded by the solution vectors of smaller target vectors.

To implement this optimization, we have to re-arrange the computation of the algorithm, namely by generating the target vectors upfront (in contrast to calculating them on the fly – iteration by iteration – as it happens in the original algorithm), so that we can sort them (by increasing norm). We have implemented both the merge sort [22] and the quicksort [23] algorithms and compared them against std::sort, the C++ standard sorting library. The latter, std::sort, performed better than the former, and therefore, we have performed the rest of the tests with this implementation (the GNU Compiler Suite also provides a parallel OpenMP version of the std::sort algorithm, which is useful for higher dimensions).

Given that we want to sort the target vectors (which are stored in a matrix, in a row-wise manner), we have to compute an auxiliary vector with the norm of each target vector. This is obviously not required, but it does avoid computing the norm of a target vector each time it is needed. With the std::sort implementation, given the nature of the library function, we store the norm of each vector in a "struct", where each element holds one target vector and its norm; in this case, the sorting procedure is done by simply swapping the memory pointers to the elements, instead of actually having to move the data around.

The performance results for combined pruning with pre-sorting are shown in Figure 4.6. As the figure shows, we obtain a speedup of as much as 76.59x by pre-sorting the target vectors in terms of increasing norm (which compares to 68.88x without sorting). As it happens without pre-sorting, the order by which the pruning techniques are applied with pre-sorting has very little significance in the execution time of the algorithm.

Evidently, it would be a very strong optimization if we were able to find a method to stop the algorithm once the shortest vector is reached, which is a common problem for many SVP-solvers. Nevertheless, we were still unable to come up with rules to stop the algorithm briefly after the shortest vector is found, as it happens with other SVP-solvers, such as sieving [24,25]. However, we push this problem to future work.

4.6 PARALLEL IMPLEMENTATIONS FOR CPUs AND GPUs

In this section, we present both CPU- and GPU-parallel versions of the RelevantVectors algorithm, the algorithm that served as the basis of this work. In theory, this algorithm is embarrassingly parallel, as there are no dependencies between iterations; i.e., we can execute several

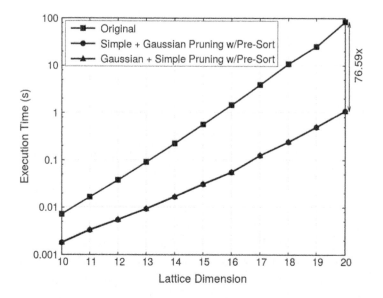

Figure 4.6 Original algorithm and the Gaussian (added margin of 15.5%) and combined pruning, by both orders, with pre-sorting, from lattice dimension 10 to lattice dimension 20, on Machine A.

*Decode*s concurrently. We used OpenMP for the parallel CPU version and CUDA for the GPU version.

4.6.1 CPU

The OpenMP compiler directives were applied to the main loop of the algorithm Line 6 in Algorithm 4.1, where the generation of the target vectors takes place, followed by the decoding of the mentioned vectors. As this process is independent between iterations, and there are no subsequent data races, threads can run concurrently.

On top of parallelizing the algorithm, we have employed other optimizations to the algorithm, regarding general memory usage/consumption and memory access.

First, the result of decoding a target vector, if valid, yields two solution vectors. As such, if we were to store every result of every decode, a matrix of dimension $2(2^n - 1) \times n$ would be required, for an n-dimensional lattice. This is impractical, as the memory requirement for this matrix grows exponentially with the lattice dimension. To solve this issue, instead of storing every solution vector, we only store the shortest vector found at the end of each decode procedure. This decreases the size of the matrix used to store the solution vector to $1 \times n$ (or $2 \times n$ if we were to store both results of each decode). It requires the use of a critical region so that threads cannot simultaneously access these variables, which would lead to data races and a potentially incorrect result.

Second, originally the matrices were implemented as an array of arrays; while this provides a very natural indexing notation, it is not very efficient from a memory standpoint. Not only it requires several memory allocations (and deallocations) for each matrix, but also there is no guarantee that the required memory is allocated continuously in RAM. Therefore, the implementation of matrices was changed (from an array of arrays) to a single, large vector. This increases indexing computation slightly, but improves memory locality considerably.

Algorithm 4.2 shows the pseudo-code of the OpenMP-based parallel version of the RelevantVectors algorithm.

Algorithm 4.2: Parallel RelevantVectors
___

Input: Basis matrix **B**
Output: Relevant Vectors **N**

$\mathbf{M} = \text{Reduce}(\mathbf{B})$; /* for example, using the LLL algorithm */
$[\mathbf{Q}, \mathbf{R}] = $ QR decomposition of $\mathbf{M}$;
$\mathbf{G} = \mathbf{R}^T$;
$\mathbf{H} = \mathbf{G}^{-1}$;
$\mathbf{N} = \varnothing$;
$\min\_\text{norm} = \infty$;

```
#pragma omp parallel for
```
forall *vectors* $\mathbf{s} \in \mathcal{M}$ **do**
    $\mathbf{X} = \text{AllClosestPoints}(\mathbf{M}, \mathbf{H}, \mathbf{Q}, \mathbf{s})$;
    ```#pragma omp critical```
    if $||2\mathbf{x} - 2\mathbf{s}|| < \min\_\text{norm}$ **then**
        $\min\_\text{norm} = ||2\mathbf{x} - 2\mathbf{s}||$;
        $\mathbf{N} = \{2\mathbf{x} - 2\mathbf{s} : \mathbf{x} \in \mathbf{X}\}$;

return N
___
    ```

4.6.1.1 Original Version (No Pruning and No Pre-Sorting)

We first parallelized the original version of the algorithm (i.e., without pruning and without pre-sorting). Given that the execution time of each iteration is different (as decoding different target vectors may be faster or slower), there may be work imbalance among threads. In preliminary tests, we tested the OpenMP static scheduler, but the results were not, unsurprisingly, optimal. For that reason, the experiments we report were conducted with the OpenMP dynamic scheduler, which assigns work to threads as they complete the previous tasks, thus balancing out the workload. Although this strategy does not guarantee perfect load balancing, it usually minimizes the imbalance substantially (usually at the cost of a given overhead, which may be smaller or bigger depending on circumstances). As such, we still expect some threads to finish ahead of others.

Figure 4.7 shows the execution time of the algorithm, on Machine A, for lattices in dimensions 16–20, and 1–56 threads. For readability purposes, we display the speedups in Table 4.4.

We achieved higher speedups for higher lattice dimensions, due to lower thread creation latency and improved the overall workload

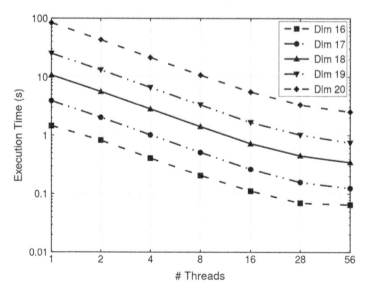

Figure 4.7 Execution time for the parallel algorithm, on lattices in dimensions 16–20, using 1–56 threads on Machine A.

TABLE 4.4 Speedups on Machine A, Parallel Non-Pruned Implementation Running with 1–56 Threads, in Comparison with the Parallel Non-Pruned Version Running with a Single Thread

Dimension	16	17	18	19	20
2 Threads	1.772	1.917	1.915	1.914	1.961
4 Threads	3.556	3.833	3.824	3.815	3.933
8 Threads	7.072	7.615	7.642	7.604	7.849
16 Threads	12.990	14.830	14.890	15.170	15.190
28 Threads	20.910	24.820	24.020	24.660	25.370
56 Threads	22.210	31.190	31.140	33.600	33.440

TABLE 4.5 Speedups of the Parallel Implementation for Gaussian and Simple Pruning, on Machine A

Dimension	25	26	27	28	29
2 Threads	1.681	1.810	1.766	1.800	1.763
4 Threads	3.322	3.514	3.419	3.667	3.581
8 Threads	6.297	6.694	6.916	7.254	7.128
16 Threads	7.085	8.856	11.412	6.706	6.040
28 Threads	5.986	9.732	9.464	19.870	11.850
56 Threads	10.630	12.050	11.220	18.020	16.190

distribution. This is particularly important because we aim at using our implementation in large dimensions – as large as possible.

We also developed a parallel version of the optimized version, with pre-sorting both turned on and off, with OpenMP. As we have seen, the order of the optimizations was not relevant for performance, so we only used one order. We also parallelized the generation of target vectors, as they can be executed independently (both with and without pre-sorting).

4.6.1.2 Pruned Version without Sorting

As shown in Figure 4.8, the parallel combined pruning version also scales well (cf. Table 4.5 for readability purposes). Nevertheless, scalability is overall a little lower than the non-optimized implementation due to the critical section necessary for the optimizations of this particular version (note the contention for more than eight threads in Figure 4.8).

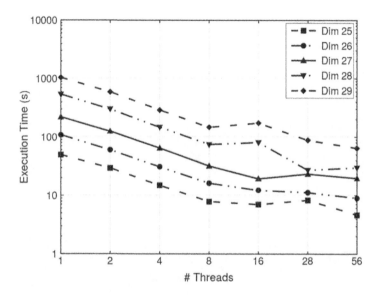

Figure 4.8 Execution time for the combined Gaussian + simple pruned version of the algorithm, on dimensions 25–29, using 1–56 threads on Machine A.

As mentioned in Section 4.5.1.2, there is the possibility that the chosen added margin may fail for some lattice bases that were not tested before, as it is impossible to know upfront which added margin guarantees the optimal solution. The number of bases that the algorithm did not return the optimal solution was still residual. We also note that arriving at a short vector, as opposed to the shortest vector, is still important, especially in the context of a relaxed version of the SVP, usually referred to as α-SVP. In this work, we will not expand on this topic, even though we note that short vectors are still an important result in this context.

4.6.1.3   Pruned Version with Sorting

Regarding the optimized version with the pre-sorting phase, in this setup, we need to generate all target vectors upfront, and sort them, before the algorithm actually computes the SVP. This uses up more memory than the original algorithm, as we will show next.

As mentioned in Section 4.5.2, the GNU Compiler Suite already implements an OpenMP version of the std::sort algorithm, which we

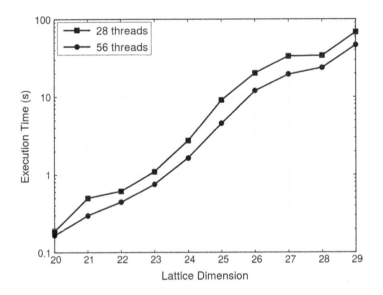

Figure 4.9 Execution time for the combined Gaussian + simple pruned version of the algorithm, with pre-sorting, for dimensions 20–29, using 28 and 56 threads on Machine A.

used in the sorting phase. This way, the procedure is entirely parallel, including the generation and sorting of the target vectors, except for the synchronization among all the threads (implemented with a critical section) to update the shortest norm found, should they find one.

Figure 4.9 shows the execution time up to dimension 29, which is the highest lattice dimension we can test with 128 GB of RAM. In dimension 29, using pre-sorting results in a speedup of almost 30% (for 28 threads) and 40% (for 56 threads), compared to the non-sorted version. With 56 threads, using pre-sorting is also faster than the non-sorting version for dimension 28, by approximately 26%. Until dimension 28 (for 56 threads) and dimension 29 (for 28 threads), the non-sorting version is faster, given that the time to generate all target vectors, store/read them from memory and sort them is higher than the gain throughout the algorithm.

It is worth noting that this version requires more memory than the previous ones. In the pruned version without pre-sorting, target vectors are decoded and generated one by one (and the algorithm should stop long before all target vectors are explored, per our optimizations). In

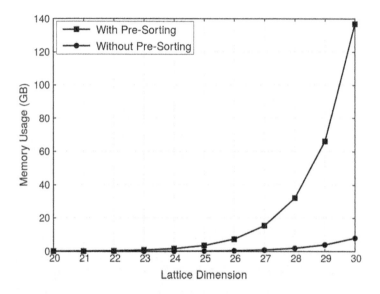

Figure 4.10 The calculated memory usage required by our combined pruning implementation (essentially for the target vector-matrix), both with and without pre-sorting. The number of threads does not make a difference.

this version, all target vectors are generated (in order to be sorted) up-front, which consumes more memory than in the non-sorted version. In essence, the pre-sorting creates a trade-off between memory and execution time (because the solution is achieved faster). The execution time to sort the vectors upfront was never relevant in our tests (i.e., even with the sorting phase, the final time to solution was always lower).

Regarding memory, we should note that in the parallel versions, the memory required increases exponentially with the lattice dimension (as per the original algorithm), but also linearly with the number of threads being used. This happens because each iteration (and thus each thread) requires its own auxiliary structures for the correct working of the decode function. These matrices are initially allocated with a certain number of rows (the number of columns is equal to the dimension of the problem) and, when needed, are extended via reallocation.

Figure 4.10 shows the (calculated) memory usage of the implementation in the worst-case scenario for a given dimension (i.e., the largest size measured among all bases in a given dimension), both when sorting

TABLE 4.6   Estimated Memory
Usage of the Combined Pruning
Implementation for Dimensions
20–80, with Pre-Sorting

Dimension	Estimated memory usage
20	83.89 MB
30	128.85 GB
40	175.92 TB
50	225.18 PB
60	276.70 EB
70	330.57 ZB
80	386.86 YB

is used and when it is not. As Machine A has 128 GB of RAM memory, we were able to test the optimized version with pre-sorting up until dimension 29. Running dimension 30 would require around 137 GB of memory available.

Table 4.6 shows the estimated memory usage of the combined pruning implementation with pre-sorting, for dimensions 20–80 in increments of 10, using 28 threads.

4.6.2   GPU

As mentioned at the beginning of Section 4.6, we also present a parallel version for GPUs, in CUDA, similar to [18]. Due to the inefficiency of software-based critical sections in CUDA, we were forced to employ a larger matrix to hold all solution vectors, similar to the original algorithm. Should we be able to implement an efficient critical section, threads would be able to compare the solution vector they arrive at, against the shortest one found so far, without the need to store the larger ones. This same reason prevented implementing a CUDA version of the pruning optimization. The results are, therefore, presented for the non-optimized algorithm. In this version, we calculate the target vectors on the fly, as in the non-pruned and pruned versions without pre-sorting (and in contrast to our CPU version with pre-sorting).

Our CUDA implementation contains a single kernel. We set up the kernel so that each thread decodes a single target vector unless

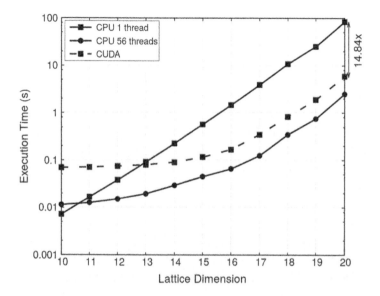

Figure 4.11 Execution time for dimensions 10–20, for the non-pruned CPU algorithm (1/56 threads on Machine A) and the parallel GPU non-pruned algorithm (on Machine B). Note: The CPU execution times are those of Section 4.6.1 for the non-pruned algorithm.

the available memory is not enough (note that each thread allocates memory for auxiliary structures). For instance, running dimension 20 on our GPU implies that each thread will decode more than one vector. The first step of the kernel is to generate the target vectors, decode them and store the solution vectors in the final matrix (list of vectors), similar to the CPU version. In the meantime, the result of the decode function is checked; if the test holds, the vector is stored in the final matrix; otherwise, the thread dies (until dimension 19) or proceeds to the following iteration (in dimension 20).

Until dimension 19, we set the number of threads equal to the target vectors (in practice, we set the number of blocks and threads per block). We set 128 threads per block, so the number of blocks changes based on the number of target vectors. As we said, each thread is responsible for generating and decoding a single target vector.

Figure 4.11 shows the execution time of our CUDA implementation, running with as many threads as target vectors (except for dimension 20, where that number is halved), for several lattice dimensions.

The figure also includes the execution time of our CPU version of the non-optimized algorithm, both with 1 and 56 threads. Up until dimension 13, the GPU implementation is slower than the CPU implementation, as the penalty for transferring memory (matrices M, H, Q and N) over the PCI Express bus to the GPU only becomes diluted/clouded for bigger dimensions and the launch time of the GPU kernel (not excluded in the results) is also diluted for bigger dimensions.

The GPU implementation is almost 15× times faster than the sequential version and about 2,34× slower than the CPU running with 56 threads. As we can see in the figure, the difference between both implementations gets smaller with the lattice dimension, which is expected due to the penalty of memory transfer and GPU initialization. Thus, we expect this GPU version to beat the CPU version with 56 threads, for a sufficiently large lattice dimension (which we cannot test due to memory limitations).

4.7 DISCUSSION

There are two different angles of our research that deserve comments. First is the algorithmic optimizations that we propose, which greatly improve the algorithm. The idea of speeding up SVP-solvers by empirical observations on vectors is not new, e.g., [26], but it was never applied to Voronoi cell-based algorithms, to our best knowledge. The study of the correlation between the norm of target vectors and their solution is, to our knowledge, unprecedented. The "simple" and the Gaussian pruning is motivated by some optimizations implemented in other SVP-solvers (for instance, the simple pruning is used in sieving algorithms, while Gaussian pruning is used in enumeration algorithms as a way to define a radius for a search space or prune the enumeration tree [27]).

Objectively, these optimizations greatly improve the algorithm, and sorting target vectors is another great optimization as it decreases time to solution even further. The sorting procedure is also very efficient and can be done in parallel; therefore, we see no concerns regarding adding this pre-processing to the overall algorithmic routines.

A second angle for discussion is the performance of our parallel versions, both for CPUs and for GPUs. Although not all of our

CPU implementations scale linearly, they do scale fairly well. We are confident that, if further developments are made to the algorithm, these implementations could be used for high lattice dimensions. The GPU implementation, on the other hand, has to be revisited in order to integrate the proposed pruning optimizations. GPUs currently lack efficient synchronization mechanisms. This prevents sharing of information (such as the current pruning norm) among threads while still maintaining scalability. An interesting line of research in this context should be to rewrite the algorithm differently so that synchronization could either be avoided or be made parallel.

4.8 CONCLUSIONS

Attacks to post-quantum lattice-based cryptosystems require solving the computationally hard shortest vector problem (SVP). Different families of SVP-solvers have been suggested over the last two decades, including Voronoi cell-based algorithms. Proposed back in 2002 by Agrell et al., this family of algorithms has not been optimized since, under the claim that its memory complexity (exponential with the number of dimensions) renders it unpractical even for low dimensions. However, Voronoi cell-based algorithms exhibit a number of characteristics that justify a thorough study of their practicality when a few optimizations are employed. In particular, their time complexity is asymptotically very interesting, which could allow them to become competitive with other SVP-solvers if the memory barrier can be overcome. Indeed, there is plenty of room for practical optimizations, which can eventually lead to tractable implementations for high-dimensional lattices, unleashing their true potential.

This work addressed the reduction in the execution time of the Voronoi cell-based "Relevant Vectors" algorithm, by tackling two different axes: (1) algorithmically reducing the number of operations required to reach a solution to the SVP and (2) parallelizing it for both GPUs and multi-core CPUs.

In order to reduce the workload, we hypothesized that there is a correlation between the norm size of the target vectors and the solution vectors. This correlation was demonstrated to hold, which allowed us to propose pruning target vectors based on the length of the shortest solution vector observed this far and/or the Gaussian heuristic. Also, we have shown that pre-sorting the target vectors by increasing norm allows for a more effective pruning (by reordering computations), accelerating our optimized version further, notwithstanding the additional sorting time. Altogether, our optimizations improved the throughput performance approximately 77× compared to the baseline implementation. Adding sorting on top of pruning provided an additional speedup of as much as 40% up to dimension 29, but we estimate that it would be considerably superior, should we be able to test higher dimensions.

The main drawback with sorting is that it currently requires storing all target vectors, which results in a huge memory consumption. Naturally, we could ignore/cut off a substantial percentage (e.g., 70%) of the largest target vectors right in the pre-processing stage, significantly reducing memory usage. However, we have not done so yet as we would like to look for a cutoff formula that translates to an approximated likelihood of still finding the shortest vector (which would be a very interesting result in the context of the approximate SVP). We note the potential of this idea, given that Voronoi is not tractable in practice solely because target vectors become a bottleneck memory-wise.

Additionally, we have shown that the algorithm and our optimizations are well suited for multi-core CPU machines, as we devised and implemented a scalable parallel version. We also optimized the algorithm's memory map and found that dynamic scheduling is mandatory since decoding time varies for different target vectors. Our implementation scales linearly on multi-core CPUs up to 28 threads and can even take advantage of SMT, although the benefit is reduced given that the problem is compute-bound. We found no reason why similar scalability will not hold for higher thread counts.

We also implemented the original algorithm on a GPU, using the CUDA framework. The optimized pruning algorithm could not be tested, since it would require recurrent use of critical sections, currently not efficiently supported by CUDA. Therefore, we could not use pruning to reduce the workload and had to store all computed solution vectors, further increasing memory consumption. Although our GPU version was never faster than our 56-thread CPU version, we observed that the gap between the CPU and the GPU generally decreases with lattice dimension. This is a very promising result, hinting that the GPU could become faster for higher lattice dimensions. Also the CPU/GPU memory transfer penalty will be diluted for such higher dimensions, further contributing to the GPU advantage. In the future, we expect to develop better data structures for the GPU and optimize the CUDA code, such that experiments with higher lattice dimensions become feasible.

This chapter represents a step forward on making Voronoi cell-based SVP-solvers practical. It has shown that there is plenty of room for algorithmic optimizations, namely workload reduction by pruning large target vectors. It has also demonstrated that multi-core CPU parallel solutions scale and are efficient. GPU solutions show a promising trend as the lattice dimensionality increases, but further support is required for synchronization primitives enabling efficient critical regions controlled access. The exponential space complexity of Voronoi cell-based algorithms remains a challenge that has not been directly addressed in this chapter. Educated discarding of a percentage of the largest target vectors on the sorting stage could represent a first step on the right direction, reducing the constants associated with this complexity.

4.8.1 Open Problems

This work leads to many lines of future work. In particular, we think that it would be interesting to:

- Find a stopping criterion so that our optimized algorithm stops shortly after the solution is found.

- Reduce the memory requirements of our GPU implementation by developing new data structures.

- Optimize our GPU implementation further, to take full advantage of the architecture.

- Implement a heterogeneous version of our algorithm.

- Reduce the parallel CPU version memory requirements, by using only a small part of the Voronoi cell.

ACKNOWLEDGMENTS

This work was financed by national funds from INESC TEC and the Portuguese funding agency, Fundação para a Ciência e a Tecnologia, within project UIDB/50014/2020. This work was also financially supported by Instituto de Telecomunicações and Fundação para a Ciência e a Tecnologia under project UIDB/50008/2020. Artur Mariano was funded by the Deutsche Forschungsgemeinschaft (DFG, German Research Foundation) – Projektnummer 382285730.

NOTES

1 A cryptosystem that supports fully homomorphic encryption can implement any operation on encrypted data, without decrypting data, which is particularly useful when, e.g., outsourcing sensitive computations on private data to a cloud server. The reader is referred to the survey [4] for a practical perspective of fully homomorphic encryption.
2 We refer the reader to papers [6,7] to learn more about lattices, especially in the context of lattice-based cryptography.
3 The diagonal elements of this matrix must be positive.
4 https://www.latticechallenge.org/svp-challenge/
5 https://www.latticechallenge.org/svp-challenge/

REFERENCES

[1] Peter Shor. Polynomial-time algorithms for prime factorization and discrete logarithms on a quantum computer. *SIAM Journal of Computing*, 26(5):1484–1509, 1997.

[2] Peter Shor. Algorithms for quantum computation: Discrete logarithms and factoring. In *Proceedings of the 35th Annual Symposium on Foundations of Computer Science SFCS'94*, pp. 124–134, Washington, DC, 1994. IEEE Computer Society.

[3] Daniel Bernstein, Johannes Buchmann, and Erik Dahmen, editors. *Post-Quantum Cryptography*. Cham: Springer, 2009.

[4] Paulo Martins, Artur Mariano, and Leonel Sousa. A survey on fully homomorphic encryption: an engineering perspective. *ACM Computing Surveys*, 50:1–33, 2017.

[5] Daniele Micciancio and Oded Regev. *Post-Quantum Cryptography, Chapter Lattice-Based Cryptography*, pp. 147–191.

[6] Oded Regev. *Lattice-Based Cryptography*, pp. 131–141. Berlin Heidelberg: Springer, 2006. Berlin, Heidelberg: Springer, 2009.

[7] Phong Nguyen and Jacques Stern. The two faces of lattices in cryptology. In *International Cryptography and Lattices Conference.* Springer, Berlin, Heidelberg, pp. 146–180, 2001.

[8] Artur Mariano, Thijs Laarhoven, Fabio Correia, Manuel Rodrigues, and Gabriel Falcão. A practical view of the state-of-the-art of lattice-based cryptanalysis. *IEEE Access*, 5:24184–24202, 2017.

[9] Artur Mariano. High performance algorithms for lattice-based cryptanalysis. PhD thesis, Technische Universität Darmstadt, Darmstadt, Germany, 2016.

[10] Joop van de Pol. Lattice-based cryptography. Master's thesis, Technische Universiteit Eindhoven, The Netherlands, 2011.

[11] Daniele Micciancio and Panagiotis Voulgaris. A deterministic single exponential time algorithm for most lattice problems based on Voronoi cell computations. In *STOC'10: Proceedings of the Forty-Second ACM Symposium on Theory of Computing*, Cambridge MA, pp. 351–358, 2010.

[12] Fabio Correia. Assessing the hardness of SVP algorithms in the presence of CPUs and GPUs. Master's thesis, University of Minho, Braga, Portugal, 2014.

[13] Erik Agrell, Thomas Eriksson, Alexander Vardy, and Kenneth Zeger. Closest point search in lattices. *IEEE Transactions on Information Theory*, 48(8):2201–2214, 2002.

[14] Thijs Laarhoven. Evolutionary techniques in lattice sieving algorithms. *CoRR*, abs/1907.04629, 2019.

[15] Martin R. Albrecht, Léo Ducas, Gottfried Herold, Elena Kirshanova, Eamonn W. Postlethwaite, and Marc Stevens. The general sieve kernel and new records in lattice reduction. In Yuval Ishai and Vincent Rijmen, editors, *Advances in Cryptology – EUROCRYPT 2019*, pp. 717–746, Cham: Springer International Publishing, 2019.

[16] Thijs Laarhoven. Sieving for shortest vectors in lattices using angular locality-sensitive hashing. In *CRYPTO*, pp. 3–22, 2015.

[17] Nicolas Gama, Phong Nguyen, and Oded Regev. Lattice enumeration using extreme pruning. In *EUROCRYPT*, pp. 257–278, 2010.

[18] Gabriel Falcao, Filipe Cabeleira, Artur Mariano, and Luís Paulo Santos. Heterogeneous implementation of a voronoi cell-based svp solver. *IEEE Access*, 7:127012–127023, 2019.

[19] Claus-Peter Schnorr and Martin Euchner. Lattice basis reduction: Improved practical algorithms and solving subset sum problems. *Mathematical Programming*, 66(2–3):181–199, 1994.

[20] Arjen Lenstra, Hendrik Willem Lenstra, and Lászlo Lovász. Factoring polynomials with rational coefficients. *Mathematische Annalen*, 261:515–534, 1982.

[21] Daniel Goldstein and Andrew Mayer. On the equidistribution of Hecke points. *Forum Mathematicum*, 15:165–189, 2003.

[22] Donald Knuth. *The Art of Computer Programming*, volume 3, Sorting and searching. Boston, MA: Addison-Wesley, 1998.

[23] Charles Hoare. Algorithm 64: Quicksort. *Communications of ACM*, 4(7):321, 1961.

[24] Phong Nguyen and Thomas Vidick. Sieve algorithms for the shortest vector problem are practical. *Journal of Mathematical Cryptology*, 2(2):181–207, 2008.

[25] Daniele Micciancio and Panagiotis Voulgaris. Faster exponential time algorithms for the Shortest Vector Problem. In *Proceedings of the twenty-first annual ACM-SIAM symposium on Discrete Algorithms (SODA)*, Society for Industrial and Applied Mathematics, Philadelphia, PA, pp. 1468–1480, 2010.

[26] Robert Fitzpatrick, Christian Bischof, Johannes Buchmann, Özgür Dagdelen, Florian Göpfert, Artur Mariano, and Bo-Yin Yang. Tuning GaussSieve for speed. In *International Conference on Cryptology and Information Security in Latin America (LATINCRYPT)*, Springer, Cham, pp. 288–305, 2014.

[27] Nicolas Gama, Phong Q. Nguyên, and Oded Regev. Lattice enumeration using extreme pruning. In *EUROCRYPT*, Monaco and Nice, French Riviera, pp. 257–278, 2010.

CHAPTER 5

Attribute-Based Secure Keyword Search for Cloud Computing

Hui Yin, Yu Zhang, and Fangmin Li

Changsha University

Keqin Li

State University of New York

CONTENTS

DOI: 10.1201/9781003155799-5

123

5.1 INTRODUCTION

Cloud computing is an overwhelming technology that indicates IT field is developing toward the trend of intensification, scale, and specialization. In the cloud computing paradigm, the IT facilities are pooled as the configurable resources, including computing power, storage, network, and services. The end-users are able to flexibly and dynamically request those resources by the on-demand network access with low expenditures anytime and anywhere. Compared to the traditional IT infrastructure, the enormous advantages such as elastic resource configuration, quick deployment, and cost saving have attracted more and more enterprises and individual users to migrating their applications and data to the cloud center. However, the security of cloud computing is always a controversial issue as outsourcing data to remote cloud servers also means that data owners no more possess the control power on the outsourced data [1]. The data stored on the cloud platform face a dual threat from the cloud server itself and external attackers. Encryption is an effective way to guarantee the security of the outsourced data [2]. However, traditional block cipher techniques make original plaintext unavailable due to the introduction of random keys. It is critical for cloud applications, as the cloud computing is characterized by not only massive data storage, but also efficient data processing. If the encrypted data are not able to be processed and operated on the cloud platform, it will greatly thwart the wide adoption of cloud computing. For example, in order to save IT infrastructure cost, a hospital would like to store their electronic medical records (EMRs) to the cloud platform in the form of the ciphertext, as EMRs contain a huge amount of confidential, sensitive information that patients are reluctant to publish, such as medical history. If in the cloud center these data cannot work just like their plaintext, the hospital may give up the cloud computing. Because encrypted EMRs have to be downloaded and decrypted when performing one search or diagnosis task, it is obviously not the original intention of using the cloud computing.

To address this problem, a long line of research has been made to realize operations directly over ciphertext, among which searchable encryption techniques are a recently vibrant research field, aiming at guaranteeing both confidentiality and searchability over encrypted data. Song et al. first introduced the idea of searchable encryption and, in Ref. [3], proposed a practical construction that supports data searching on ciphertext through the specified query trapdoor (encrypted query keywords). According to the adoptions of different encryption mechanisms, searchable encryption can be divided into symmetric (private-key) searchable encryption (SSE) [4,5] and public-key encryption with keyword search (PEKS) [6]. Recently, with the rapid development and increasing popularity of cloud computing, from the point of practicability, searchable encryption has been extended to solve how to achieve efficient and functionally rich search over encrypted cloud data [7–9]. These techniques promote the practical application of searchable encryption in the cloud computing environment.

While those schemes provide a powerful capacity to perform the keyword search over encrypted data, they have a lack of the data access control. In the data-shared cloud environment, performing access control over outsourced data can effectively prevent data from being illegally accessed by unauthorized entities. The practical requirement reclaims a new research topic, called attribute-based keyword search. The attribute-based keyword secure search schemes [10–12] are able to achieve fine-grained access control and private search over encrypted data simultaneously by taking full advantage of searchable encryption and attribute-based encryption (ABE) [13], which is very applicable to the cloud computing environment. In this chapter, we first briefly introduce the key techniques to achieve ABKS scheme, such as necessary components used in the attribute-based encryption. Then, by several existing ABKS schemes, we describe how to design a practical and efficient ABKS construction in the cloud computing environment (by combining the attribute-based encryption primitive and searchable encryption primitive as well as some other key techniques). Further, we show some interesting experiment results to explain the key factors affecting the search complexity in ABKS schemes and present some ideas to design a truly practical and high-performance ABKS scheme. Also, we present future directions in this research field.

5.2 KEY TECHNIQUES IN ABKS

5.2.1 Attribute-Based Encryption

ABE allows one to enforce flexible and fine-grained data access control in the Internet or open distributed computing environment, meanwhile guaranteeing data confidentiality via cryptographic means. Due to the dramatic reduction in the cost of network bandwidth and sending nodes operation in data sharing, ABE has a broad prospect of application in the area of fine-grained access control. The first ABE scheme was proposed by Sahai and Water in [13], referred to as fuzzy identity-based encryption (FIBE). In FIBE, one encrypts a message to the ciphertext associating a set of attributes ω and an authority generates a private key by embedding a set of attributes ω' into the private key. When decrypting, if and only if $|\omega \cap \omega'| \geq d$, the private key can work on the ciphertext, where d is a threshold value. The flaw of this scheme is that the expressivity of the access policy is deficient and inflexible due to the only adoption of the intersection operation between two attribute sets to enforce the decryption control. This feature was greatly improved by using an access tree to express the access control policy. Depending on where the access tree is in the ciphertext or in the private key, the subsequently proposed ABE schemes can be generally classified into two categories: key-policy ABE (KP-ABE) [14] and ciphertext-policy ABE (CP-ABE) [15]. In KP-ABE, an authority specifies an access tree to generate a private key and an encrypter encrypts a message associating a set of attributes. When decrypting, if and only if the attribute set in the ciphertext component satisfies the access tree in the key component, the key can recover the message. We give an example of KP-ABE as shown in Figure 5.1. Obviously, the data user is able to successfully decrypt the encrypted outsourced files, since the attribute set in ciphertext satisfies the access tree in the key, which can recover the plaintext.

Compared with KP-ABE, in the CP-ABE schemes [15], the ciphertext is associated with an access tree and a set of attributes is embedded

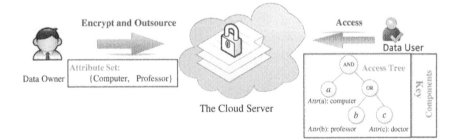

Figure 5.1 KP-ABE.

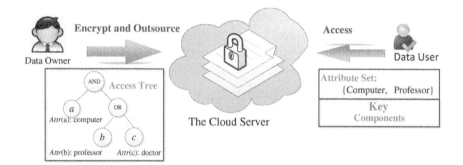

Figure 5.2 CP-ABE.

into the private key. When decrypting, if and only if the attribute set in the key satisfies the access tree in the ciphertext, the private key can recover the encrypted message. We give an example as shown in Figure 5.2. Obviously, the data user can successfully decrypt the encrypted outsourced files, since the attribute set in the key satisfies the access tree in the ciphertext, which can be decrypted by using the key.

5.2.1.1 Preliminaries in ABE

Next, we introduce some important background knowledge used for the attribute-based encryption. These techniques are also necessities for designing the attribute-based keyword search schemes.

5.2.1.1.1 Bilinear Map   We use notations $\mathbb{G}_1$ and $\mathbb{G}_2$ to denote two multiplicative cyclic groups with the prime order q. Let g be a generator of $\mathbb{G}_1$. A bilinear map $e : \mathbb{G}_1 \times \mathbb{G}_1 \to \mathbb{G}_2$ follows the properties:

1. Efficiently computational: For all $x, y \in \mathbb{G}_1$, $e(x, y) \in \mathbb{G}_2$ can be efficiently computed in the polynomial time.

2. Bilinear: For all $x, y \in \mathbb{G}_1$ and $a, b \in \mathbb{Z}_q^*$, $e(x^a, y^b) = e(x, y)^{ab}$ holds.

3. Non-degenerate: $e(g, g) \neq 1$, g is a generator of $\mathbb{G}_1$.

5.2.1.1.2 Access Tree   In ABE, an access tree is widely used to describe an access structure due to its flexible and rich expressivity.

Given an access tree T, a non-leaf node in T is a threshold gate of "m of n", where m is a threshold value and n is the number of children of the node. More specifically, for any node $x \in T$, let k_x and num_x be threshold value and the number of children of x. If x is a non-leaf node, $k_x = 1$ means x is an OR gate, $k_x = num_x$ indicates it is an AND gate, and $1 < k_x < num_x$ represents x is a threshold gate. If x is a leaf node, then $k_x = 1$ and $num_x = 0$. For ease of description, several notations are defined as follows.

1. $parent(x)$: the parent of node x.

2. $index(x)$: x is a child of its parent node; $index(x)$ denotes the index number of x. The index number of the leftmost child node is set to be 1, and correspondingly, the index number of the rightmost child node is set to be num.

3. $attr(x)$: x is a leaf node; $attr(x)$ denotes an attribute associated with x.

Here, we see an example, as shown in Figure 5.3. According to our definition, we have $num_R = 3$, $num_{N_1} = 2$, $num_{N_2} = 2$, $num_{N_3} = 3$, $k_R = 3$, $k_{N_1} = 2$, $k_{N_2} = 1$, $k_{N_3} = 2$, $parent(A) = N_1$, $index(A) = 1$, $index(B) = 2$, $index(C) = 1$, $index(G) = 3$. The nodes R and N_1 are AND gates, N_2 is an OR gate, and N_3 is a threshold gate; nodes $A - G$ are leaf nodes. Also, nodes R, N_1, and N_2 can be presented as 3 of 3, 2 of 2, and 1 of 2 threshold gate, respectively.

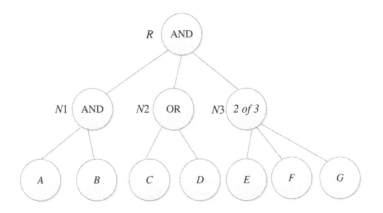

Figure 5.3 Access tree.

5.2.1.1.3 Satisfying an access tree Let $\mathbb{A}$ be a set of attributes and T be an access tree with root r. For a subtree T_x of T rooted at the node x, we define

$$\begin{cases} T_x(\mathbb{A}) = 1 & \text{If } \mathbb{A} \text{ satisfies } T_x \\ T_x(\mathbb{A}) = 0 & \text{Otherwise.} \end{cases} \tag{5.1}$$

We can compute $T_x(\mathbb{A})$ by following recursive algorithm. If x is a non-leaf node, evaluate $T_{x'}(\mathbb{A})$ for all children x' of node x. If at least k_x children return 1, then $T_x(\mathbb{A})$ returns 1. If x is a leaf node, if $attr(x) \in \mathbb{A}$, then $T_x(\mathbb{A})$ returns 1. Thus, if $\mathbb{A}$ satisfies T, then $T_r(\mathbb{A}) = 1$; otherwise, $T_r(\mathbb{A}) = 0$. For example, the attribute sets $\{A, B, C, E, G\}$ and $\{A, B, D, F, G\}$ satisfy the access tree, but $\{A, C, E\}$, $\{A, B, E, F\}$, and $\{A, B, C, E\}$ do not satisfy it. For simplicity, here we use the same notations to denote the leaf nodes and their associated attributes.

5.2.1.1.4 Access Structure Let $\{P_1, P_2, ..., P_n\}$ be a set of parties. A collection $\mathbb{A} \subseteq 2^{\{P_1, P_2, ..., P_n\}}$ is monotone if $\forall B, C$: If $B \in \mathbb{A}$ and $B \subseteq C$, then $C \in \mathbb{A}$. An access structure is a collection $\mathbb{A}$ of non-empty subsets of $\{P_1, P_2, ..., P_n\}$, i.e., $\mathbb{A} \subseteq 2^{\{P_1, P_2, ..., P_n\}} \setminus \{\emptyset\}$. The sets in $\mathbb{A}$ are called the authorized sets, and the sets not in $\mathbb{A}$ are called the unauthorized sets.

In the attribute-based encryption system, we use the attributes to represent the role of the parties. Thus, $\mathbb{A}$ is an access policy usually expressed by an access tree, organized by different attributes from the authorized sets of attributes.

5.2.1.2 A CP-ABE Construction

Now, we state the construction of the famous ABE scheme proposed in [15], which is a CP-ABE scheme and composed of four polynomial-time algorithms: Setup, Encrypt, KeyGen, and Decrypt. The following are several important tools used to implement those algorithms.

A bilinear map is denoted as $e : \mathbb{G}_1 \times \mathbb{G}_1 \to \mathbb{G}_2$ with the three aforementioned properties, where $\mathbb{G}_1$ and $\mathbb{G}_2$ are two cyclic multiplicative groups with large prime order q. A cryptography hash function $H : \{0,1\}^* \to \mathbb{G}_1$ converting a bit string into a group element in $\mathbb{G}_1$. The Lagrange coefficient is as follows:

$$\Delta_{i,S}(x) = \prod_{j \in S, j \neq i} \frac{x - j}{i - j}, \tag{5.2}$$

where S denotes a set of elements in $\mathbb{Z}_q^*$ and $i, j \in \mathbb{Z}_q^*$.

5.2.1.2.1 **Setup** The algorithm sets up the system running environment. It first generates two groups $\mathbb{G}_1, \mathbb{G}_2$ of prime order q and establishes the bilinear computation environment. Let g be the generator of $\mathbb{G}_1$. Next, it chooses elements α, β from $\mathbb{Z}_q^*$ at random and calculates $h = g^\beta, e(g,g)^\alpha$. Finally, the algorithm creates the public key to be $\mathbf{PK} = \{\mathbb{G}_1, g, h = g^\beta, e(g,g)^\alpha\}$ and the master key to be $\mathbf{MK} = \{\beta, g^\alpha\}$.

5.2.1.2.2 **Encrypt($\mathbf{PK}, M, T$)** On inputting the public key $\mathbf{PK}$, a message M, and an access tree T, the algorithm outputs the ciphertext $\mathbf{CT}$ of the message M. First, for each node x in T_w, it generates a polynomial q_x. Starting from the root node R, these polynomials are generated in a top-down manner. Specifically, for each polynomial q_x of x, it sets the degree d_x of polynomial q_x to be $d_x = k_x - 1$, where k_x is the threshold value of the node x. Then, for the root node R, it chooses a random element $s \in \mathbb{Z}_q^*$ and sets $q_R(0) = s$ and sets d_R other points of q_R randomly to completely define it. For any other node x in T_w, it sets $q_x(0) = q_{p(x)}(index(x))$ and chooses d_x other points to completely define q_x. Let Y be the set of leaf nodes in tree T_w; finally, the algorithm outputs $\mathbf{CT}$ as:

$$\mathbf{CT} = (T, \tilde{C} = Me(g,g)^{\alpha s}, C = h^s,$$
$$\forall y \in Y : C_y = g^{q_y(0)}, C_y' = H_2(attr(y))^{q_y(0)}) \qquad (5.3)$$

5.2.1.2.3 **KeyGen($\mathbf{MK}, S$)** On inputting the master key $\mathbf{MK}$ and a set S of attributes, the algorithm outputs private key $\mathbf{SK}$. Specifically, it first chooses an element $r \in \mathbb{Z}_q^*$ at random and calculates $D = (g^\alpha g^r)^{1/\beta}$, and then chooses an element $r_a \in \mathbb{Z}_q^*$ at random for each attribute $a \in S$ and computes $D_a = H(a)^{r_a}, D_a' = g^{r_a}$. The private key can be written as

$$\mathbf{SK} = (D = g^{\frac{\alpha+r}{\beta}}, \forall a \in S, D_a = H(a)^{r_a}, D_a' = g^{r_a}) \qquad (5.4)$$

5.2.1.2.4 **Decrypt($\mathbf{CT}, \mathbf{SK}$)** On inputting the ciphertext $\mathbf{CT}$ and the private key $\mathbf{SK}$, the algorithm decrypts $\mathbf{CT}$ and outputs the original message M if decryption succeeds; otherwise, it outputs $\perp$. The decryption process is as follows.

Let x be a node from T_w.

1. For each leaf node x, let $a = attr(x)$ denote the attribute associated with x, if $a \in S$, then compute:

$$F_x = \frac{e(D_a, C_x)}{e(D'_a, C'_x)} = \frac{e(g^r \cdot H(a)^{r_a}, g^{q_x(0)})}{e(g^{r_a}, (H(a)^{q_x(0)}))}$$

$$= \frac{e(g^r, g^{q_x(0)}) \cdot e(H(a), g)^{r_a \cdot q_x(0)}}{e(H(a), g)^{r_a \cdot q_x(0)}}$$

$$= e(g, g)^{r q_x(0)} \tag{5.5}$$

If $a \notin S$, it defines $F_x = \perp$.

2. For each non-leaf node x, if there exists an arbitrary k_x-sized set of child nodes z, denoted by S_x, we define $F_z \neq \perp$; if no such set exists, then this means that the node is not satisfied by the attribute set S and define $F_x = \perp$. If $F_z \neq \perp$, the algorithm further calculates using Lagrange interpolation:

$$F_x = \prod_{z \in S_x} F_z^{\Delta_{i, S'_x}(0)}$$

$$= \prod_{z \in S_x} (e(g, g)^{r \cdot q_z(0)})^{\Delta_{i, S'_x}(0)}$$

$$= \prod_{z \in S_x} (e(g, g)^{r \cdot q_{parent(z)}(index(z))})^{\Delta_{i, S'_x}(0)}$$

$$= \prod_{z \in S_x} e(g, g)^{r \cdot q_x(i) \cdot \Delta_{i, S'_x}(0)}$$

$$= e(g, g)^{r \cdot q_x(0)} \tag{5.6}$$

where $i = index(z), S'_x = (\forall z \in S_x : index(z))$, and Δ_{i, S'_x} is the Lagrange coefficient.

3. For the root node R of the access tree T, if $F_R = \perp$, then this means that T is not satisfied by the attribute set S; otherwise, according to the recursive calculation, we have $F_R = e(g, g)^{r \cdot q_R(0)} = e(g, g)^{rs}$.

4. If S satisfies T, the algorithm recovers the message M by computing

$$\frac{e(C,D)}{F_R} = \frac{e\left(h^s, g^{\frac{\alpha+r}{\beta}}\right)}{e(g,g)^{rs}} = \frac{e\left(g^{\beta s}, g^{\frac{\alpha+r}{\beta}}\right)}{e(g,g)^{rs}}$$

$$= \frac{e\left(g^s, g^\alpha \cdot g^r\right)}{e(g,g)^{rs}} = \frac{e\left(g^s, g^\alpha\right) e\left(g^s, g^r\right)}{e(g,g)^{rs}}$$

$$= e(g,g)^{\alpha s}$$

$$\frac{\widetilde{C}}{e(C,D)/F_R} = Me(g,g)^{\alpha s}/e(g,g)^{\alpha s} = M \qquad (5.7)$$

5.2.2 Searchable Encryption

Searchable encryption (SE) is an attractive cryptographic primitive as it enables a keyword-based search over encrypted data just like the information retrieval in the plaintext data. Figure 5.4 depicts a standard system model of SE. The model consists of three entities and demonstrates the following application scenario: Data owners encrypt data and build the secure index for ensuring the confidentiality and searchability. Encrypted data and secure index are uploaded to a remote server. After search authorization via secure communication channels, a data user is allowed to submit encrypted query keywords to the server to request goal data. Upon receiving the encrypted query

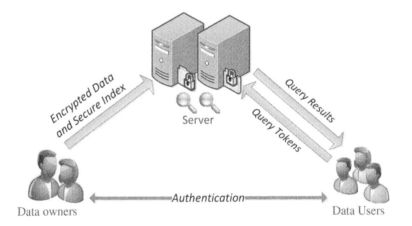

Figure 5.4 The system model of SE.

keywords, the server carries out a private search on secure index and returns all search results to the data user. Of course, the data user may also be the data owner. In this case, the search authorization can obviously be unnecessary.

Song et al. [3] designed the first practical searchable encryption construction in the private-key setting. In this scheme, a special three-layer encryption is used to encrypt each keyword of a document and linearly scan each encrypted keyword using the encrypted query to achieve private search, which leads to the linear search complexity. In order to achieve sub-linear search complexity, Curtmola et al. [4] constructed a searchable encryption construction based on an encrypted inverted index structure that the search time is only related to the number of data files containing the query. Kamara et al. [16] introduced the dynamic SE and discussed the problem of how to dynamically add and delete data files with low computation and communication cost and small leakage. On the other hand, to prevent the unreliable server from tampering search results (maliciously modify or even delete search results), verifiable SE was introduced by Kurosawa and Ohtaki [17]. Combining blockchain, Ref. [18] proposed the decentralized SE, which can guarantee that the server always returns the correct and complete search results. Recently, with the rapid development and increasing popularity of cloud computing, from the point of practicability, searchable encryption has been extended to solve how to achieve efficient and functionally rich search over encrypted cloud data [7–9,19]. They focus on how to achieve over encrypted data multi-keyword ranked search, fuzzy search, personalized search, etc. These schemes above are realized in the private-key environment, i.e., SSE. Boneh et al. [6] proposed the first public-key encryption with keyword search technique. Later, PEKS schemes supporting conjunctive and range search were also studied in [20–22].

Next, we present how to construct a searchable encryption scheme in the private-key environment and in the public-key environment, respectively. Here, we only provide a basic implementation skeleton and the details can be found in [4,16,22].

5.2.2.1 *SE in the Private-Key Setting*

We first introduce the basic cryptographic primitives and definitions used to construct the SE scheme in the private-key setting.

5.2.2.1.1 Cryptographic Primitives Let SKE = (Gen, Enc, Dec) be a private-key encryption scheme, in which Gen is a probabilistic algorithm that returns a secret key K on inputting a security parameter; Enc is a probabilistic algorithm that encrypts a message m under a key K and outputs a ciphertext c; Den is a deterministic algorithm that decrypts the ciphertext c using a K that was exactly used to produce c and returns m. A pseudo-random function F is computationally efficient function. It takes a key K and a bit string of arbitrary length as input and outputs a random string of fixed length, which is undistinguishable from the output of a real random function by any probabilistic polynomial-time adversary.

5.2.2.1.2 Definitions We write $x \overset{\$}{\leftarrow} X$ to represent an element x being sampled uniformly from a set X. The output x of an algorithm F is denoted by $x \leftarrow F$. The notation $a||b$ refers to the concatenation of two strings a and b. Let $a := b$ be an assignment operation. We use DB and EDB to denote a set of documents and its ciphertext version. Each document is identified by notation id. W is defined to be a keyword dictionary, and $w \in W$ denotes a keyword. We write $DB(w)$ to represent the documents containing the keyword w. We need a list data structure L, and each element in L is a label–data pair (l, d). One can invoke method add to insert (l, d) into L. In addition, we define an algorithm $Get(L, l)$, which indicates from L taking the label–data pair (l, d).

5.2.2.1.3 Basic Implementation Now, we give a basic implementation skeleton of SE scheme in the private-key setting, as shown in Figure 5.5. There are two key algorithms, i.e., SetUp and Search. The data owner runs SetUp to encrypt plaintext documents and construct a secure searchable index. Search algorithm consists of two sub-algorithm. On the one hand, on inputting a search keyword w and key K, the data user invokes this algorithm to generate a query token. Upon receiving the query token, the server is responsible for performing search over EDB on behalf of the data user and returns search results to the data user.

5.2.2.2 SE in the Public-Key Setting

We first introduce several cryptographic tools used to construct the SE scheme in the public-key setting and then describe a basic implementation skeleton.

SetUp(DB)

Data owner:

1. Compute $K \xleftarrow{\$} \{0,1\}^\lambda$ and generate an empty List L
2. For each keyword $w \in W$:
   (1) Compute $K_1 \leftarrow F(K, w\|1)$ and $K_1 \leftarrow F(K, w\|2)$
   (2) Define a counter and initialize $c := 0$
   (3) For each $\texttt{id} \in \texttt{DB}(w)$:
       1) Compute $l \leftarrow F(K_1, c)$ and $d \leftarrow \texttt{Enc}(K_2, \texttt{id})$ and $c := c+1$
       2) Add (l, d) to L by algorithm add
3. Send the key K to the data user and output the encrypted DB as EDB

Search$(K, w, \texttt{EDB})$

Data user: On input (K, w)
1. Compute $K_1 \leftarrow F(K, w\|1)$ and $K_1 \leftarrow F(K, w\|2)$
2. Send (K_1, K_2) to the server.

Server: On input EDB, message (K_1, K_2)
1. Generate an empty list R
2. For $c = 0$ until Get returns $\bot$
   (1) $d \leftarrow \texttt{Get}(\texttt{EDB}, F(K_1, c)); \texttt{id} \leftarrow \texttt{Dec}(K_2, d)$
   (2) Add id to R by algorithm add
3. Return R to the data user

Figure 5.5 The implementation skeleton of SE in the private-key setting

5.2.2.2.1 Cryptographic Tools   Let $\mathbb{G}_1$ and $\mathbb{G}_2$ be two multiplicative groups of prime order q. Specify a bilinear map $e : \mathbb{G}_1 \times \mathbb{G}_1 \to \mathbb{G}_2$ with three important properties defined in Section 5.2. We in addition need two hash functions $H_1 : \{0,1\}^* \to \mathbb{G}_1$ and $H_2 : \mathbb{G}_2 \to \{0,1\}^{\log q}$.

5.2.2.2.2 Basic Implementation   Now, we give a basic implementation skeleton of SE scheme in the public-key setting, as shown in Figure 5.6. Compared with SE in the private-key setting, the data owner uses the public key to encrypt index keyword in Enc algorithm and the data user uses private key to encrypt query keyword in Search algorithm. Because $H_2(e(\widetilde{q}, g^r)) = H_2(e(H_1(\mathcal{Q})^\alpha, g^r)) = H_2(e(H_1(\mathcal{Q}), g)^{\alpha r})$ and $H_2(t) = H_2(e(H_1(w), h^r)) = H_2(e(H_1(w), g)^{\alpha r})$, if $w = \mathcal{Q}$, we have

---

$\texttt{KeyGen}(1^\lambda)$

Data user:
1. Pick a random element $\alpha \in \mathbb{Z}_q^*$
2. Find a generator g of $\mathbb{G}_1$
3. Output public key $pub = [g, h = g^\alpha]$ and private key $priv = \alpha$

$\texttt{Enc}(pub, w)$

Data owner:
1. Pick a random element $r \in \mathbb{Z}_q^*$
2. Compute g^r, h^r, $t = e(H_1(w), h^r)$, and $H_2(t)$
3. Output w's ciphertext $\widetilde{w} = [g^r, H_2(t)]$

$\texttt{Search}(priv, \mathcal{Q}, \widetilde{w})$

Data user: On input $(priv, q)$, where $\mathcal{Q}$ is a query keyword.
1. Output q's ciphertext $\widetilde{q} = H_1(\mathcal{Q})^\alpha$

Server: On input $(\widetilde{w}, \widetilde{q})$
1. Check if $H_2(e(\widetilde{q}, g^r)) = H_2(t)$
2. If so, output "yes"; otherwise, output "no".

Figure 5.6 The implementation skeleton of SE in the public-key setting.

$H_2(e(\widetilde{q}, g^r)) = H_2(t)$. The derivation shows that the $\texttt{Search}$ algorithm is correct.

5.3 ABKS CONSTRUCTION

The attribute-based keyword search (ABKS) technique by taking full advantage of the searchable encryption and the attribute-based encryption is able to simultaneously achieve fine-grained access control and private data searching over ciphertext, which is very applicable to the cloud computing environment. Like ABE schemes, ABKS can also be divided into two categories: CP-ABKS [10–12] and KP-ABKS [23]. In CP-ABKS, a data owner embeds the access policy into the secure searchable index and issues the private key to a data user according to the attribute information of the data user. By using the private key, the data user can encrypt the search query to generate legal query trapdoor. On the contrary, in KP-ABKS, the access policy is embedded into the private key and a set of attributes is specified in the secure searchable index. In this section, we first introduce a CP-ABKS construction and then discuss how to perform search privilege revocation dynamically with a low cost.

5.3.1 System Model and Threat Model

First of all, we give the system model and the threat model in a CP-ABKS scheme.

5.3.1.1 System Model

As shown in Figure 5.7, the system model of a CP-ABKS for cloud computing involves three entities. They are the cloud server, the data owner, and the data users. This system model describes the following application scenario: The data owner intends to outsource his data to the remote cloud platform for enjoying low-cost data storage and processing. For confidentiality guaranteeing, before uploading the data, the data owner employs a semantically secure encryption scheme such as AES to encrypt the data and a CP-ABE to build searchable secure index for data access control. Via secure communication channels, the data owner sends some secret information to a data user, by which the data user can generate a legal query trapdoor he wants to search.

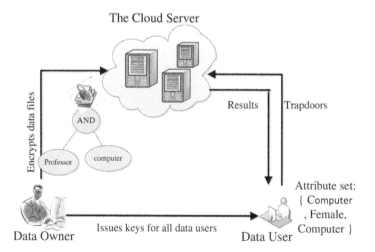

Figure 5.7 The system model of CP-ABKS for cloud computing.

The cloud server stores the encrypted data and index and, upon receiving a query trapdoor, performs the search over encrypted data on behalf of the data user. In a CP-ABKS scheme, if and only if a data user has access to a certain index and his submitted trapdoor matches the index, a successful search will complete.

5.3.1.2 Threat Model

The threat model of a CP-ABKS for cloud computing is generally modeled as "honest-but-curious" passive adversary. In this model, the cloud server provider promises that it would comply with the service and security contracts for maintaining company reputations. However, we cannot rule out the possibility that it may try to infer or steal information from outsourced data. This assumption is reasonable, since the cloud server is usually operated by a third-party commercial company, which is outside of the trusted domain of the data providers. In other words, the data owner cannot absolutely give assurance that the remote cloud server does not access the outsourced data. On the other hand, this threat model assumes that the data owner and the data users are fully trusted. Moreover, a data user does not leak the secret information such as private key to others such that the unauthorized data access will never occur. In addition, to secure the key distribution, there exist secure communication channels between the data owner and the data users.

5.3.1.2.1 Adaptively Chosen Keyword Attack Game   In general, the formal security proof of a CP-ABKS scheme relies on a game between a challenger $\mathcal{B}$ and an adversary $\mathcal{A}$, called the adaptively chosen keyword attack game, which is described below.

Setup. $\mathcal{B}$ initializes running environment and sends public parameters to the adversary $\mathcal{A}$.

Phase 1. $\mathcal{A}$ adaptively requests search trapdoor $\mathcal{T}_{\mathcal{A}}(w)$ for any keyword w for polynomially many times from $\mathcal{B}$ with the attribute sets $S_1, ..., S_q$.

Challenge. $\mathcal{A}$ defines a challenge access tree T^* such that none of the attribute sets $S_1, ..., S_q$ from Phase 1 satisfy T^*. $\mathcal{A}$ submits two keywords w_0, w_1 and T^* to $\mathcal{B}$. $\mathcal{B}$ flips a random binary coin $b \in \{0, 1\}$ and encrypts w_b with T^* as $\mathcal{I}_{w_b}$, which is sent to $\mathcal{A}$.

Phase 2. $\mathcal{A}$ continues to query the search trapdoor $\mathcal{T}_\mathcal{A}(w)$ for chosen keyword w (including w_0 and w_1) with the attribute set S_{q_w} from $\mathcal{B}$. The only restriction is that if the attribute set S_{q_w} in $\mathcal{T}_\mathcal{A}(w)$ satisfies T^*, then $w \neq w_0, w_1$ (in other words, if $w = w_0$ or $w = w_1$, then $S_{q_{w_0}}$ or $S_{q_{w_1}}$ does not satisfy T^*).

Guess. Finally, $\mathcal{A}$ outputs a guess b' of b.

The advantage that a probabilistic polynomial-time adversary $\mathcal{A}$ wins the above game is defined as $Adv = \mathbf{Pr}[b' = b] - \frac{1}{2}$.

5.3.2 Basic Algorithm

5.3.2.1 Algorithm Definition

A CP-ABKS scheme consists of five polynomial-time algorithms: Setup, Keygen, Enc, Trap, and Search.

1. Setup$(1^\lambda) \rightarrow (\mathbf{PK}, \mathbf{MSK})$. The algorithm generates system public parameter and system master key. On inputting a security parameter λ, it outputs the system public parameters $\mathbf{PK}$ and the master private key $\mathbf{MSK}$.

2. KeyGen$(\mathbf{PK}, \mathbf{MSK}, S_u) \rightarrow \mathcal{K}_u$. The algorithm generates a private key for a data user u. On inputting $\mathbf{PK}$, $\mathbf{MSK}$, and u's attribute set S_u, it outputs the private key $\mathcal{K}_u$.

3. Enc$(\mathbf{PK}, w, T_w) \rightarrow \mathcal{I}_w$. The algorithm encrypts an index keyword. On inputting $\mathbf{PK}$, an index keyword w, and a specified access tree T_w, it outputs w's ciphertext $\mathcal{I}_w$.

4. Trap$(\mathbf{PK}, \mathcal{K}_u, q) \rightarrow \mathcal{T}_u$. The algorithm encrypts a search query for data user u. On inputting $\mathbf{PK}$, a search query q, and $\mathcal{K}_u$, it outputs search trapdoor $\mathcal{T}_u(q)$.

5. Search$(\mathbf{PK}, \mathcal{I}_w, \mathcal{T}_u(q)) \rightarrow \mathbf{True}$. The algorithm performs the search over the encrypted data index. On inputting $\mathbf{PK}$, $\mathcal{I}_w$, and $\mathcal{T}_u(q)$, it outputs $\mathbf{True}$ if S_u satisfies T_w in $\mathcal{I}_w$ and $w = q$, simultaneously; otherwise, it outputs $\mathbf{False}$.

5.3.2.1.1 Correctness We say a CP-ABKS scheme is correct if given Setup$(1^\lambda) \rightarrow (\mathbf{PK}, \mathbf{MSK})$, Keygen$(\mathbf{PK}, \mathbf{MSK}, S_u) \rightarrow \mathcal{K}_u$,

$\text{Enc}(\mathbf{PK}, w, \mathcal{T}_w) \rightarrow \mathcal{I}_w$, and $\text{Trap}(\mathbf{PK}, \mathcal{K}_u, q) \rightarrow \mathcal{T}_u$, then $\text{Search}(\mathbf{PK}, \mathcal{I}_w, \mathcal{T}_u(q))$ always returns 1.

5.3.2.2   Algorithm Implementation

Here, we introduce a concrete construction of a CP-ABKS scheme by implementing the five polynomial-time algorithms defined above: Setup, KeyGen, Enc, Trap, and Search. In the system model of CP-ABKS for cloud computing, the data owner runs the three algorithms Setup, KeyGen, and Enc; the data user runs the Trap algorithm; and the cloud server runs the Search algorithm.

5.3.2.2.1   Setup Let $e : \mathbb{G}_1 \times \mathbb{G}_1 \rightarrow \mathbb{G}_2$ be a bilinear map with the three aforementioned properties, where $\mathbb{G}_1$ and $\mathbb{G}_2$ are two cyclic multiplicative groups with large prime order q. g is a generator of group $\mathbb{G}_1$. We define two one-way hash functions $H_1 : \{0,1\}^* \rightarrow \mathbb{Z}_q^*$ converting a bit string into an element in $\mathbb{Z}_q^*$ and $H_2 : \{0,1\}^* \rightarrow \mathbb{G}_1$ converting a bit string to an element in $\mathbb{G}_1$. Further, the Lagrange coefficient is defined as shown in Equation (5.2). On inputting a security parameter λ, the algorithm chooses two random elements α, β from $\mathbb{Z}_q^*$ and outputs $\mathbf{PK} = \{\mathbb{G}_1, \mathbb{G}_2, H_1, H_2, e(g,g)^\alpha, h = g^\beta\}$ and $\mathbf{MSK} = \{\beta, g^\alpha\}$.

5.3.2.2.2   KeyGen Suppose that there is a data user u with an attribute set S. The algorithm takes as input $\mathbf{PK}$, $\mathbf{MSK}$, and S, and outputs the private key $\mathcal{K}_u$ for u as follows:

$$\mathcal{K}_u = (G_1 = g^{\frac{\alpha}{\beta}}, G_2 = g^{\frac{1}{\beta}}$$
$$\forall a \in S, G_a = H_2(a)^{r_a}, G_a' = g^{r_a}) \qquad (5.8)$$

where r_a is randomly chosen from group $\mathbb{Z}_q^*$ for each attribute $a \in S$.

5.3.2.2.3   Enc The algorithm takes as input the master key $\mathbf{MSK}$ and an index keyword, and outputs the ciphertext of the index keyword. Specifically, the algorithm takes the following two steps to encrypt an index keyword w.

1. It defines an access tree $\mathcal{T}_w$ and, for each node x in $\mathcal{T}_w$, generates a polynomial q_x. Starting from the root node R, these polynomials are generated in a top-down manner. Specifically,

for each polynomial q_x of x, it sets the degree d_x of q_x to be $d_x = k_x - 1$, where k_x is the threshold value of the node x. Then, for the root node R, it chooses a random element $s \in \mathbb{Z}_q^*$ and sets $q_R(0) = s$ and sets d_R other points of q_R randomly to completely define it. For any other node x in T_w, it sets $q_x(0) = q_{p(x)}(index(x))$ and chooses d_x other points to completely define q_x.

2. Let Y be the set of leaf nodes in T_w, and w is encrypted under **MSK** as follows:

$$\mathcal{I}_w = (T_w, \tilde{\mathcal{I}}'_w = e(g,g)^{\alpha s H_1(w)}, \tilde{\mathcal{I}}''_w = h^{s H_1(w)},$$
$$\forall y \in Y : I_y = g^{q_y(0)}, I'_y = H_2(attr(y))^{q_y(0)}) \qquad (5.9)$$

5.3.2.2.4 Trap Assume a data user u with private key $\mathcal{K}_u$ wishes to search data files containing search query $\mathcal{Q}$; the algorithm takes as input **PK**, q, and $\mathcal{K}_u$, and outputs q's ciphertext by doing the following three steps.

1. It chooses a random element r from group $\mathbb{Z}_q^*$ and computes $\lambda_1 = r \cdot H_1(\mathcal{Q}), \lambda_2 = g^{\lambda_1} = g^{r H_1(\mathcal{Q})}, T_1 = G_1(G_2)^r = g^{\frac{\alpha}{\beta}} \cdot g^{\frac{r}{\beta}} = g^{\frac{\alpha+r}{\beta}}$.

2. For each $a \in S$, it computes $T_a = \lambda_2 G_a = g^{r H_1(\mathcal{Q})} H_2(a)^{r_a}$.

3. The algorithm encrypts the query keyword $\mathcal{Q}$ as

$$\mathcal{T}_u(q) = (T_1 = g^{\frac{\alpha+r}{\beta}},$$
$$\forall a \in S : T_a = g^{r H_1(\mathcal{Q})} H_2(a)^{r_a}, T'_a = G'_a = g^{r_a}) \qquad (5.10)$$

5.3.2.2.5 Search Given the query trapdoor $\mathcal{T}_u(\mathcal{Q})$ and an encrypted index keyword $\mathcal{I}_w$, the algorithm can be regarded as two sub-procedures. The first sub-procedure is that the cloud server performs an access privilege match between the attribute set S in $\mathcal{T}_u(\mathcal{Q})$ and the access tree T_w in $\mathcal{I}_w$. If S satisfies the access tree T_w, then this indicates u has the search privilege to $\mathcal{I}_w$. The algorithm continues to run the second sub-procedure to judge whether the search query $\mathcal{Q}$ is equal to w in a secret manner. In the whole search process, the cloud server cannot obtain any plaintext information about the search query and the index keywords.

The detailed process can be described as follows.
Let x be a node from T_w.

1. For each leaf node x, let $a = attr(x)$ denote the attribute associated with x; if $a \in S$, then compute:

$$
\begin{aligned}
F_x &= \frac{e(T_a, I_x)}{e(T'_a, I'_x)} = \frac{e(g^{rH_1(\mathcal{Q})} \cdot H_2(a)^{r_a}, g^{q_x(0)})}{e(g^{r_a}, H_2(a)^{q_x(0)})} \\
&= \frac{e(g^{rH_1(\mathcal{Q})}, g^{q_x(0)}) \cdot e(H_2(a), g)^{r_a \cdot q_x(0)}}{e(H_2(a), g)^{r_a \cdot q_x(0)}} \\
&= e(g, g)^{rH_1(\mathcal{Q})q_x(0)}
\end{aligned}
\tag{5.11}
$$

If $a \notin S$, we define $F_x = \perp$.

2. For each non-leaf node x, if there exists an arbitrary k_x-sized set of child nodes z, denoted by S_x, we define $F_z \neq \perp$; if no such set exists, then this means that the node is not satisfied by the attribute set S and define $F_x = \perp$. If $F_z \neq \perp$, the algorithm further calculates using Lagrange interpolation:

$$
\begin{aligned}
F_x &= \prod_{z \in S_x} F_z^{\Delta_{i, S'_x}(0)} \\
&= \prod_{z \in S_x} \left(e(g, g)^{rH_1(\mathcal{Q}) \cdot q_z(0)} \right)^{\Delta_{i, S'_x}(0)} \\
&= \prod_{z \in S_x} \left(e(g, g)^{rH_1(\mathcal{Q}) \cdot q_{parent(z)}(index(z))} \right)^{\Delta_{i, S'_x}(0)} \\
&= \prod_{z \in S_x} e(g, g)^{rH_1(\mathcal{Q}) \cdot q_x(i) \cdot \Delta_{i, S'_x}(0)} \\
&= e(g, g)^{rH_1(\mathcal{Q}) \cdot q_x(0)}
\end{aligned}
\tag{5.12}
$$

where $i = index(z)$, $S'_x = (\forall z \in S_x : index(z))$, and Δ_{i, S'_x} is the Lagrange coefficient.

3. For the root node R of T_w, after finishing the above recursive operations, if $F_R = \perp$, then this indicates T is not satisfied by S and the Search will terminate in advance; otherwise, we can get

$$
F_R = e(g, g)^{rH_1(\mathcal{Q}) \cdot q_R(0)} = e(g, g)^{rH_1(\mathcal{Q})s}
$$

Next, the second sub-procedure is performed to check whether the search query $\mathcal{Q}$ is equal to w by verifying:

$$\widetilde{I}'_w = \frac{e(\widetilde{I}''_w, T_1)}{F_R} \tag{5.13}$$

If Equation (5.13) returns true, we have $w = \mathcal{Q}$ by the following derivation:

$$\frac{e(\widetilde{I}''_w, T_1)}{F_R} = \frac{e(h^{sH_1(w)}, g^{\frac{\alpha+r}{\beta}})}{e(g,g)^{rH_1(\mathcal{Q})s}} = \frac{e(g^{\beta sH_1(w)}, g^{\frac{\alpha+r}{\beta}})}{e(g,g)^{rH_1(\mathcal{Q})s}}$$

$$= \frac{e(g^{sH_1(w)}, g^{\alpha+r})}{e(g,g)^{rH_1(\mathcal{Q})s}} = \frac{e(g^{sH_1(w)}, g^{\alpha})e(g^{sH_1(w)}, g^r)}{e(g,g)^{rH_1(\mathcal{Q})s}}$$

$$= \frac{e(g,g)^{\alpha sH_1(w)}e(g,g)^{rH_1(w)s}}{e(g,g)^{rH_1(\mathcal{Q})s}}$$

If the search query $\mathcal{Q}$ is identical to w (i.e., $H_1(\mathcal{Q}) = H_1(w)$), then we can further get:

$$\frac{e(\widetilde{I}''_w, T_1)}{F_R} = \frac{e(g,g)^{\alpha sH_1(w)}e(g,g)^{rH_1(w)s}}{e(g,g)^{rH_1(\mathcal{Q})s}}$$

$$= e(g,g)^{\alpha sH_1(w)}$$

$$= \widetilde{I}'_w$$

5.3.3 Search Privilege Revocation

The cloud computing is a dynamic and open environment. Therefore, dynamically and flexibly revoking a data user's search privilege is a significant property in an ABKS scheme. We introduce two approaches to explain in ABKS how to revoke a data user's search privilege with a low computation and communication overhead. The two approaches achieve search privilege revocation from different grains. The first approach is to revoke the whole user (in a coarse-grained manner), and the second is to revoke certain attributes of a data user (in a fine-grained manner).

5.3.3.1 Coarse-Grained Revocation

The coarse-grained revocation indicates revoking a data user's whole search privilege, which means the data user no more has the ability to generate a legal query trapdoor. Without the legal query trapdoor, he cannot retrieve the data from the cloud server; i.e., the search privilege has been invoked.

Here, we introduce a coarse-grained search privilege revocation approach based on symmetric key sharing and dynamic update. Given the traditional symmetric encryption scheme SE=(Gen, Enc, Dec) (such as AES), the cloud server runs algorithm SE.Gen to generate a key k, which is shared between the cloud server and data users. After a data user generates the query trapdoor $\mathcal{T}_u(\mathcal{Q})$, $\mathcal{T}_u(\mathcal{Q})$ is re-encrypted using algorithm SE.Enc under the shared key k as $\mathcal{T}_u(\mathcal{Q})' =$ SE.Enc$(g^{\frac{\alpha+r}{\beta}}||\{\forall a \in S : g^{rH_1(q)}H_2(a)^{r_a}, g^{r_a}\})$, where $||$ denotes the concatenation of two strings. Obviously, before performing search algorithm, the cloud server can recover $\mathcal{T}_u(\mathcal{Q})$ by encrypting SE.Dec$(k,$ $\mathcal{T}_u(\mathcal{Q})')$. When the system needs to revoke an authorized data user, it asks the cloud server to update key k to k' and distributes it to unrevoked data users via secure channels. As a result, the revoked data user cannot generate a valid trapdoor component without the updated key k'. To guarantee the user experience, when a worker is revoked, the cloud server will send a notification to the revoked data user.

5.3.3.2 Fine-Grained Revocation

The fine-grained revocation means revoking certain attributes from a data user, which only incurs the degradation of the data user's search privilege. After certain attributes have been revoked from a data user, the data user may still hold search privilege for some index keywords, as long as the remaining attributes satisfy the access policies embedded in the index keywords.

Here, we introduce a fine-grained search privilege revocation approach based on the re-encryption idea.

5.3.3.2.1 Index keyword re-encryption   Let $\mathbb{A}$ be the attribute universe in the system and, for any an attribute $a \in \mathbb{A}$, define an attribute key K_a to generate an attribute key universe, denoted by $\mathbb{AK} = \{\forall a \in$ $\mathbb{A} : K_a\}$, which is shared between the cloud server, the data owner, and data users. When receiving the encrypted index keyword $\mathcal{I}_w$ from the data owner, the cloud server uses $\mathbb{AK}$ to re-encrypt $\mathcal{I}_w$ as follows:

$$\mathcal{I}_w^* = (T_w, \widetilde{I}_w' = e(g,g)^{\alpha s H_1(w)}, \widetilde{I}_w'' = h^{s H_1(w)},$$

$$\forall y \in Y \wedge \forall K_{attr(y)} \in \mathbb{AK} : I_y = g^{q_y(0)},$$

$$I_y' = (H_2(attr(y))^{q_y(0)})^{K_{attr(y)}}) \tag{5.14}$$

5.3.3.2.2 Private key re-encryption When a data user u receives the private key $\mathcal{K}_u$ from the data owner, the data user re-encrypts it. To achieve this re-encryption, based on S and $\mathbb{AK}$, the data user first generates an attribute key subset as $\overline{\mathbb{AK}} = \{K_a | a \in S, K_a \in \mathbb{AK}\}$, where S denotes $u's$ attribute set, which has been embedded into the private key $\mathcal{K}_u$. Then, u employs the attribute key subset $\overline{\mathbb{AK}}$ to *re-encrypt* the $\mathcal{K}_u$ as follows:

$$\mathcal{K}_u' = (G_1 = g^{\frac{\alpha}{\beta}}, G_2 = g^{\frac{1}{\beta}},$$

$$\forall a \in S \wedge \forall K_a \in \overline{\mathbb{AK}} : G_a = H_2(a)^{r_a},$$

$$G_a' = (g^{r_a})^{\frac{1}{K_a}}) \tag{5.15}$$

5.3.3.2.3 Query trapdoor re-encryption When a data user u generates the query trapdoor $\mathcal{T}_u(\mathcal{Q})$ of query keyword $\mathcal{Q}$, the data user further re-encrypts $\mathcal{T}_u(\mathcal{Q})$ using $\mathcal{K}_u'$ as:

$$\mathcal{T}_u(q)' = (T_1 = g^{\frac{\alpha+r}{\beta}},$$

$$\forall a \in S \wedge \forall K_a \in \overline{\mathbb{AK}} : T_a = g^{r H_1(\mathcal{Q})} H_2(a)^{r_a},$$

$$T_a' = G_a' = (g^{r_a})^{\frac{1}{K_a}}), \tag{5.16}$$

which will be submitted to the cloud server.

Note that the re-encryption operations mentioned above have no influence on the search algorithm; interested readers can verify the conclusion by substituting those re-encryption ciphertext components into the Search algorithm.

Now, we explain how to perform the fine-grained attribute revocation operations based on an attribute revocation protocol among the cloud server, the data owner, and the data users. Assume that an attribute a will be revoked from a data user u by the system, the attribute revocation protocol works as follows.

1. Data Owner. For the attribute a, the data owner first generates a new attribute key K'_a and updates $\mathbb{AK}$ by computing $\mathbb{AK} := (\mathbb{AK} - \{K_a\}) \bigcup \{K'_a\}$ and then sends K'_a to the cloud server and data users who have been assigned the attribute a except u.

2. Cloud Server. Upon receiving the K'_a, the cloud server first updates $\mathbb{AK}$ by computing $\mathbb{AK} := (\mathbb{AK} - \{K_a\}) \bigcup \{K'_a\}$. Then, for each encrypted index keyword w, if existing one leaf node in the access tree T_w associates with the attribute a, then the cloud server updates the value I'_a of $\mathcal{I}^*_w$ as $(I'_a)^{K'_a}$ for the attribute a and keeps other leaf nodes unchanged. The new $\mathcal{I}^*_w$ is denoted as follows (assume that the lead node x in T_w associates with the attribute a, i.e., $a = attr(x)$):

$$
\begin{aligned}
\mathcal{I}^*_w &= (T_w, \tilde{I}'_w = e(g,g)^{\alpha s H_1(w)}, \tilde{I}''_w = h^{s H_1(w)}, \\
I_x &= g^{q_x(0)}, I'_x = (H_2(attr(x))^{q_x(0)})^{K_{attr(x)} K'_{attr(x)}} \\
&\forall y \in Y \wedge \forall K_{attr(y)} \in \mathbb{AK} \setminus \{x\} : I_y = g^{q_y(0)}, \\
I'_y &= (H_2(attr(y))^{q_y(0)})^{K_{attr(y)}})
\end{aligned}
\tag{5.17}
$$

3. Data Users. When a data user u' who has been assigned the attribute a receives the updated attribute key K'_a from the data owner, he first updates his attribute key subset $\overline{\mathbb{AK}}$ by computing $\overline{\mathbb{AK}} := (\overline{\mathbb{AK}} - \{K_a\}) \bigcup \{K'_a\}$ and then updates the previous G'_a as $(G'_a)^{\frac{1}{K'_a}}$ and keeps the other attribute keys unchanged. The new $\mathcal{G}^*_{u'}$ is denoted by:

$$
\begin{aligned}
T'_{u'} t &= (G_1 = g^{\frac{a}{\beta}}, G_2 = g^{\frac{1}{\beta}}, G_a = H_2(a)^{r_a}, G'_a = (g^{r_a})^{\frac{1}{K_a K'_a}} \\
&\forall b \in S \wedge \forall K_b \in \overline{\mathbb{AK}} \setminus \{a\}, G_b = H_2(b)^{r_b}, G'_b = (g^{r_b})^{\frac{1}{K_b}})
\end{aligned}
\tag{5.18}
$$

Revoking certain attributes from a data user incurs that the data user's attribute set no more satisfies the access policy associated with an index keyword. This is because the original attribute keys of the revoked attributes have been updated after running the attribute revocation protocol. These updated attribute keys are unknown to the data user. Without the newly updated attribute keys, the data user cannot recover the information F_R for the root node R in the access tree in the **Search** algorithm.

5.4   EXPERIMENTAL RESULT ANALYSIS

The search performance is of paramount importance in practice for a search system, which directly affects user experiences. In this section, we analyze the practicality of the ABKS scheme by a group of search cost evaluation experiments over a real data set. The experiments were conducted in Java platform, and the configuration of the search server is an Ubuntu 16.04 system with 3.60 GHZ Inter Core i7-7700 CPU and 16GB memory. In these experiments, we mainly consider the search performance trend affected by the size of data files and index keywords and ignore the number of attributes and set it to be a constant.

Figure 5.8 shows the time cost of search for different numbers of encrypted index keywords when fixing the size of data files to be 4000. We can observe that the search complexity of the ABKS scheme is proportional to the number of the encrypted index keywords. The more the index keywords are, the more time would be spent on search over encrypted index keywords. This is because the linear scanning on the index keywords causes the time-consuming pairing and exponentiation operations to be linear with the number of index keywords. We can see that when the number of index keywords is 800, the average time of search is about 50s. Such a search efficiency is obviously impractical in real applications, especially in the big data environments. Therefore, we can say that the current ABKS researches are more of theoretic interest.

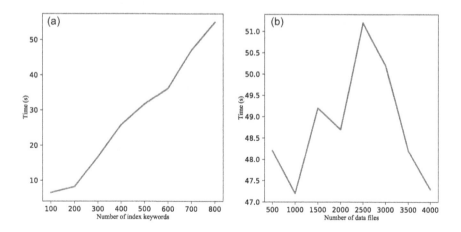

Figure 5.8   Search performance evaluation.

On the other hand, our experimental results also shows the time cost of search for different numbers of encrypted data files when fixing the size index keywords to be 800. We can observe that the size of data files has little influence on the search overhead, since the keyword-based index structure is widely used in the ABKS schemes, not the file-level index.

5.5 CONCLUSIONS AND FUTURE DIRECTIONS

The ABKS techniques provide a feasibility that simultaneously achieves searching and fine-grained access control over encrypted data, which are very applied to the cloud computing environment characterized by data storage and sharing. In this chapter, we first introduce the key techniques to achieve an ABKS technique and then we give an ABKS construction and discuss how to revoke a data user's search privilege in the coarse-grained and fine-grained manners. Finally, we run the CP-ABKS scheme present in Section 5.3.2 over a real data set and evaluate the average search complexity of this scheme. From the experimental results, we can see that existing ABKS schemes are not suitable to use in the real data set due to the high search complexity. How to eliminate the gap is still an important research topic.

Based on the literature review, we present the future research directions for the ABKS technique as follows.

1. Search Complexity Optimization. At present, in the existing ABKS schemes, the reason for high search overhead is that the time-consuming pairing and exponentiation operations are linear in the number of encrypted index keywords. Designing the encrypted index structure and search algorithm with constant or no pairing and exponentiation operations is the key point to improve the search overhead of ABKS schemes.

2. Dynamic ABKS Technique. As far as we know, there are no dynamic ABKS schemes in the existing literature. A dynamic ABKS technique will provide the ability to dynamically add or delete the data files from the server side with a strong security guarantee and a low computation and communication overhead. The feature is attractive, especially in the open and elastic cloud computing environment, since it will facilitate the data owner to dynamically update their cloud data.

REFERENCES

[1] K. Ren, C. Wang, and Q. Wang. Security challenges for the public cloud. *IEEE Internet Computing*, 16(1):69–73, 2012.

[2] S. Kamara and K. Lauter. Cryptographic cloud storage. In *Springer RLCPS*, Berlin/Heidelberg, January 2010.

[3] D. Song, D. Wagner, and A. Perrig. Practical techniques for searches on encrypted data. In *IEEE Symposium on Security and Privacy*, vol. 8, pp. 44–55, Berkeley, CA, 2000.

[4] R. Curtmola, J. Garay, S. Kamara, and R. Ostrovsky. Searchable symmetric encryption: improved definitions and efficient constructions. In *ACM CCS*, vol. 19, pp. 79–88, Alexandria, VA, 2006.

[5] S. Sun, X. Yuan, J. K. Liu, and R. Steinfeld. Practical backward-secure searchable encryption from symmetric puncturable encryption. In *ACM Conference on Computer and Communications Security*, pp. 763–780, Toronto, ON, 2018.

[6] D. Boneh, G. D. Crescenzo, R. Ostrovsky, and G. Persiano. Public-key encryption with keyword search. In *EUROCRYPR*, pp. 506–522, Berlin/Heidelberg, 2004.

[7] Z. Fu, X. Sun, Q. Liu, L. Zhou, and J. Shu. Achieving efficient cloud search services: Multi-keyword ranked search over encrypted cloud data supporting parallel computing. *IEICE Transactions on Communications*, E98-B(1):190–200, 2015.

[8] W. Zhang, S. Xiao, Y. Lin, J. Wu, and S. Zhou. Privacy preserving ranked multi-keyword search for multiple data owners in cloud computing. *IEEE Transactions on Computers*, 65(5):1566–1577, 2016.

[9] Z. Fu, X. Wu, Q. Wang, and K. Ren. Enabling central keyword-based semantic extension search over encrypted outsourced data. *IEEE Transactions on Information Forensics and Security*, 12(12):2986–2997, 2017.

[10] W. Sun, S. Yu, W. Lou, Y. T. Hou, and H. Li. Protecting your right: Attribute-based keyword search with fine-grained owner-enforced search authorization in the cloud. In *IEEE INFOCOM*, pp. 226–234, Toronto, ON, 2014.

[11] J. Li, X. Lin, Y. Zhang, and J. Han. Ksf-oabe: Outsourced attribute-based encryption with keyword search function for cloud storage. *IEEE Transactions on Services computing*, 10(5):715–725, 2016.

[12] Y. Miao, J. Ma, X. Liu, X. Li, Z. Liu, and H. Li. Practical attribute-based multi-keyword search scheme in mobile crowdsourcing. *IEEE Internet of Things Journal*, 5(4):3008–3018, 2018.

[13] A. Sahai and B. Waters. Fuzzy identity-base encryption. In *EUROCRYPT*, pp. 457–473, Berlin/Heidelberg, 2005.

[14] V. Goyal, O. Pandey, A. Sahai, and B. Waters. Attribute-based encryption for fine-grained access control of encryption data. In *ACM Conference on Computer and Communications Security*, pp. 89–98, Alexandria, VA, 2006.

[15] J. Bethencourt, A. Sahai, and B. Waters. Ciphertext-policy attribute-based encryption. In *IEEE Symposium on Security and Privacy*, pp. 321–334, Berkeley, CA, 2007.

[16] S. Kamara, C. Papamanthou, and T. Roeder. Dynamic searchable symmeteric encryption. In *ACM Conference on Computer and Communications Security*, pp. 965–976, Raleigh, NC, 2012.

[17] K. Kurosawa and Y. Ohtaki. Uc-secure searchable symmetric encryption. In *Financial Cryptography and Data Security*, pp. 285–298. Springer Berlin Heidelberg, 2012.

[18] Y. Zhang, R. H. Deng, J. Shu, K Yang, and D. Zheng. Tkse: Trustworthy keyword search over encrypted data with two-side verifiability via blockchain. *IEEE Access*, 6:31077–31087, 2018.

[19] N. Cao, C. Wang, M. Li, K. Ren, and W. Lou. Privacy-preserving multi-keyword ranked search over encrypted cloud data. *IEEE Transactions on Parallel and Distributed Systems*, 25(1):222–233, 2014.

[20] P. Golle, J. Staddon, and B. Waters. Secure conjunctive keyword search over encrypted data. In *Springer ACNS*, pp. 31–45, Berlin/Heidelberg, 2004.

[21] D. Boneh and B. Waters. Conjunctive, subset, and range queries on encrypted data. In *Springer TCC*, pp. 535–554, Berlin/Heidelberg, 2007.

[22] H. Yin, Z. Qin, J. Zhang, L. Ou, F. Li, and K. Li. Secure conjunctive multi-keyword ranked search over encrypted cloud data for multiple data owners. *Future Generation Computer Systems*, 100:689–700, 2019.

[23] H. Zhu, L. Wangand, H. Ahmad, and X. Niu. Key-policy attribute-based encryption with equality test in cloud computing. *IEEE Access*, 5(1):20428–20439, 2018.

CHAPTER **6**

Understanding Cybersecurity Risk in FMI Using HPC

Gurdip Kaur
University of New Brunswick (UNB)

Ziba Habibi Lashkari
Universidad Politécnica de Madrid

Arash Habibi Lashkari
University of New Brunswick (UNB)

CONTENTS

DOI: 10.1201/9781003155799-6

6.1 INTRODUCTION

Financial market infrastructure (FMI) serves as the backbone of financial markets. It allows financial transactions to take place between people, financial institutions, and businesses in a cheaper and more efficient manner. It is the key component between financial institutions that exchange payments, securities, and derivatives. It allows customers and financial firms to purchase goods and services safely. It strengthens financial stability and economic growth by recording, clearing, and settling monetary and other financial transactions.

Simple examples of FMI include depositing salary into an employee's account, taking cash from an ATM machine, and paying for online purchases. It is estimated that payments worth 360 billion pounds take place every day in the UK through FMIs [1]. FMIs also play some other important functions such as transferring shares between traders and stock market, helping banks to borrow money from other banks and financial institutions in the market, and lending and borrowing loans to buy houses and invest in business.

FMIs can be a source of liquidity risk and credit losses, if not managed properly [2]. In addition, FMIs are prone to general business risk and financial, legal, operational, and systemic risks. All these risks pose threat to the security of data and systems in FMIs. Consequently, adequate supervision of FMIs is necessary for the proper functioning of the financial institutions [3].

Since FMIs undergo millions of financial transactions every day, it is important that these transactions are processed at a much faster and accurate rate. This brings high-performance computing (HPC) into picture. HPC enables distributed parallel computing of huge amounts of data. It allows organizations, especially FMIs, to derive significant and meaningful value from unusable information [4]. It possesses high computational ability not only to process financial transactions at a higher speed, but also to identify fraudulent transactions as soon as they take place.

Financial fraud is a severe threat for FMIs that can incur a huge number of financial losses. With the integration of HPC, FMIs can maintain a big dataset that can be used to detect suspicious transactions immediately by correlating meaningful information from data stored in a data lake. Cloud implementation of HPC plays a pivotal role in order to maintain the big data. According to Hyperion research, HPC server market grew over 15% to generate a record revenue of 13.7 billion dollars. It is expected to reach 44 billion dollars by 2023 [5].

HPC is transforming innovation and revenue for organizations across industries. With the adoption of cloud-based HPC solutions, financial institutions strive to keep pace with innovation in the market [6]. The continuous growth of HPC speaks high of its value to the scientific community which carries a high-risk potential. This makes HPC a prime target of security breaches. Some popular security issues associated with HPC consist of confidentiality and integrity of data, data security, malicious insiders, and external cyber-threats [7].

Focusing on FMIs, cyber-threats have emerged as a persistent systemic risk. Its persistence makes it difficult to detect and eradicate completely. It is equally difficult to measure the breadth of damage caused by cyberattacks [8]. The primary motivation behind these attacks is to make money, disrupt services to cause financial losses, and steal sensitive data.

The rest of the chapter is organized as follows: Section 6.2 provides an overview of various components of FMIs. Section 6.3 introduces high-performance computing. It is followed by HPC's power to transform financial industry in Section 6.4. Section 6.5 delineates the association of high-performance computing with FMIs. Section 6.6 reviews the current works on cybersecurity issues related to HPC in FMIs as reported in the literature. Section 6.7 introduces financial risks in FMIs and is followed by common security objectives in Section 6.8. Various cybersecurity issues in each component of the infrastructure and their mapping with common security objectives of cybersecurity are presented in Section 6.9. Section 6.10 brings forward cybersecurity risks in FMIs. Finally, Section 6.11 concludes the chapter.

6.2 WHAT IS FINANCIAL MARKET INFRASTRUCTURE (FMI)?

Financial market infrastructures are defined as a multilateral system designed to record, clear, or settle payment systems among participating financial institutions. Apart from handling payment systems, they also include settlements, securities, derivatives, or other financial transactions [9]. The participating financial institutions are referred to as buyers and sellers. FMIs establish a set of common rules and procedures for participating entities that considers specialized risk management framework to deal with risks that may occur. It ensures financial stability and economic growth by effectively managing risks that may occur in the financial system [10]. Financial stability and market functioning rely on the continuity of services provided by FMIs [11]. A complete structure of FMI along with essential components is presented in Figure 6.1.

6.2.1 Payment Systems

A payment system is a set of rules and procedures used to transfer funds between participating entities. It operates based on an agreement

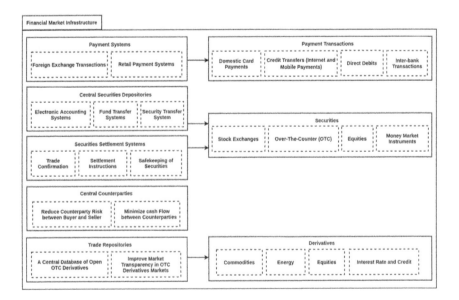

Figure 6.1 Essential components of FMI.

between the entities and the operator. It enables lending and repayment of money, payments for goods and services offered, salaries, and benefits for general public [11]. It is generally categorized as either a foreign exchange transaction, or a retail payment system. Foreign exchange (FX) transactions are the most liquid sector of payment systems in the financial market. It primarily deals with international trade and investments through exchange rates of currencies and transfer of funds. It generates the largest number of payments every day. It is estimated that the daily turnover of the foreign exchange market is 5.3 trillion dollars.

On the other hand, a retail payment system handles large volumes of low-value funds transfer in the form of cash, checks, credits, debits, and debit card transactions. It primarily deals with payments and transfers within the country. It is operated by private or public sector real-time gross settlement (RTGS) or deferred net settlement (DNS) mechanism.

The types of payment transactions covered by payment systems include domestic card payments, credit transfers (Internet and mobile payments), direct debits, and inter-bank transactions [12]. Domestic card payments are used to make payments within the country. It uses credit or debit card issued by the bank and merchant's registered account. Credit transfers works like a direct cash transfer between a payee and a payer. It is also called e-transfer or electronic transfer that makes use of Internet services and mobile payments. Credit transfer can be used to pay electricity and water bills, purchase and sell goods and services, and shop online. It provides a fast mode of payment where the payee does not need to wait for the payment.

In contrast, direct debits or debit transfers begin with the delivery of the payment. In a debit transfer, the bank notifies if the payment is not successful. Thus, it works on the principle of "no news is good news". Despite the popularity of credit transfers, debit transfers are used predominantly by many countries [13].

Inter-bank transactions provide great liquidity to financial markets. It describes monetary transactions between banks. For example, national banks seeking loan from the central bank or central banks seeking loan from the World Bank are classified as inter-bank transactions. They also include payment transactions between two banks for transferring an amount from one user account registered with one bank to the other user account registered with another bank.

Inter-bank transactions can be carried out through RTGS or National Electronic Funds Transfer (NEFT).

6.2.2 Central Security Depositories

A central security depository holds a security account for fund transfer in either a certificated or uncertificated form. It plays an important role in ensuring the integrity of security issues. It may maintain a record of legal ownership for security. The functions performed by a central security depository may vary depending upon the jurisdiction in which it is operating. It is responsible for electronic accounting of assets and services, fund transfer, and security transfer system. It includes stock exchanges, over-the-counter (OTC) derivatives, equities, and money market instruments.

A stock exchange is a centralized location where government and corporations can buy and sell equities. Equities and stocks are sometimes used interchangeably. It acts as an investment hub for two counterparties involved in an investment. The New York Stock Exchange (NYSE) and Nasdaq are the two most popular stock exchanges in the world. All the trading activities in a stock exchange take place through a broker. In addition to physical exchanges, electronic exchanges use an electronic platform to avoid a centralized physical location for trade.

OTC derivatives are private financial contracts that are not traded on an asset exchange. A derivative is a security with a price that depends on or is derived from an underlying asset. The most common underlying assets include stocks, bonds, commodities, currencies, interest rates, and market indexes. Derivatives which can be traded are called exchange-traded, while non-traded derivatives are called OTC derivatives. An OTC derivative is a financial contract arranged between counterparties (buyer and seller) by following minimal regulations [14].

Money market instruments allocate short-term funding to financial institutions. It is a type of mutual fund that is invested in low-risk securities such as government securities, certificates of deposit, and commercial paper. Money market instruments maintain a stable net asset value for a share. The value of a share may increase or decrease depending on the business of a firm in the market [14].

6.2.3 Security Settlement Systems

A security settlement system is a critical component of FMIs. It enables securities for a settlement between the trading parties. It acts as an intermediator between borrowers and lenders to secure the flow of funds and maintain their security portfolios [15]. It allows transfer of payment either free of cost or against a payment. When the transfer is made against a payment, delivery of the security is taken care of, if and only if payment is made. It also ensures safekeeping of securities by providing additional security clearing and settlement instructions.

With the soaring cross-border trades and settlements, the integration of global markets is also increased. Like central security depositories, it also includes stock exchanges, OTC derivatives, equities, and money market instruments. Any lapse in security settlement system may result in systemic risks to securities markets. It may further cause liquidity or credit losses for the participating entities [15].

6.2.4 Central Counterparties

A central counterparty acts as an intermediator by acting buyer to the seller and vice versa. It interposes itself between counterparties to financial contracts traded in the financial market [16]. It is used by derivatives exchanges, security exchanges, and trading systems. It has the potential to reduce risks between buyers and sellers by binding on them through legal procedures and imposing effective risk control measures. Due to this, it is feasible to reduce systemic risk as well.

The effectiveness of risk controls is critical to minimize cash flow between counterparts and achieve risk reduction benefits. Central counterparties' failure to control risk has the potential to disrupt not only the financial market, but the other settlement systems also. It also tends to enhance the liquidity of the financial market by supporting anonymous trading in some cases [16].

6.2.5 Trade Repositories

A trade repository maintains a central database of transactions and data. It is a new component of FMIs and is gaining importance in the OTC derivatives market. By centralizing the transactions and dissemination and storage of collected data, it enhances the transparency of information to relevant authorities and the public. An important function performed by trade repositories is to provide information that supports risk reduction, operational efficiency, and cost savings for the participating entities and the market [9]. Trade repositories store commodities, energy, equities, interest rate, and credit. Since the data stored by trade repositories are used by several stakeholders, it is critical to maintain accuracy, reliability, and availability of data. Trade repositories can be characterized by the following benefits:

- The centralization of data provides a transparent market infrastructure.

- Timely and reliable access to data stored in trade repositories significantly improves the ability to identify the risks posed to the financial system.

- Trade repositories provide a common platform for various stakeholders to support consistency of data formats and representations.

- Centralized and reliable data increase its usefulness.

The concept of FMIs was started after the financial crisis in 2009. G20 leaders agreed on a stricter regulation of "over-the-counter" derivatives [17]. As a result, the European Union passed the European Market Infrastructure Regulation ("EMIR") in 2012 [18]. The regulation was approved in 2015 in the form of the Financial Market Infrastructure Act (FMIA). FMIA entered into force on New Year of 2016. It includes rules and regulations for derivatives trading, operational functioning of FMIs, and existing market behavior rules from the Stock Exchange Act [19]. The FMIA is supplemented by two ordinances: the Federal Council's Financial Market Infrastructure Ordinance ("FMIO") and FINMA's Financial Market Infrastructure Ordinance ("FMIO-FINMA"). These ordinances support rules and regulations for trading and post-trading (clearing, settlement, and custody) events.

6.3 WHAT IS HIGH-PERFORMANCE COMPUTING?

High-performance computing can be defined as "the practice of aggregating computing power in a way that delivers much higher

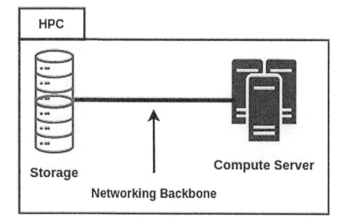

Figure 6.2 HPC components.

performance than one could get out of a typical desktop computer or workstation in order to solve large problems in science, engineering, or business" [20].

In other words, HPC is the ability to process data and perform complex calculations at a much higher speed. One of the best HPC computers is a supercomputer that contains thousands of nodes that work together to complete a task. This is called parallel processing. HPC is the foundation to various scientific, business, and industrial innovations by processing data. HPC solutions have three main components: (1) compute, (2) network, and (3) storage. Figure 6.2 presents these components and their functions in a nutshell.

To build a HPC architecture, compute servers are clustered together in a network. These servers run software and applications that perform fast computations. The cluster is networked to a data storage component that captures the output [21]. Putting all these components together allows HPC to perform diverse sets of tasks in minimal time period.

Further, to achieve the best performance, all these components pace together. To substantiate, storage component feeds and ingests data to and from compute servers as fast as possible. Similarly, networking components support the high-speed transmission of data between compute servers and storage devices. If any component fails to maintain

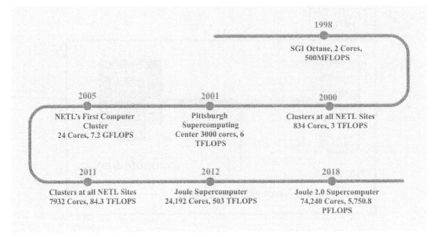

Figure 6.3 Evolution of HPC [22].

pace with rest of the components, the HPC architecture fails to achieve its objective of high performance.

Figure 6.3 shows the evolution of HPC over the years. The concept started in 1998 with a two-core processor that evolved to first computer cluster in 2005. From then onward, HPC has revolutionized the computing world with high-performance supercomputers such as Pittsburgh, NETL, and Joule supercomputer. The most recent supercomputer is Joule 2.0, which contains 74,240 cores and is an advanced version of 2012 supercomputer with the same name having 24,192 cores.

6.4 HOW HPC COULD TRANSFORM THE FINANCIAL INDUSTRY

HPC possesses the potential to provide a deep insight into financial market predictions, especially in the FMIs [23]. The trend commenced in 2,000 with the launch of the first supercomputer that was installed in Wall Street. This installation accelerated the investment in applications such as fraud detection, derivative pricing, and econometrics. The computational sector is equipped with high-frequency trading and zero latency. HPC also supports facilities to compute risk and safeguard the financial system [24]. These characteristics could help in transforming the financial industry.

According to the statistics published by the Intersect360 Research [25], financial services gained biggest profits in 2017 by integrating HPC. The total revenue for HPC market was 35.4 billion dollars in 2017. It was attributed to commercial vertical markets. The report also predicted a 6.9% compound annual growth rate (CAGR) for HPC from 2017 to 2022.

HPC's ability to perform high-quality quantitative analysis has been recognized as a key factor for banks, brokers, funds, and participating entities in FMIs. These analyses help financial industry to speed up their activities and prediction of share prices in stock exchanges [26]. HPC also enables businesses to use new innovations such as Internet of things (IoT) and artificial intelligence (AI). Interwinding AI with HPC facilitates financial industry to scale to accommodate increasing workloads [27].

6.5 HPC IN FMIs

Financial services around the globe are adopting HPC to reduce the risk of a global pandemic and beat the market [23]. According to a survey conducted by Intersect360 Research, financial industry is the largest commercial market for HPC solutions [28]. The importance of HPC in finance is attributed to the insights provided by HPC. These insights help investment firms to predict the stock market trends within a fraction of second. Banking is one of the largest FinTech (financial technology) sectors that use HPC to detect frauds and reduce lending risks. Figure 6.4 presents the activities performed by HPC in financial services industry.

- Customer Engagement: HPC facilitates drafting customer-oriented, personalized marketing strategies. Many FinTech institutions use chatbots and voice recognition technologies to interact with customers. These technologies effectively understand the needs of customers and automate quality assurance monitoring [29]. All this is possible due to the depth of user profiling done by HPC. HPC does not only have advantages for financial institutions, but for customers also. From the customers' perspective, they can make more money by utilizing stock

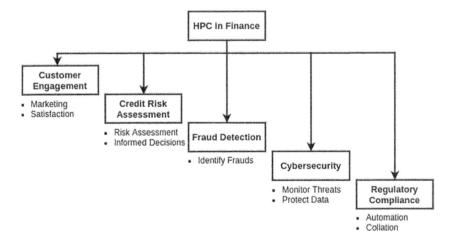

Figure 6.4 HPC in financial services.

market predictions made by HPC. Furthermore, it ensures that customers are satisfied with banking services that verify credit card details and bank accounts for any purchase and activity performed by the customers.

- Credit Risk Assessment: HPC is used in combination with artificial intelligence to speed up risk assessment of load applications received by retail banking institutions. It helps make informed risk decisions to reduce losses associated with loans. The financial sector, especially the FMI, is known for its fast-computing needs for monetary transactions, payment systems, trade activities, and security of central settlement systems. All these needs vary for every type of financial firm and depends on its market value. Financial institutions such as banks use HPC for real-time risk management, as they handle thousands of customers every moment.

- Fraud Detection: Fraudulent transactions have become an inseparable part of financial institutions. It is the prime need of the hour to detect such transactions to keep the business going. HPC-driven solutions are helping banks and payment systems to detect suspicious and potentially fraudulent transactions as they are taking place. For example, Mastercard leverages HPC systems to process large number of transactions to immediately identify and combat fraudulent transactions.

- Cybersecurity: HPC can detect cybercrimes for the millions of financial transactions taking place in the shortest time span. Financial services industry is prone to internal and external cyber-threats. Internal cyber-threats come in the form of malicious insiders determined to take revenge and cause harm to the employer. On the other hand, external threats include denial-of-service (DoS) attacks, distributed denial-of-service (DDoS) attacks, malware, and phishing attempts to disrupt services. Overall, the entire financial sector is dependent on HPC to perform high-intensity quantitative analyses to tackle the internal and external threats and protect sensitive information and systems [30].

- Regulatory Compliance: FinTech industry has witnessed several national and international regulations in the recent years. HPC-driven artificial intelligence solutions can automate the process of identifying, collating, and analyzing data from different components to follow regulatory compliance.

On the onset, HPC offers several benefits to financial institutions. However, it comes with certain security issues and challenges. The availability of HPC devices is the key to reap the benefits provided by it. If the device is down, every second is counted as catastrophic for time-based financial transactions. For example, a downtime for a stock market or investment firm can cost millions of dollars to the traders. HPC devices need to handle extreme work pressure, and it is not that easy to deploy, manage, and scale. The next section focuses on the security issues related to HPC in FMIs.

6.6 CURRENT WORKS ON CYBERSECURITY ISSUES RELATED TO HPC IN FMIs

HPC facilitates financial institutions to reduce financial risks by predicting market trends in advance. It provides several benefits that help the financial market flourish. However, there are some important security issues in HPC related to financial services industry. This section reviews the related works on cybersecurity issues related to HPC when integrated with FMIs, as reported by researchers.

One of the most important cybersecurity issues in HPC is the theft or misuse of HPC resources by unauthorized personnel. Malicious users gain unauthorized access to HPC resources that can shut down the critical devices to disrupt services, steal data, and launch further attacks. Dozens of HPC facilities used for COVID-19 research in Germany, the UK, and Switzerland were forcefully shut down by cyberattackers. Furthermore, the scalability of consequences in bringing down the HPC device can cost heavily to the business as HPC devices perform millions of computations every second. Security breaches involving computer malware such as Trojans and worms steal data from HPC nodes to impact confidentiality, integrity, and availability of data [31].

Like data theft, data modification is a serious threat that can result in loss of data integrity and pose risk to applications. Tampered data could impact critical data processing facilities and regulatory compliance used by essential services. Integrity and availability issues are caused by malicious insiders who misuse computing cycles, especially in bitcoin transactions. Although HPC provides protection against internal and external threats, the menace is never-ending. New tidal waves of changing regulations for national and international business practices are a continuous challenge for HPC [31].

Cybersecurity threats disrupt businesses and hence financial stability, especially in FMIs [32]. FMI serves as the backbone of financial markets [33]. It is also one of the popular targets of cyberattacks that have the potential to cause systemic risks in FMIs [34]. According to Li and Perez-Saiz [35], Canadian FMIs are exposed to credit risks and there are large differences in the level of systemic risks among participants. FMIs comprise essential components for processing FinTech transactions. Since large amounts of money is involved, these components are prone to several cybersecurity threats, including fraudulent transactions [9]. As the number of payment systems increases, the risk of fraud grows with the number of payment systems in the market [36].

Cyber-threats have emerged as a growing systemic risk to FMIs over the years. The reasons for this surge can be attributed to technological innovations, degree of inter-dependency between various components of financial markets, and diversified motivations of cyberattackers [36]. Cybercriminals are motivated by financial gain to cause financial instability. One of the major challenges in making FMIs cyber-resilient is to manage their complexities and inter-dependencies [37]. Cyber-attacks pose unique challenges to FMI's operational risk management framework.

Although the development of mobile payment systems provides a convenient payment infrastructure compatible with traditional pay-ment services, security of sensitive user information is a key challenge. Security of payment systems in FMI ensures that information about payment systems is not exposed to unauthorized third parties. Other security challenges for payment systems include mutual authentication, authorization, integrity, privacy, atomicity, and availability [38]. These security challenges pose security risks, threats, financial privacy issues, and other emerging issues in FinTech [39].

The technological transformations focus on the use of hard information and help financial markets grow, increase competition, and reduce frictions between lenders and borrowers. However, these changes bring some policy-related challenges to the traditional business models [40]. Financial systems are more reliant on hard information and, hence, prone to more financial and cyber-risks. These changes push authorities to strengthen FMIs to support cross-border transactions [41]. Table 6.1 summarizes the cybersecurity issues related to HPC in FMIs as reported by researchers.

To summarize, internal and external threats and cyberattacks/ cyber-risks are the most discussed cybersecurity issues by the researchers. In addition, theft, misuse of resources, confidentiality, in-tegrity, availability, cyber-fraud, authentication, authorization, privacy, atomicity, and security breach are some other issues discussed briefly. However, it does not mean that the less discussed issues are not of much importance. The losses caused by these less discussed issues can be much more disastrous compared to the most discussed issues. Based on this analysis, this chapter focuses on bringing forward the less discussed cybersecurity issues by mapping FMI risks with the security issues.

6.7 FINANCIAL RISKS IN FMIs

FMI handles enormous financial transactions dealing with huge amounts of money. Although it provides an effective risk management component to secure the transactions by using a central security repository, there are certain key financial risks faced by FMIs. These

TABLE 6.1 Summary of Cybersecurity Issues Related to HPC in FMIs

Issue/Work	[9]	[31]	[32]	[34]	[36]	[37]	[38]	[39]	[40]	[41]
Theft		X								
Misuse of resources		X								
Data theft		X								
Confidentiality		X								
Integrity		X					X			
Availability		X					X			
Internal and external threats	X	X	X					X		
Cyber-fraud	X	X			X					
Cyber-attacks/cyber-risks				X		X			X	X
Authentication							X			
Authorization							X			
Privacy							X			
Atomicity							X			
Security breach	X									

non-security risks are the outcome of centralized activities that create dependencies among financial institutions. This section instigates these non-security financial risks and their subcategories.

Systemic Risks: Systemic risks are the results of inter-dependencies among participating banks and inability of banks to meet their obligations and perform as expected. This may have an adverse effect on FMIs. Systemic risks can lead to reversed transactions or deliveries, delayed settlements, and disruption of services in financial systems. Furthermore, if one participating entity depends on other entities for payments, clearance, and settlements, it will spread the disruptions more quickly to reach out the broader economy. Systemic risks are prominent in payment systems of FMIs. Inter-dependencies can be grouped into three broad categories: system-based, institution-based, and environmental dependencies [42]. In system-based dependencies, FMIs are directly linked. They can be vertical (inter-dependence between different essential components of FMIs, such as between a payment system and trade repository) and horizontal (inter-dependence within the same component, such as within two payment systems). In institution-based inter-dependencies, FMIs are indirectly linked by a financial institution. Finally, environmental dependencies include broad factors such as physical infrastructure and network providers. Figure 6.5 shows schematic interconnections between different categories of inter-dependencies.

Legal Risks: Financial transactions between different countries are liable to legal terms and regulations. Legal risks arise if an application is unlawful, involves different law bodies, and involves delays in recovering financial assets. Different bodies of law are applicable not only to

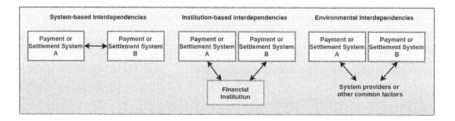

Figure 6.5 Categories of inter-dependence. (BIS 2008.)

international transactions, but to different jurisdictions also. Legal risks affect the central counterparties of FMIs the most.

Credit Risks: Credit risks may occur due to several reasons such as unsettled transactions between entities, inability of a participating entity to meet financial obligations within stipulated time, and failure of settlement banks itself. FMIs may face replacement cost risk due to unsettled transactions with an entity. As a result, FMIs need to replace the original transaction at the current market price. Credit risks are prevalent in security settlement systems of FMIs [43].

Liquidity Risks: Liquidity risks are related to the possession of insufficient funds to complete a transaction by the participating entities. Other types of liquidity risk can be seller not receiving funds and buyer not receiving product on time. Failure of settlement banks is also treated as a liquidity risk in FMIs. Liquidity risks have the potential to cause systemic risks. They are mostly found in central counterparties and security settlement systems of FMIs.

General Business Risks: General business risks are related to operational and administration activities performed by FMIs. These risks include financial losses due to increased debts and falling growth, resulting in an imbalanced revenue and cost curve. Severe financial losses may result in reputation loss, losses in other operations, poor execution strategy, and other business factors. Failure to manage business risks can lead to operational and legal risks. General business risks can occur in any essential component of FMIs.

Custody and Investment Risks: FMIs face a lot of custody risks including losses due to assets held in custody, financial fraud, poor administration, inadequate record-keeping, and negligence. Investment risks comprise losses due to investing their own resources in market, credit, or liquidity risks. These risks are also responsible for the safety and reliability of FMI's risk management systems. Custody and investment risks target central security depositories, central counterparties, security settlement systems, and trade repositories of FMIs.

Operational Risks: As evident from the name itself, operational risks are caused by irresponsible data and finance handling habits. Some common causes of operational risks include erroneous human transactions, data losses, information leakage, and deficiency in the information system. The erroneous operations may lead to internal and external threats to data security, failure of management systems that rely on information, fraudulent transactions, and incomplete settlements. Operational risks affect the trade repositories of FMIs.

6.8 COMMON SECURITY OBJECTIVES

To understand the security issues that can arise in FMI components owing to the financial risks faced by them, it is mandatory to be aware of the CIAAA principle of cybersecurity that ensures confidentiality (C), integrity (I), availability (A), accountability (A), and authenticity (A) of data for any organization. The level of importance varies for every organization depending upon its security goals and requirements. Figure 6.6 presents the CIAAA principle for data security.

Confidentiality: It refers to the protection of secret data, objects, or resources. The goal of confidentiality is to prevent or minimize unauthorized access to data. It ensures that only authorized users can access data and resources. Simply put, confidentiality ensures protection of data from unauthorized access, use, or disclosure while in storage, process, or transit. Several cyberattacks focus on violating confidentiality.

Integrity: It ensures the correctness and reliability of data. It prevents unauthorized users from modifying data. Proper implementation of integrity means authorized changes are allowed on sensitive data.

Figure 6.6 CIAAA principle.

Integrity loss may result from human errors such as when an authorized user makes an unintentional change to data.

Availability: It refers to timely and uninterrupted access to authorized objects, data, or resources. Some of the pertinent threats to availability of data include system failures, power loss, software errors, and environmental issues (natural calamities). In addition to that, sometimes, the accidental deletion of files, over-utilizing a resource, or mislabeling a classified object can also result in unavailability of data.

Accountability: It is referred to as the responsibility of a person to protect an asset, material, or key information. The person is held accountable for safeguarding the equipment in his custody. If a data breach, loss, or misuse of that equipment takes place, that person is held accountable for it. Accountability is an essential part of a cybersecurity plan. For example, let us assume that an organization has a policy that lists legitimate software or applications that the employees can install on their computers. If an employee installs software or applications not listed in the policy, the IT administrator is held accountable for not verifying the software or applications downloaded and installed on computer systems owned by the organization.

Authenticity: It is the validation of messages transmitted between a sender and receiver. It ensures that an authenticated sender originates from a message, the message is authenticated, and only an authentic receiver can receive the message. It helps to prevent an unauthorized person from sending or receiving a message. In technical terms, this principle prevents an impersonator from intercepting transmission. It requires users to establish their identities before getting involved in communication. Once the sender and receiver confirm their identities, they can access the system to communicate with each other. Authenticity is established by using usernames, passwords, smart cards, biometrics, e-mails, and tokens.

6.9   CYBERSECURITY ISSUES AND FINANCIAL RISKS IN FMIs

This section puts forward security issues faced by FMIs by mapping financial risks faced by FMIs with the security objectives to identify data security issues in FMIs.

1. Systemic Risks:

   - Inter-Dependency among Participating Entities: Systemic risks bring down the entire enterprise. When participating entities are dependent on each other for completing transactions, it poses an accountability issue in case the transaction is not completed due to any reason.

2. Custody and Investment Risks:

   - Loss of Assets Held by Custodian: From the data security point of view, assets in FMIs include data and information related to clients, participating entities, buyers, sellers, monetary transactions, and third-party entities involved. The loss of any of these assets can cause issues with confidentiality, authenticity, and availability of data.

   - Fraud: Financial fraud in FMIs refers to illegitimate monetary transactions that can cause harm to the business. The participating entities (buyers and sellers) may not possess legitimate sources to prove their identity. This type of risk can be mapped with authenticity and integrity issues in the CIAAA principle.

   - Poor Administration: Management is responsible for administering financial settlements and exchanges between entities. It is held responsible for poor administration which can be mapped with accountability issues in the CIAAA principle.

   - Inadequate Record-Keeping: Inadequate record-keeping may result in incomplete information or data classification. Data classification is the process of labeling data based on their sensitivity. Data may be classified as public, confidential, private, and restricted. Inadequate record-keeping poses confidentiality and integrity issues to data security.

   - Negligence: Negligence is somehow related to data handling, data classification, and record-keeping. Therefore, it can be mapped with authenticity and integrity issues in the CIAAA principle.

- Investing Own Resources to Market: Investing own resources to market is highly vulnerable and poses accountability issue as the owner is solely responsible for any financial losses.

- Credit or Liquidity Risks: Credit or liquidity risks explained below pose all security issues in the CIAAA principle.

3. Liquidity Risks:

- Insufficient Funds: Insufficient funds may result in incomplete transactions, which poses the availability issue in the CIAAA principle.

- Seller Does not Receive Funds: Any type of unavailability of data or funds in a settlement or transaction is treated as an availability issue in the CIAAA principle. Further, there are issues with its confidentiality as the originality of the funds may not be certain. It means that funds can be tampered within transit.

- Buyer Does not Receive Product: A product is an OTC derivative contract that is exchanged between the participating entities. Like a seller not receiving funds, any type of unavailability of data or funds in a settlement or transaction is treated as an availability issue in the CIAAA principle.

- Failure of Settlement Banks: Failure of settlement banks is a high-level liquidity risk. It can result in disruption of services for an unspecified time. A person from the management is also held responsible for this failure. Therefore, this risk can be mapped with availability and accountability issues in the CIAAA principle.

4. Credit Risks:

- Replacement Cost Risks: Replacement cost risks occur in case of failure of a transaction and the responsible entity returns the cost of the failed transaction. This type of risk can be mapped with authenticity and confidentiality issues in the CIAAA principle.

- Unsettled Transactions: It is the root cause of replacement cost risks and can be mapped with confidentiality and integrity issues in the CIAAA principle.

- Failure of Settlement Banks: Failure of settlement banks is a high-level credit risk. It can result in disruption of services for an unspecified time. This type of risk can be mapped with availability and accountability issues in the CIAAA principle.

5. Legal Risks:

- Different Law Bodies: FMI business with participating entities that belong to two different jurisdictions or legal regulations can be mapped with accountability issue in the CIAAA principle because law bodies are to be held accountable for financial transactions.

- Cross-Border Transactions: International financial business transactions pose risk to confidentiality and integrity of information in addition to accountability issue in the CIAAA principle.

- Delay in Recovery of Financial Assets: Any type of unavailability issue is treated as an availability issue in the CIAAA principle. Moreover, delays in recovery may cause authenticity issues also.

6. Operational Risks:

- Data Loss: Data loss indicates incorrect data which can be attributed to integrity issue in the CIAAA principle.

- Leakage: Just like data loss, information leakage is also attributed to integrity issue in the CIAAA principle.

- Deficiency in Information System: Information systems are responsible for handling data, entities, and transfer of transactions by using a central repository. Deficiency in information systems may result in integrity issue in the CIAAA principle.

- Insufficient Capacity: This type of risk can be mapped with availability and integrity issues in the CIAAA principle as insufficient capacity may lead to loss of data.

- Internal and External Threats: Cyber-threats have the potential to exploit vulnerabilities in the software systems, especially central repositories used to store sensitive data. Internal and external threats cause harm to confidentiality, integrity, and availability of data.

- Management Failure: Management is responsible for overall administration such as taking decisions, handling settlement issues, transfer of money, and transfer of other miscellaneous information. Management failure can be mapped with accountability issues in the CIAAA principle.

- Human Errors: Humans are prone to errors and can be held responsible for the type of data or assets they are managing. It can be mapped with accountability issues in the CIAAA principle.

- Fraud: Financial fraud in FMIs refers to illegitimate monetary transactions that can cause harm to the business. The participating entities (buyers and sellers) may not possess legitimate sources to prove their identity. This type of risk can be mapped with authenticity and integrity issues in the CIAAA principle.

- Incomplete Settlement: Incomplete settlement can be mapped with authenticity and confidentiality issues in the CIAAA principle.

Figure 6.7 presents an overview of the mapping of different categories of financial risks with security objectives to summarize security issues in FMIs.

The following observations are drawn from Figure 6.7:

- As per the current works discussed in Section 6.6, confidentiality, integrity, availability, accountability, and authenticity are less discussed cybersecurity issues in FMIs. However, a quantitative analysis of Figure 6.5 reveals that these issues are equally important. Integrity is the most common security issue in FMI risks. It is followed by availability, accountability, confidentiality, and authenticity.

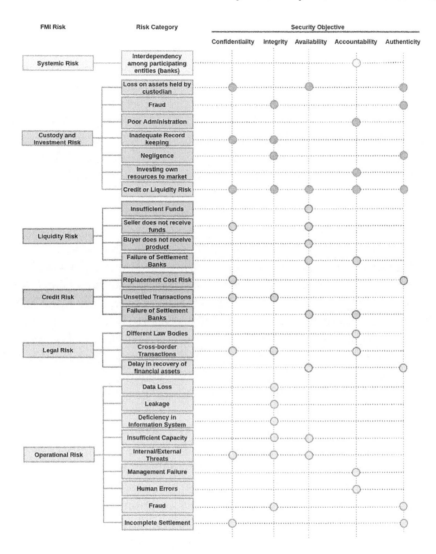

Figure 6.7 Security issues identified in FMI risks.

- Integrity, accountability, and authenticity equally impact most of the custody and investment risks.

- Availability is the only issue that impacts all types of liquidity risks.

- Integrity impacts most types of the operational risks.

6.10   CYBERSECURITY RISKS IN FMIs

After identifying cybersecurity issues in FMIs, this section introduces cybersecurity risks faced by FMIs, assessment, analysis, monitoring, reporting, and mitigation of these risks. FinTech has improved its products and services with time, but the risks still exist. This is the primary reason why FinTech institutions perform risk management tasks to protect personally identifiable information (PII). There are several cyber-risks faced by FinTech industry, especially FMIs.

6.10.1   Cybersecurity Risks

According to a BIS Bulletin report in 2021 [44], the finance sector is the worst affected sector by cyber-events during the rise of the COVID-19 pandemic. The number of cyberattacks increased from fewer than 5,000 per week in February 2020 to more than 200,000 per week in April 2020. Furthermore, one-fifth of the financial firms reported that their network operation activities were interrupted during the pandemic. The report further indicates that the financial sector's cyber-risk is small but is growing relative to operational risk. In another survey conducted by the Financial Services Information Sharing and Analysis Center (FS-ISAC) among financial institutions [45], there is a substantial rise in phishing, suspicious scanning, and malicious activity against web pages. The most common cyber-risks faced by FMIs include cyberattacks, risks to third-party vendors, data breaches, money laundering, digital identity risks, and cloud-based cybersecurity risks.

Cyber-Attacks: With the digital transformation comes the menace of cyberattacks that attempt to disrupt financial transactions, breach sensitive information, perform credit card fraud, and carry out fraudulent money transfers. Some of the most threatening cyberattacks experienced by FinTech have affected economic infrastructures, especially FMIs. As reported by Carnegie Endowment for International Peace [46], data breach, malware, and distributed denial-of-service (DDoS) attacks are the most common cyberattacks that resulted in significant financial losses for various financial institutions. Nonetheless, the list of individual security risks is never-ending. FinTech institutions are reluctant to report and admit being targeted by cyberattacks most of the times to protect their loss of reputation among competitors.

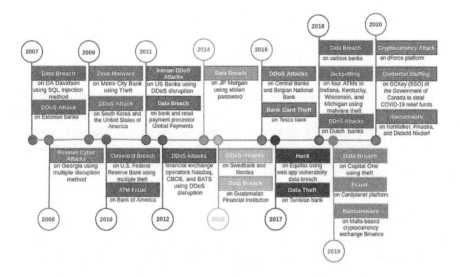

Figure 6.8 Timeline of prominent categories of cyberattacks on FinTech across the globe.

Figure 6.8 presents a glimpse of reported cyberattacks on FinTech that resulted in significant financial losses to financial institutions.

Evidently, payment systems including banks, stock exchanges, and other financial firms are the primary targets of cyberattacks. Even the major FinTech institutions suffer the menacing cyberattacks over the years. These statistics reveal that cyberattacks are one of the biggest challenges that FinTech is facing in the past couple of years. Advanced persistent threats intend to steal sensitive and valuable data from financial industries [47]. It is the most critical threat to financial stability, especially the FMIs that provide the fundamental support for payment systems, security of transactions, and agreements between the involved parties.

Data Breaches: FinTech is experiencing unprecedented changes. Two key issues that challenge FinTech are risk management, and security and privacy [48]. There are several financial and operational risks to FinTech start-ups. Depending on the size of FinTech and the specialization of financial activities performed by it, the tendency of risk management varies for every financial institution. The security and privacy of a consumer's sensitive information are pertinent. For FinTech applications, stolen and compromised mobile devices are one of the critical issues. FinTech companies need to develop appropriate measures to protect sensitive information from data breaches. Figure 6.6 highlights several data breaches reported by FinTech institutions.

Risks to Third-Party Vendors: Data breaches are difficult to prevent when third-party vendors are involved. If the services are not provided by a trusted third party, business is at risk. In FMIs, participating counterparties, security settlements, and payment institutions (banks, stock exchanges, foreign exchanges, etc.) act as vendors. Untrusted third-party vendors also pose risk to reputation. Eliminating third-party cyber-risks is the key element of every financial institution's risk management protocol.

Money Laundering: Money laundering or cyber-frauds are very common cyber-risks to FMIs. Cryptocurrency is frequently used in cross-border financial transactions owing to its ease of use. It does not need to be exchanged. The risk associated with cryptocurrency transactions is that it is not governed by any regulatory compliance or authority. This makes it vulnerable to cyber-risks as attackers can launder it through legitimate financial institutions, especially in FMIs.

Digital Identity Risk: Digital transformation brings the risk of stolen digital identity. Attackers can steal username and password of legitimate users to masquerade as legitimate users and make illegitimate financial transactions. Credentials can be stolen by launching malware attacks on target institutions.

Cloud-Based Risks: With the introduction of HPC in FMIs, cloud-based FinTech transactions have gained importance. Cloud-based storage services are considered secure until adequate protocols are used. If cloud-based risks are not managed properly, misuse of HPC resources and data theft become prevalent.

6.10.2 Risk Assessment

Risk management is a cyclic process that commences with assessing risks. Figure 6.9 presents the risk management process and its different phases.

The objective of the risk assessment is to identify and measure the risks in order to obtain accurate and relevant information to assist the decision-making process. It is imperative to assess risks due to possible threats that may have adverse effects on the information

Figure 6.9 Risk management cycle.

system. These threats attack the vulnerabilities by virtue of which the successful attacks result in financial losses. Risk assessment identifies all the vulnerabilities and potential threats that can exploit those vulnerabilities in the system. For computing the risk assessment, a vulnerability is defined as the probability of a successful attack, while a threat is treated as the intention to cause harm or exercise the vulnerability in the FinTech industry. Whenever a threat exploits a vulnerability, it has some consequences, which represent the negative impact as a result of exploiting vulnerability. All these definitions are derived from the International Organization for Standardization and the International Electrotechnical Commission (ISO/IEC) 27000 series standards and National Institute of Standards and Technology (NIST) guidelines [49].

To substantiate, a cybercrime gang named "OldGremlin" targeted a Russian bank with a ransomware attack in 2020. The gang used spear phishing e-mails to enter the bank's network and then encrypted its data. The gang demanded a ransom of around USD 50,000 to provide the decryption key [46]. In this incident, ransomware is the cyberattack (threat), spear phishing is the method of reaching the network and executing remote code (vulnerability) which was later used to encrypt data, and the encrypted data act as the consequence of this attack. All such vulnerabilities that are exercised by threats and their consequences are added to assess risk.

Risk assessment can be performed in a qualitative and quantitative manner. Qualitative risk assessment is subjective in nature and assigns intangible values to the losses. Qualitative methods use various levels of appraisement according to expert decisions. On the other hand, quantitative risk assessment measures losses in numbers and assigns monetary value to it. It also assigns severity value to losses (low, medium, and high). It makes use of matrices, numerical values, and mathematical formulae to compute loss due to risk. A combination of qualitative and quantitative assessment is also used and is called hybrid risk assessment.

The primary challenge in FinTech risk assessment is the unavailability of historical data related to cyber-threats. Since every financial institution has a market value and reputation among competitors, it does not want to reveal to the world at first that it became a victim of a cyberattack. If some financial institutions accept being a target, they do not share the cyberattack data due to several reasons, including sensitivity of customer financial data, legal policies, compliance with financial standards, and reputation.

6.10.3   Risk Analysis

Risk analysis is a three-step procedure that (1) identifies critical resources, (2) determines threats that can exploit the vulnerabilities to put the resources at stake, and (3) evaluates risk by assigning a rating to them. This section addresses the step-by-step procedure used to analyze risks and puts forward the existing risk analysis strategies for FinTech.

Risk analysis measures the likelihood of occurrence of all threats and vulnerabilities, and the magnitude of the impact of all risks on the FinTech industry. A qualitative risk analysis performs subjective analysis in which risk matrix is created as per NIST guidelines as shown in Table 6.2 [49]. Risk matrix maps the likelihood of threats and vulnerabilities to the magnitude of impact to determine an overall risk

TABLE 6.2   Sample Risk Matrix

Likelihood	Impact		
	Low	Medium	High
High	Low	Medium	High
Medium	Low	Medium	Medium
Low	Low	Low	Low

rating. On the other hand, a quantitative risk analysis is objective in nature and follows the scientific and data-intensive approach to analyze the impact of risks in terms of cost, time, and critical infrastructure consumption.

Based on the exemplary risk matrix, if the likelihood of occurrence of a threat is high, and the magnitude of the impact is low, then the risk level is considered low. Similarly, if both the likelihood and impact are high, then the risk level is high. The risk matrix facilitates the upper management to prioritize risks and take the appropriate actions based on the level of risk.

6.10.4   Risk Monitoring, Reporting, and Mitigation

Monitoring cybersecurity risks is important to collect cyber-data for future risk analyses. There are certain standard risk policies and guidelines for effective risk monitoring and reporting.

- Organizational Policies: At the beginners' level, every organization has its own risk monitoring policy which is designed by the upper management and followed by the middle-level management. This policy covers several basic rules and regulations related to cyber-risks that the employees must abide by. The depth of rules and safety measures to protect sensitive information depends on several crucial factors such as organization size, budget, importance of financial data, risk acceptance level, and exposure to vulnerabilities. Organizational policies such as strong passwords, knowledge of social engineering, trained staff, and confidentiality of sensitive financial data are some of the fundamental practices that need to be followed to reduce cyber-risks. Some organizations might prefer to avoid or accept the risk, while others may prefer to mitigate it. The analogy of implementing cybersecurity risk monitoring and review policy varies for every FinTech industry.

- Risk Guidelines: Apart from organizational policies, FinTech firms also prepare risk guidelines that define the extent to which a risk can be tolerated and what actions are required in case that risk exceeds a certain threshold value.

- International Cybersecurity Risk Management Standards: To monitor cyber-thefts, the financial sector must stringently implement cybersecurity risk management standards released by international organizations such as NIST and ISO/IEC.

There are four ways to address a cyber-risk as part of the mitigation policy [50–52]:

- Risk acceptance is the strategy adopted by a financial organization to accept risk after understanding its consequences for the business.

- Risk avoidance is used to avoid altogether the activities posing a minor risk to a business.

- Risk transfer is a two-step policy in which some part of the risk is accepted in the first step and the rest is transferred to another party in the second step.

- Risk mitigation is the procedure to control the risk and its consequences to reduce it, that is below the threshold value of risk acceptance to business.

Handling risks in the financial sector involves using a combination of all these ways; that is, some risks are avoided, some are transferred, some are mitigated, and the rest are accepted.

Risk mitigation is a plan that comprises preparing a new cybersecurity policy (in case it is not available) or updating an existing policy document to reduce the negative impact of risk. Since every country and each company in a country has different cybersecurity risk challenges, the policy to mitigate risks also varies depending on the type of company and its requirements for cybersecurity defense. The impact of risk is a weighted factor associated with each vulnerability based on the severity of that vulnerability. The mitigation strategies aim to accept, avoid, transfer, share, or mitigate the risk depending on the scope of risk response decisions delegated by the organizational management.

In order to compute the impact and find the severity of the vulnerability, the Common Vulnerability Scoring System (CVSS) provides a variety of measures for scoring each vulnerability. CVSS assigns a score to vulnerabilities to prioritize them and execute the mitigation policy to alleviate them. Once the impact is computed, the vulnerabilities are prioritized to perform response actions according to mitigation policies. CVSS score is represented by a CVSS vector containing several parameter–value pairs separated by a forward slash, and each parameter and value are separated by a colon.

For example, WannaCry vulnerability (vulnerability identifier: CVE-2017-0144 [53]) is identified by the CVSS vector AV:N/AC:H/ PR:N/UI:N/S:U/C:H/I:H/A:H, where AV represents the attack vector (N – network); AC is the attack complexity (H – high); PR means the privilege required (N – none); UI is the user interaction (N – none); S represents the scope (U – unchanged); and C (H – high), I (H – high), and A (H – high) denote confidentiality, integrity, and availability impact, respectively. The values of these parameters for this example are specified in the brackets.

CVSS v3.1 calculator computes the base score of this vulnerability by using the following equations:

Impact Sub Score $(ISS) = 1 - [(1 - C) * (1 - I) * (1 - A)]$

$$= \begin{cases} 6.42 * ISS, & \text{If scope is unchanged} \\ 7.52 * (ISS - 0.029) & \\ -3.25 * (ISS - 0.02), & \text{If scope is changes} \end{cases} \quad (6.1)$$

$$\text{Exploitability (Exp)} = 8.22 * AV * AC * PR * UI \quad (6.2)$$

Base score $= 0\&$ if impact ≤ 0

$$= \begin{cases} \text{Roundup} & \\ (\min[(\text{impact} + \text{Exp}), 10]), & \text{If scope is unchanged} \\ \text{Roundup} & \\ (\min[1.08 \times (\text{impact} + \text{Exp}), 10]), & \text{If scope is changed} \end{cases}$$

$$(6.3)$$

The metric values of all the variables in the equation are available at [54]. For this example, we compute the CVSS score as follows:

$$ISS = 1 - [(1 - 0.56) * (1 - 0.56) * (1 - 0.56)] = 0.914816 \qquad (6.4)$$

$$\text{Impact} = 6.42 * 0.914816 = 5.87311872 \qquad (6.5)$$

$$\text{Exp} = 8.22 * 0.85 * 0.44 * 0.85 * 0.85 = 2.2211673 \qquad (6.6)$$

$$\text{Base score} = \text{Roundup}\,(\min\,[(5.87311872 + 2.2211673)\,, 10]) = 8.1$$
$$\qquad (6.7)$$

Finally, the outcomes of a risk mitigation plan and lessons learned from mitigating risks are repeatedly fed into the risk analysis phase to tackle future vulnerabilities.

Effective risk management on various levels is crucial to ensure that cybersecurity investments are commensurate with the underlying risk. As with other financial risks, firms must decide how to manage their exposure to cyber-threats. The risk identified, analyzed, and evaluated in the risk assessment needs to be actively managed, including reducing, transferring, and avoiding risk.

Indeed, FinTech risk management represents a central point of interest for regulatory authorities and require research and development of novel measurements. Across the world, there is a strong need to improve the FinTech sector's competitiveness, introducing a risk management framework that can supervise FinTech innovations without stifling their economic potential. A structure that can help both FinTech and supervisors: on the one hand, FinTech firms need advice on how to identify opportunities for innovation procurement such as in advanced regulatory technology (RegTech) solutions. On the other hand, the supervisory bodies' ability to monitor innovative financial products proposed by FinTech is limited, and advanced supervisory technology (SupTech) solutions are required. A crucial step in transforming compliance and supervision is to develop uniform and technology-driven risk management tools, which could reduce the barriers between FinTech and supervisors [55].

6.11 CONCLUSIONS

Financial market infrastructures refer to critical financial institutions that are involved in clearing, settlement, and recording of monetary transactions in the form of payments, securities, custody activities, and trading. There are five essential components of FMIs, including payment systems, central security depositories, security settlement systems, central counterparties, and trade repositories. Secure and fast monetary transactions help in economic growth of the global financial industry. This can be achieved by integrating HPC with FMIs. The participating entities can be exposed to several types of financial risks such as systemic, legal, credit, liquidity, custody and investment, and operational risks. These risks can further lead to cybersecurity issues that can be exploited to cause cybersecurity risks to FMIs. Furthermore, HPC also comes equipped with certain cybersecurity issues. To understand these cyber-issues, the financial risks are associated with security objectives such as confidentiality, integrity, availability, accountability, and authenticity. This chapter mapped various types of financial risks with cybersecurity objectives to identify cybersecurity issues in FMIs. It further presented diverse cyberattacks launched against financial institutions, especially FMIs, with an objective to steal sensitive information, disrupt essential services, modify information, and make money. These cyberattacks instigate cyber-risks that can be catastrophic for the financial industry. Therefore, it is pertinent to assess, analyze, monitor, report, and mitigate cybersecurity risks in FMIs to maintain financial stability and improve economic growth of the financial market. Finally, the chapter detailed cyber-risk mitigation processes by taking WannaCry ransomware as an example to remedy cybersecurity risks in FMIs.

REFERENCES

[1] Financial market infrastructures – what happens when you pay? https://www.bankofengland.co.uk/knowledgebank/financial-market-infrastructures-what-happens-when-you-pay.

[2] Bank for International Settlements, Guidance on cyber resilience for financial market infrastructures, pp. 1–32, 2016.

[3] Serafin Martinez-Jaramillo, Jose Luis Molina-Borboa, and Bernardo Bravo-Benitez, The role of financial market infrastructures in financial stability: An overview, analyzing the economics of financial market infrastructures, pp. 21, 2016.

[4] How zero trust privilege addresses five high-performance computing security risks, https://www.somerfordassociates.com/wp-content/uploads/

2020/01/how-zero-trust-privilege-addresses-five-high-performance-computing-security-risks.pdf.

[5] HPC market five-year forecast bumps up to $44 billion worldwide, https://insidehpc.com/2019/06/hpc-market-five-year-forecast-bumps-up-to-44-billion-worldwide/#:~:text=HPC%20Market%20Five%2DYear%20Forecast%20bumps%20up%20to%20%2444%20Billion%20Worldwide,-June%2017%2C%202019&text=At%20ISC%202019%20in%20Frankfurt,35%20billion)%20for%20that%20year.

[6] Challenging the barriers to high performance computing in the cloud, https://d1.awsstatic.com/HPC2019/Challenging-Barriers-to-HPC-in-the-cloud-Oct2019.pdf.

[7] Karthik Paladugu and Sumanth Mukka, Systematic literature review and survey on high performance computing in cloud, Master's Thesis, School of Computing, Blekinge Institute of Technology, Sweden, 2012.

[8] Cyber Resilience for Financial Market Infrastructures, Financial inclusion global initiative, The World Bank, https://pubdocs.worldbank.org/en/189821576699037673/FIGI-ECB-OperationalCyber-FinalWeb-12-13.pdf, 2019.

[9] Bank for International Settlements, Principles for financial market infrastructures, Consultative report, pp. 1–148, 2011.

[10] Nephil Matangi Maskay, Analytical framework in assessing systemic financial market infrastructure: Interdependence of financial market infrastructure and the need for a broader risk perspective, The South East Asian Central Banks (SEACEN), Research and Training Centre, Malaysia, pp. 1–370, 2014.

[11] Oversight Framework for Financial Market Infrastructures (FMIs) and Retail Payment Systems (RPSs), Reserve Bank of India, Version 2.0, pp. 1–77, 2020.

[12] Supervision and Systemic Risk Management of Financial Market Infrastructures – Technical Note, International Monetary Fund, Washington, D.C., pp. 1–37, 2016.

[13] Payment Systems, Monetary Policy, and the role of the Central Bank, International Monetary Fund, https://asean.elibrary.imf.org/doc/IMF071/05174-9781557756268/05174-9781557756268/Other_formats/Source_PDF/05174-9781455246670.pdf, pp. 1–273, 1998.

[14] Financial Market Infrastructure & Reform, Federal Reserve Bank of New York, https://www.newyorkfed.org/financial-services-and-infrastructure/financial-market-infrastructure-and-reform.

[15] Bank for International Settlements, Recommendations for securities settlement systems, https://www.bis.org/cpmi/publ/d46.pdf, pp. 1–55, 2001.

[16] Bank for International Settlements, Recommendations for Central Counterparties, Consultative Report, https://www.bis.org/cpmi/publ/d61.pdf, pp. 1–55, 2004.

[17] Financial Market Infrastructure Act (FMIA), Swiss Derivative Regulation, https://www2.deloitte.com/content/dam/Deloitte/ch/Documents/financial-services/ch-en-fs-fmia-brochure.pdf, pp. 1–16.

[18] Regulation (EU) No 648/2012 of the European parliament and of the Council of 4 July 2012 on OTC derivatives, central counterparties and trade repositories ("EMIR").

[19] Public Law 111-203- Dodd-Frank Wall Street Reform and Consumer Protection Act, https://www.govinfo.gov/app/details/PLAW-111publ203.

[20] What is High Performance Computing? https://insidehpc.com/hpc-basic-training/what-is-hpc/.

[21] What is High-Performance Computing? https://www.netapp.com/data-storage/high-performance-computing/what-is-hpc/.

[22] History of HPC, https://hpc.netl.doe.gov/about/history-of-hpc/.

[23] Julie Fagan, Why HPC is important to the financial services industry, https://blog.netapp.com/why-hpc-is-important-to-financial-services-industry/.

[24] Addison Snell, HPC and AI at the Forefront of Finance, Intersect360 Research, https://www.hpcwire.com/2018/09/26/hpc-and-ai-at-the-forefront-of-finance/, 2018.

[25] Worldwide High Performance Computing 2017 Total Market Model and 2018–2022 Forecast: Vertical Markets, https://intersect360.world securesystems.com/reports/worldwide-high-performance-computing-2017-total-market-model-and-2018-2022-forecast-vertical-market.

[26] HPC strategies for financial services: The playing field widens, https://www.therealizationgroup.com/portfolio/hpc-strategies-for-financial-services-the-playing-field-widens/.

[27] Libby Plummer, How Combining AI with High Performance Computing (HPC) Could Transform the Finance Industry, https://www.intel.ca/content/www/ca/en/financial-services-it/article/ai-hpc-banking.html.

[28] Intersect360 Research White Paper: AI and the new HPC: Revolutionizing Finance, Dell Technologies and Intel Corp., 2019.

[29] Cashing in on HPC and AI in the Financial Services Industry, https://www.hpcwire.com/2019/05/13/cashing-in-on-hpc-and-ai-in-the-financial-services-industry/, 2019.

[30] HPC strategies for financial services: The playing field widens, https://www.therealizationgroup.com/portfolio/hpc-strategies-for-financial-services-the-playing-field-widens/.

[31] An action plan for high performance computing security, https://www.nist.gov/system/files/documents/2018/03/15/working_draft_actionplanhpc.pdf, 2016.

[32] Ron J. Berndsen, Carlos León, and Luc Renneboog, Financial stability in networks of financial institutions and market infrastructures, *Journal of Financial Stability*, Vol. 35, pp. 120–135, 2018.

[33] Shaofang Li, and Matej Marinč, Economies of scale and scope in financial market infrastructures, *Journal of International Financial Markets, Institutions & Money*, Vol. 53, pp. 17–49, 2018.

[34] Emanuel Kopp, Lincoln Kaffenberger, and Christopher Wilson, Cyber risk, market failures, and financial stability, International Monetary Fund working paper, pp. 1–36, 2017.

[35] Fuchun Li, and Hector Perez-Saiz, Measuring systemic risk across financial market infrastructures, *Journal of Financial Stability*, Vol. 34, pp. 1–11, 2018.

[36] Bruce Nikkel, Fintech forensics: Criminal investigation and digital evidence in financial technologies, *Forensic Science International: Digital Investigation*, Vol. 33, pp. 1–7, 2020.

[37] Bank for International Settlements, Cyber resilience in financial market infrastructures, pp. 1–19, 2014.

[38] Jungho Kang, Mobile payment in Fintech environment: Trends, security challenges, and services, *Human-centric Computing and Information Sciences*, Vol. 8(32), pp. 1–16, 2018.

[39] Sobia Mehrban, Muhammad Waqas Nadeem, Muzammil Hussain, Mohammad Masroor Ahmed, Owais Hakeem, Shazia Saqib, Miss Laiha Binti Mat Kiah, Fakhar Abbas, Mujtaba Hassan, and Muhammad Adnan Khan, Towards secure FinTech: A survey, taxonomy, and open research challenges, *IEEE Access*, Vol. 8, pp. 23391–23406, 2020.

[40] Keke Gai, Meikang Qiu, and Xiaotong Sun, A survey on FinTech, *Journal of Network and Computer Applications*, Vol. 103, pp. 262–273, 2018.

[41] Arnoud Boot, Peter Hoffmann, Luc Laeven, and Lev Ratnovski, FinTech: What's old, what's new? *Journal of Financial Stability*, Vol. 53, pp. 1–37, 2021.

[42] Bank for International Settlements. The interdependencies of payment and settlement systems, https://www.bis.org/cpmi/publ/d84.pdf, pp. 1–83, 2008.

[43] Financial Market Infrastructure Risk, Current report of the financial market infrastructure risk task force, New York, pp. 1–19, 2007.

[44] Covid-19 and cyber risk in the financial sector, BIS Bulletin, No. 37, 2021, https://www.bis.org/publ/bisbull37.pdf.

[45] Financial Services Information Sharing and Analysis Center (FS-ISAC) (2020): COVID-19 effects on cybersecurity survey, July, 2020.

[46] Timeline of Cyber Incidents Involving Financial Institutions, 2020. https://carnegieendowment.org/specialprojects/protectingfinancial stability/timeline.

[47] Wiem Tounsi, and Helmi Rais, A survey on technical threat intelligence in the age of sophisticated cyberattacks, *Computers & Security*, Vol. 72, pp. 212–233, 2018.

[48] In Lee, and Yong Jae Shin, Fintech: Ecosystem, business models, investment decisions, and challenges, *Business Horizons*, Vol. 61, Number 1, pp. 35–46, 2018.

[49] Guide for Conducting Risk Assessments, NIST special publication 800-30 revision 1, pp. 1–95, 2012.

[50] Shon Harris, and Fernando Maymi, *CISSP All-in-One Exam Guide*, 8th edition. New York: McGraw-Hill, 2018.

[51] Douglas Landoll, *The Security Risk Assessment Handbook: A Complete Guide for Performing Security Risk Assessments*, 2nd edition, Boca Raton, FL: Auerbach Publications, 2006.

[52] Evan Wheeler, *Security Risk Management: Building an Information Security Risk Management Program from the Ground Up*. Waltham: Syngress, 2011.

[53] CVE-2017–0144 Detail, https://nvd.nist.gov/vuln/detail/cve-2017-0144.

[54] Common vulnerability scoring system version 3.1: Specification document, https://www.first.org/cvss/specification-document.

[55] Paolo Giudici, Fintech risk management: A research challenge for artificial intelligence in finance, *Frontiers in Artificial Intelligence*, Vol. 1, pp. 1, 2018.

Live Migration in HPC

Anil Kumar Gupta and Amarjeet Sharma

Centre for Development of Advanced Computing (CDAC)

Aditi Pandey, Kaustubh Patil, and Sanskar Sharma

MIT Academy of Engineering

CONTENTS

DOI: 10.1201/9781003155799-7

7.1 INTRODUCTION

7.1.1 Introduction to Live Migration

The live migration technique is a very trending topic in today's era in connection with the virtualization technology in development, which is widely used in different computing environments from the single-processor computers to the large cloud solutions and data centres at present. **Live migration** means the process of transferring a running virtual machine/application among varying physical machines, but without disconnecting the application or the client. Storage, memory, and network connectivity of the VM are transferred from the original guest machine to the destination. It is also referred as low-latency migration that does not disrupt the TCP connections to the direct-access device being migrated.

The main goal of a VM live migration is to enable maintenance or upgrades to be executed on a VM without letting any of the virtual machine's user experience downtime during the migration. Live migrations are also known as seamless live migrations where there's no apparent downtime to the end user during the migration process.

7.1.1.1 Needs

Migration of **VM** is acquiring more **importance** in today's world, for improving the utilization of resources, load balancing the processing nodes, isolating the applications, and tolerating the faults in virtual machines to increase the portability of nodes and to rise the efficiency of the physical server. **Live migration** enables administrators to easily add, on the fly, new hosts to a Hyper-V cluster and also allows to instantly increase resources required by **VM** workloads. **Live migration** can also be **used** to enable administrators to access various service hosts during the normal business hours and without affecting business-related **services** and applications.

7.1.1.2 Applications

There are various applications of live migration. Live migration allows users to keep their instances running during regular infrastructure upgrades and maintenance, and hardware failures, such as memory, network, and power grid maintenance in the data centres, and the failure of CPU, NIC, disks, power, and so on. Updates related to security need to respond quickly along with system configuration changes, including the change in the size of the host root partition, for the storage of packages and host image.

7.1.1.3 Efficiency

Live migration has proved to be more efficient than offline migration in terms of maintenance, reachability, load balancing, and offloading. There might be several servers in the network experiencing heavy load due to their position in a dense area or because of the service type they run. In this scenario, it is beneficial to distribute the load among other servers in the network via live migration of VMs.

The performance of migration process depends on many other factors, such as the size of workload it serves, the memory allocated to the VM, and the transmission rate at which the migration is occurring. The time taken by the migration process degrades the network performance. Transferred VMs increase the latency factor, leading to more imposed link delay and network performance degradation. Overhead cost of live migration is considerable, but in total, it results as a disadvantage.

7.1.1.4 Security

Live migration is a quite peculiar and unique idea, and aspects related to its security are not fully discovered. The prevalence of cloud computing has gained the attention of many hackers and their attacks. These attacks may vary from man-in-the-middle (MITM) attacks to denial-of-service (DoS) attacks. Bandwidth stealing, falsely advertising, passive snooping, and active manipulation are some of the active and passive attacks possible while migration is under process.

To address the above issues, we use various cryptographic algorithms that help in encryption and decryption of data, thereby detecting and preventing such attacks. Also, certain steps must be considered at both ends when migration is initiated, such as authenticity of person initiating migration, stepwise entities security perseverance, and confidentiality of migration information.

7.1.2 Introduction to Cloud Computing

"Cloud computing is the on-demand availability of computer system resources, especially data storage (cloud storage) and computing power, without direct active management by the user", as written on *Wikipedia*.

Cloud computing is maybe the foremost most flamboyant technological innovation of the 21st century. It is rising as an important paradigm shift; however, computing demands will be met in future. It is remodelling the role of IT in business in recent years. As virtualization, that is a crucial technology part in cloud computing and has become more and more crucial in many actions of the IT field, as services and applications are always running on virtual machines, and in order to assure a maximum of availability and a satisfying quality of service (QoS) to shoppers/clients and users, the idea of virtual machines live migration proves to be extraordinarily important, given its utility and edges. Cloud computing is not just simply meant for a few organizations and specific businesses; it's additionally helpful for a normal person as well. It permits one to run software programs without installing them on his computers; it permits him to store and modify/access his multimedia or transmission content via the Internet; it permits him to introduce, develop, and check programs while not essentially having servers; and what not. Cloud computing is a 21st century marvel that holds its importance in almost every field you'll be able to think about.

Cloud computing is predicted to get rid of the software piracy forever. Software piracy is not a healthy habit for the economic development of the country. And this will be removed or stopped solely by software firms, publishers, and distributors by using and implementing cloud computing within the business system. The simple methodology they will use is to prevent selling the software online for downloading and offline for selling. Instead, charge it on a monthly or yearly basis. The adoption of cloud computing infrastructure will also cut back the cost of conducting business. Now firms/companies can store, back up the data or information, and launch a personal cloud network by using the existing infrastructure of cloud computing at a lower cost. They don't need to get any physical parts to manage and store information or data.

The growing age of cloud computing permits us to access and share computing and storage resources over the Internet. Conversely, the infrastructure cost of the cloud reaches an improbable limit. Therefore, virtualization concept is applied in cloud computing systems to assist users and owners to gain higher usage and economical and efficient management of the cloud with the least possible cost. And live migration of VMs further helps us to better use the cloud resources with their benefits mentioned previously.

There are numerous examples that how technology has modified our lives to be easier, quick, and comforting. And cloud computing is the next massive thing in information technology that will make life even easier than it is currently. That's why we have a tendency to use machines to make life easier. In the end, change is always challenging for everyone. Similarly, it's challenging to go from an in-house network to virtual personal or cloud networks, particularly when in-house information or data security and user piracy are the biggest considerations.

7.2 LIVE MIGRATION IN VM

"A **virtual machine** is a **virtual** representation, or emulation, of a physical computer", by IBM, is the official definition of the virtual machine. Various systems available in the market help in performing virtualization tasks. That is, they can help in running multiple virtual machines on the same system in parallel. To name a few, there are VirtualBox, KVM, and Microsoft Hyper-V. As discussed previously, cloud computing associated with various features such as networking tools, storage spaces, server, and applications can undoubtedly increase the efficiency and play a key role in high-performance computing by taking a step towards virtualization. Virtualization comes bearing gifts such as resource utilization, reliability, portability, application security by application isolation, and hence improved synchronization and resistance to fault tolerance. As virtualization allows multiple VMs to run concurrently, it also provides the service of live migration of VM from one node to another node in a cluster of nodes. As it gives isolation, it hence provides a clean separation between hardware and software. Technically, there are two types of migrations in VM: One is live migration and the other is cold migration. Let's discuss how one differentiates from the other: In cold migration, the machine loses its state and hence becomes noticeable like an interrupt from users' point of view, while in live migration, on the other hand, the state of the VM is preserved and the migrating process is not noticeable from the user's perspective.

Here's where live migration in VM comes in handy:

1. Load Balancing: This prevents a server from overloading or overheating by migration of their workloads to other servers.

2. Server Consolidation: These are conditions where servers that need maintenance can be brought down by migrating their works to other servers.

3. Energy Distribution Control: As the workload is balanced, for efficient utilization of energy the servers that are currently not in use can be shut down to save energy and thus guarantee green cloud services.

7.2.1 Live VM Migration Techniques in Cloud

A cloud administrator migrates applications so that the load can be balanced among the clusters to increase efficiency. Hence, live migration turns out to be a very important facility for management purposes. To perform live migration, the current state of the VM such as the CPU states and memory pages must be migrated to the destination where it can then be resumed.

Along with being able to migrate our VM, it's also needed to be ensured that the VM live migration process occurs efficiently. For this, we have different performance metrics that can help us to compare different techniques and adopt the one that suits our application more. For this, we have some defined key metrics that help in understanding the performance of a VM migration technique. These are as follows [1]:

1. Preparation Time: The time when the migration is initiated and pages are transferred to the destination VM.

2. Downtime: The time during which the machine's runtime is stopped.

3. Resume Time: The time between the start of execution of VM at destination and the end of migration is called resume time.

4. Pages Transferred: The total number of pages transferred from source to destination including the duplicated.

5. Total Migration Time: The total time between the start of migration from source from preparation till the end of migration by transfer of the last page at the destination.

6. Application Degradation: The degradation of the performance of the applications within VM during migration.

After knowing the various performance metrics, it is now time to discuss several live VM migration approaches. We have mainly two approaches used in VM live migration: post-copy memory migration and pre-copy memory migration. Let us discuss these live migration approaches one by one.

7.2.1.1 Post-Copy Approach

In the post-copy approach, the VM at the sending node is halted until the required minimal CPU states are migrated to destination node, and once transferred, the VM is resumed and the remaining memory pages are sent over the network to the destination. The post-copy approach is a combination of four prime modules that include demand paging, active pushing, pre-paging, and dynamic self-ballooning that jointly make the post-copy approaches more methodical.

Let's have a quick review of each of the modules:

1. Post-Copy Using Demand Paging: In this type of technique, once the VM launches at the target, the page is requested for every memory access fault occurred. However, a disadvantage associated with this method is that requesting for the page at each fault causes the VM to slow down and also leaves long-term dependencies unfetched. Hence, we use other approaches along with demand paging so as to lessen the network latency issue [1].

2. Post-Copy Using Active Pushing: Using active pushing, the pages are pre-emptively transmitted to the destination VM and any future page faults that occur are serviced separately by sending the requested page using demand paging. Along with this, to prevent sending of the same page multiple times, it makes sure that the page which is serviced separately is not sent again with active pushing [1].

3. Post-Copying Using Pre-paging: Pre-paging technique aims at minimizing the page faults arising at the destination VM by anticipating the possible page references that can be made in future by analysing the sequence of memory access made. By minimizing the page faults and indirectly minimizing the page requests made, it makes the system more efficient.

   Pre-paging strategy is imposed using the bubbling algorithm. The different strategies are:

   (a) Bubbling with a Single Pivot: In this type of strategy, a particular page is selected as pivot. Around this pivot, active pushing of the page that is located close to it is done at each iteration. As this strategy involves expanding the reach around a point similar to a bubble, therefore it is known as bubbling. Whenever a page fault arises and is requested by the destination, the pivot is now shifted to this new requested page in the memory and the selection of next pages to be pushed is done that according to this newly selected pivot.

(b) Bubbling with Multiple Pivots: As the term itself implies, this approach utilizes multiple pivots instead of a single pivot. It is quite usual that multiple processes can run at a time and hence concurrently memory access at different locations is possible. Hence, in this context, having multiple pivots helps us to capture the locality of reference across multiple processes and helps in appropriate paging so as to decrease the number of subsequent page faults. Here, similar to the previous approach bubbling strategy is employed, however in this at once multiple pivots are expanded and all the memory pages which are symmetrically located around it are pushed one by one. Deciding an appropriate limit on the number of pivots is important as because having too many pivots can affect the system performance. Once we decide with the upper limit for the number of pivots for any subsequent page fault, the least recently used policy can be used to replace a pivot with the new pivot as the demanded page.

Along with the pivot selection, determining the direction of bubble expansion is essential in both single- and multiple-pivot approaches and, in this case, the bidirectional expansion has been proved to be beneficial as compared to forward or backward unidirectional expansions. While expansion of the bubble continues, this approach also ensures that a given page has not been transmitted previously by a previous pivot or by either of the neighbouring pivots, thereby reducing waste work and maintaining coherency [1].

4. Dynamic Self-Ballooning: The source virtual machine can have a huge amount of free unallocated pages, and migrating all of these to destination can be a waste of network as well as of the CPU resources, making the overall migration process inefficient by increasing the total migration time. To overcome this problem, we have a technique called ballooning that helps in resizing the allocated memory of a VM. To implement this, a balloon driver

resides in the guest kernel. The task of this balloon driver is either to retrieve the least important pages from the kernel and send them to hypervisor (inflating the balloon), or to request some pages from hypervisor and return them to the kernel (deflating the balloon). In this way, any VM to be migrated can be deflated and any destination VM that requires more memory can be inflated. This type of ballooning occurs at every iteration and is known as dynamic self-ballooning. This way the dynamic self-ballooning approach helps to reduce the number of free pages, thereby making our migration process more efficient. Dynamic self-ballooning reacts dynamically to each invocation by inflating when memory is needed and by deflating when memory can be released or transferred. Hence, by determining the ideal interval of ballooning, we can optimize the overall performance of our process [1].

7.2.1.2 Pre-Copy Approach

In the pre-copy approach, all the memory pages are migrated to the destination while the VM is still executing at source. And if memory change or overwrite occurs, then those modified pages or the dirtied pages are retransmitted to the destination. Until the application's writable working set becomes small or reaches to maximum limit of iterations, the VM is halted and all the remaining dirty pages and CPU state are then transferred. Pre-copy approach method tries to decrease the downtime of the source machine while increasing the migration time.

Numerous techniques have been developed under the pre-copy approach. Below are few of those techniques:

1. Improved Pre-Copy Approach: Among the several improved pre-copy approaches, this one includes keeping the track of the commonly updated pages with the help of bitmaps such as TO_SEND which marks the memory pages that have been dirtied in previous iteration and need not be transferred in this particular iteration, TO_SKIP which records the pages that can be skipped over, and TO_FIX which tracks the pages that need to be sent at last. Along with this, it includes another bitmask

TO_SEND_LAST that marks the pages which are updated frequently and are to be sent at last. Such kind of method reduces the pages to be transferred and hence lowers the migration time. However, this has higher downtime in comparison with the traditional pre-copy approach [2].

2. Two-Phase Strategy: Basically, in one-phase strategy, the page is sent once it is dirtied in the prior iterations. On the other hand, in the case of two-phase strategy, the scheduler holds a bit more patience. It sees if the current page is not being dirtied for two consecutive iterations and then only it sends that particular page. This approach tries to decrease the unnecessary retransmitting of a page to decrease the amount of memory being transferred. However, it has a bounding condition according to which if the number of iterations performed are less or the number of dirty pages are less then it tries to remain in the one-phase strategy and if either of these conditions are not followed, then it shifts to two-phase strategy [3].

3. Pre-Copy Using Memory Compression: The given technique aims at reducing both the migration time and downtime. It follows a memory compression-based technique to compress the memory pages with the aid of a characteristic-based compression (CBC) algorithm and then transfer the pages, helping to reduce the migration time. However, the compression ratio, i.e. the amount by which a given memory should be compressed, needs to be chosen wisely as compressing the data requires an additional overhead of time, and hence, choosing the best compression ratio that maintains a balance between compression overhead and memory migration time is necessary [4].

4. Combined Checkpoint–Restore/Trace–Replay Technique: This method makes use of checkpoint–restore and trace–replay methods to maintain synchronization between the source and the destination. The CR and TR helps provide a syncing mechanism by sending the log files of the source to the destination to emulate the working state at destination. While the log files are being executed at destination, the CPU scheduler adjusts the log generation rate. This way it helps to reduce the downtime and has an acceptable total migration time [5].

202 ■ Cybersecurity and High-Performance Computing Environments

5. Integrated Replication with Scheduling: It proposes the architecture required to overcome the challenges of VM migration over WAN. In this, it replicates a VM image over different cloud sites and then chooses a copy of the image as the primary copy and propagates the additional changes over it. The replication strategy of VM is factored on the basis of the de-duplication techniques that try to reduce the migration latencies over WAN [6].

6. Delta Compression Technique for Large VMs: This pre-copy approach uses compression techniques to compress the memory page before transmitting so that the required time to transmit pages reduces. It aims at increasing the network throughput for shortening migration downtime rather than reducing dirtying rate, which degrades the performance of the VM. It uses an XOR binary run-length encoding compression technique for faster compression of the pages, thereby increasing the migration throughput [7].

7. Optimized Pre-Copy Live Migration: This optimized version of iterative pre-copy approach is aimed at meeting a faster optimal convergence point. Convergence point is the state in migration when the live migration is stopped and finally stop and copy migration is used. The algorithm helps in deciding the convergence points by analysing the memory access patterns. It monitors the number of page changes per constant time interval and then uses linear regression to estimate the pages to be sent to determine the same page sampling interval at each iteration [8].

7.2.2 Research Challenges in VM Migration

Despite various developments, there are still some challenges in the field of VM migration:

i. Reducing Both Downtime and Migration Time: Any of the approaches discussed is able to improvise either of the aspects, but not both, and hence to increase the overall efficiency, there is still the need to find a better approach.

ii. VM Dependencies Are not Considered: The current methods do not focus on the inter-VM dependencies and do not take into the account the underlying topology being used.

iii. Migration at Low Bandwidth over WAN: The task of migrating a large-sized VM at a high latency and low bandwidth over WAN at different geographical locations is not time efficient.

iv. VMs with High Workload: When VMs are performing some computation- and memory-intensive tasks, then the migration speeds become quite low.

v. Security in Live VM Migration: This is ensuring the security of VM at the same time not compromising on the performance.

vi. Address Wrapping: Address wrapping from source to destination VM is quite intricate.

7.2.3 Security in Live VM Migration

Security is an essential factor to be taken care of while considering VM live migration. Live migrations can be quite susceptible to foreign attacks. Any third person in the same subnet can easily capture the migrating packets, and even direct attacks on the host VM are possible, which makes it lose its confidentiality, hence becoming a major concern. For this, there is the requirement of security systems to prevent these issues and here are some of the security approaches in live migration of VM:

1) Security in Live VM Migration with IPsec Tunnelling: Here, the use of a secured channel through which the VM can be migrated is emphasized. With the help of IPsec tunnel, a secured channel can be established through which every packet that is transferred through the network would be encrypted and then sent. Due to this process, we have an overhead in execution time. However, this comes with a benefit of security of the system. To reduce the migration time, memory pages can be compressed and then sent to reduce the total migration time. One can think of encrypting the entire VM and then send it; however, it increases

the migration cost considerably and hence it's not one of the best methods to choose for security [9].

2) Security in Live VM Migration with IPsec Tunnelling and Onion Routing Algorithm: The given method can be supposed as an upgraded approach over the VM migration with IPsec tunnelling. The additional security feature it incorporates is the use of TOR onion routing that helps in protecting the data by maintaining anonymity of the migration transactions [10].

3) Role-Based Mechanism for Secure Migration: This mechanism is based on identifying the valid role of any user/machine, and the migration is proceeded if and only if the given constraints are satisfied. It's a hardware- and software-based solution for creating a secure mechanism. The architecture consists of following features:

- Attestation Service: This feature helps the source VM hypervisor to cryptographically introduce itself to the destination VM hypervisor by communicating what application is running inside it and thereby helping the destination to identify trusted applications for further communication.

- Seal Storage: TPM (Trusted Platform Module) is responsible for encrypting data for attestation service. It also includes the hash along with the encrypted data. The TPM only allows the OS with the same hash to unseal it, thereby maintaining protection of the data.

- Policy Service: Policy service defines and manages the role-based policies for migration-related decisions such as who has the authority to migrate VM or at which hosts the migration is allowed.

- Migration Service: Migration service is responsible for all the migration-related tasks. It initiates the attestation requests to the destination to check if it meets all the security requirements after which only the migration can take place.

- Secure Hypervisor: This helps to protect the process of guest OS by runtime memory management. It provides the service of encrypting and storing keys and data and also provides with remote attestation ability to ensure the trustworthy environment is invoked [11].

4) Lightweight Authentication Framework for Securing VM Migration: Most of the VM migration securing mechanisms are not suitable for voluminous message transfer. Prior methods involving encrypting and decrypting the message or source and host authentication mechanism can increase the transmission delay. This given approach illustrates the use of lightweight authentication framework in a data centre network. It includes three modules: authentication, migration management, and migration analysis and monitoring.

- Authentication: Before participating in migration, authentication protocols such as Diffie–Hellman and IKE can be used for data centre authentication. Authentication frameworks consist of a lightweight handshake mechanism using the Diffie–Hellman method between a physical machine and the data centre, which is done with the help of a pair of keys – private and public keys – of the corresponding machine.

- Migration Management: Migration management consists of two sections – data encryption and decryption and host-to-host protection. The data encryption and decryption part is carried out using cryptography techniques such as RSA, AES, and DES, whereas host-to-host protection is provided by IPsec tunnelling.

- Migration Analysis and Monitoring: Data centre will act as a monitor for migration analysis and monitoring. The data centre will be equipped with IDS (intrusion detection system) to detect any suspicious and malicious activity, and if a potential threat is recorded, then in that case, it communicates a protected server for patch [12].

7.3 LIVE CONTAINER MIGRATION

Stepping one level up towards the process of live migration! The use of containers. The underlying processes of VM migration of having the image of OS processed first and then applying that instant make the process less portable and more redundant.

Containers similar to virtual machines provide the virtual environment that encases all the required dependencies required for any application to run on it. However, containers do not require the extra bulky OS; instead, they are just wrappers that directly request the kernel for accessing the resources. Application and process isolation are provided with the use of Linux resource isolation features such as control groups and namespaces that allow processes to work independently. Hence, not having the overhead of an extra hypervisor or OS makes containers a very lightweight and portable migration option as compared to virtual machines. Let's completely understand the process of live container migration.

7.3.1 Migration

The process of moving a container which might have an application, a program, or a website running in it from one server to another sever is called **live container migration**. Migration can help in creating in a sense of security in the context of fault tolerance while running the application as when a system failure occurs the container can be painlessly migrated to another host. Apart from fault tolerance, this technique can also provide services such as load balancing, scaling the applications and reallocating the resources accordingly, and tackling hardware failures. Similar to virtual machines, the live container migration also includes three main classes, which include

1) Memory migration

2) Process migration

3) Disk migration

Considering this technique to be used in high-performance computing, it is expected that the migration process performs with zero downtime. For all the applications running in the container and the container itself, it should appear that the container is in the same location even during migration. Although we have a high expectation, we assume there would be a slender decrement in the performance during the migration process, still making sure the overall effect is quite profitable.

In the following, we will discuss different migration and replication procedures. Preferably, it is assumed that during the process of migration there is transfer of the complete state of the original container that is the state of disk, memory, and network connections [13].

7.3.1.1 Memory Migration

Memory Migration can again be divided into two types:

1) Post-copy

2) Pre-copy.

Post-copy: The memory migration via post-copy approach takes place such that the memory is transferred after the state of the process is transferred to the target location.

Steps to accomplish the post-copy migration are the following:

1) Stop the running container at the source.

2) Send the register state, process state, and devices' states to the target location.

3) Resume the container that reached the destination without memory.

4) When the container is trying to run when it tries to access the memory that is not present, the required memory is transferred to the target location via the page fault mechanism.

Pre-copy: The memory migration via pre-copy approach takes place such that the memory is transferred on a continuous repeat first; after that, the state of the process is transferred to the target location.

Steps to accomplish the pre-copy migration are as follows:

1) The container at the source continues to run; during this time, the memory pages are transferred to the destination.

2) The memory transfer here is a repetitive process; in order to maintain consistency, only the pages last modified are copied to the destination.

3) Then the container at the source is stopped and then the register state, process state, and the devices' states are transferred to the target location.

4) Finally, the destination container is started.

Similar to post-copy, pre-copy follows similar steps, with the only difference of the transferring memory step ahead in one and later in the other [13].

7.3.1.2 Network Migration

With memory and CPU states, there should also be migration of the network connection states that is by preserving the open connections that the application in the container was using. These states can be achieved by retaining the original IP address, if the migration is happening on the same LAN. Otherwise, an ARP protocol can be generated to broadcast the destination address. But in the case where migration is happening over a large network such as WAN, then the existing technologies such as virtual private network (VPN), tunnelling, and DNS can be used.

7.3.2 Type of Migration to Manage Cache Transfers

7.3.2.1 Suspend/Resume Migration

In order to achieve mobility in a secured manner, the strategy of suspend/resume migration is used. In this technique, the container is transferred in an inactive mode to the target location. The underlying processes that take place in the container migration are listed as follows:

- The network connections are disconnected at the sources and then reconnected at the target host.

- Then the processor state, register state, and devices' states are sent to destination host.

- Then the images, local persistent state, and ongoing network connections are migrated; also, the support for disconnected operation is offered.

- Then apply delta disk operations to optimize the migration process of disk.

Delta Disk Operations: The disk migration process can be enhanced with the delta abstraction. The methodology of this notion is that the write operation in the source is seized and various deltas are created. Here deltas are the communication units containing information such as written data, size of the data, and location on the disk. The first step of the process is keeping track of the stored data and locating data blocks that have changed due to recent updates, i.e. the last write. The latest updated data are then sent to the target host via WAN or LAN. Another recognizable feature of suspend/resume technique is the disconnected operations. In this type of operation, the clients have access to critical data during the unfortunate event of failures of data repository through the use of contents of the cache. The updates in the cache can be transferred when disconnection ends.

7.3.2.2 Record–Replay Migration

The technique of record–replay is majorly used for recovering the states. The methodology used to implement this technique is as follows:

1) Find the last checkpointed state.

2) From the logs obtained, repeat the events to get the desired results.

Events: The events mentioned in the above technique can be categorized into deterministic and non-deterministic. In non-deterministic events, replaying is needed, which requires logging that could in turn affect the computation. However, deterministic events are the regular events such as memory, branching instruction, and arithmetic instructions, and the outcome of these events can be deterministic. Non-deterministic events are the interrupts that are caused by the input devices such as keyboard and mouse, and network and clock outcome cannot be determined when the process is repeated. This non-deterministic event can be further categorized into two classes as external input and time. The time events are the exact point during the execution when the event would occur, and the external input is data from other devices or human input requirements.

For replaying of a container, the non-deterministic events that help in the computation are needed to be logged. As deterministic events can be determined, they are not logged and can be computed during replay. Finally, putting all things together that is replaying the non-deterministic events from the log and computing deterministic events can get the container to the desired state. However, the record–replay technique should try to minimize the challenges such as maximizing trace completeness, reducing log file size, and trying to avoid low performance due to large overhead [13].

7.3.3 Case Study

7.3.3.1 Checkpointing and Restoring in CRIU

The essential phases in the process of live migration are checkpointing and restoring. This can be achieved using open-source project CRIU and P.Haul in OpenVZ. The CRIU here is a low-level technique that manages the saving and restoring of the checkpointed state. Similarly, it can perform the memory pre-copy or post-copy accordingly. Moreover, when P.Haul is implemented on top of CRIU, it helps in managing all checkpointing and restoring procedures and deals with file systems simultaneously.

- Checkpoint: During the checkpointing process, the CRIU freezes the container to ensure consistency and also dumps the process memory state. Hence, the checkpoint time includes the time taken to collect the process tree, and then freezing it, and then collecting the process resources which include memory mappings, timers, file descriptors, and threads, and then finally writing the resources in dump files over the network to a remote page-server (the target location). From experimental evaluations, the checkpoint time for the MySQL container at stages with different numbers of records is different, resulting in a linear increase in the pagemap dump file size from 100 to 250 MB. Hence, the checkpoint time increases linearly with the size of the application's memory state. In the microservice-type architecture, the expected memory usage of individual containers is <1 GB, which limits the checkpoint time to be <2 seconds.

- Restore: During the restoring process, the CRIU reads the
  files that were dump during checkpointing, resolves the shared
  resources, forks the process tree, and restores the process'
  resources. From experimental evaluations, the restore time for the
  MySQL container is ≈ 0.7−0.8 seconds for <250 MB dump size.
  Hence, the total expected application downtime is between 2 and
  3 seconds. With the recent incorporation in CRIU's incremental
  memory, checkpointing capabilities should help in lowering the
  application downtime.

As future work, there is a scope to evaluate this optimization and also
to instrument CRIU to measure both the checkpoint and restore times
at a per-resource requirement, so that we can prioritize and optimize
for the individual resources [14].

7.3.3.2 Checkpointing and Restoring in OpenVZ

OpenVZ also uses checkpointing and restoring methodology in order
to achieve live migration. During the checkpointing process, the state
of the running container is checkpointed and then restored later on
the same or different system (target location). The whole process
of checkpointing and restoring is transparent for the applications
and the network connections. The container has the capability to
reboot independently, given that it is provided with the required IP
addresses, users, root accesses, memory, processes, and filesystem. As
the container is an isolated entity, all the inter-process communications
and the parent–child relationships are within container boundaries.
Hence, it becomes very handy when the complete state is to be saved
in a disk file. As we know, the process of saving the complete state of
a container is known as checkpointing. The saved disk file is used to
restart the container. The first step of checkpointing and the last step
of restarting are freezing the process. It helps to maintain consistency
in the process and also reconstructing a frozen process is effortless. This
freezing is achieved by sending a TIF FREEZE signal to all the process
threads. In this, all the dependencies should be saved, which include
identifiers, process hierarchy, and shared resources such as the opened
files and the shared objects. Finally, these states should be restored
when restarting is required at the target host. The network should be
disabled by dropping all incoming packets, but at the same time, should

be preserved. Resources are restored from the process states, and this facilitates a special function called hook, which is added on top of each process stack during the restarting. The process then first runs hook on restart and thus restores all of its resources. Simultaneously, for the init process of container, this hook restores networking state, which includes the interfaces, iptables, route tables, IPC objects, and mount points, and starts the process tree construction [14].

7.3.4 Performance

The Voyager is a novel filesystem-agnostic and vendor-agnostic migration service that provides consistency in full-system migration. The Voyager combines CRIU-based memory migration together with the data federation capabilities of union mounts, which in turn helps in the minimization of the migration downtime. In Voyager, once a container is resumed at the target, it is provided with immediate access to its respective data storage with the help of Voyager's data federation layer. This layer incurs performance overhead, which is measured using YCSB for different types of workload profiles, including inserts, updates, reads, and scans. For each profile, in the YCSB's load stage, we insert 1 M records to a database table, and in the run stage, we perform 1M record operations of respective types. The records were accessed using the Zipfian distribution for the popularity-based long-tail access patterns. For each workload profile, average application throughput (operations/sec) is measured every 10 seconds.

Each experiment was performed via two application states:

1) Baseline: The application state at the source host before it is migrated.

2) Federation: The application state after it is migrated to the destination host, also having access to data through the federation layer.

For common application read/write workload, the patterns observed are with 0%–3% overhead in steady state. The performance impact on the individual workload profiles is as follows:

The initial low throughput is attributed to the cache warming phase, and then in the steady-state phase it is observed to have relatively stable performance. Every read operation via the federation layer makes the data access over NFS at the source. As a result, in the federation state, the read throughput drops by 20% during cache warming and by 1% in steady state. Unlike reads where a Zipfian pattern accesses popular records frequently, this workload accesses records in order, starting at a randomly chosen record key, and generates more unique read requests. Thus, even in steady state, we record a performance overhead of 10% for read accesses over NFS.

Updates: In federation state, an update is essentially a CoW operation; that is, a file is read from source over NFS, copied at the target, and then updated locally. MySQL stores its InnoDB tables and indexes in separate.ibd data files. Thus, during the federation state when a record is updated, the respective index and tablespace file is CoW'ed at the target host. Then, every subsequent update to the records is completed locally. Conclusively, it is observed that there is almost 75% performance overhead at the start and, in steady state, the update performance is on a par with baseline.

Inserts: In federation state, each write operation that results in the creation of new files is performed locally. Thus, we observe similar performance for baseline and federation state. The size of the table slows down the insertion of indexes by log N, assuming B-tree indexes; thus, a steady performance drop is observed for both states.

Read/Update/Insert: In this profile, the IO workload is split into 60:20:20 for read:update:insert. Finally, it observes 65% performance overhead at the start attributed to file-copy during updates and NFS access for reads, and 3% overhead in steady state [14].

7.3.5 Comparing VMs vs. Containers via High-Availability/Fault Tolerance (HA/FT) Solutions

In the wake of digitalization, optimization in virtualization technologies in the past decades has led to their widespread acceptance and a growing trend towards hosting workload in virtualized platforms. Although the virtualization technology promises a reduction in the cost and complexity through various abstractions of physical resources, they also raise questions on the availability of applications hosted on the virtualized platforms. Virtualization retailers propose different HA/FT solutions to their customers. Among these solutions, the HA is implemented by forming multiple levels of fault tolerance capabilities. A standard HA solution consists of a collection of loosely coupled servers that are self-contained and continuously monitored with the heartbeat methodology. In the event of host failure, VMs or containers can failover from one server to others. To guarantee service continuity, a secondary replica is required to be tightly coupled and reliable with the primary replica such that in case of failure, the replica is always ready to take over without service interruption and data loss.

The HA/FT solutions may be significantly different at the time of implementation; they share the same principle, which is duplicating critical components through redundancy in an attempt to remove single points of failure.

7.3.5.1 HA in Hypervisor-Based Platforms

7.3.5.1.1 **HA Solutions** HA features are provided by three main vendors: VMware, Citrix XenServer, and Marathon everRun MX. It has been observed that most of the retailers such as Microsoft Azure, Red Hat HP Serviceguard, and Enterprise Linux OpenStack Platform in the market provide integrated HA using failover clustering strategies that are discussed further in this chapter. VM live migration is supported by VMware and XenServer through vMotion and XenMotion, respectively. Still, CPU compatibility is required to make sure that the VM can perform normally on the target system after migration. The CPUs on the source and destination systems are expected to provide the same set of configurations to the VM so that the applications running on the VM do not crash. Simultaneously, checkpoint–restore is also supported by all of them, assisting in the capability of VM snapshotting [15].

7.3.5.1.2 *FT: Checkpointing vs. Record-and-Replay* Unlike HA that can be achieved by standard failover clustering, FT is a more complex procedure to be achieved in virtualized platforms as efficiently synchronizing a secondary VM with a primary VM is a complex task. This problem can be solved by two main strategies. One of them is record-and-replay, which basically records all input data in the source VM, sends them over a corresponding link to the secondary replica, and then replays them in the replica on the destination location. Implementing this strategy for a uniprocessor VM is comparatively pretty straightforward as all instructions executed by the vCPU in the source VM are replayed deterministically on the vCPU in the destination VM. However, the question of performance in the current CPU architectures is still a concern because modern CPU architectures usually consist of multiple processors and provide techniques such as branch speculation, prediction, and out-of-order execution, introducing non-deterministic behaviour across program executions. This non-determinacy increases the difficulty level of synchronizing a replica with a primary execution. Because of this reason, VMware that applies this strategy can currently only provide FT for uniprocessor VMs. This problem is known as symmetric multiprocessing fault tolerance (SMP FT). Intel argued that the problem of an efficient record-and-replay system targeting must be provided by the hardware support. Then Marathon everRun MX announced that they have found a solution to this problem. An alternative strategy, that is checkpointing the state of the VM after the inputs are provided, sends it to the clone and keeps the clone VM frequently synchronized with the original VM. Unlike record-and-replay, checkpointing has its upper hand in its simplicity and SMP support. But still its performance mainly depends on the checkpointing rate and the amount of data that need to be checkpointed and transferred to the clone side. While Marathon everRun MX provides all HA/FT features, it only supports Microsoft Windows as the guest OS, creating a monopoly in the market [15].

7.3.5.1.3 HA in VMware The VMware platform makes use of the VMware Distributed Resource Scheduler (DRS), VMware HA, VMware FT, and vMotion for achieving virtual environment high availability. VMware HA is also constructed on failover clustering strategy. All the VM disk images are needed to be present on the shared storage. The HA agents that are installed on all ESXi hosts are in charge of maintaining heartbeats between hosts in the cluster, that is heartbeats between applications and the vCenter server, and the heartbeats between VMs and the vCenter server.

VMware HA protects against three types of failures, which include ESXi host failure, that the heartbeat signal is no longer transmitted from the host, and the failure of the guest OS. For the first two, VMware HA restarts the VMs on remaining surviving hosts. In case of the third type of failure, the heartbeat signal is sent between the VM and the vCenter server. But in the third problem, VM fails or the guest OS within the VM freezes, the VM tools installed inside the VM also freezes, and this makes the vCenter sever unable to send the heartbeat signals. In order to solve this problem, the vCenter server resets the VM on the same host [15].

The failure on application level is identified by checking the heartbeat between the application and the vCenter server. So at the time of application failure, the vCenter server simply restarts not just the application, but the entire VM on the same host followed by the application that failed previously. For planed or predictable scenarios such as host maintenance or upgradation, HA for VMs can be achieved through live migration by vMotion. For migration of restarting strategies, the decision of the new location for a VM is made by VMware DRS according to information such as the resource consumption of a VM over time, state of hosts in the cluster, and anti-affinity rules.

If VMs are in the powered off state, then they can coexist on the same system. But when anyone of the VM is powered on, the host-level anti-affinity check is performed and the other VM has to be started on a different host according to the results obtained. With the initiation of vLockStep, the hypervisor on the two hosts coordinates a system of heartbeat signals and mutual monitoring. In case of failure on either host, the other host can take over and continue running the protected VM seamlessly through transparent failover.

However, as we previously discussed, VMware has FT capabilities based on the current implementation, but only a single logical processor on the VM is supported. So in order to protect multiprocessor VMs, VMware is developing a new protocol known as the SMP FT protocol, with a huge network requirement of at least 10 GB link. This increase in bandwidth is not only used for synchronization of multiple vCPUs, but also to eliminate the requirement on shared storage between the primary and secondary VMs. However, the performance overhead introduced by SMP FT is very large.

7.3.5.1.4 HA in XenServer Platform   The XenServer platform also offers HA protection for VMs similar to VMware, but it can only handle failures on host level. XenServer can be accompanied with third-party products such as HA-Lizard to deliver HA capabilities to address failures on VM level and application level. Also, the support for FT is not available in the XenServer platform. One potential way to integrate FT in XenServer is to enable Remus, which has been a part of XEN hypervisor.

Remus uses the active–passive technique where the state of the VM is continuously replicated from the primary host to the secondary host. Remus also allows speculative execution to simultaneously run the active VM slightly ahead of the replicated VM state. This in turn helps the primary server to be productive, while synchronization with the replicated server is performed asynchronously, which helps in improving the performance of the primary VM. However, XEN hypervisor is with Remus support, but still it is not included with XCP and XenServer [15].

7.3.5.2   HA in Container-Based Platforms

As opposed to hypervisor-based virtualization, container-based virtualization also known as operating system-level virtualization is not targeted to emulate an entire hardware environment, but rather providing the modern Linux kernel to manage isolation between applications. With OS-level virtualization technique, multiple isolated Linux containers can run on a single host by sharing a single kernel instance. Each container can have its own process and network. Systems such as LXC (Linux Containers), Docker, and OpenVZ are few well-known implementations of containers.

In fact, a container is a set of processes usually with a storage associated that could be completely isolated from other containers. In order to provide the HA facilities the capability to process, checkpoint–restore is required. There have been a large amount of techniques devoted to targeting this challenge, including few implementations such as BLCR, DMTCP, and ZAP. However, these systems either lack one feature or another, or usually only support a limited set of applications, and none of them has been a part of the mainstream Linux kernel due to the complexity of implementations.

An additional high-level feature such as versioning and sharing on top of LXC+ Docker is becoming a most used platform for container hosting. For checkpointing and restarting, one can snapshot a running container using the commit command, which saves the container's file

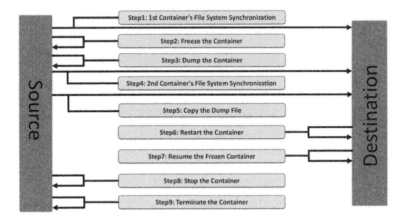

Figure 7.1 A diagram of live migration sequence in CRIU [16].

changes and settings into a new image, with no concern on the state of the running processes. Then another container can be restarted based on the snapshot image of the hosts. However, the state of running processes in the previous container is not preserved.

Features of live migration and checkpoint–restore in OpenVZ are implemented as loadable kernel modules plus a set of user space utilities. However, the major shortcoming of OpenVZ is the lack of official integration with upstream Linux kernel. Issues such as security and compatibility are faced by the users when using old kernels. To tackle this problem, a new working direction CRIU is implemented, that is, moving most of the checkpointing complexity out of the kernel and into the user space, thus minimizing the amount of required kernel changes. There is no other container-based platform that supports features of automatic state synchronization between the active and standby, failure detection, and failover management [15].

The plus point of this implementation is that the migration process can roll back to source and resume the container on the source when there is a failure in the synchronization of file system or in case of network disconnectivity during the transfer of memory pages. The availability mostly depends on the time consumed in Steps 3 to 5 in Figure 7.1 [16]. These include three optimizations: file system changes tracking, lazy migration, and iterative migration, and are implemented to reduce the service downtime.

7.3.5.2.1   File System Changes Tracking   The basic idea here is to reduce the time for file system synchronization in Step 4 in Figure 7.1. This can be achieved by tracking the file system changes and continuously synchronizing the changes only. The current optimization in CRIU is implemented on a block device similar to Linux loop device, but specifically designed for containers known as ploop. The important feature of ploop is that it has a write tracker, which helps the kernel to memorize a list of modified data blocks. This list formed enables us to efficiently migrate a ploop device to destination host, with minimal container downtime. In the vzmigrate utility, the user space support is implemented in the ploop copy tool.

7.3.5.2.2   Lazy Migration   Mainly lazy migration is to only migrate a minor subset of memory pages to the target host, then resume the container on the target, and finally pull the remaining pages from the source on demand. With the help of lazy migration, the container can be resumed at the target location without waiting for entire memory copy from the source. On the event of page fault, the container sends a request to the page-in swap device that then redirects the request to the page-out daemon that resides on the source to pull in the missing page. Accordingly, the requested page is transferred and loaded into the memory on the target host. Then finally whenever the container is idle for a certain time, a last swap-out action is applied and all remaining pages are transferred from the source to the target location.

The main setback of lazy migration is that neither the source nor the target holds an integral state of the container, meaning that the source and the destination as well as the network connection in between must be reliable until the full migration process is completed. However, the container restored on the target location can be malfunctioning due to incomplete pulling of memory pages in case of network failure between the source and the destination. Also, rollback is inapplicable under such scenarios [15].

7.3.5.2.3   Iterative Migration   Another optimization technique is to perform memory pages transfer and file system synchronization prior to freezing the container; this helps to reduce the amount of data needed to mitigate after the freeze of the container. Still as the pages are being dirtied and file systems might also be dynamically changing during the data transfer, this process needs to be executed iteratively. Hence, in this strategy, the file system is needed to be iteratively synchronized, along with the dirtied memory pages transfer in each iteration.

7.3.5.3 Clustering Efforts for Containers

The power of Linux containers can be fully explored when there is a complete orchestration of them in a well-synchronized manner. These are known as clustering of the containers. As their individual working becomes insignificant, a collective functionality to build services with multiple building blocks is required. In order to achieve this, various efforts to build cluster-level management for containers are going on. Docker Swarm is a well-known Docker-native clustering system that aims at creating a cluster of Docker hosts as a single virtual host. Kubernetes is another significant clustering solution to containers, in which tightly coupled containers are grouped into pods and the loosely coupled cooperating pods are organized into key/value pair labels. These labels are considered metadata describing the semantic structure of the service composed by multiple pods. Kubernetes works on the notion of a Replication Controller in which a pre-defined number of replicas of a given pod is always running; this helps in providing fault tolerance. In case of a failure of a pod, it can be restarted on another healthy host.

7.4 ATTACKS ON LIVE MIGRATION

Based on the various researches conducted on the attacks on the live migration strategies, a few categories are identified on the basis of the causes that let the attack happen. The categories of attacks are as follows:

1) The improper access control policies.

2) The unprotected transmission channel.

3) The loopholes in the migration module.

7.4.1 Improper Access Control Policies

Unsuited or inapt access control policies give access to an unauthorized user to start, transfer, and terminate a virtual machine by themselves with concern of the governing host. This policy provides access to hypervisor, governs the isolation between VMs on the same machine and the resource sharing among them, etc. Lack of security can help a malicious attacker to perform the following attacks:

1) Denial-of-Service Attack: This unauthorized attacker can start a large number of outgoing transfers onto a virtualized host server. This results in the overloading of the target server, decreasing its performance or at worst establishing havoc in the service it provides. As the VM is providing its services, it is possible for an unauthorized attacker to make the VM to migrate from server to server that reduces the performance of service provided by it.

2) Internal Attacks: This can be the result of an unauthorized attacker transferring VM with malicious code in it to the main target hypervisor. This provides a platform for malicious VM to perform numerous internal attacks on the target system that might also include the control over the target hypervisor and then finally the other guest VMs.

3) Guest VM Attack: In this, the attacker sends a request for an incoming migration of a VM; during the mitigation of this request, the attacker gains control over the migrated VM and then performs an attack by executing a malicious code on it or crashing it or in many other ways.

4) False Resource Sharing: An attacker system can pass wrong reports of the available resources, influencing other VMs to migrate to this unauthorized VM.

5) Inter-VM Attack: The VMs running on the same machine can communicate with each other. If a policy for communication between VMs is not defined, then an unauthorized VM can attack other VMs running on the same machine.

Solution: To block these attackers from performing the above activities, appropriate access control policies (acls) must be defined. Access control policies define perfect rules guiding who can migrate out a VM, who can request to migrate in a VM, who can suspend a VM, whether a user can terminate VM, and more similar decisions. And these acls must first be authenticated and should provide opposition to tampering. The Xen provides sHype with the mandatory access control for Xen, whereas the guidelines for the configuration of sHype are given in Xen user manual. Moreover, acls can also be accompanied with a firewall to check that migration is from authorized source and to authorized destination systems. This firewall rule will be very helpful in checking each packet for allowed and rejected source, destination, and protocol, and accordingly, the specified actions are taken. These actions include accepting the packet, forwarding the packet, or rejecting the packet [17].

7.4.2 Unprotected Transmission Channel

The endangered and exposed transmission channel is the result of the improper migration protocol. The migration protocol does not encrypt the data during their migration over the network, which results in making the data susceptible to active and passive attacks. An attacker can gain access to the transmission channel using known methodologies such as DNS poisoning, ARP/DHCP poisoning, and IP/route hijacking to perform passive or active attacks. Passive attacks include eavesdropping of messages for sensitive data, such as the passwords and keys, and then capturing the authenticated packets and replying them later. Active attacks are more dangerous comparatively. This may include manipulating authentication services such as /bin/login, pam, and sshd; manipulating kernel memory such as slip root kits into kernel memory; etc.

Solution: One simple solution is to assign a VM or group of VMs to a VLAN so that the VLAN isolates migration traffic from other network traffic and provides a secure transmission channel for migration of data. Other solutions include encryption of the data to provide anonymity such that integrity can be maintained using digital signatures, MAC, and checksums [17].

7.4.3 Loopholes in Migration Module

Vulnerabilities in migration include heap overflow, stack overflow, and integer overflow. Such vulnerabilities become an advantage point for an attacker to inject malicious code or even freeze the process. The virtualization software can be huge and complex with a large number of LOC. Xen hypervisor has about 200 K LOC and XEN emulator has about 600 K LOC and the host almost include 1,000 LOC. With such a large code, lots of bugs tend to exist. Bug reports such as those listed in the NIST's National Vulnerability Database show how hard it is to ship a bug-free hypervisor code. A malicious user can take advantage of these bugs to attack the virtualization software. Exploiting such an attack gives the attacker the ability to get unauthorized access to the other virtual machines and therefore breach system's integrity, and also the availability of the other virtual machine's code or data. The virtualization software migration code must be structured such as to remove such vulnerabilities.

Solution: The release of new virtualization software includes patch of such types of vulnerabilities. Hence, the system must be updated with the recent releases and patches to be protected from attacks via the migration module. Moreover, secure programming methods must be used. The following section projects more light on the details of some major approaches to secure live migration [17].

7.5 APPROACHES

7.5.1 Isolating the Migration Traffic

For secure live migration against all such attacks, it is important to assign a small group of VMs or even a single VM to its own host-based virtual LAN (VLAN). The VLAN isolates migration traffic from other network traffic and thus provides a secure transmission channel for migration process. A major drawback of the VLAN-based security approach is the growth in complexity and administrative costs as the number of VMs grows. The main complexity lies in constructing such a network and also maintaining VLANs for each VM, simultaneously synchronizing VLANs configuration on virtual and physical switches, with troubleshooting and fix configuration errors, and also managing the growth and complexity of acls as the number of VMs increases, ensure compatibility between physical network and virtual network security policies is in all a very complicated problem. Moreover, with migration, the things become more complicated because then there is the VM continuously needed to be moved between the hosts and virtual switches. Hence, using VLAN because it has no traffic monitoring and filtering mechanism; thus, inter-VM communication within the VLAN remains invisible [17].

7.5.2   Network Security Engine-Hypervisor (NSE-H)

NSE-H is based on hypervisors that are included with the network security engines to prevent intrusions occurring in a virtual network. NSE includes intelligent packet processing capability, intrusion detection systems, firewall, and intrusion prevention system to provide security to a virtualized environment. The NSE firewall works in the state-full procedure, thus manage to maintain security context for each packet and make decisions in the context of security and packet content. There are two modules in the NSE firewall: CTM (connection tracking module) and PMM (policy matching module). The CTM keeps track of transport layer connection status using a database similar to the hash table. When a packet arrives, it looks up the database based on packet header; if a match is found with the existing connection, then the packet is accepted; otherwise, the packet is forwarded to PMM for further instruction to be processed on whether to accept the package or not. This PMM stores a set of packet filtering policies defined by the administrator; these filtering policies are basically a set of rules which consist of sequence of descriptors that are matched with packet content; and accordingly, the actions are taken. The problem with live migration implementation is that it only encapsulates the VM execution context for transmission and not the security context which results the destination VM to be rejected because of the missing or not matching which is the required security procedure. The solution to this problem is to include security context (SC) along with VM execution context in the migration data, thus making use of the components of architecture such as VMMA, SCMA, LMC, NSE, and hypervisor core. To transmit the VM encapsulated states to the target hypervisor, the virtual machine migration agent (VMMA) interacts with the destination hypervisor's VMMA. Security context migration agent (SCMA) encapsulates and sends VM-related security context set through a dedicated channel such that the live migration coordinator (LMC) collaborates with the destination hypervisor's LMC and schedules the two agents to perform migration tasks in parallel.

Live migration extends the four phases of live migration implementation which are as follows:

1) Preparation: The LMC on source informs the destination LMC to start reserving resources. Thus, VMMA and SCMA

both reserve the required resources and get prepared for migration.

2) Iterative Synchronization: The VMMA on source iteratively transfers the execution context of VM to be migrated to the destination. Similarly, the SCMA transfers the security context of VM to be migrated.

3) Final Synchronization: This phase is concerned with the transfer of the recently written pages to migrated VM after the first phase of synchronization. Both the execution context and the security context are transferred by VMMA and SCMA, respectively. The migrated VM is then suspended on the source hypervisor, and the VM-related network is redirected to target server through unsolicited ARP replay adverting. The VMMA and SCMA copy the execution instructions and security set.

4) Resumption: The migrated VM is restarted form the point it was frozen on the target hypervisor, and the VM instance of the source is discarded. In this way, the above discussed approach makes it possible for traditional security approaches such as firewall and IDS to be effective in the context of live migration [17].

7.6 SUMMARY

In the wake of digitalization, the need for high efficiency and high availability in all aspects increases. This makes any application or a program lengthy. Hence, it rises the need for fault tolerance, load balancing, and also the urgency to take care of the applications during a blackout. In this chapter, we've learnt the basics of **Live Migration** and its needs, applications, security aspects, and role in **HPC (High-Performance Computing)**. It also highlights one of the most flamboyant technologies – "**Cloud Computing**" – and its importance in context with live migration and its various techniques.

This chapter basically covers two approaches: "**Live Migration with Virtual Machine**" and "**Live Container Migration**". This chapter introduces live migration in virtual machines and its performance metrics, followed by covering two general techniques used for virtual machine live migration, namely **Post-Copy Approach** and

Pre-Copy Approach. It also includes the research challenges faced while implementing the VM live migration and also addresses the cost and performance vs energy requirements for the same. The second half of the chapter explains the container live migration and its types in order to manage cache transfers. This chapter covers two case studies: **Checkpointing and Restoring** in "CRIU" and "OpenVZ" for container live migration.

It also compares live migration in virtual machines with live container migration with respect to various attributes such as performance, challenges, and security. This chapter not only underlines the role of live migration in high-performance computing, but also discusses security breaches and possible threats to it, and it concludes with suggesting various approaches to overcoming the same.

REFERENCES

[1] M.R. Hines, U. Deshpande, and K. Gopalan (2009). Post-copy live migration of virtual machines. *SIGOPS Oper. Syst. Rev.* 43(3), 14–26. doi: 10.1145/1618525.1618528.

[2] F. Ma, F. Liu, and Z. Liu (2010). Live virtual machine migration based on improved pre-copy approach. *In 2010 IEEE International Conference on Software Engineering and Service Sciences*, pp. 230–233. doi: 10.1109/ICSESS.2010.5552416.

[3] C.-C. Lin, Y.-C. Huang, and Z. Dejian (2012). A two phase iterative pre-copy strategy for live migration of virtual machines. *In Proceedings of ICCM*, Taiwan, pp. 29–34.

[4] H. Jin, L. Deng, S. Wu, X. Shi, and X. Pan (2009). Live virtual machine migration with adaptive memory compression. *In Proceedings of Cluster Computing and Workshop*, China, pp. 1–10.

[5] W. Liu and T. Fan, et al. (2011). The live migration of virtual machine based on recovering system and CPU scheduling. *In Proceedings of ITAIC*, China, pp. 1088–1096.

[6] S. Bose, S. Brock, R. Skeoch, S. Nisaruddin, and S. Rao (2011). Optimizing live migration of virtual machines across wide area networks using integrated replication and scheduling. *2011 IEEE International Systems Conference*, Montreal, QC, Canada. doi: 10.1109/SYSCON.2011.5929040.

[7] P. Svärd, B. Hudzia, J. Tordsson, and E. Elmroth (2011). Evaluation of delta compression techniques for efficient live migration of large virtual machines. *SIGPLAN Not*, 46(7), 111–120. doi: 10.1145/2007477.1952698.

[8] K.Z. Ibrahim, S. Hofmeyr, C. Iancu, and E. Roman (2011). Optimized pre-copy live migration for memory intensive applications. *In Proceedings of 2011 International Conference for High Performance Computing, Networking, Storage and Analysis (SC'11)*. Association for Computing Machinery, New York, Article 40, pp. 1–11. doi: 10.1145/2063384.2063437.

[9] A. Tamrakar (2014). Security in live migration of virtual machine with automated load balancing, *International Journal of Engineering Research & Technology (IJERT)*, December 2014, ISSN: 2278–0181.

[10] G. Naravanan and K. Saravanan (2018). Securing VM migration through IPSec tunneling and onion routing algorithm. *2018 Second International Conference on Intelligent Computing and Control Systems (ICICCS)*, pp. 364–370. doi: 10.1109/ICCONS.2018.8663094.

[11] W. Wang, Y. Zhang, B. Lin & X. Wu, and K. Miao (2010). Secured and reliable VM migration in personal cloud. *2nd International Conference on Computer Engineering and Technology (ICCET)*, pp. V1–705. doi: 10.1109/ICCET.2010.5485376.

[12] S.K. Majhi and S. Dhal (2016). An authentication framework for securing virtual machine migration. *In 2016 International Conference on Advances in Computing, Communications and Informatics (ICACCI)*, Jaipur, India, pp. 1283–1286. IEEE.

[13] W. Li and A. Kanso (2015). Comparing containers versus virtual machines for achieving high availability. *2015 IEEE International Conference on Cloud Engineering*, pp. 353–358. doi: 10.1109/IC2E.2015.79.

[14] S. Nadgowda, S. Suneja, N. Bila, and C. Isci (2017). Voyager: Complete container state migration. *2017 IEEE 37th International Conference on Distributed Computing Systems (ICDCS)*, pp. 2137–2142. doi: 10.1109/ICDCS.2017.91.

[15] D. Kapil, E.S. Pilli, and R. C. Joshi (2013). Live virtual machine migration techniques: Survey and research challenges. *2013 3rd IEEE International Advance Computing Conference (IACC)*, pp. 963–969. doi: 10.1109/IAdCC.2013.6514357.

[16] L. Helali and M.N. Omri (2021). A survey of data center consolidation in cloud computing systems. *Computer Science Review*, 39. doi: 10.1016/j.cosrev.2021.100366.

[17] A. Strunk (2012). Costs of virtual machine live migration: A survey. *2012 IEEE Eighth World Congress on Services*, pp. 323–329. doi: 10.1109/SERVICES.2012.23.

CHAPTER 8

Security-Aware Real-Time Transmission for Automotive CAN-FD Networks

Ruiqi Lu and Guoqi Xie
Hunan University

Junqiang Jiang
Hunan Institute of Science and Technology

Renfa Li
Hunan University

Keqin Li
State University of New York

CONTENTS

DOI: 10.1201/9781003155799-8

8.1 INTRODUCTION

8.1.1 Background and Motivation

The rapid advancement and introduction of new processing technologies for computing have facilitated the development of high-performance embedded computing systems, which are widely applied in critical scenarios such as mobile communication devices, smart health care, and intelligent vehicles. High-performance embedded computing systems consist of various physical devices and advanced communication technologies. Notonly do they complete a large number of computations, but they also have to coordinate hardware and software in real time in terms of security, low overhead requirements, etc. High-performance embedded systems are all over people's lives and are integral parts of modern life. In different application fields, high-performance embedded systems have different characteristics. Figure 8.1 shows the classification of high-performance embedded systems by application areas, such as industrial control, consumer electronics, wireless sensors, and network/communication. In this chapter, we focus on intelligent vehicles in industrial control in terms of real-time and security-aware issues.

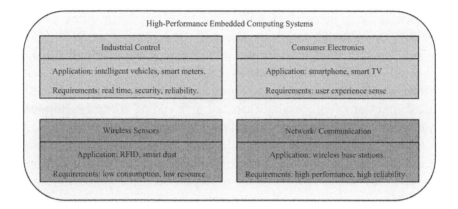

Figure 8.1 Classification of high-performance embedded systems by application areas.

Modern intelligent vehicles not only facilitate people's travel, but also give a comfortable and pleasant experience on the road. While intelligent vehicles bring these conveniences to people, they also raise various security issues for automotive networks. With the development of modern communication and networking technologies (e.g., 4G/5G), and the increase in external interfaces (e.g., OBD, Bluetooth, and WiFi), automotive networks suffer from various cyberattacks (e.g., DoS attack, injection attack, and masquerade attack). Attackers could intrude internal systems and maliciously steal internal confidential communication information. For example, Charlie Miller and Chris Valasek have spent months successfully hacking the automotive systems of the Toyota Prius and Ford Impala by the OBD interface, allowing the hacked vehicle to slam the brakes or change direction beyond the driver's control in 2015 [1]; Samy Kamkar adopted OwnStar to intrude GM OnStar's mobile app RemoteLink, successfully accessing the driver's authentication information and remotely controlling the vehicle's ignition and unlocking functions in 2015 [2]; in 2017, Jay Turla launched an open-source cyberattack project against Mazda Motors, which allows anyone to execute malware code on Mazda cars using a USB flash when the vehicle is in device mode or the engine is running [3]. These attacks seriously threaten the security of automotive networks, thereby affecting the safety of vehicles and humans. There are some automotive networks for automotive communications, such as controller area network (CAN), Time-Sensitive Networking (TSN), FlexRay, and Media Oriented Systems Transport (MOST). CAN, which is a serial, synchronous, non-preemptive, and half-duplex bus, is widely used in automotive networks. CAN is primarily used for communication and control between electronic control units (ECUs) of safety-critical functions (e.g., brake, throttle, and engine control). However, CAN lacks any security-aware methods, making it vulnerable to malicious attacks, which could result in a huge loss of economy. Moreover, the low payload (up to 8 bytes) and low bandwidth (up to 1 Mbps) characteristics make CAN difficult to deploy security-aware methods.

In addition, a large number of automated driving applications such as adaptive cruise control (ACC), automated parking system (APS), and advanced driver-assistance system (ADAS) are being added to intelligent vehicles. As a result, the number of automated driving technologies and ECUs continues to increase, which generates a huge amount of dependent messages in automotive networks. The high data volume brings a great challenge to the real-time requirement. Therefore, the traditional CAN is not suitable for this high data volume transmission with the real-time requirement. In 2012, CAN Flexible Data-Rate (CAN-FD) was proposed by BOSCH to improve the transmission rate and bandwidth of the current CAN bus. CAN-FD combines the core features of CAN with a high bandwidth (up to 12 Mbps) and data field length (up to 64 bytes), thereby providing the possibility of real-time transmissions in automotive networks. Meanwhile, these features make CAN-FD more feasible than CAN to deploy security methods.

8.1.2   Contributions and Outline

At present, there is no investigation to classify security-aware real-time transmission for automotive CAN-FD networks in terms of confidentiality-aware real-time transmission methods, integrity-aware real-time transmission methods, and availability-aware real-time transmission methods. Figure 8.2 shows the overview of recent advances in security-aware real-time transmission for automotive CAN-FD networks discussed in this chapter. For security-aware real-time transmission for automotive CAN-FD networks, this chapter provides the following contributions:

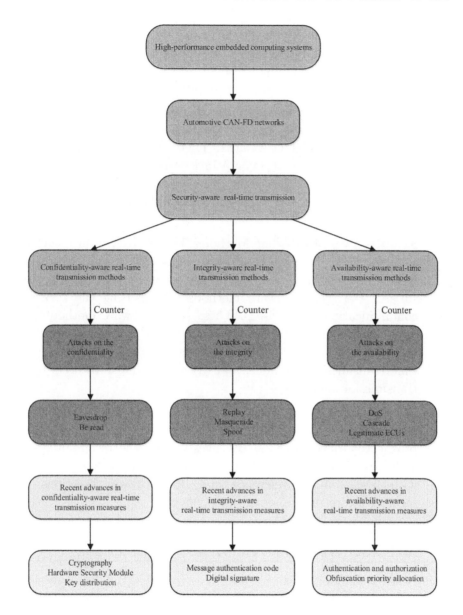

Figure 8.2 Overview of recent advances in security-aware real-time transmission for automotive CAN-FD networks discussed in this chapter.

1. Preliminaries of Automotive CAN-FD Networks: This chapter provides the preliminaries of automotive CAN-FD networks, mainly including (1) differences between CAN-FD and CAN, and (2) CAN-FD networks security vulnerabilities.

2. Cyber-Attacks Model: Automotive networks lack security protection mechanisms for automotive applications, which makes them vulnerable to malicious attacks. This chapter surveys common and serious automotive cyberattacks that threaten the proper functioning of vehicles. The cyberattacks mainly attack the confidentiality, the integrity, and the availability of automotive CAN-FD networks.

3. Security-Aware Real-Time Methods: The security-aware method ensures the security of automotive networks. Considering that CAN-FD does not take security into account, this chapter surveys the security-aware methods for ensuring the security communication in CAN-FD. These security-aware methods are mainly investigated in the following items: (1) confidentiality-aware real-time transmission methods, (2) integrity-aware real-time transmission methods, and (3) availability-aware real-time transmission methods.

4. Future Trends: This chapter introduces the future trends in security-aware real-time methods in terms of new demands and prospective developments. By investigating the recent progress and presenting the future trends, we hope to provide researchers with a systematic reference and development directions in security-aware real-time methods.

8.2 AUTOMOTIVE CAN-FD NETWORKS PRELIMINARIES

To facilitate the understanding of security-aware real-time transmission for automotive CAN-FD networks, this section provides a basic introduction to automotive CAN-FD networks preliminaries. We first introduce the differences between CAN-FD and CAN. Then, we investigate the security vulnerabilities in CAN-FD. Finally, we survey the automotive cyberattacks, which mainly attack the confidentiality, the integrity, and the availability of automotive CAN-FD networks based on the security vulnerabilities of CAN-FD.

8.2.1 Differences between CAN-FD and CAN

With the rapid development of automotive electronics and the demand for high bandwidth, CAN-FD was proposed by Bosch in 2012 and was officially approved by the International Organization for Standardization (ISO) in ISO 11898-1 in 2015. CAN-FD, with the advantages of high bandwidth and long data length, inherits the main characteristics of the traditional CAN. CAN-FD adopts two-wire serial communication protocol and is based on non-destructive arbitration technology, distributed real-time control, reliable error handling, and detection mechanism. It is fully compatible with CAN and can be used on the same physical connections due to a less modified physical layer. Based on these features and advantages, CAN-FD is regarded as the next generation of mainstream automotive bus system. Considering that CAN-FD is an upgraded version of CAN, we first introduce the data frame format of CAN and CAN-FD, and then we present the obvious advantages of the CAN-FD networks compared with CAN.

In CAN and CAN-FD networks, different nodes adopt data frames for communication. The different messages are encoded according to the message ID. Nodes can receive data frames according to their needs (message ID) and filter the messages they are not interested in. According to the number of identifier bits, CAN data frames can be divided into standard frames and extended frames. The former uses 11-bit identifiers, and the latter uses 29-bit identifiers. According to the length of the data field, CAN data frames can be divided into CAN Classical and CAN-FD. The maximum data load of CAN Classical is 8 bytes, and the maximum data load of CAN-FD is 64 bytes. The comparison between CAN-FD and CAN data frame formats is illustrated in Figure 8.3. In CAN standard frames, 11-bit identifiers are used. The value of the identifier can range from 0x000 to 0x7FF, so a total of 2048 message types can be encoded. In the data frame, the IDE bit identifies the standard frame or the extended frame. When the IDE is 0, it means that the data frame is the standard frame, and when the IDE is 1, it means that the data frame is the extended frame. FDF identifies CAN Classical or CAN-FD. When FDF is 0, it means CAN Classical. When FDF is 1, it means CAN-FD. DLC identifies the length of the data field. The content of the CRC field is to perform CRC check on the data frame. In CAN Classical, DLC ranges from 0 to 8, so the

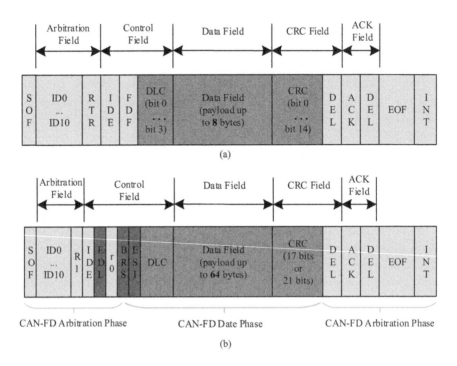

Figure 8.3 Comparison between CAN-FD and CAN data frames.

data field length of CAN Classical can range from 0 bytes to 8 bytes. CAN Classical uses 15-bit CRC for CRC check. In CAN-FD, FDF is 1. The length of CAN-FD data field can be 8, 12, 16, 20, 24, 32, 48, and 64 bytes according to the value of DLC. When the length of the data field does not exceed 16 bytes, a 17-bit CRC check code is used. When the data field length is between 20 bytes and 64 bytes, a 21-bit CRC check code is used. When IDE is 1, it means that the data frame is an extended frame. The extended frame uses a 29-bit identifier, with a value range from 0x00000000 to 0x1FFFFFFFF, which can represent 229 different message types, about 530 million.

Based on the differences between CAN and CANFD data frames, we summarize the obvious advantages of CAN-FD networks as follows.

1. CAN-FD Improves Frame Structure: CAN-FD adds three new control bits: EDL (extended data length: 0 denotes CAN frame and 1 denotes CAN-FD frame), BRS (bit rate switch: 1 denotes convertible data-phase rate and 0 denotes non-convertible

data-phase rate), and ESI (error status indicator: 1 denotes error passive and 0 denotes error active).

2. CAN-FD Has a Flexible Transmission Rate: CAN-FD adopts two kinds of bit rates: The data rate of data transmission phase (from BRS to ACK) is up to 12 Mbps and the data rate of arbitration and ACK phase is up to 1 Mbps; however, the bit rates of CAN are up to 1 Mbps in data transmission phase, arbitration phase, and ACK phase.

3. CAN-FD Has Longer Data Fields Than CAN: Compared to the traditional CAN data fields of 8 bytes, CAN-FD has greatly expanded the data field length, whose maximum data field length can reach 64 bytes. When the data length code (DLC) of CAN-FD is less than or equal to 8, it is consistent with the original CAN bus; when it is greater than 8, it is non-linear growth. This greatly increases the valid message in the data frame, which means that CAN-FD has a higher payload for transmission than CAN.

4. CAN-FD Optimizes Checksum Fields: In addition to adding stuff bits from SOF to the data field, CAN-FD also adds stuff bits in CRC with a higher frequency. The CRC field always starts with a stuff bit complementary to its predecessor. After every four bits, a stuff bit is inserted complementary to the predecessor. If the stuff bit is not complementary to the previous bit, an error will be reported for processing when format checking is performed.

8.2.2 Security Vulnerabilities in CAN-FD

CAN-FD initially works in an isolated environment and lacks cybersecurity-aware mechanisms. However, with the development of intelligent vehicles, CAN-FD, which carries the key function of controlling vehicle safety, is becoming the target of cyberattacks. The main security vulnerabilities of CAN-FD networks are listed as follows:

1. Physical Structure Characteristics: The physical layer of CAN-FD networks is twisted-pair cables, which lack abnormal access detection and can be easily accessed illegally by malicious attackers. Therefore, these physical structure characteristics cannot guarantee the availability and integrity of automotive CAN-FD networks.

2. Broadcast: CAN-FD messages are broadcast messages, which can be received by all the ECUs in CAN-FD bus because CAN-FD is not segmented. As a message-oriented protocol, CAN-FD does not define any fields specifying information related to the sending or receiving ECUs. For a CAN-FD message, the receiving ECU only checks the identifier of the message to decide whether it should be received or discarded. In this way, attackers can attach a compromised ECU and easily eavesdrop and read the content of the CAN-FD messages. The broadcast mechanism makes CAN-FD networks a challenge to guarantee the confidentiality of CAN-FD messages.

3. No Message Encryption: The CAN-FD protocol does not introduce any encryption mechanism in communication; that is, messages are transmitted in plaintext in the CAN-FD bus. Any node connected to the CAN-FD (including compromised node) can read the message directly, making the CAN-FD messages vulnerable to eavesdropping attacks, thus affecting the confidentiality of the automotive network.

4. Arbitration Field Mechanism: Arbitration field mechanism of CAN-FD is based on the priority of the identifier. When the bus is free, all ECUs can send messages. Conflicts can occur when multiple ECUs try to send messages at the same time. CAN-FD protocol provides an arbitration field mechanism to determine which ECU access CAN-FD. The message with the lowest ID (i.e., the frame with the highest priority) wins arbitration and accesses the CAN-FD bus. The ECU that fails arbitration will try to send the message again when the CAN-FD bus is free again. However, if a malicious node sends a message with the highest priority continuously to CAN-FD, the CAN-FD bus will be collapsed and other ECUs will not be able to communicate with each other, thus enabling denial-of-service (DoS) attacks. Therefore, the arbitration rule makes it difficult for CAN-FD to guarantee the availability of CAN-FD messages.

5. No authentication: CAN-FD messages transmitted between ECUs in CAN-FD have no authentication mechanism as they are just identified and filtered by message ID. There is no field in CAN-FD message identifying the sending ECU. CAN-FD

only provides CRC for message integrity and error verification. Therefore, in the absence of security methods, any malicious node in the CAN-FD bus can easily perform DoS, replay, forgery, and other attacks since the receiving ECU cannot verify the origin of the messages. Therefore, no authentication mechanism makes it impossible for CAN-FD to ensure the integrity and the availability of CAN-FD messages.

6. No Freshness: The frame structures of CAN-FD messages have no time stamp or random number. A malicious attacker can perform a replay attack to control the behavior of the vehicle.

8.2.3 Automotive Cyber-Attack Model

Initially, automobiles were relatively isolated electro-mechanical systems that did not need to interact with the outside world, so CAN-FD was originally designed without any security mechanisms in mind. However, with the increment in interconnections of sensors, actuators, and devices, various communication technologies and interfaces are embedded in modern vehicles, opening a door to a wide variety of cyberattacks. As a result, the vehicle is no longer considered to be a closed system.

Koscher et al. [4] first assessed the cybersecurity analysis of automotive safety-critical CAN networks based on real vehicle platforms, demonstrating the vulnerability of automotive networks in the face of malicious attacks. In particular, CAN-FD is an upgraded version of CAN and inherits the core features of CAN; thus, the cybersecurity analysis of CAN is similar to the cybersecurity analysis of CAN-FD. In addition, Ref. [4] analyzed the inherent weaknesses of the CAN protocol, including broadcast characteristics, inability to resist DoS attacks, lack of message authentication mechanisms, and weak access control. By exploiting these protocol flaws, an attacker can launch targeted sniffing detection or obfuscation attacks to compromise ECUs in the CAN bus.

In general, confidentiality, integrity, and availability are the three elements of security [5]. When it comes to message transmission in automotive CAN-FD networks, confidentiality represents the security of CAN-FD message from being read by malicious attackers; integrity represents the security of CAN-FD message from being created

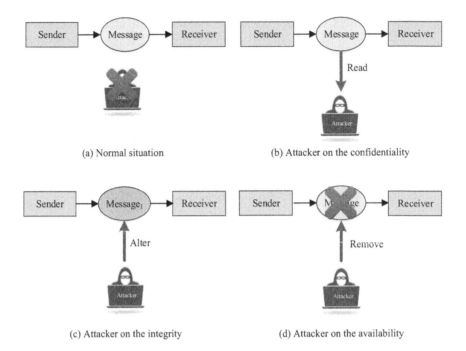

(a) Normal situation   (b) Attacker on the confidentiality

(c) Attacker on the integrity   (d) Attacker on the availability

Figure 8.4 Security principles of confidentiality, integrity, and availability of messages in automotive CAN-FD networks. (a) Message is sent from the sender to the receiver without being attacked. (b) Message is read by an attacker when it is sent from the sender to the receiver, and this attack affected the confidentiality of the message. (c) Message is tampered with by an attacker when it is sent from the sender to the receiver, and this attack affected the integrity of the message. (d) Message is removed by the attacker when it is sent from the sender to the receiver, i.e., the normal message could not be sent to the receiver from the sender.

or modified by malicious attackers; and availability represents the security of CAN-FD message from being removed and interrupted by malicious attackers [5]. Figure 8.4 shows the security principles of the confidentiality, the integrity, and the availability of messages in automotive CAN-FD networks.

We focus on the three elements of security to introduce the cyberattack models on automotive CAN-FD networks, namely attacks on the confidentiality, attacks on the integrity, and attacks on the

TABLE 8.1 Automotive Cyber-Attack Model Based on Confidentiality, Integrity, and Availability

Security Elements	CAN-FD Vulnerabilities	Attacks
Confidentiality	Broadcast Unencrypted [6]	Eavesdrop Be read
Integrity	CRC [6] No authentication [6,7]	Replay [6,9] Masquerade [7] Tamper [10] Spoof [9]
Availability	Arbitration field [11] No ECU authentication [10] Intrusion detection [12]	DoS [11] Cascade [13] Legitimate ECUs [10]

availability. Table 8.1 shows the automotive cyberattack model based on the confidentiality, the integrity, and the availability.

Attacks on the Confidentiality: When a message broadcasts in CAN-FD without encryption, CAN-FD cannot ensure only legitimate ECU receives the message, thereby providing the potential of eavesdropping for malicious attackers. In this way, the message could be read by attackers, thus attacking the confidentiality of the CAN-FD message [6].

Attacks on the Integrity: As CAN-FD lacks a message authentication mechanism, the receiving ECU can only identify CAN-FD messages based on the message ID, which paves the way for an attacker to masquerade as the sending ECU and send messages in the CAN-FD networks. The current CAN-FD just relies on a CRC to guarantee transmission error detection; thus, it cannot prevent replay attacks [7,8]. In this way, the message is created or modified by attackers, thus attacking the integrity of the CAN-FD message.

Attacks on the Availability: When two nodes (ECUs) in the CAN-FD bus have messages to send at the same time, the arbitration mechanism of CAN-FD allows the message with high priority to be transmitted, while the message with low priority must wait for the next idle state. Therefore, a malicious attacker can easily use messages with high priority to launch DoS attacks. In this way, the message is removed and interrupted by attackers, thus attacking the availability of the CAN-FD message.

8.3 AUTOMOTIVE CAN-FD SECURITY-AWARE REAL-TIME TRANSMISSION METHODS

Based on the analysis and discussion of the cybersecurity attack models of automotive CAN-FD networks in the previous section, we will focus on automotive CAN-FD security-aware real-time transmission in this section. We first survey the constraints of automotive CAN-FD security-aware real-time transmission. Then, we research security-aware real-time transmission methods, namely confidentiality-aware real-time transmission methods, integrity-aware real-time transmission methods, and availability-aware real-time transmission methods.

8.3.1 Automotive CAN-FD Security-Aware Real-Time Transmission Constraints

Although the concepts and methods of security on the Internet can be applied in automotive networks, their physical environments are different from computers. When designing security methods for automotive networks, we need to consider the characteristics of vehicles. Constraints of automotive CAN-FD security-aware real-time transmission are listed below.

Software and Hardware Architecture: The automotive architecture consists of a large number of heterogeneous and complex software and hardware components, whose communication is based on different network protocols such as CAN, CAN-FD, and MOST. This heterogeneous and complex architecture not only adds uncertainty elements in functional safety and cybersecurity of vehicles, but also makes it difficult to perform security-aware testing and verification.

Real-Time Sensitivity and Resource Limitations: Compared with commercial computers, computing resources in a vehicle have many limitations such as storage and communication bandwidth, which directly affect the deployment and implementation of security-aware methods. Implementing complex security methods could take a long time. In addition, the critical functions and applications of the vehicle are real-time sensitive, and these functions and applications must be completed within a specific time to ensure the safety of the vehicles and passengers. Therefore, real-time sensitivity and hardware resource limitations make a secure real-time transmission difficult. For example, simple cryptography requires less time to execute, but it is not secure enough; however, complex cryptography consumes significant computing resources and time overhead, but it is more secure than the simple one.

Lifecycle and Compatibility: The automotive lifecycle is typical about 20 years, which is longer than the computer lifecycle. Additional security methods inside the vehicle should be easily updated rather than outright obsolete during the lifecycle. In addition, this security equipment should be able to withstand the physical conditions inside the vehicle, such as shock, high temperature, and humidity. Meanwhile, the security methods should not only be of low cost and can be installed at a low cost, but also be compatible with the internal protocols and external resources of vehicles.

8.3.2 Confidentiality-Aware Real-Time Transmission

The messages transmitted in CAN-FD are broadcast without any encryption mechanism to all the ECUs connected to the CAN-FD bus as mentioned before. There is no proper way of authenticating the sending ECU of a message. Cryptographic algorithms are widely used in automotive CAN-FD networks to provide secure communication channels while enhancing message confidentiality and ECU authentication and preventing messages from being read by ECUs that do not possess the appropriate keys. Cryptographic algorithms are usually distinguished as symmetric-key and asymmetric-key algorithms (also called public-key cryptography). These two types are explained and depicted in Figure 8.5.

8.3.2.1 Symmetric-Key Cryptography

Symmetric-key cryptography, which is a predistribution key cryptography, is usually used to encrypt messages in automotive CAN-FD networks. In the symmetric-key cryptography, the symmetric key is shared among all communication participants. Each participant encrypts or decrypts the message based on the same symmetric key. Symmetric-key cryptography can be implemented with few resources. It is widely used as a core part of many encryption protocols due to its high efficiency. To maintain the confidentiality of the communication, the symmetric key must be obtained and stored in a secure manner by communication participants. When the communication node changes, the predistribution manner requires the new communication node to be predistributed with the key again. This leads to increased coupling between nodes

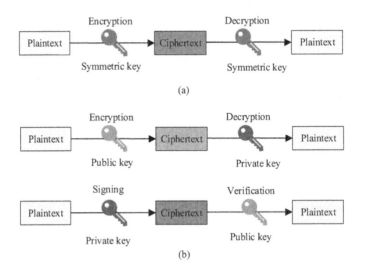

Figure 8.5 Comparison of symmetric-key cryptography and asymmetric-key cryptography.

in the system. Secure storage imposes requirements on the storage capacity of the node. Common symmetric-key algorithms include Data Encryption Standard (DES), 3DES, Advanced Encryption Standard (AES), International Data Encryption Algorithm (IDEA), RC5, and RC6. In [14], RC6 was adopted as symmetric-key cryptography for the sending and the receiving ECU to encrypt and decrypt CAN-FD messages. Considering that symmetric-key cryptography requires additional computing overhead, the authors first adopted the pre-allocation method to pre-allocate a reasonable encryption level for CAN-FD messages, which is to select a suitable encryption level while meeting the real-time requirements; then, they selected the maximum number of rounds to improve the encryption strength on the premise of ensuring real-time requirement. In this way, it's effective to enhance the confidentiality by protecting against eavesdropping attacks, while guaranteeing real-time requirements of CAN-FD message transmission.

8.3.2.2 Asymmetric-Key Cryptography

In asymmetric-key cryptography, each communication participant has two unique keys: One is a private key, which is to be kept secret, and the other is a public key, which is public to all the communication participants. These keys are mathematically related that a message encrypted with one key can only be decrypted with the other key. If a participant knows one of the keys, the participant does not calculate the private key based on the public key. Therefore, even if the asymmetric-key algorithm discloses the public key, it does not affect the confidentiality of the private key. Asymmetric keys can be used to authenticate the identity of communication participants. The sender encrypts a message with its private key, and the receiver can verify the sender's identity with the sender's public key, but this method also requires distributing public keys in advance; that is, the keys are exchanged in a predistribution scheme. It has the same drawback as symmetric-key cryptography, i.e., the increased coupling between nodes in the system. At the same time, the storage requirements are higher than those of symmetric keys, as the length of asymmetric keys is often larger than that of symmetric keys. The computational complexity of asymmetric-key cryptography is also higher than that of symmetric-key cryptography. In addition, digital certificates can be used to distribute asymmetric keys, which can avoid increasing the coupling among participants. Instead of storing the public keys of other participants, each participant only needs to hold a public key certificate signed by a trusted authority (e.g., the vehicle manufacturer), and the authentication and session key generation among participants can be achieved. However, this method also has some drawbacks. Asymmetric-key cryptography tends to be more complex and have longer computation time than symmetric-key cryptography, making it difficult to meet the real-time requirements of automotive networks. Common asymmetric-key cryptography includes RSA, ElGamal encryption algorithm, and elliptic-curve cryptography (ECC). For example, Ref. [15] implemented key exchange and encrypt engine in hardware with ECC as asymmetric-key cryptography. In Ref. [10], asymmetric algorithms are used in ECU authentication for the session key distribution, while symmetric keys are used in stream authorization for session communication.

8.3.2.3 Key Distribution

Cryptographic algorithms are public, and the security of the algorithms depends on the security protection of the keys; thus, key management is critical for cryptographic algorithms. The key management includes

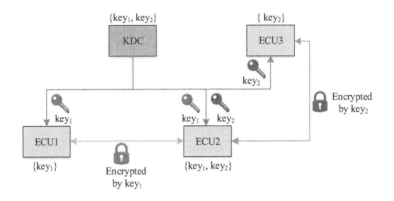

Figure 8.6 KDC working process.

key generation, key distribution, key injection, key authentication, and key use. For secure automotive transmission, an ECU usually contains multiple keys, such as a key for encryption, a key for MAC/HASH, and a key for signature. In addition, an ECU may be involved in more than one communication; thus, there are various keys in an ECU. Therefore, key distribution is particularly important in secure automotive transmission. Security mechanisms are needed in the key distribution. In addition, symmetric keys are also used for key distribution with additional mechanisms, such as time stamp, random numbers, and counters [9,10]. One of the most widely used methods of key distribution is key distribution center (KDC), which is a trusted institution to temporarily assign a session key (used only once) to users who need to communicate secretly. Figure 8.6 illustrates the KDC working process. There are two keys in the KDC. key_1 is the session key for ECU1 and ECU2, and key_2 is the session key for ECU2 and ECU3. When KDC receives a request from EUC1 to communicate with EUC2 (or when EUC2 requests to communicate with EUC1), KDC would distribute the session key key_1 to ECU1 and ECU2. When KDC receives a request from EUC2 to communicate with EUC3 (or when EUC3 requests to communicate with EUC2), KDC would distribute the session key key_1 to ECU2 and ECU3. In [6], the authors developed a practical architecture for CAN-FD networks. This architecture adopts key Management to enhance the confidentiality and the integrity of CAN-FD networks. Key Management has two properties, which are key freshness, and forward and backward secrecy. Forward and backward secrecy means that the architecture uses an authentication session key and an encryption session key to offer authentication and confidentiality for CAN-FD messages, respectively. Specifically, the two keys are different for each CAN-FD message. Key freshness means that the seeds used for session keys generation are constantly updated to ensure the freshness of the generated keys, thereby countering replay attacks. Furthermore, this architecture can also enhance the integrity of CAN-FD messages due to authentication session keys and key freshness. In [9], the authors implemented a key security mechanism for CAN/CAN-FD messages authentication to counter spoofing attack and replay attack, thereby enhancing the confidentiality and the integrity of transmission. The key security mechanism includes an AUTOSAR-compliant key management architecture that includes a baseline session key distribution protocol (SKDC) and a secret-sharing-based protocol (SSKT). This architecture reduces the storage for predistribution message and distinguishes sessions. SSKT reduces the overall protocol runtime and improves the efficiency of computation and communication, but it increases the memory footprint of the ECU.

8.3.2.4 Hardware Security Module

Consider that the automotive system is a resource- and time-sensitive system and that strong encryption and decryption could consume a large number of computational resources and time. This issue can be addressed by deploying a hardware module called hardware security module (HSM) [16] at ECU to reduce ECU resource consumption and time overhead while ensuring secure communication. HSM is conceived by EVITA, and it is used for secure key generation, storage, and management, as well as hardware cryptography acceleration in various key scenarios. For example, some kinds of HSM have already supported ECC with shorter keys and possessing the same level of security as ECC without deploying HSM. Schweppe et al. [17] deployed the HSM on each ECU to speed up encryption while providing a secure environment for key storage. Ref. [18] integrated HSM into automotive existing infrastructure to accelerate the encryption process and establish symmetric-key cryptography-based trust between ECUs. There are many benefits of using hardware encryption, such as fast encryption, no additional overhead for the chip responsible for the main function, minimal impact on the performance of the original network, and no changes to the logic between the nodes that communicate with each other. The disadvantages of the hardware encryption module are obvious. Its installation requires changing the hardware structure of the network nodes. In particular, long-term experiments are required before installing hardware security modules; otherwise, many unknown problems will be introduced in automotive networks. In addition, the cost of upgrading hardware is great. The automotive industry is relatively strict and conservative, so the implementation of hardware encryption is slow and not easily accepted. Moreover, it is not very realistic for OEMs to recall and modify hardware for models that are already on the market. Ref. [19] displayed a CAN encryption design architecture to enhance the confidentiality and the integrity of CAN-FD messages, and this architecture was tested and verified on a Xilinx FPGA chip using Verilog HDL. The design adopted the symmetric-key cryptography AES-128 algorithm to enhance the confidentiality of CAN-FD messages and the HMAC algorithm SHA-1 to enhance the integrity and ensure the authentication of CAN-FD messages. To reduce the extra time overhead caused by cryptographic operations in automotive networks, lightweight hardware acceleration is usually adopted in automotive networks, such as using programmable logic devices for AES and ECC [20]. Ref. [21] implemented a trimmed version of hash with field-programmable gate arrays (FPGAs).

8.3.3 Integrity-Aware Real-Time Transmission

Integrity checks of messages transmitted in automotive networks are one of the key factors to ensure the security of automotive networks. CRC is adopted by CAN-FD to check if messages have been modified or transmitted incorrectly; this mechanism can detect message transmission faults, such as loss, repetition, delay, and incorrect sequence [52]. However, CRC is inefficient in preventing from modifying correct messages and masquerade attacks, as it is an easy way for a fake message to spoof the right CRC. Therefore, it is essential to adopt message authentication mechanisms to ensure the integrity of messages. Message authentication code (MAC) and digital signature are two common types of methods for message authentication. Digital signatures are usually more than 40 bytes in length, while MACs can be as long or as short as desired.

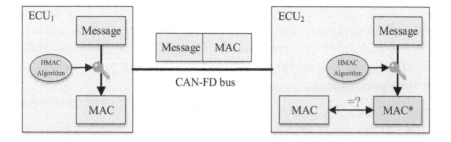

Figure 8.7 Process of attaching HMAC into CAN-FD message.

8.3.3.1 Hash-Based Message Authentication Code

Hash-based message authentication code (HMAC), which was created by Krawezyk, Bellare, and Canetti in 1996, is widely used in automotive networks for message authentication to enhance the integrity of CAN-FD transmission [6]. Figure 8.7 illustrates the process of attaching an HMAC into a CAN-FD message. HMAC added in the data field of a message would occupy the position of the message and reduce the message length. HMAC inputs would increase the bus load rate and the message transmission delay as more frames could be used to transmit messages. The length of HMAC inputs and the type of HAMC algorithms both affect the transmission delay. The longer the size of the inputs of HMAC, the longer the computation time [23]. MD5 takes less time than SHA256 for computation [24]. Ref. [7] adopted a pre-shared secret key to populate messages by MAC in the sending ECU and the receiving ECU to enhance the integrity of the CAN-FD messages. If there is a message that needs to be transmitted from one ECU to another ECU in CAN-FD, the sending ECU first uses a MAC algorithm to calculate the MAC value of the message and then attach the MAC value to the end of this message. Then, the sender sends the new message to the receiver. After receiving the new message, the receiver splits it into two parts (the original message and the MAC value), calculates the MAC value by MAC algorithm with the pre-shared secret key, and obtains a new MAC value; if the new MAC value is equal to the MAC value calculated by the sender, it shows that the message is not tampered with and is transmitted in CAN-FD securely. However, the added MAC to counter tampering attacks increases the processing and transmission delay of CAN-FD messages, which affects the guarantee of real-time performance. To solve this problem, the authors quickly found the lower bound of the application by prefix and suffix pruning and then increased the MAC by round accumulation to extend the lower bound, while still guaranteeing the real-time performance.

8.3.3.2 Cipher-Based Message Authentication Codes

Cipher-based message authentication code (CMAC), which is another type of MAC, is generally used as a signature of a message. Consider that the calculation result of CMAC-128 is 128 bits, which is the same size as the AES key. We can calculate multiple 128-bit outputs by CMAC-128 with a 128-bit AES key. These outputs can be used as different keys when we need multiple keys involved in a module. However, it takes a long time for CMAC to calculate. Hardware-based acceleration is used to reduce the calculated delay of CMAC. What's more, consider that AES has the restriction of delay $< 2\mu$ per block based on the SHE specification [24,25]. NXP MPC5748G uses internal core HSMv2 to perform and accelerate AES-128. When the block number is 32 or more, the calculated delay of AES can meet the SHE specification and real-time requirement restriction of automotive networks. The payload size of AES-128 is 16 bytes, which is larger than the data field of CAN (8 bytes). If the length of MAC is not truncated, it cannot be used in CAN. But it can be used in CAN-FD because its data field is up to 64 bytes as mentioned before. Park et al. [26] adopted CMACs to enhance the integrity of the message of gateway systems with security features and used HSM in the MCU to quickly generate and validate CMAC. Zalman et al. contributed a reliable, secure, and low-delay solution for automotive networks by using CMAC and combining CRC [27].

8.3.3.3 Digital Signature

Digital signature is one of the security mechanisms for message authentication as MAC. Digital signature is a security method to achieve signature, authenticate data authenticity, and assure integrity. It has the property of non-repudiation because it is a valid proof of the

TABLE 8.2   Comparison between Digital Signature and MAC

Features	Digital Signature	MAC
Message authentication	Yes	Yes
Non-repudiation	Yes	No
Cryptography	Asymmetric key	Symmetric key
Execution time	Long	Short
Applicability	CAN-FD, FlexRay, Ethernet	CAN, CAN-FD, FlexRay, Ethernet

authenticity of the message sender, while MAC does not have this property. The digital signature is based on asymmetric-key cryptography, and it is also known as a public-key digital signature. Considering that asymmetric-key cryptography is a computationally expensive task, the digital signature can be used in Ethernet, FlexRay, and CAN-FD. If a digital signature is used in CAN, it will increase the bus load rate and data frames. MAC is based on symmetric-key cryptography, which needs low computation effort. Therefore, it is suitable to use in CAN, Ethernet, FlexRay, and CAN-FD. The digital signature is signed by a private key and verified by a public key. The public key only needs to be generated once to be verified by all communication participants because the public key can be known by anyone. However, in the symmetric way of MAC, the shared key between each two communication entities must be different. In addition, the digital signature can also be used to prevent malicious software download and update, while guaranteeing the integrity, authentication of origin, and non-repudiation. For secure software downloading, Kocher employed a digital signature to ensure secure software download in the SDR functioning [28,29]. For secure software updates, the security level of over-the-air (OTA) is much higher than that of the onboard networks. Digital signature is necessary for OTA in terms of the communication process (security protocols [30] and security architectures), downloaded firmware, and related update repository [31]. Table 8.2 concludes the differences between digital signature and MAC.

8.3.4   Availability-Aware Real-Time Transmission

As described in the previous section, arbitration rules are originally designed to avoid message blocking on the automotive bus, but these rules increase the potential malicious attacks, which continuously send high-priority messages in CAN-FD, thereby preventing legitimate message transmission in CAN-FD, i.e., DoS attacks. Therefore, it seriously affects the availability of automotive CAN-FD networks.

8.3.4.1 Authentication and Authorization

Mundhenk et al. [10] presented a Lightweight Authentication for Secure Automotive Networks (LASAN) that is a full lifecycle secure framework. LASAN divides the security operations into two processes: ECU authentication and stream authorization, which are based on two types of security operations. ECU authentication is based on asymmetric-key cryptography, which requires a larger amount of computation. But asymmetric operations (ECU authentication) are performed only when the car is not in use to avoid affecting the real-time performance of the vehicle. Stream authorization is based on symmetric-key cryptography, which can be executed quickly on resource-limited ECUs. The required security level is achieved by a rational allocation of symmetric and asymmetric operations while ensuring real-time performance. In addition, Ref. [10] demonstrated how LASAN enables the protection of the entire lifecycle of a vehicle, including the production, maintenance, and software update phases of the vehicle. LASAN ensures that only legitimate ECUs can participate in the communication and that only valid message streams can be transmitted, which enhances the availability of automotive networks. Meanwhile, the rational use of cryptography also guarantees real-time requirement of automotive networks. To implement key distribution and management, Woo et al. [32] proposed a complete set of authentication protocols suitable for automotive networks. These protocols include the Initial Session Key Distribution Protocol (ISDP), Data Frame Transfer Protocol (DFP), session key update protocol (SKUP), and Vehicle-to-External Device Connection Protocol (VCP). Palaniswamy et al. [33] analyzed the security of these protocols and designed the Remote Frame Transfer Protocol (RTRP) for the security vulnerabilities caused by insecure remote frames. In addition, a new session key update protocol (NSKUP) is introduced to enhance the security of key updates when the vehicle is connected to an external device.

8.3.4.2 Obfuscating Priority Assignment

In addition, the availability of automotive networks is closely related to the automotive industry. Taking the current actual automotive industry mass production model, for example, millions of cars produced in this mass production model adopt the same message execution stream for an automotive application. If the message execution stream of one car is cracked by attackers, other cars that also adopt this stream are then exposed to cascade attacks. In 2015, Jeep and BMW were both forced to recall 2.2 and 1.4 million vehicles of cascade attacks, respectively, due to a cascading exposure from an information security vulnerability in one vehicle [34]. To enhance the availability by protecting against cascading attacks, Ref. [35] exploited an obfuscating priority assignment method to generate different message executions of the same application in millions of vehicles (more than 10 million available real-time obfuscated message streams), while still ensuring the functional integrity and real-time constraints of the application. The authors quickly generate valid streams by message swapping to avoid obtaining all streams in advance and adopt affix matching (prefix, midfix, and suffix matching) technique to obtain as many available streams as possible. In this way, these available message streams ensure the timing relationships between messages and guarantee the real-time performance of the application.

8.3.4.3 Intrusion Detection

Intrusion detection (ID) is a simple and efficient security-aware method that can monitor the data flow transmitted in the in-vehicle networks in real time. Intrusion detection can detect anomalies and report network attacks when the vehicle is running. Compared with security-aware methods based on cryptographic methods, intrusion detection methods are based on the observation and analysis of network traffic to achieve anomalous behavior. It does not interfere with the existing data flow and does not encroach on the limited message load and bandwidth resources (e.g., CAN). The attack detection patterns of intrusion detection are diverse, such as intrusion detection method based on message timing information, intrusion detection method based on message data values, and intrusion detection method based on message physical layer characteristics. Hoppe et al. [36] first introduced the concept of intrusion detection systems to automotive networks. The authors created the detection methods based on the features of increased CAN message frequency, observation of physical layer electrical communication characteristics, and misuse of CAN message IDs. Larson et al. [37] extracted security specifications based on the requirement of in-vehicle networks communication protocol to describe the normal behavior patterns of the vehicle. When the current behavior pattern of the vehicle system is not consistent with the desired behavior, it would indicate that the vehicle system is under attack.

Intrusion detection is often adopted in the CAN bus because it does not add additional data frames to CAN. Nowadays, it is also used in CAN-FD networks to counter potential cyberattacks in vehicles. In Ref. [38], an anomaly intrusion detection based on a support vector machine was exploited for automotive CAN-FD networks. Under the Common Intrusion Detection Framework (CIDF), anomaly intrusion detection adopts message identifiers, periods, and data field data as intrusion detection features. The authors use the binary classification property and small sample feature of the support vector machine algorithm to achieve the identification of intrusion message in the CAN-FD networks environment. The simulation experimental results show that the offered method has a high correct rate of intrusion detection and can be used for both periodic and non-periodic messages. To enhance the security of automotive CAN-FD networks, a novel intrusion detection method based on network topology verification was proposed in Ref. [12]. This method can reliably detect XIDs through a simple random walk-based network topology and follow-on verification. When intrusion attacks are detected by the method, secure modes would be activated to further protect the network from attacks. These intrusion detection approaches effectively enhance the availability of CAN-FD networks while ensuring real-time requirement because they do not affect CAN-FD messages and do not occupy the limited bus load and bandwidth resources.

Table 8.3 summarizes the above security-aware real-time methods based on confidentiality-aware real-time methods, integrity-aware real-time methods, and availability-aware real-time methods.

TABLE 8.3 Security-Aware Real-Time Methods of CAN-FD Networks

References	Security Methods	Attack Model	Security Elements
[19]	Asymmetric-key cryptography, Hardware security module	Eavesdrop, Be read	Confidentiality
[15]	Asymmetric-key cryptography	Eavesdrop, Be read	Confidentiality
[5]	HMAC, Asymmetric-key cryptography, Symmetric-key cryptography	DoS, Legitimate ECU	Availability
[26]	CMAC	Spoof, Masquerade	Integrity
[6]	AES-128, HMAC, SHA256	Replay, Spoof	Confidentiality, Integrity
[32]	Key distribution	DoS, Legitimate ECU	Availability
[9]	Key distribution, Symmetric-key cryptography	Spoof, Replay	Confidentiality, Integrity
[35]	Obfuscating priority assignment	Cascade	Availability
[14]	RC6	Eavesdrop	Confidentiality
[7]	HMAC	Masquerade	Integrity
[38]	Intrusion detection	Legitimate messages	Availability
[12]	Intrusion detection	Legitimate messages	Availability

8.4 FUTURE TRENDS

People's increasing requirements for automotive safety, comfort, and convenience have accelerated the rapid development of intelligent automotive. The continuous changes in the new generation of automotive networks have made cybersecurity a challenge. Cybersecurity has attracted widespread attention from industry and academia. Combining the development trend of the modern vehicle and the current latest research security-aware methods described before, this chapter presents the future research fields below.

Intrusion Detection Accuracy and Response Time: In terms of the serious functional safety threats brought by the untimely detection of malicious attacks on vehicle networks, intrusion detection technology has become an important security-aware method for vehicles. Therefore, it is an urgent issue to improve intrusion detection accuracy, reducing false-positive rate, shortening detection response time, and improving system robustness for intrusion detection technologies.

Attack Analysis and Cybersecurity Evaluation: Attack analysis is the basis of automotive cybersecurity research. Security vulnerabilities and security requirements can be found by the comprehensive attack analysis.

Security-Aware Methods and Resource Consumption: Given the limited communication and computational resources of the vehicle, it makes functional security and information security compete in design.

8.5 CONCLUSIONS

As an indispensable part of people's lives, the intelligent vehicle not only brings convenience to people's travel, but also brings more and more serious cyber-threats to automotive networks. This chapter first provides the preliminaries of automotive CAN-FD networks, including the differences between CAN-FD and CAN as well as their security vulnerabilities and the corresponding classification of cyberattacks. Then, security-aware real-time CAN-FD transmission methods are summarized based on the three elements of security such as confidentiality-aware real-time transmission, integrity-aware real-time transmission, and availability-aware real-time transmission. Finally, this chapter discusses the further trends of security-aware real-time

CAN-FD transmission methods, including intrusion detection accuracy and response time, attack analysis and cybersecurity evaluation, and security-aware methods and resource consumption. Cryptographic algorithms are primarily used to ensure confidentiality-aware transmission, and HSM and key distribution are used to assist the cryptographic algorithm by providing fast and secure cryptographic operations. MAC and digital signatures are used to ensure integrity-aware transmission. Authentication and authorization framework and obfuscation priority assignment are used to ensure availability-aware transmission. However, when implementing these security-aware methods, we need to consider the actual vehicle requirements, such as network latency, real-time performance, bus load factor, algorithm complexity (cryptography, MAC, and digital signatures), key management (cryptography), and implementation cost. We hope this chapter can help researchers to understand and grasp the status and research of automotive CAN-FD networks quickly and comprehensively and give reference directions for automotive CAN-FD networks-related research in the future.

REFERENCES

[1] Charlie Miller and Chris Valasek. Adventures in automotive networks and control units. *Def Con*, 21(260-264):15–31, 2013.

[2] Kamkar Samy. OwnStar—hacking cars with OnStar to locate, unlock and remote start vehicles. https://www. youtube. com/watch. 2015.

[3] Some mazda models can be hacked with a flash drive, 2017.

[4] Karl Koscher, Alexei Czeskis, Franziska Roesner, Shwetak Patel, Tadayoshi Kohno, Stephen Checkoway, Damon McCoy, Brian Kantor, Danny Anderson, Hovav Shacham, et al. Experimental security analysis of a modern automobile. In *The Ethics of Information Technologies*, pp. 119–134. Routledge, 2020.

[5] Philipp Mundhenk, Andrew Paverd, Artur Mrowca, Sebastian Steinhorst, Martin Lukasiewycz, Suhaib A Fahmy, and Samarjit Chakraborty. Security in automotive networks: Lightweight authentication and authorization. *ACM Transactions on Design Automation of Electronic Systems (TODAES)*, 22(2):1–27, 2017.

[6] Samuel Woo, Hyo Jin Jo, In Seok Kim, and Dong Hoon Lee. A practical security architecture for in-vehicle can-fd. *IEEE Transactions on Intelligent Transportation Systems*, 17(8):2248–2261, 2016.

[7] Guoqi Xie, Laurence T. Yang, Wei Wu, Xiangzhen Xiao, and Renfa Li. Security enhancement for real-time parallel in-vehicle applications by CAN FD message authentication. *IEEE Transactions on Intelligent Transportation Systems*, pp. 1–12, 2020.

[8] Yong Xie, Gang Zeng, Ryo Kurachi, Hiroaki Takada, and Guoqi Xie. Security/timing-aware design space exploration of can fd for automotive cyber-physical systems. *IEEE Transactions on Industrial Informatics*, 15(2):1094–1104, 2018.

[9] Yang Xiao, Shanghao Shi, Ning Zhang, Wenjing Lou, and Y. Thomas Hou. Session key distribution made practical for can and can-fd message authentication. pp. 681–693. Association for Computing Machinery, 2020.

[10] Philipp Mundhenk, Andrew Paverd, Artur Mrowca, Sebastian Steinhorst, Martin Lukasiewycz, Suhaib A. Fahmy, and Samarjit Chakraborty. Security in automotive networks: Lightweight authentication and authorization. *ACM Transactions on Design Automation of Electronic Systems (TODAES)*, 22(2):1–27, 2017.

[11] Luiz Quintino and Alexei Machado Machado. Protection against attack dos in can and can-fd vehicle networks. In *Anais do XXXV Simpósio Brasileiro de Redes de Computadores e Sistemas Distribuídos*. SBC, 2017.

[12] Tianqi Yu and Xianbin Wang. Topology verification enabled intrusion detection for in-vehicle can-fd networks. *IEEE Communications Letters*, 24(1):227–230, 2020.

[13] Guoqi Xie, Renfa Li, and Shiyan Hu. Security-aware obfuscated priority assignment for can fd messages in real-time parallel automotive applications. *IEEE Transactions on Computer-Aided Design of Integrated Circuits and Systems*, 39(12):4413–4425, Dec. 2020.

[14] Guoqi Xie, Kehua Yang, Haibo Luo, Renfa Li, and Shiyan Hu Reliability and confidentiality co-verification for parallel applications in distributed systems. *IEEE Transactions on Parallel and Distributed Systems*, 32(6):1353–1368, 2021.

[15] Bogdan Groza and Pal-Stefan Murvay. Identity-based key exchange on in-vehicle networks: CAN-FD & FlexRay. *Sensors*, 19(22), 2019.

[16] Marko Wolf and Timo Gendrullis. Design, implementation, and evaluation of a vehicular hardware security module. In *International Conference on Information Security and Cryptology*, pp. 302–318. Springer, 2011.

[17] Hendrik Schweppe, Yves Roudier, Benjamin Weyl, Ludovic Apvrille, and Dirk Scheuermann Car2x communication: Securing the last meter - a cost-effective approach for ensuring trust in car2x applications using

in-vehicle symmetric cryptography. In *2011 IEEE Vehicular Technology Conference (VTC Fall)*, pp. 1–5, 2011. San Francisco, CA, USA.

[18] Marco Steger, Carlo Alberto Boano, Thomas Niedermayr, Michael Karner, Joachim Hillebrand, Kay Roemer, and Werner Rom. An efficient and secure automotive wireless software update framework. In *IEEE Transactions on Industrial Informatics*, 14(5): 2181–2193, 2017.

[19] Tri P Doan and Subramaniam Ganesan. CAN crypto FPGA chip to secure data transmitted through CAN FD bus using AES-128 and SHA-1 algorithms with a symmetric key. Technical report, SAE Technical Paper, 2017.

[20] Feng Luo and Shuo Hou. Cyberattacks and countermeasures for intelligent and connected vehicles. *SAE International Journal of Passenger Cars-Electronic and Electrical Systems*, 12:55–66, 2019.

[21] Sigrid Gürgens and Daniel Zelle. A hardware based solution for freshness of secure onboard communication in vehicles. In *Computer Security*, pp. 53–68. Springer, 2018.

[22] ISO. Road vehicles – Functional safety– Part 6: Product Development at the Software Level, 2011.

[23] Bogdan Groza, Stefan Murvay, Anthony Van Herrewege, and Ingrid Verbauwhede. Libra-can: A lightweight broadcast authentication protocol for controller area networks. In *International Conference on Cryptology and Network Security*, pp. 185–200. Springer, 2012.

[24] Qiang Hu and Feng Luo. Review of secure communication approaches for in-vehicle network. *International Journal of Automotive Technology*, 19(5):879–894, 2018.

[25] R Escherich, I Ledendecker, C Schmal, B Kuhls, C Grothe, and F Scharberth. She–secure hardware extension–functional specification version 1.1. *Hersteller Initiative Software (HIS) AK Security*, 2009.

[26] Jin Seo Park, Dae Hyun Kim, and Il Hong Suh. Design and implementation of security function according to routing method in automotive gateway. *International Journal of Automotive Technology*, 22(1):19–25, 2021.

[27] Rafael Zalman and Albrecht Mayer. A secure but still safe and low cost automotive communication technique. In *Proceedings of the 51st Annual Design Automation Conference*, pp. 1–5, 2014.

[28] Didier Bourse, Markus Dillinger, Tim Farnham, Raquel Navarro, Nikolas Olaziregi, and Thomas Wiebke. SDR equipment in future mobile networks. In *IST Summit*, pp. 189–193, 2002.

[29] V. Jeyalakshmi and G. Vijayakumari. Secured reconfigurable software defined radio using ota software download. *International Journal of Advanced Networking and Applications*, 3(4):1276, 2012.

[30] Benjamin Weyl, Marko Wolf, Frank Zweers, Timo Gendrullis, M. Sabir Idrees, Y. Roudier, H. Schweppe, H. Platzdasch, R. El Khayari, O. Henniger, et al. Secure on-board architecture specification. *Evita Deliverable D*, 3:2, 2010.

[31] Trishank Karthik, Akan Brown, Sebastien Awwad, Damon McCoy, Russ Bielawski, Cameron Mott, Sam Lauzon, André Weimerskirch, and Justin Cappos. Uptane: Securing software updates for automobiles. In *International Conference on Embedded Security in Car*, pp. 1–11, 2016. Escar, Europe.

[32] Samuel Woo, Hyo Jin Jo, and Dong Hoon Lee. A practical wireless attack on the connected car and security protocol for in-vehicle can. *IEEE Transactions on Intelligent Transportation Systems*, 16(2):993–1006, 2014.

[33] Basker Palaniswamy, Seyit Camtepe, Ernest Foo, and Josef Pieprzyk. An efficient authentication scheme for intra-vehicular controller area network. *IEEE Transactions on Information Forensics and Security*, 15:3107–3122, 2020.

[34] Fiat chrysler to recall 1.4 million vehicles following remote hack, 2015.

[35] Guoqi Xie, Renfa Li, and Shiyan Hu. Security-aware obfuscated priority assignment for can fd messages in real-time parallel automotive applications. *IEEE Transactions on Computer-Aided Design of Integrated Circuits and Systems*, 39(12):4413–4425, 2020.

[36] Tobias Hoppe, Stefan Kiltz, and Jana Dittmann. Security threats to automotive can networks-practical examples and selected short-term countermeasures. In *SAFECOMP: International Conference on Computer Safety, Reliability, and Security*, pp. 235–248. Springer, 2008.

[37] Ulf E Larson, Dennis K Nilsson, and Erland Jonsson. An approach to specification-based attack detection for in-vehicle networks. In *2008 IEEE Intelligent Vehicles Symposium*, pp. 220–225. IEEE, 2008. Eindhoven, Netherlands.

[38] Vinayak Tanksale. Intrusion detection for controller area network using support vector machines. *2019 IEEE 16th International Conference on Mobile Ad Hoc and Sensor Systems Workshops (MASSW)*. IEEE, 2019. Monterey, CA, USA.

OntoEnricher

A Deep Learning Approach for Ontology Enrichment from Unstructured Text

Lalit Mohan Sanagavarapu, Vivek Iyer, and Y. Raghu Reddy

IIIT Hyderabad

CONTENTS

9.1 INTRODUCTION

In recent times, there is an exponential increase in the number of content providers and content consumers on the internet due to various reasons like improved digital literacy, affordable devices, better network, etc. Further, the number of internet-connected devices per

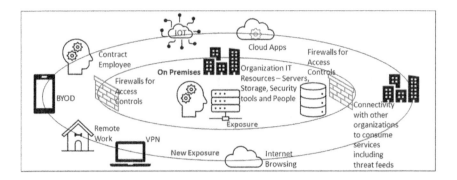

Figure 9.1 Changing Attack Surface.

person is expected to increase even more with adoption of emerging technologies such as Internet of Things and 5G. This change in users and usage is leading to an increase in data breaches[1]. In many cases, realization of an impact happens long after the attack. Figure 9.1 shows changing attack surface for organizations with remote work force and connected devices.

Typically, organizations invest in security tools and infrastructure that are based on rules, statistical models and machine learning (ML) techniques to identify and mitigate the risks arising from the threats. Firewalls, intrusion detection and prevention systems, authentication and authorization mechanisms to data and servers, encryption layers, anti-virus software, endpoint controls and permissions are some of the tools and processes are used to protect Information Technology (IT) systems. Apart from these controls and processes, IT systems are regularly patched to mitigate the risks.

In addition, organizations purchase threat intelligence feeds to continuously monitor IT infrastructure for anomaly detection. The subscription fee of threat intelligence feeds from service providers is expensive and to a large extent, it contains threat intelligence that is already available in public forums. Public forums such as blogs, discussion forums, government sites, social media channels including Twitter and others contain unstructured threat intelligence on vulnerabilities, attacks, and controls. Tech-savvy internet users interested in information security access public forums, search, and browse on security products, their configurations, reviews, vulnerabilities and other related content for awareness and to protect IT assets.

In recent years, organization's information security infrastructure use Structured Threat Information eXchange (STIX)/Trusted Automated Exchange of Intelligence Information (TAXII) knowledge representation from OASIS[2] to represent observable objects and their properties in the cyber domain. However, automated processing of unstructured text to generate STIX format is a formidable challenge [35]. Interestingly, there are transformations available to convert from XML based STIX format to ontological 'OWL' or 'RDF' formats, which in part, has influenced OASIS to adopt ontology for representations.

Evidently, the research to use unstructured security related content to enrich ontologies is gaining ground to mitigate risks related to zero-day attacks, malware characterization, digital forensics and incidence response and management [1,12,35]. Security ontologies are used to analyze vulnerabilities and model attacks [9,12,15,39]. The concepts, relationships and instances of security ontologies are used to validate level of defence-in-depth to protect IT assets, map security product features to controls which leads to assurance of the security infrastructure. The constraints and properties of ontologies allow root cause analysis of attacks. Additionally, given that security-related data is in structured, semi-structured or unstructured forms, unifying them with ontologies aids in situational awareness and readiness to defend an attack [35].

Traditionally, domain experts constructed and maintained ontologies. Given the extent of effort and cost involved, access to domain content and ability to process text with advanced natural language processing (NLP) techniques and ML models on powerful IT infrastructure opens up research opportunities to construct and manage ontologies. The information security ontologies can be constructed or enriched from unstructured text available on public forums, vulnerability databases such as National Vulnerability Database (NVD)[3] and other information security processing systems [2,31] sources. Also, standards and guidelines from ISO/IEC [13], NIST from US, ENISA from European Nation, Cloud Security Alliance (CSA) and others to protect confidentiality, integrity and availability of IT assets, contain embedded concepts. The ISO 27001:2015 [9] based security ontologies that encompass most of these guidelines are being extensively explored for protection, auditing and compliance checking. Hence, enrichment of ISO 27001 based ontology provides wider acceptance, easier management and interoperability.

In this work, we propose to enrich a widely accepted information security ontology instead of constructing a new ontology from text. This avoids inclusion of trivial concepts and relations. The success of enrichment also enables wider acceptance and usage by domain experts. However, the available literature on ontology enrichment from text is based on approaches utilizing word similarity and supervised ML models [12,32]. These ontology enrichment approaches, albeit useful to extract word-level concepts, are limited with respect to (a) extraction of longer concepts embedded in compound words and phrases (b) factoring context while identifying relevant concepts and (c) extracting and classifying instances [14].

In the proposed approach (*OntoEnricher*), we implemented a supervised sequential deep learning model that: a) factors context from grammatical and linguistic information encoded in the dependency paths of a sentence, and then b) utilizes sequential neural networks, such as Bidirectional Long Short Term Memory (LSTM) [34] to traverse (forward and backward directions) dependency paths and learn relevant path representations that constitute relations. Bidirectional LSTM model has ability to forget unrelated stream of data to identify related concepts that are available in the form of a word, a phrase or a sentence in the text. In addition, we utilized pre-trained transformer-based architecture of Universal Sentence Encoder (USE) [4] to handle distributional representations of compound words, phrases, and instances.

The proposed *OntoEnricher* is implemented on information security ontology. As availability of information security datasets is a concern, a semi-automatic approach with a training dataset of 97,425 related terms (hypernyms, hyponyms and instances) is extracted from DBpedia for all concepts of a information security ontology [9]. To learn syntactic and semantic dependency structure in sentences, a 2.6 GB training corpus on information security is extracted from Wikipedia of all terms in the ontology and the DBpedia dataset. The curated dataset and corpus are used to train bidirectional LSTM model in the proposed ontology enrichment approach. The trained model is tested to enrich concepts, relations, and instances in information security ontology from unstructured text on the internet. The *OntoEnricher* is also tested with 10% of training dataset, knocking out terms from ontology and unstructured text from web pages and achieved an average accuracy of 80%, which is better than current state-of-the-art approaches. As the text in corpus is multi-dimensional and dependency path gets generated for very matching pair of dataset terms, we used a high performance computing (HPC) cluster for training and testing of model faster [19]. The code and documentation of ontology enrichment pipeline are publicly available on GitHub for reuse and extension. The subsequent sections includes (a) an elaboration of *OntoEnricher* approach along with an example; (b) Experiment and Results; (c) Discussion and potential future work.

9.2 RELATED WORK

This section discusses related work on enrichment of ontologies from unstructured text as well as approaches to create and maintain information security ontologies. The work on enrichment of knowledge graphs (KG) from unstructured text is also discussed as it represents knowledge and contains similarities with ontologies.

Researchers worked on knowledge acquisition from text to construct ontologies for past couple of decades [3,20]. The last decade witnessed significant progress in the field of information extraction from web with projects such as DBpedia, Freebase and others. The work of Mitchell et. al [23] known as 'NELL' states that it is a never-ending system to learn from web, their work bootstraps knowledge graphs on a continuous basis. Tools such as ReVerb [8] and OLLIE [33] are based on open information systems to extract a triple from a sentence using syntactic and lexical patterns. Although these approaches extract triples from unstructured text using shallow and fast models, they do not handle ambiguity while entity mapping and do not learn expressive features compared to deep and multi-layer models.

The ML models based on probabilistic, neural networks and others are also explored for ontology enrichment from text [20,27,28]. In 2017, Wang et al [37] conducted a survey on knowledge graph completion, entity classification and resolution, and relation extraction. The study classified embedding techniques into translational distance models and semantic matching models. The study also stated that additional information in the form of entity types, textual descriptions, relation paths and logical rules strengthen the research. Deep learning models such as CNN [5], LSTM [18,25] and variants are used to construct knowledge graphs from text as they carry memory cells and forget gates to build the context and reduce noise. The work of Vedula et al. [36] proposed an approach to bootstrap newer ontologies from related domains.

Some of the recent approaches are based on Word2Vec [38] and its variants such as Phrase2Vec or Doc2Vec that use distributional similarities to identify concepts to enrich an ontology. However, these approaches underperform in the extraction of concepts embedded in words, phrases and sentences due to their inability to adequately characterize context. Compared to Word2Vec and its variants, Universal Sentence Encoder (USE) [4] stands promising to identify concepts in long phrases as it encodes text into high dimensional vectors for semantic similarity. Lately, researchers [10] are exploring USE to produce sentence embeddings and deduce semantic closeness in queries. Although, transformer-based models such as BERT and XLNet [7,21] are of interest to ontology enrichment researchers, training them to a domain is effort intensive.

The literature to enrich security ontologies from text drew attention with OASIS's STIX/TAXII standardization and open source threat intelligence. Most of the current work on security ontologies from text (construction or enrichment) are based on usage of string, substring, pre-fix and post-fix matching of terms, Word2Vec and other basic ML models [26,28,35]. In ontologies as well, the deep learning approaches based on recurrent neural networks are trending because of their ability to build the context over multiple words [11,15]. The research of Houssem et al. [11] used LSTM for population of security ontologies. However, the details to create corpus, handle phrases and robustness of the approach are not elaborated, only 40 entities are used in the model. The literature revealed that security ontologies based on ISO 27001 [9] and MITRE Corporation's cyber security effort [35] are most referred.

9.3 ONTOLOGY ENRICHMENT APPROACH

In the proposed approach, whenever a new concept is introduced, current memory state of LSTMs are updated to replace old concept, or add new concept by multiplying with forget gates as needed. The concept in current memory are mapped to instances and relations

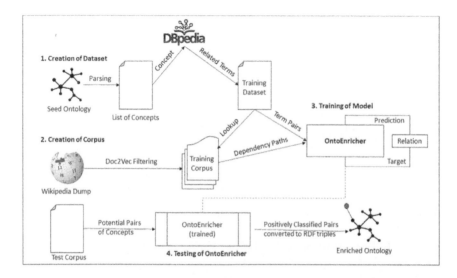

Figure 9.2 Ontology Enrichment Approach.

between concepts in current state are constructed. Concepts extracted are used to update the ontology automatically or after manual validation by a domain expert.

The *OntoEnricher* enriches a seed ontology with concepts, relations and instances extracted from unstructured text. As shown in Figure 9.2, the ontology enrichment approach consists of four stages: (i) *DatasetCreation* : creates training dataset by extracting and curating related terms from DBpedia for all concepts in the ontology (ii) *CorpusCreation* : creates domain-specific training corpus by parsing Wikipedia dump using various filtering measures (iii) *Training* : trains *OntoEnricher* for relation classification of term pairs using training dataset and corpus, and (iv) *Testing* : tests the approach by enriching the ontology from domain-specific web pages.

9.3.1   Stage 1: Creation of Dataset

The information security seed ontology is based on ISO 27001 [9]. The standard ISO 27001:2015 [13] contains 114 controls across 14 groups. These groups are 'Human Resources', 'Asset Management', 'Access Control', 'Cryptography', 'Physical and environmental', 'Operations', 'Communications', 'System development and acquisition', 'Business

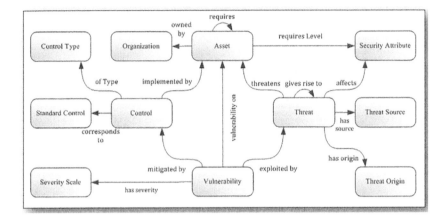

Figure 9.3 Information Security Upper Ontology [9].

Continuity', 'Supplier relations', 'Information security incident management', 'Compliance', 'Security Policies' and 'Security organisation'. These groups and controls are represented as 408 concepts in the security ontology to protect assets from vulnerabilities and threats. The upper ontology of the seed ontology is shown in Figure 9.3 and the ontology is available on GitHub.

These 408 concepts are extracted from security ontology 'to query related terms, namely hypernyms and hyponyms from DBpedia. DBpedia contains over 5 million entities, allows querying of semantic relationships, concepts and properties encoded in the form of RDF triples.

Typically, the RDF triples (subject-verb-object) in an ontology contain a 'verb' relationship between concepts. Verbs are typically domain-specific and unavailable in general-purpose knowledge graphs like DBPedia. Hypernyms and hyponyms that denote 'is-a' relationship between concepts, are easily available in DBPedia and widely used in ontologies, making these relations an ideal choice to demonstrate *OntoEnricher* approach. The SPARQL queries (query 9.3.1) to extract hypernyms and hyponyms from DBpedia for concepts in information security ontology are:

SELECT * WHERE {<http://dbpedia.org/resource/""""+ concept + """"> <http://purl.org/linguistics/gold/hypernym> ?hypernyms}

SELECT * WHERE {?hypernyms <http://purl.org/linguistics/gold/hypernym> <http://dbpedia.org/resource/""""+ concept + """">}

TABLE 9.1 Composition
of the Dataset

Relationship	Count
Hypernymy	2,939
Hyponymy	794
Instances	2,685
Concepts	1,187
None	4,490
Total	12,096

The extracted terms with SPARQL queries are converted to triples of the form $(a, b, label)$ where a denotes the ontology concept, b denotes the DBPedia term and $label$ determines the DBPedia relation between a and b. This leads to a dataset of 97,425 triples. These triples are then curated by three domain experts and authors to mark unrelated terms as 'none'. This includes pairs that are not related to the domain and pairs that are not related to each other, as both these cases are not needed for ontology enrichment. In addition, since DBPedia often categorizes ontological instances under 'hyponyms', some pairs are separately labelled as 'instances' if b is an instance of a or as a 'concept' if b denotes the concept of which a is an instance. The terms classified include names of experts, organizations, products and tools, attacks, vulnerabilities, malware, virus and many others. Finally, since the number of 'none' pairs (89,820) is significantly higher than the number of 'non-none' (7,605) pairs, 'none' pairs are sorted in order of increasing similarity. The first 5% of 'none' pairs are filtered out, this is experimentally determined to yield better results. Table 9.1 shows composition of dataset after extraction, curation and filtration.

9.3.2 Stage 2: Creation of Corpus

Once the training dataset is created, a training corpus to provide linguistic information for all terms in the dataset is extracted. Wikipedia is used as it is moderated and structured for model training. The DBPedia is a part of the Wikipedia project, and therefore assures unambigous articles of all extracted dataset terms. As a first step, all corresponding Wikipedia articles for terms in the dataset are extracted and added to the corpus. In addition, other articles related to the information security ontology domain are also extracted. This is done by comparing Doc2Vec [17] similarity of each article with the Wikipedia article on 'Information Security'[4] and then filtering in articles with a similarity score higher than a certain threshold (0.27 after manual validation). This threshold is determined to optimize classification accuracy after a validation with a sample corpus. The two-step filtering yielded a 2.6 GB size information security training corpus.

9.3.3 Stage 3: Training *OntoEnricher*

Training dataset and corpus are parsed to generate various dependency paths to connect each pair of terms provided in the training dataset. Here, 'dependency paths' refers to the multi-set of all paths that connect a pair of terms in the training corpus. These paths are encoded as a sequence of nodes, where each node is a 4-tuple of the form $(word, POS\_tag, dep\_tag, dir)$. The POS_tag and dep_tag denote POS and dependency tags of the word respectively, while dir denotes the direction of the edge connecting it to the next node in that dependency path. The term pairs along with extracted dependency paths between them are passed to *OntoEnricher* for training.

Figure 9.4 shows the architecture diagram of *OntoEnricher*. The first layer in proposed model is the embedding layer. The distributional embeddings for the terms (words) are obtained using a pre-trained state-of-the-art Universal Sentence Encoder (USE) [4] model. This model is preferred over other vocabulary-based distributional models such as Word2Vec, Glove and others as it returns distributional embeddings for not just single words, but also compound words, phrases and sentences. In addition, USE is pretrained on Wikipedia along with other corpora, making it suited for this task. Apart from pre-trained word embeddings, embeddings for POS tags, dependency tags and direction tags are obtained from trainable embedding layers. The node embeddings constructed from the concatenation of words, POS, dependency, and direction tag embeddings are arranged in a sequence to obtain path embeddings. A dropout layer is applied after each embedding. The path embeddings for each path connecting the term pair are then input to a bidirectional, two-layer LSTM which trains on a sequence of linguistically and semantically encoded nodes and learns the type of sequences that characterize a particular kind of relation. The bidirectional LSTM allows the network to have both

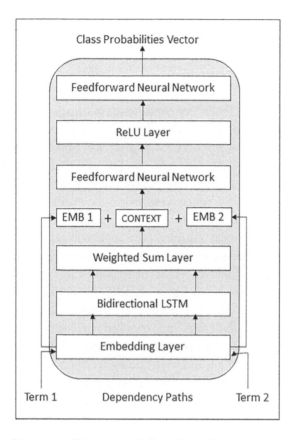

Figure 9.4 Architecture Diagram of OntoEnricher.

backward and forward information about the path embeddings at every time step, while the two layers enable capturing of complex relations among dependency paths.

The output of last hidden state of LSTM is taken as the path representation. Since a pair of terms may have multiple paths between them, a weighted sum of these path representations is taken by using path counts as weights, to yield a final context vector. This context vector encodes syntactic and linguistic information, is passed through a dropout layer and then concatenated with distributional embeddings of both terms in order to encode semantic information. The concatenated vector is then passed through two Feedfoward Neural Networks with a Rectifier Linear Unit (ReLU) layer in between, to yield final class probability vector. The class with maximum probability is output as predicted relation between the term pair.

9.3.4 Stage 4: Testing *OntoEnricher*

The procedure to extract concepts and instances from (web page) text, during testing stage is detailed here. To avoid usage of every unstructured (web page) text to enrich an ontology, a lightweight evaluation technique [30] that checks for sufficiency of new security terms is deployed. After passing the sufficiency evaluation as a pre-processing stage, co-reference resolution is applied and then noun chunks are extracted from web page. A cartesian product (nC_2) is taken of extracted noun chunks to construct potential term pairs. However, a cartesian product to *OntoEnricher* is computationally expensive and also leads to error propagation. A two-stage filtering is applied to validate (a) if noun chunks are 'sufficiently' related to Information Security and (b) if they are 'sufficiently' related to each other. Both these conditions are checked to compare distributional similarity using USE against experimentally determined threshold values. The sufficiently similar term pairs are then input to pre-trained model to classify the relationship. The pairs classified as 'None' are discarded and the rest are converted to RDF triples for information security ontology enrichment.

9.3.5 Example

Figure 9.5 illustrates ontology enrichment approach with an example. 'Real-time adaptive security' (R-TAS) is a concept present in information security ontology. The corresponding article in DBPedia, 'Real-time adaptive security' has 'model' as its hypernymy entry, which is returned using a SPARQL query. The information security corpus extracted from Wikipedia dump using Doc2Vec filter contains multiple paired mentions of these terms, out of which one article contains two mentions. The corpus, the aforementioned sentences, are passed to SpaCy[5] dependency parser and all corresponding dependency paths to connect are extracted for every term pair. These dependency paths which contain encoded linguistic information are passed to a serialization layer that converts the dependency graph into a series of nodes to form the input to *OntoEnricher*.

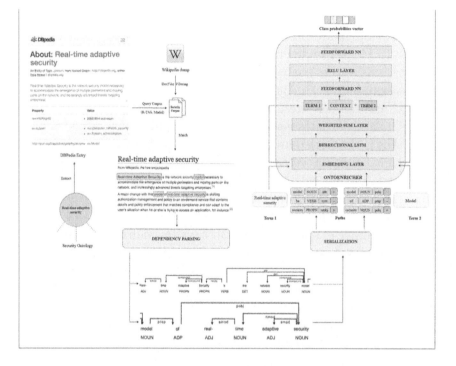

Figure 9.5 An Example Illustrating Ontology Enrichment Approach.

The serialization layer reduces the word in every node in the dependency path to its lemma, a root word to enable meaningful training and generalization. Thus, 'Real-time adaptive security' is reduced to 'security' and 'is' is reduced to 'be'. It also converts every node to a feature vector. The 'Real-time adaptive security' is converted to a feature vector that uses 'security' as the word, 'PROPN' as POS tag, 'nsubj' as dependency tag and '+' denotes the direction of the edge connecting it to the lowest common root node between the term pair. Similarly, the next word 'be' is a verb and a root word of 'is' does not have any direction '∼'. The last word of this path, 'model', has 'NOUN' as POS tag, 'attr' as dependency tag and '+' as direction of the arrow going away from 'model' to 'is'.

The same approach is followed for second dependency path and nodes are sequenced similarly. These two paths are then passed to the embedding layer that calculates (i) USE embedding for word (ii) POS tag embedding (iii) dependency tag embedding and (iv) direction embedding. The last 3 embeddings are trainable while word embeddings are pre-trained using USE. These are concatenated together to yield a node embedding. All paths (node sequences) that connect term pair are passed as input to Bidirectional two-layer LSTM. In this example, both the paths connecting 'Real-Time Adaptive Security' and 'model' are input to LSTM, post which the last hidden state is taken as path-wise contextual output. A weighted sum of these paths is then calculated using frequency of occurrence as weights to yield final context vector, this has encoded linguistic information of paths that connect 'R-TAS' and 'model'. This context vector is concatenated with distributional embeddings of 'Real-Time Adapative Security' and 'model'. Reducing words to their root form during serialization stage enables to construct a contextualized representation. The characterized paths constitutes a specific relation and the most frequent ones, while distributional word and phrase embeddings enable semantic relevance and specificity at a conceptual level. This concatenated vector denotes semantic and linguistic information that are passed to 2 Feedforward Neural Networks with a ReLU layer in between, yielding a final class probability vector as output. This class probability vector is trained to identify relationship between 'model' and 'Real-Time Adapative Security' as hypernymy.

9.4 EXPERIMENTAL SETTINGS AND RESULTS

The experiment is conducted with two ontologies, namely the ISO 27001-based information security and Stanford pizza ontologies. While the former is focus of this section and use case to build knowledge base, pizza ontology is used to demonstrate generalizability of the approach. Table 9.2 shows the composition of information security and pizza datasets respectively. While the information security corpus is 2.8 GB in volume, interestingly, the pizza corpus is significantly smaller and only 95 MB. This can be attributed to the fact that the pizza ontology represents a very narrow domain ('pizza' out of food domain) and thus contains few relevant Wiki articles. Information security ontology contains broader, systems-level concepts, information about assets, controls etc. that return a variety of related articles.

The *OntoEnricher* is implemented using deep learning library Pytorch with '0' as random seed number for consistency in results.

TABLE 9.2   Dataset Composition

Parameters	Security	Pizza
# of Concepts	408	143
Dataset size	12,096	7,119
Corpus size	2.8GB	95MB

Also, various other Python libraries such as Pronto[6] to extract ontology terms, Wikiextractor[7] to extract articles from Wikipedia dump, spaCy for dependency graph extraction, and Tensorflow-Hub to load Universal Sentence Encoder are used. The deployed HPC expedites training and testing performance of *OntoEnricher*, this also aids in parallel processing of adding or retrieving concepts, relations and instances from ontology. The performance of *OntoEnricher* is evaluated on three diverse test datasets:

1. DBPedia test dataset: This is created by randomly extracting 10% of the training dataset extracted from DBpedia. It mostly consists of small-medium length words.

2. 'Knocked-out' test dataset: This is created by knocking out concepts and relations from the seed ontology. This evaluates the ability of *OntoEnricher* to identify multi-word or phrase-level concepts, as is common in information security ontology, and identification of highly-domain specific, non-English terms as in pizza ontology.

3. Instance dataset: This is created by extracting text from security-domain related web pages. The top 10 vulnerability related web pages from OWASP and product pages on 'firewall' are extracted to test the model. The ability to identify concepts and instances from web pages confirms that *OntoEnricher* can use text from public forums and other unstructured data sources. This evaluation is done without factoring sufficiency requirement [30] of new terms in text to evaluate identification of ontology terms by *OntoEnricher*.

Table 9.3 shows optimized hyper parameters after tuning *OntoEnricher*. Grid search is used to experiment with and arrive at optimal values of various hyper parameters. It includes hidden dimensions (120,

TABLE 9.3   Hyperparameters of the Model

Hyperparameters	Security	Pizza
Activation Function	Log Softmax	Log Softmax
Number of Layers	2	2
Hidden Dimension of LSTM	180	250
Input Dimension (2nd NN)	120	90
Embedding layer Dropout	0.35	0.35
Hidden layer Dropout	0.8	0.8
Hidden layer Dropout	0.8	0.8
Optimizer	AdamW	AdamW
Loss function	NLL Loss	NLL Loss
Epochs	200	200
Learning Rate	0.001	0.001
Weight Decay	0.001	0.001
Weight Initialization	Xavier	Xavier

TABLE 9.4   Security Ontology Enrichment Results

Metrics	DBPedia	Knocked Out	Web Page
Terms	1197	5538	153
Accuracy	0.81	0.77	0.83
Precision	0.76	0.84	0.84
Recall	0.76	0.77	0.73
F1-Score	0.76	0.80	0.78

180, 200, 250, 300, 500, 900), input dimension of 2nd NN (60, 90, 120, 180, 300, 500), number of LSTM layers (1,2), activation functions (Softmax, ReLU, LogSoftmax), loss functions (NLL Loss, Cross Entropy loss), and learning and weight decay rates (0.001, 0.01). The experimentation data with various embeddings, epochs, learning rate, activation functions, hidden layers and the related results are available as spreadsheet on GitHub.

The evaluation results of *OntoEnricher* on information security and pizza ontologies are shown in Tables 9.4 and 9.6 respectively. A competent and comparable scores on information security ontology enrichment with all three datasets are achieved. The test results with 10% test dataset performed better, while test results on knockout concepts or information security related web pages are not far apart, proving that performance did not dip in extraction of phrases, multi-word concepts and instances which is a key component missing from previous ontology enrichment approaches. As input and output format of existing approaches are different, only a qualitative comparison is performed and shown in Table 9.5. Additionally, in *OntoEnricher*, the number of terms and the size of the corpus used for training and testing are much larger. It is observed that the difference between precision and recall value is less, indicates that terms are not skewed towards domain and establishes robustness of the proposed *OntoEnricher* approach.

Interestingly, the pizza enrichment results shown in Table 9.6 are better than security enrichment results, presumably due to domain being narrow as mentioned earlier and concepts are easily identifiable as a consequence.

Most of the existing ontology evaluation metrics [29] are extensions of Precision and Recall information retrieval metrics. Hence, precision score for k documents (shown in Table 9.7) is measured to validate consistency in ontology enrichment with web pages. The scores indicate that the proposed approach can identify concepts for any large number of domain documents. Figure 9.6 shows the relationship accuracy for each of the classes. It is observable that all relationships are classified equally and hypernymy classification seems to be relatively higher.

9.5 CONCLUSION AND FUTURE WORK

The implemented information security ontology enrichment approach is comprehensive with the ability to handle new terms, changing domain content that includes concepts, relations and instances. Usage of well accepted ISO 27001 based security ontology, an exhaustive data source such as DBpedia and Wikipedia, Universal Sentence Encoder for distributional embeddings and Bidirectional LSTM for sequential learning makes it extensible to other domains as well. In the implemented enrichment approach, concepts in seed ontology can be a single or multiple words, is an improvement from state-of-the-art. The approach also incorporated instances from unstructured text (web pages) so that organizations or individuals have flexibility to reason information security ontologies for mitigation strategies, vulnerabilities assessment, attack graphs detection and many other use cases. The enriched security ontology can also be used by search

TABLE 9.5 Comparison of Ontology Enrichment Approaches

Approach	Dataset	Model	Evaluation Metric	Observation
Relation between two named entities identified using NER technique [28]	Open source threat intelligence	Neural Network and Word2Vec	96% as accuracy	Single words are only handled and there is no base ontology. Evaluation is performed on pre-trained data
Dual Iterative Pattern Relation Expansion for relation extraction [16]	Security related articles from web page	Semi-supervised learning models	82% as accuracy	Not enough volume of training data to validate scalability and generalizability. Ontology and dataset details are not available
Named Entity recognition to identify vulnerabilities and relations [24]	NVD, DBPedia and other open source threat intelligence	Support Vector Machines	90% as accuracy	Only vulnerability related words are handled and there is no base ontology. Evaluation is performed on pre-trained data

TABLE 9.5 (*Continued*)
Comparison of Ontology Enrichment Approaches

Approach	Dataset	Model	Evaluation Metric	Observation
Malware text classification [22]	Malware-TextDB	Convolutional Neural Network and Conditional Random Field	25 – 36% as accuracy	Used Glove for word embeddings that is not fully context sensitive
Named Entities are considered as concepts in security content [11]	NVD, Microsoft Bulletins	Long Short Term Memory and Conditional Random Field	96% as accuracy	The dataset was similar and there are no references to handle multi-word and instances
Entity extraction from DBPedia [6]	Wikipedia and DBPedia	Semantic Role Labeler and co-reference resolution	66.3% as F1 score	No base ontology and references to handle multi-words or instances

TABLE 9.6   Pizza Ontology Enrichment Results

Metrics	DBPedia	Knocked Out	Web Page
Terms	791	85	99
Accuracy	0.99	0.79	0.88
Precision	0.81	0.99	0.84
Recall	0.91	0.79	0.81
F1-Score	0.86	0.88	0.82

TABLE 9.7   Precision Scores for 20 Random Web Pages in Information Security

Web pages	P@5	P@10	P@15	P@20
Score	0.89	0.80	0.82	0.84

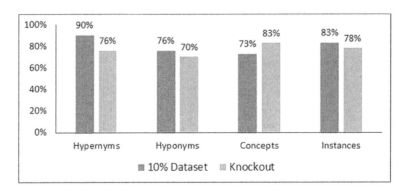

Figure 9.6 Accuracy on Class Identification in Information Security Ontology.

engines to display relevant results, top trends in vulnerabilities, threats, attacks and controls. The implemented *OntoEnricher* is trained on 408 information security ontology terms, 97,425 DBpedia terms and 2.8 GB size Wikipedia articles with a HPC cluster. The *OntoEnricher* is tested with 20 random information security related web pages extracted from internet with an accuracy of 80% and an F1-score of 78%. While state-of-the-art results are achieved in this work, the following activities are being explored as future work -

- Optimize effort required to create DBPedia dataset such as filtering out irrelevant terms.

- Test the approach with other security ontologies and extend training corpus beyond Wikipedia.

- Compare results with other knowledge graph and ontology enrichment approaches after curation of input and output format of dataset and corpus.

- While there is a need for domain experts to evaluate an enriched ontology, it is effort intensive and brings in other dependencies. A syntactic and semantic evaluation with a easily configurable rules and AI models to reduce effort.

NOTES

1 https://digitalguardian.com/blog/history-data-breaches
2 https://www.oasis-open.org/
3 https://nvd.nist.gov
4 https://en.wikipedia.org/wiki/Information_security
5 https://spacy.io/
6 https://pypi.org/project/pronto/
7 https://github.com/attardi/wikiextractor

REFERENCES

[1] Fatima N Al-Aswadi, Huah Yong Chan, and Keng Hoon Gan. Automatic Ontology Construction from Text: a Review from Shallow to Deep Learning Trend. *Artificial Intelligence Review*, pages 1–28, 2019.

[2] AlienVault. *Open Threat Intelligence*, February 2021. https://otx.alienvault.com/.

[3] Paul Buitelaar, Philipp Cimiano, and Bernardo Magnini. *Ontology Learning from Text: Methods, Evaluation and Applications*, volume 123. IOS Press, 2005.

[4] Daniel Cer, Yinfei Yang, Sheng-yi Kong, Nan Hua, Nicole Limtiaco, Rhomni St John, Noah Constant, Mario Guajardo-Cespedes, Steve Yuan, Chris Tar, et al. Universal Sentence Encoder. *ArXiv preprint arXiv:1803.11175*, 2018.

[5] Tim Dettmers, Pasquale Minervini, Pontus Stenetorp, and Sebastian Riedel. Convolutional 2D Knowledge Graph Embeddings. In *32nd AAAI Conference on Artificial Intelligence*, 2018.

[6] Peter Exner and Pierre Nugues. Entity Extraction: From Unstructured Text to DBpedia RDF Triples. In *Proceedings of the WoLE@ ISWC*, pages 58–69, 2012.

[7] Aysu Ezen-Can. A Comparison of LSTM and BERT for Small Corpus. *arXiv preprint arXiv:2009.05451*, 2020.

[8] Anthony Fader, Stephen Soderland, and Oren Etzioni. Identifying Relations for Open Information Extraction. In *Proceedings of the Conference on Empirical Methods in Natural Language Processing*, pages 1535–1545. ACL, 2011.

[9] Stefan Fenz and Andreas Ekelhart. Formalizing Information Security Knowledge. In *Proceedings of the 4th International Symposium on Information, Computer, and Communications Security*. ACM, 2009.

[10] Balaji Ganesan, Riddhiman Dasgupta, Akshay Parekh, Hima Patel, and Berthold Reinwald. A Neural Architecture for Person Ontology Population. *arXiv preprint arXiv:2001.08013*, 2020.

[11] Houssem Gasmi, Jannik Laval, and Abdelaziz Bouras. Cold-start Cybersecurity Ontology Population using Information Extraction with LSTM. In *International Conference on Cyber Security for Emerging Technologies*, pages 1–6. IEEE, 2019.

[12] Michael Iannacone, Shawn Bohn, Grant Nakamura, John Gerth, Kelly Huffer, Robert Bridges, Erik Ferragut, and John Goodall. Developing an Ontology for Cyber Security Knowledge Graphs. In *Proceedings of the 10th Annual Cyber and Information Security Research Conference*, pages 1–4, 2015.

[13] ISO/IEC 27001. *Information Security Management*, February 2021. https://www.iso.org/isoiec-27001-information-security.html.

[14] Vivek Iyer, Lalit Mohan, Y Raghu Reddy, and Mehar Bhatia. A Survey on Ontology Enrichment from Text. *Proceedings of the 16th International Conference on Natural Language Processing*, 2019.

[15] Yan Jia, Yulu Qi, Huaijun Shang, Rong Jiang, and Aiping Li. A Practical Approach to Constructing a Knowledge Graph for Cybersecurity. *Engineering*, 4(1):53–60, 2018.

[16] Corinne L Jones, Robert A Bridges, Kelly MT Huffer, and John R Goodall. Towards a Relation Extraction Framework for Cyber-security Concepts. In *Proceedings of the 10th Annual Cyber and Information Security Research Conference*, pages 1–4, 2015.

[17] Jey Han Lau and Timothy Baldwin. An Empirical Evaluation of Doc2Vec with Practical Insights into Document Embedding Generation. *arXiv preprint arXiv:1607.05368*, 2016.

[18] Diya Li, Lifu Huang, Heng Ji, and Jiawei Han. Biomedical Event Extraction based on Knowledge-driven Tree-LSTM. In *NAACL-HLT 2019: Annual Conference of the North American Chapter of the Association for Computational Linguistics*, pages 1421–1430, 2019.

[19] Robert Lim. Methods for Accelerating Machine Learning in High Performance Computing. *University of Oregon—Area-2019-01*, 2019.

[20] Kaihong Liu, William R Hogan, and Rebecca S Crowley. Natural Language Processing Methods and Systems for Biomedical Ontology Learning. *Journal of Biomedical Informatics*, 44(1):163–179, 2011.

[21] Qi Liu, Matt J Kusner, and Phil Blunsom. A Survey on Contextual Embeddings. *arXiv preprint arXiv:2003.07278*, 2020.

[22] R Manikandan, Krishna Madgula, and Snehanshu Saha. Cybersecurity Text Analysis using Convolutional Neural Network and Conditional Random Fields. In *Proceedings of the 12th International Workshop on Semantic Evaluation*, pages 868–873, 2018.

[23] Tom Mitchell, William Cohen, Estevam Hruschka, Partha Talukdar, Bishan Yang, Justin Betteridge, Andrew Carlson, Bhanava Dalvi, Matt Gardner, Bryan Kisiel, et al. Never-Ending Learning. *Communications of the ACM*, 61(5):103–115, 2018.

[24] Varish Mulwad, Wenjia Li, Anupam Joshi, Tim Finin, and Krishnamurthy Viswanathan. Extracting Information about Security Vulnerabilities from Web Text. In *Proceedings of the IEEE/WIC/ACM International Conferences on Web Intelligence and Intelligent Agent Technology*, volume 3, pages 257–260. IEEE, 2011.

[25] Binling Nie and Shouqian Sun. Knowledge Graph Embedding via Reasoning over Entities, Relations, and Text. *Future Generation Computer Systems*, 91:426–433, 2019.

[26] Leo Obrst, Penny Chase, and Richard Markeloff. Developing an Ontology of the Cyber Security Domain. In *STIDS*, pages 49–56, 2012.

[27] Georgios Petasis, Vangelis Karkaletsis, Georgios Paliouras, Anastasia Krithara, and Elias Zavitsanos. Ontology Population and Enrichment: State of the Art. In *Knowledge-driven Multimedia Information Extraction and Ontology Evolution*, pages 134–166. Springer, 2011.

[28] Aditya Pingle, Aritran Piplai, Sudip Mittal, Anupam Joshi, James Holt, and Richard Zak. RelExt: Relation Extraction using Deep Learning Approaches for Cybersecurity Knowledge Graph Improvement. In *Proceedings of the 2019 IEEE/ACM International Conference on Advances in Social Networks Analysis and Mining*, pages 879–886, 2019.

[29] Marta Sabou, Chris Wroe, Carole Goble, and Gilad Mishne. Learning Domain Ontologies for Web Service Descriptions: An Experiment in Bioinformatics. In *Proceedings of the 14th International Conference on World Wide Web*, pages 190–198, 2005.

[30] Lalit Sanagavarapu, Sai Gollapudi, S. Chimalakonda, Y. Reddy, and Venkatesh Choppella. A Lightweight Approach for Evaluating Sufficiency of Ontologies. In *SEKE*, 2017.

[31] Lalit Mohan Sanagavarapu, Neeraj Mathur, Shriyansh Agrawal, and Y Raghu Reddy. SIREN-Security Information Retrieval and Extraction eNgine. In *European Conference on Information Retrieval*, pages 811–814. Springer, 2018.

[32] Carla Sayan, Salim Hariri, and George L Ball. Semantic Knowledge Architecture for Cyber Security. In *Proceedings of the International Conference on Security and Management (SAM)*, pages 69–76. The Steering Committee of The World Congress in Computer Science, Computer Engineering, and Applied Computing, 2019.

[33] Michael Schmitz, Robert Bart, Stephen Soderland, Oren Etzioni, et al. Open Language Learning for Information Extraction. In *Proceedings of the Joint Conference on Empirical Methods in Natural Language Processing and Computational Natural Language Learning*, pages 523–534. Association for Computational Linguistics, 2012.

[34] M. Schuster and K. K. Paliwal. Bidirectional Recurrent Neural Networks. *IEEE Transactions on Signal Processing*, 45(11):2673–2681, 1997.

[35] Zareen Syed, Ankur Padia, Tim Finin, Lisa Mathews, and Anupam Joshi. UCO: A Unified Cybersecurity Ontology. In *Workshops at the 30th AAAI Conference on Artificial Intelligence*, 2016.

[36] Nikhita Vedula, Pranav Maneriker, and Srinivasan Parthasarathy. BOLT-K: Bootstrapping Ontology Learning via Transfer of Knowledge. In *The World Wide Web Conference*, pages 1897–1908, 2019.

[37] Quan Wang, Zhendong Mao, Bin Wang, and Li Guo. Knowledge Graph Embedding: A Survey of Approaches and Applications. *IEEE Transactions on Knowledge and Data Engineering*, 29(12):2724–2743, 2017.

[38] Gerhard Wohlgenannt and Filip Minic. Using Word2Vec to Build a Simple Ontology Learning System. In *International Semantic Web Conference*, 2016.

[39] Huangjie Zheng, Yuchen Wang, Chen Han, Fangjie Le, Ruan He, and Jialiang Lu. Learning and Applying Ontology for Machine Learning in Cyber Attack Detection. In *17th IEEE International Conference On Trust, Security And Privacy In Computing And Communications/ 12th IEEE International Conference On Big Data Science And Engineering*, pages 1309–1315, 2018.

Intelligent Connected Vehicles

Wufei Wu

Nanchang University

Ryo Kurachi and Gang Zeng

Nagoya University

Yuhao Wang

Nanchang University

Hiroaki Takada

Nagoya University

Keqin Li

State University of New York

CONTENTS

DOI: 10.1201/9781003155799-10

10.1 INTRODUCTION

With the rapid development of information and communication technology, more and more intelligent connected vehicles are entering people's lives. While intelligent connected vehicles bring safety, efficiency, comfort, and convenience to people's travel, due to the increase in external communication interfaces and bandwidth, cybersecurity issues have become one of the key issues that intelligent networked vehicles need to solve urgently.

10.1.1 Intelligent Connected Vehicle (ICV)

From the perspective of the network, as a mobile terminal in the Internet of vehicles architecture, the intelligent connected vehicle (ICV) is a heterogeneous, distributed, real-time system, as shown in Figure 10.1. The in-vehicle electronic control units (ECUs) are connected via a network bus such as controller area network (CAN), local interconnect network (LIN) and FlexRay. The in-vehicle information exchange between different networks is realized through gateways. The network architecture presents the characteristics of heterogeneous, real-time, safety-critical and cost-sensitive [1]. Therefore, its main features can be summarized as follows:

1. Rich External Interfaces: With the development of vehicle wireless communication technology (V2X, vehicle to everything), intelligent networked vehicles have the characteristics of interconnection; that is, the vehicle will no longer be an independent electronic system, but a mobile terminal under the framework of Internet of vehicles. To realize the information exchange between

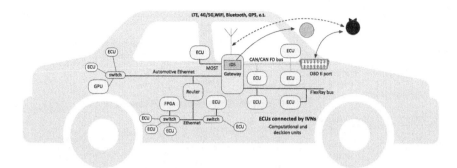

Figure 10.1 The electronic system structure of the intelligent connected vehicle from the network perspective.

vehicle and X (other vehicles, road, person, cloud computing platform, etc.), it will be equipped with a wealth of external communication interfaces (Bluetooth, GPS, 4G/5G, Wi-Fi, etc.). At the same time, the increase in communication demand and the abundance of external interfaces will lead to the diversification of entry and forms of cyberattacks.

2. A Large Amount of Real-Time Data: In-vehicle infotainment (IVI), electronic cockpit (e-cockpit), advanced driver-assistance system (ADAS), autonomous driving driven by cameras, artificial intelligence (AI), and sensors (such as LiDAR and radar) will generate a large amount of data that require real-time transmission and processing. However, the existing in-vehicle network protocol cannot meet its bandwidth requirements, and general-purpose Ethernet (Ethernet) cannot provide deterministic delay protection. In order to meet the ever-increasing bandwidth requirements of automotive functions, in recent years, high-speed vehicle network protocols with deterministic delay characteristics have been developed rapidly, such as time-sensitive vehicle Ethernet, FlexRay [2], and Ethernet TSN [3], among which FlexRay is used in the drive-by-wire system to take advantage of its deterministic time delay.

3. Heterogeneous Network Environment: For a long time, due to the balance of cost and performance, automotive electronic systems have been in a state of coexistence of multiple network protocols.

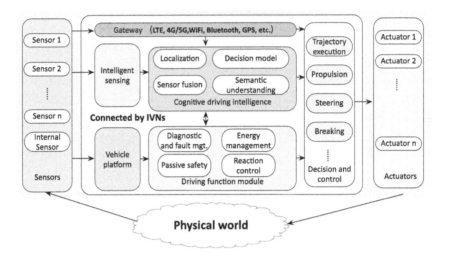

Figure 10.2 Intelligent connected vehicles' decision-making framework.

Different network protocols are used in different functional domains. For example, the FlexRay [2] is used as backbone, the high-speed CAN [4] is used for power train and diagnosis systems, and the low-cost LIN [5] is used for body control. These different networks are interconnected through a gateway to build an overall vehicle network architecture.

4. Lack of Cybersecurity Protection Mechanism: The traditional vehicle is a relatively independent and closed individual, and the in-vehicle network design did not consider external network security threats at the beginning; that is, the existing network protocol lacks basic security mechanisms (such as authentication, encryption, and message authentication). Intelligent connected vehicles' decision-making framework is shown in Figure 10.2. From the framework, we can find that due to the increase in communication between the in-vehicle network and the external network, the cybersecurity threats faced by intelligent networked vehicles may come from various network layers. With the development of the intelligent networked vehicle architecture, the intelligent networked vehicle will be more like a mobile terminal node. It is urgent to carry out research on the cybersecurity enhancement technology of the terminal node of the ICVs to improve cybersecurity.

10.1.2   Contributions and Chapter Organization

This chapter provides the following contributions: review of the cybersecurity issues in the ICV environment; evaluation of the current cryptographic, authentication, and intrusion detection approaches used for protecting ICV; and challenges and potential future research directions for ICV cybersecurity. The contents of this chapter are as follows: Section 10.2 reviews the cybersecurity issues in the ICV environment. Section 10.3 summarizes and compares the current major ICV cybersecurity enhancement countermeasures. In Section 10.4, we introduce the current research status of intrusion detection for IVNs. Section 10.5 summarizes the current trend and describes the future outlook of intrusion detection for IVNs.

10.2   CYBERSECURITY ANALYSIS OF IN-VEHICLE NETWORK

The existing in-vehicle networks such as CAN and FlexRay lack mechanism design at the beginning of the design, which makes the in-vehicle network extremely vulnerable to different types of attacks such as DoS (Denial-of-Service), fuzzing, spoofing and replay. Its vulnerability is mainly reflected in the following three aspects.

1) Weak Access Control: The physical layer of the in-vehicle network is a twisted-pair or coaxial cable, which has the characteristics of simple access and lack of abnormal access detection functions. It is easy to be accessed illegally and cannot guarantee availability and integrity.

2) No Data Encryption Guarantee: The internal message transmission is only encoded according to the function, and the lack of encryption protection in terms of information security can easily lead to theft and tampering of the message, and the authenticity of the message cannot be guaranteed.

3) No Message Authentication Mechanism: Messages are only calibrated by the message ID and used as a receiving filter, which is vulnerable to attacks such as DoS (denial of service), replay, and fuzzing. For example, the current CAN and FlexRay specifications only provide cyclic redundancy check (CRC) codes for message integrity and error verification functions and lack a node authentication mechanism.

10.2.1   In-Vehicle Networks of ICV

Moreover, the in-vehicle network has the characteristics of hetero-geneous, distributed, safety-critical and real-time. Its heterogeneity not only is reflected in the hardware platform, but also includes the heterogeneity of the network [1]. A structure diagram of an in-vehicle network composed of multiple functional domains interconnected through a gateway is shown in Figure 10.3. In order to ensure functional safety, intelligent networked vehicles require the vehicle network to prioritize deterministic delay and hard real-time performance at the data link layer and, at the same time, have a higher anti-interference ability at the physical layer. In-vehicle networks can be divided into two types: time-triggered (TT) and event-triggered (ET). TT refers to the time point as the communication trigger condition, which is generally realized by means of timing and time synchronization. ET means that the communication trigger condition is the occurrence of a certain event. For example, when an automobile airbag system detects a collision event, the ECU where the trigger sensor is located sends a data frame containing control parameters to detonate the airbag.

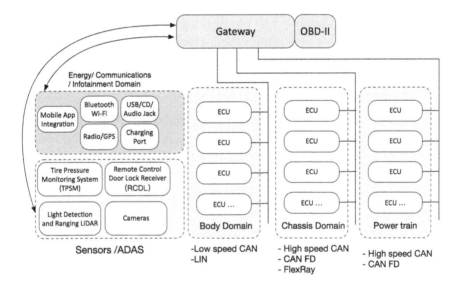

Figure 10.3   In-vehicle network structure diagram, which is composed of multiple functional domains interconnected through gateways.

The current time-triggered networks in vehicle networks mainly include TTEthernet [6], TTP/C [7], and TTCAN [8]. The TT network has the characteristics of high bandwidth and deterministic transmission delay, which makes up for the lack of deterministic delay of the ET network. It can be applied to the field of wire-controlled braking, but it also has high node deployment costs and relatively high system scalability. ET-type networks such as LIN and CAN have better performance in terms of flexibility, scalability and cost.

According to the difference in bandwidth and functional domain, the Society of Automotive Engineers (SAE) classifies network protocols into four categories: A, B, C, and D. As shown in Table 10.1, different network protocols are different in node cost, bandwidth, minimum response time, and scalability, and are suitable for different automotive functional domains [9]. For example, Class A bus is generally used for body control, such as luggage opening and closing, window control, and other occasions with small data volume. As a new generation of in-vehicle network protocol standard, FlexRay can be used in fields that require high real-time and reliability of message transmission, such as brake-by-wire. It is worth mentioning that FlexRay is a TT and ET hybrid in-vehicle network.

TABLE 10.1 Classification of In-Vehicle Networks

Class	Protocol	Domain	Robustness	Cost
A	LIN	Vehicle body control	Low	Low
B	Low-speed CAN CAN2.0 TTP/A	Body electronics non-diagnostic and safety-critical data	Medium	Low
C	High-speed CAN TTP/C CAN-FD	Transmission device mobile device diagnosis wire control	High	Medium
D	FlexRay	Power train chassis domain	High	High
	MOST Ethernet	Multimedia (audio, video)	Low	High
	Safe-by-wire Byte-flight	Safety-related real-time and reliable areas	High	High

10.2.2   Vulnerabilities and Cybersecurity Requirements

The current in-vehicle network standard protocol CAN lacks message authentication and data encryption mechanisms at the beginning of its design. As more consumer electronic products can be easily accessed, intelligent networked vehicles make automobiles become smart mobile devices with wheels, and the advancement of software and data services has gradually become the core competitiveness of automobiles. If the research and deployment of in-vehicle network security enhancements are not carried out in time, they will suffer from various malicious attacks due to potential security vulnerabilities [10].

From the perspective of attack entry, in recent years, cybersecuiry threats to automobiles can be divided into three implementation methods: direct physical access attacks, short-range wireless attacks, and long-range wireless attacks. As shown in Figure 10.4, direct physical attacks are mainly through illegal access to CAN, OBD diagnostic interfaces, etc. As shown in Figure 10.5, short-range wireless attacks are mainly through illegal access of Bluetooth and wireless sensor channels, and remote attacks are mainly through Wi-Fi and mobile digital cellular network ports to achieve illegal access, as shown in Figure 10.6.

10.2.3   Attack Model and Vulnerabilities from External Interface Layer

Attacks from the sensing layer (physical layer). With the development of ICV technology, more and more smart sensors will be assembled on

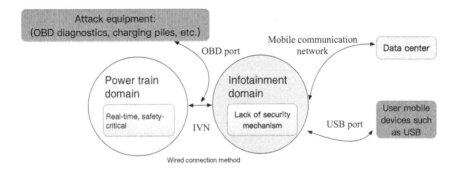

Figure 10.4 Direct physical access attacks through USB, OBD-II, and other interfaces.

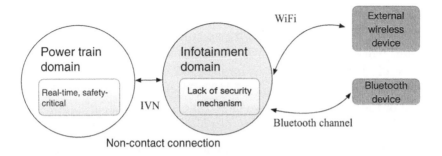

Figure 10.5 Short-range wireless access attacks through wireless interfaces such as Bluetooth and Wi-Fi.

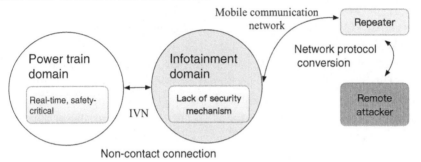

Figure 10.6 Use of repeater to achieve remote intrusion and vehicle control.

vehicles, such as LiDAR, millimeter-wave radar, cameras, and GPS, which can collect external environment perception information and provide the ability to perceive the environment for autonomous driving decision making. Therefore, attacking the vehicle through the physical layer will become a new threat to the security of the in-vehicle network. For example, in Ref. [11], Rouf et al. proposed an attack that interfered with the tire pressure monitoring system through a radio channel, causing the vehicle tire pressure monitoring system to fail. In Ref. [10], Tao et al. used a radio channel to achieve an attack on the keyless start system and illegally started the target vehicle.

10.2.4 Attack Model and Vulnerabilities from Network Layer

Due to the lack of data encryption and message authentication mechanisms in the in-vehicle network, once an attacker can access the network device, the attack can be easily carried out. The attack modes of the data link layer include frame injection, frame forgery, frame sniffing, pause, and DoS attacks. The availability of the network will be severely threatened. For example, Cho et al. implemented a DoS attack on the data link layer of the vehicle CAN, which led to the failure of the entire automotive electronic system [12].

10.2.5 Attack Model and Vulnerabilities from Application Layer

In recent years, there have been many reports on exploiting vulnerabilities in external network interfaces and equipment to implement remote network attacks on vehicles [13–15]. Attack entrances include Bluetooth, OBD-II, and Wi-Fi. At the application layer of IVN, attackers can conduct more targeted attacks that are not easily detected, such as remotely controlling or braking a vehicle [16–18]. Since this type of attack has no illegal access to nodes and obvious data frame anomalies, it is more difficult to detect. In response to this type of attacks, researchers mainly focus on the design of intrusion detection methods based on machine learning [11,19]. Currently, there are mainly problems such as excessive consumption of computing resources, lack of test data sets, and model evaluation.

10.3 OVERVIEW OF INTELLIGENT CONNECTED VEHICLE CYBERSECURITY ENHANCEMENT COUNTERMEASURES

Cybersecurity is one of the problems that ICV needs to solve urgently. However, due to the cost and real-time constraints of the in-vehicle network, automotive electronic systems are sensitive to bandwidth and computing resources, which results in many traditional information security enhancement technologies that cannot be directly applied to the in-vehicle network environment. In recent years, in response to this problem, relevant researchers have carried out a series of research work. As shown in Table 10.2, there are many classic methods, such as encryption, digital signatures, and message authentication. The method of data encryption can improve the integrity and correctness of network message transmission, but faces the problem of balancing security and computing resources. Message authentication can improve the accuracy of network message transmission, but it mainly faces

TABLE 10.2 Comparison and Analysis of In-Vehicle Network Security Enhancement Technologies

Technology	Network Layer	Representative Literature and Technology	CIA
Data encryption	Data link layer	Lightweight AES [20] Hardware cartographic acceleration module [21] MAC decomposition transmission [22]	Security Integrity Correctness
MAC	Physical layer, data link layer	TESLA [17] MAuth-CAN [23] One-way hash linked list [24]	Correctness
IDS	Physical layer Data link layer Application layer	One-class SVM [25] Deep neural network [26] Bayesian network [27] RNN-LSTM [28]	Availability Completeness

design constraints brought by network bandwidth. Intrusion detection can enhance the protection of network availability and integrity. The current main challenge is to improve detection accuracy and robustness and to reduce false alarm rate and detection response time. The remaining sections focus on the cybersecurity threats of in-vehicle networks in the intelligent networked vehicle environment and summarize the following three technologies.

10.3.1 Hardware Security Module

Encryption and authentication are widely used in the security field of communication channels, and this technology is also widely used on in-vehicle network environments (where MAC technology has been included in the AUTOSAR protocol specification). However, the traditional message encryption and authentication technology faces the problems of heterogeneous architecture, and limited bandwidth and computing resources on in-vehicle network environment. Therefore, in order to reduce the additional time overhead caused by encryption operations, message authentication and encryption on in-vehicle network usually adopt lightweight and hardware acceleration methods, such as the use of programmable logic device for Advanced Encryption Standard (AES), elliptic-curve ciphers, etc. For example, the use of programmable logic devices to implement the Advanced Encryption Standard (AES) arithmetic module to achieve the purpose of acceleration. In [20], Hou et al. realized elliptic curve cryptography (ECC) operation acceleration. In Ref.[21], Zelle et al. realized a tailored version of the hash algorithm through the field programmable gate array (PFGA). In Ref. [22], Mertol transmitted multiple messages to one MAC, etc.

In view of the shortage of computing resources on in-vehicle network environment and the additional time overhead caused by message encryption for network communication, in Ref. [29], Wang et al. used the addition of hardware modules to solve the problem of the calculation time of the encryption algorithm, which effectively reduces the effect of message encryption on the network. The disadvantage of performance impact is that it will increase the cost of hardware deployment.

In order to deal with the vulnerabilities and attack models of various vehicle-mounted ECUs, in Ref. [30], Siddiqui et al. proposed a hardware-based secure and trusted framework. In addition, a two-way authentication and encryption technology based on lightweight physical unclonable functions is implemented on the vehicle CAN. At the same time, a lightweight security encryption algorithm for non-secure communication channels is designed. Experimental results show that the time overhead for sending an encrypted data frame at 1 Mbit/s on-board CAN is 108 μs. In Ref. [31], Gu et al. optimized information such as digital signatures and authentication codes through the optimization of the message distribution layer from the level of message encapsulation and scheduling, and distributed tasks to the vehicle ECU, thereby reducing the impact of message encryption and authentication on network time performance. At the same time, no additional hardware cost overhead is generated, and its disadvantage is that the network protocol is extremely complicated.

10.3.2 Message Authentication

In Ref. [32], Herrewege et al. proposed a variety of lightweight message authentication protocols for in-vehicle CAN to protect vehicles from camouflage attacks. In Ref. [23], Jo et al. designed a new authentication protocol – MAuth-CAN, which can achieve a balance between the network bandwidth consumption and the prevention of masquerading attacks without modifying the CAN hardware controller. In addition, in Ref. [24], Kang Ki Dong proposed a lightweight source authentication protocol using a one-way hash chain in CAN, which has an attack elastic tree algorithm and can be deployed through ECU firmware updates. Analysis shows that the protocol has high security. The experimental platform combined with virtual ECU (implementation on CANoe) and FreescaleS12XF shows that the protocol has obvious advantages in terms of authentication time, response time, and service delay.

The lightweight message authentication protocol design can solve the problem of the lack of security authentication design of the CAN protocol and ensure the authenticity of in-vehicle network communication. Considering the current in-vehicle network bandwidth resources and message response time requirements, there exist problems in the design of the existing message authentication protocol, and the main challenge lies in how to improve the security of message authentication while avoiding the reliability and real-time problems caused by message scheduling due to communication bandwidth consumption.

10.3.3 Intrusion Detection System (IDS)

Intrusion detection systems have the characteristics of small bandwidth resources and easy deployment of existing vehicles and are more suitable for resource- and cost-constrained in-vehicle networks. IDS can be divided into host-based IDS and network-based IDS according to the data source. According to the detection technology, it can be divided into methods based on information theory and statistical analysis, feature observation, machine learning, etc. In the following sections, we will focus on the technical progress of intrusion detection technology for in-vehicle networks.

10.4 STATE-OF-THE-ART IN-VEHICLE NETWORK INTRUSION DETECTION APPROACHES

Compared with other cybersecurity enhancement methods such as data encryption and message authentication. Intrusion detection has the characteristics of small bandwidth resources and easy deployment of existing vehicles. It is more suitable for in-vehicle networks with limited resources and costs. According to the data source, intrusion detection can be divided into host-based IDS and network-based IDS. According to detection technology, it can be divided into methods based on information theory and statistical analysis, detection methods based on feature observation, and detection methods based on machine learning, as shown in Figure 10.7. This chapter mainly focuses on the realization

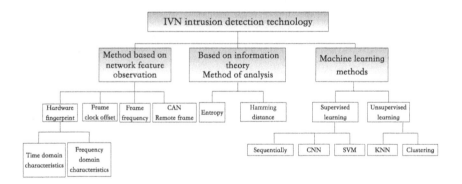

Figure 10.7 Classification of intrusion detection technologies for existing in-vehicle networks.

method of intrusion detection technology for in-vehicle networks. The following will summarize and analyze the existing research work from three different aspects.

10.4.1 Feature-Based Observation Approaches

Feature observation is one of the commonly used methods of intrusion detection and is currently widely used in the research of intrusion detection on in-vehicle networks [33]. Through the analysis of the in-vehicle network architecture and network protocol, it is found that the network features that can be used for intrusion detection and observation mainly include device fingerprints (extracted by time-domain and frequency-domain information) [34], clock offset [35], message period [36], and remote frame [37]. For example, in Ref. [38], Zeng designed a vehicle-mounted CAN intrusion detection technology based on Snort rules on the basis of fully analyzing the byte- and bit-level characteristics of the CAN network and designed and implemented a complete vehicle-mounted CAN intrusion detection technology. The validity of abnormal rule detection is verified by experiments.

In recent years, using the uniqueness of ECU electrical character-istics to establish device fingerprint information has become a popular method for tracing the source of in-vehicle network attacks and has widely been used on in-vehicle network intrusion detection research. This method was first proposed by Cho et al. in [39], and then in Ref. [40], Song et al. realized intrusion detection through the extraction and statistics of network signal features. In Ref. [37], Lee et al. used the return value delay and time interval of CAN network periodic messages as the source of device fingerprint information and achieved good detection results. In Ref. [28], Yang et al. used the RNN-LSTM classifier to construct the ECU fingerprint signal in the frequency domain. Experiments show that this method can effectively detect flooding attacks. In Ref. [41], Ning and Liu proposed a LOF-based attack detection scheme, which uses the voltage physical characteristics of the CAN frame to determine whether the message is sent by a legitimate electronic control unit (ECU). The proposed algorithm has low time and space complexity. Experimental data obtained under real in-vehicle network environment show that the recognition accuracy of specific attack models can reach more than 98%.

Methods based on the observation of network characteristics can often achieve high detection accuracy for specific attack models, with short response time and low network bandwidth overhead [42]. However, considering the characteristics of the long life cycle of automobiles (about 20 years) and the dynamic changes of the network environment, the robustness and adaptive ability of detection methods need to be further strengthened.

10.4.2 Statistical Analysis-Based Approaches

By collecting 667.3 million CAN messages and analyzing the information entropy, it is found that the average value of the information entropy in the vehicle CAN network is 11.436 [29]. When malicious attacks occur (such as DoS and replay), the information entropy of the vehicle CAN network will be significantly reduced. This feature is widely used in resource-constrained vehicle network intrusion detection research [43–45]. For example, in Ref. [43], Marchetti et al. evaluated intrusion detection algorithms for vehicle networks based on information theory, and their research found that using a single information theory model can only be effective against a single flooding attack in vehicle network intrusion detection and evaluation. In Ref. [44], Muter and Asaj used the concept of information entropy for the intrusion detection of vehicle-mounted network for the first time and limited the evaluation range of information entropy to CAN message ID. Using this feature, the intrusion state can be quickly detected. For identification, it has the characteristics of short detection response time (the fastest intrusion attack can be found within 0.01 ms). In Ref. [42], Wu et al. proposed a sliding window strategy based on a fixed number of messages. Compared with the traditional sliding window strategy with a fixed time window, this scheme can effectively avoid the problem of the on-board CAN network. The improved method effectively solves the problem of information entropy jitter caused by periodic messages. Experiments show that this scheme can effectively improve the detection accuracy of intrusion detection for vehicle network based on information entropy in response to flooding and replay attacks, and the detection response time is evaluated.

Qin et al. carried out a series of research works on vehicle network anomaly detection using the method of information theory. First of all, in Ref. [46], their theoretical analysis and experiments proved the effectiveness of using information entropy to detect attacks such as replay and flooding on the in-vehicle CAN network. Then in Ref. [47], Yan improved CAN bus anomaly detection method based on Renyi information entropy, which effectively improved the detection accuracy, but is still limited to the detection of replay and flooding attack models. In addition, in Ref. [48], a CAN message anomaly detection method based on the random forest model was proposed and a large amount of data collected by real vehicles were used to construct the random forest classification algorithm for many adjustments. Experiments show that appropriate network feature parameters have a significant impact on improving the effectiveness of vehicle network anomaly detection.

The existing research on vehicle network intrusion detection methods based on information theory often ignores the impact of vehicle network information entropy jitters caused by different states of vehicles on the detection results. The detection model has high detection accuracy under limited vehicle states, but the robustness to different vehicle states needs to be improved. These problems cause such methods to fail to meet the current Automotive Safety Integrity Level (ASIL) and high-level security requirements. Therefore, the optimization of in-vehicle network intrusion detection algorithm for state awareness by sensing vehicle state is worthy of future research.

10.4.3 Artificial Intelligence-Based Approaches

Machine learning, neural network, and other theories have also become popular directions for research on intrusion detection technology for in-vehicle networks [49–51]. For the first time, in Ref. [25], Andreas et al. proposed to use an SVM with a radial basis function (RBF) kernel to learn baseline normal behavior and classify deviations as anomalies. The generated classifier is suitable for message time series. Later, in Ref. [26], Kang and Kang designed a vehicle network intrusion detection technology that uses a deep neural network (DNN). By training the vehicle network packet messages exchanged between ECUs, low-dimensional features are extracted and used to distinguish normal and hacker groups. In Ref. [27], the author uses the Bayesian network method to quickly identify malicious message attacks on the CAN network and uses CARLA to simulate CAN network messages in

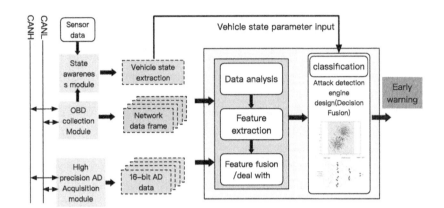

Figure 10.8   Artificial intelligence-based IDS for IVNs.

various operating states of real cars. Its shortcoming lies in its detection accuracy, only 86%, which resulted in the inability to meet the functional safety-critical requirements of the ISO26262 specification [52].

The experimental results of the above methods show that machine learning has a good effect on the intrusion detection of unknown attack models in the vehicle network. As shown in Figure 10.8, the artificial intelligence-based IDS used for IVNs needs to process a large amount of data in real time, which places higher requirements on the computing resources and network bandwidth of the automotive electronic system. However, in the in-vehicle network environment, due to the limitations of computing, storage, and communication bandwidth, how the existing machine learning-based intrusion detection method can reduce the computational complexity and the consumption of the in-vehicle network communication bandwidth is a problem that needs to be further solved. At the same time, the intrusion detection system is also required to improve the detection accuracy, reduce the false alarm rate, and reduce the detection response time. Improving the robustness of the system is also the direction that the intrusion detection system needs to be further improved. Moreover, for Automotive Cyber-Physical Systems (ACPS), due to its key functional safety attributes, the authenticity and reliability of the network are the most important information security requirements. In order to solve the above problems, it is urgent to carry out research on intrusion detection model and algorithm design of in-vehicle networks.

10.5 SUMMARY AND FUTURE RESEARCH

In recent years, the security of the ICV has aroused widespread concern in the industry and academia. One of the focuses is the development of anti-attack algorithms and architectures around the vehicle network. Combining the development trend of intelligent networked vehicles mentioned above and the latest research progress in the current in-vehicle network security, this chapter further puts forward some open issues in the field of intelligent networked vehicle cybersecurity. Regarding the security issues of the intelligent networked vehicle network, some open issues and future research directions are summarized as follows.

1. How to improve the accuracy of intrusion detection and reduce the response time? The failure to detect malicious attacks on the vehicle network in time brings serious functional security threats. Intrusion detection is used as an important means of enhancing the cybersecurity of intelligent networked vehicles to improve detection accuracy, reduce false alarm rate, shorten detection response time, and improve system robustness. It is one of the most urgent problems to be solved in the research of intrusion detection technology for in-vehicle network in the future.

2. How to achieve accurate network security testing and evaluation? Due to the increasing complexity of heterogeneous software and hardware components used in intelligent networked vehicles in the future, new attacks against in-vehicle networks will continue to appear. The complexity of these new components and on-board systems brings more challenges to the development of efficient and adaptable on-board cybersecurity mechanisms, but also brings difficulties to cybersecurity testing and verification; for example, to verify an intrusion detection model and algorithms, it is necessary to simulate the vehicle network information flow in the case of cyberattacks in the real vehicle network environment. The acquisition and generation of test data will further affect the accuracy and effect of detection. How to evaluate the security of the in-vehicle networks has not yet formed a unified solution.

3. How to deal with unknown cyberattacks on ICVs? Taking into account the characteristics of the long life cycle of automobiles

(about 20 years) and the dynamic changes of the network environment, there are three main problems in the existing research. The first is that the detection method often corresponds to a specific attack model, the second is that the robustness of the detection effect is not strong (there are many prerequisites, and the perception of the state of the vehicle is lacking), and the third is the lack of evaluation of the detection response time and functional safety. In view of the impact, considering the key attributes of ACPS functional safety, it is urgent to solve the above problems through optimization research of intrusion detection models and algorithms, so as to avoid serious safety crisis of intelligent networked vehicles caused by cybersecurity problems.

REFERENCES

[1] Wufei Wu. Research on intrusion detection and cybersecurity enhancement design for new in-vehicle network environment. PhD thesis, Hunan University, 2018.

[2] Robert Shaw and Brendan Jackman. An introduction to flexray as an industrial network. In *2008 IEEE International Symposium on Industrial Electronics*, pp. 1849–1854, Cambridge, 2008.

[3] Lin Zhao, Feng He, Ershuai Li, and Jun Lu. Comparison of time sensitive networking (TSN) and ttethernet. In *2018 IEEE/AIAA 37th Digital Avionics Systems Conference (DASC)*, pp. 1–7, London, 2018.

[4] Bosch. Can specifications. 1991.

[5] AUTOSAR. Specification of lin interface. 2017.12.

[6] Miladin Sandic, Bogdan Pavkovic, and Nikola Teslic. Ttethernet mixed-critical communication: Overview and impact of faulty switches. *IEEE Consumer Electronics Magazine*, 9(4):97–103, 2020.

[7] Howard Curtis and Robert France. Time triggered protocol (ttp/c): A safety-critical system protocol, 1999.

[8] B.T. Fijalkowski., 2011. *Time Triggered Controller Area Networking*. Springer, Netherlands, 2011.

[9] Xuezhe Wei, Zhechang Sun and Juexiao Chen. Classification method of networks in automotive and developing trend of corresponding main protocols. *Journal of Tongji University*, 6:762–766, 2004.

[10] Internet of Vehicles Network Security Committee. White paper on Internet of vehicles network security. Internet of Vehicles Network Security Committee, China, 2016.

[11] Ishtiaq Rouf, Rob Miller, Hossen Mustafa, Travis Taylor, Sangho Oh, Wenyuan Xu, Marco Gruteser, Wade Trappe, and Ivan Seskar. Security and privacy vulnerabilities of in-car wireless networks: A tire pressure monitoring system case study. In *Proceedings of Usenix Security Symposium*,pp. 323–338, Washington, DC, August 11–13, 2010.

[12] Kyong-Tak Cho and Kang G. Shin. Error handling of in-vehicle networks makes them vulnerable. In *Proceedings of the 2016 ACM SIGSAC Conference on Computer and Communications Security CCS'16*, pp. 1044–1055, New York. Association for Computing Machinery, 2016.

[13] Ian Foster, Andrew Prudhomme, Karl Koscher, and Stefan Savage. Fast and vulnerable: A story of telematic failures. In *9th USENIX Workshop on Offensive Technologies (WOOT 15)*, Washington, DC. USENIX Association, August 2015.

[14] Karl Koscher, Alexei Czeskis, Franziska Roesner, Shwetak Patel, Tadayoshi Kohno, Stephen Checkoway, Damon McCoy, Brian Kantor, Danny Anderson, Hovav Shacham, and Stefan Savage. Experimental security analysis of a modern automobile. In *2010 IEEE Symposium on Security and Privacy*, pp. 447–462, Oakland, CA, 2010.

[15] Joey Sun, Shahrear Iqbal, Najmeh Seifollahpour Arabi, and Mohammad Zulkernine. A classification of attacks to in-vehicle components (IVCS). *Vehicular Communications*, 25:100253, 2020.

[16] Stephen Checkoway, Damon McCoy, Brian Kantor, Danny Anderson, Hovav Shacham, Stefan Savage, Karl Koscher, Alexei Czeskis, Franziska Roesner, and Tadayoshi Kohno. Comprehensive experimental analyses of automotive attack surfaces. In *20th USENIX Security Symposium (USENIX Security 11)*, San Francisco, CA, USENIX Association, August 2011.

[17] Keen Security Lab. Car hacking research: Remote attack tesla motors, 2017.

[18] Samuel Woo, Hyojin Jo, and Dong Hoon Lee. A practical wireless attack on the connected car and security protocol for in-vehicle can. *IEEE Transactions on Intelligent Transportation Systems*, 16(2):993–1006, 2015.

[19] Adrian Taylor, Sylvain Leblanc, and Nathalie Japkowicz. Anomaly detection in automobile control network data with long short-term memory networks. In *IEEE International Conference on Data Science and Advanced Analytics*, pp. 130–139, Montreal, QC, 2016.

[20] Shuo Hou and Feng Luo. Cyberattacks and countermeasures for intelligent and connected vehicles. *Cars-Electronic and Electrical Systems*, 12(1):55–66, 2019.

[21] Zelle Daniel and Gürgens Sigrid. A hardware based solution for freshness of secure onboard communication in vehicles. In *InComputer Security*, pp. 53–68, Berlin, DE. Springer, 2018.

[22] Sarp Mertol. Secure message authentication protocol for CAN. PhD thesis, Middle East Technical University, Ankar, Turkey, 2020.

[23] Hyo Jin Jo, Jin Hyun Kim, Hyon Young Choi, Wonsuk Choi, Dong Hoon Lee, and Insup Lee. Mauth-can Masquerade-attack-proof authentication for in-vehicle networks. *IEEE Transactions on Vehicular Technology*, 69(2):2204–2218, 2020.

[24] Kang Ki Dong. A practical and lightweight source authentication protocol using one-way hash chain in can. Master thesis, DGIST University, 2017.

[25] Andreas Theissler. Anomaly detection in recordings from in-vehicle networks. *Big Data and Applications*, 3:23–29, 2014.

[26] Min-Ju Kang and Je-Won Kang. A novel intrusion detection method using deep neural network for in-vehicle network security. In *2016 IEEE 83rd Vehicular Technology Conference (VTC Spring)*, pp. 1–5, Nanjing, China, 2016.

[27] Mario Casillo, Simone Coppola, Massimo De Santo, Francesco Pascale, and Emanuele Santonicola. Embedded intrusion detection system for detecting attacks over can-bus. In *2019 4th International Conference on System Reliability and Safety (ICSRS)*, pp. 136–141, 2019.

[28] Yun Yang, Zongtao Duan, and Mark Tehranipoor. Identify a spoofing attack on an in-vehicle can bus based on the deep features of an ECU fingerprint signal. *Smart Cities*, 3(1):17–30, 2020.

[29] Wang Eric, Xu William, Sastry Suhas, Liu Songsong, and Zeng Kai. Hardware module-based message authentication in intra-vehicle networks. In *Proceedings of the 8th International Conference on Cyber-Physical Systems*, pp. 207–216. ACM, 2017.

[30] Ali Shuja Siddiqui, Yutian Gui, Jim Plusquellic, and Fareena Saqib. Secure communication over canbus. In *2017 IEEE 60th International Midwest Symposium on Circuits and Systems*, pp. 1264–1267, Boston, MA. IEEE Press, August 2017.

[31] Zonghua Gu, Gang Han, Haibo Zeng, and Qingling Zhao. Security-aware mapping and scheduling with hardware co-processors for flexray-based distributed embedded systems. *IEEE Transactions on Parallel and Distributed Systems*, 27(10):3044–3057, 2016.

[32] Anthony Van Herrewege, Dave Singelee, and Ingrid Verbauwhede. Canauth-a simple, backward compatible broadcast authentication protocol for can bus. In *ECRYPT Workshop on Lightweight Cryptography*, vol. 2011, Louvain-la-Neuve, Belgium, 2011.

[33] Wufei Wu, Renfa Li, Guoqi Xie, Jiyao An, Yang Bai, Jia Zhou, and Keqin Li. A survey of intrusion detection for in-vehicle networks. *IEEE Transactions on Intelligent Transportation Systems*, 21(3):919–933, 2020.

[34] Kyong-Tak Cho and Kang G. Shin. Fingerprinting electronic control units for vehicle intrusion detection. In *Proceedings of the 25th USENIX Conference on Security Symposium SEC'16*, pp. 911–927. USENIX Association, Austin, TX, 2016.

[35] Subir Halder, Mauro Conti, and Sajal K. Das. Coids: A clock offset based intrusion detection system for controller area networks. In *Proceedings of the 21st International Conference on Distributed Computing and Networking, ICDCN 2020*, New York. Association for Computing Machinery, 2020.

[36] Cao Yongwei. Researh and design of intrusion detection. PhD thesis, Chongqing University of Posts and Telecommunications, 2019.

[37] Hyunsung Lee, Seong Hoon Jeong, Huy Kang Kim. OTIDS: A novel intrusion detection system for in-vehicle network by using remote frame. *2017 15th Annual Conference on Privacy, Security and Trust (PST) IEEE*, 2018.

[38] Fan Zeng. Research and implementation of networked vehicle intrusion detection system. PhD thesis, University of Electronic Science and Technology of China, 2018.

[39] Kyong-Tak Cho and Kang G. Shin. Viden: Attacker identification on in-vehicle networks. In *Proceedings of the 2017 ACM SIGSAC Conference on Computer and Communications Security, CCS 2017*, pp. 1109–1123, Dallas, TX, October 30 to November 03, 2017.

[40] Hyun Min Song, Ha Rang Kim, and Huy Kang Kim. Intrusion detection system based on the analysis of time intervals of can messages for in-vehicle network. In *2016 International Conference on Information Networking (ICOIN)*, pp. 63–68. IEEE, Kota Kinabalu, Malaysia, 2016.

[41] Jing Ning and Jiajia Liu. An experimental study towards attacker identification in automotive networks. In *2019 IEEE Global Communications Conference (GLOBECOM)*, pp. 1–6, Waikoloa, HI, 2019.

[42] Wufei Wu, Yizhi Huang, Ryo Kurachi, Gang Zeng, Guoqi Xie, Renfa Li, and Keqin Li. Sliding window optimized information entropy analysis method for intrusion detection on in-vehicle networks. *IEEE Access*, 6:45233–45245, 2018.

[43] Mirco Marchetti, Dario Stabili, Alessandro Guido, and Michele Cola-janni. Evaluation of anomaly detection for in-vehicle networks through information-theoretic algorithms. In *2016 IEEE 2nd International Forum on Research and Technologies for Society and Industry Leveraging a Better Tomorrow (RTSI)*, pp. 1–6, Bologna, Italy, 2016.

[44] Michael Müter and Naim Asaj. Entropy-based anomaly detection for in-vehicle networks. In *2011 IEEE Intelligent Vehicles Symposium (IV)*, pp. 1110–1115, Baden-Baden, German, 2011.

[45] Franco van Wyk, Yiyang Wang, Anahita Khojandi, and Neda Masoud. Real-time sensor anomaly detection and identification in automated vehicles. *IEEE Transactions on Intelligent Transportation Systems*, 21(3):1264–1276, 2020.

[46] Yu He, Qin Hegui, Sun Minghui, yan Xin, and Wang Xuanze. On-board can bus network security issues and anomaly detection methods. *Journal of Jilin University(Engineering and Technology Edition)*, 46(04):2016–1253, 2016.

[47] Yan Xin. CAN bus anomaly detection method based on Renyi information entropy. PhD thesis, Jilin University, 2017.

[48] Wu Lingyun, Qin Guihe, and Yu He. Anomaly detection method of vehicle can bus based on random forest. *Journal of Jilin University(Engineering and Technology Edition)*, 56(3):663–668, 2018.

[49] Yi Wang, Dan Wei Ming Chia, and Yajun Ha. Vulnerability of deep learning model based anomaly detection in vehicle network. In *2020 IEEE 63rd International Midwest Symposium on Circuits and Systems (MWSCAS)*, pp. 293–296, Springfield, MA, 2020.

[50] Yubin Lin, Chengbin Chen, Fen Xiao, Omid Avatefipour, Khalid Alsubhi, and Arda Yunianta. An evolutionary deep learning anomaly detection framework for in-vehicle networks - can bus. *IEEE Transactions on Industry Applications*, pp. 1–1, 2020.

[51] Zadid Khan, Mashrur Chowdhury, Mhafuzul Islam, Chin-Ya Huang, and Mizanur Rahman. Long short-term memory neural network-based attack detection model for in-vehicle network security. *IEEE Sensors Letters*, 4(6):1–4, 2020.

[52] ISO. Road vehicles-functional safety, ISO 26262. *International Organization for Standardization in ISO 26262*, 2011.

Toward Robust Deep Learning Systems against Deepfake for Digital Forensics

Hongmei Chi and Mingming Peng

Florida A&M University

CONTENTS

DOI: 10.1201/9781003155799-11

11.1 INTRODUCTION

The past three years witnessed a flourishing development of deepfake technology and deepfake products. As an open-source, low-cost, high-fun technology, deepfake closely integrates with the rapid development of social media and mobile economy and has quickly become a threat to challenge the law, personal privacy, and even national security. The booming of this technology has alerted law enforcement and practitioners. The past president of Society of Police Futurists International Joseph Schafer [2] has written about his concerns that it will profoundly implicate the policing if people could control the video with the help of deepfake technology. He mentioned that deepfake users could easily eliminate citizen's resistance in a video of police use of force. He calls for attention and action on deepfake issues among the law enforcement "before matters escalate beyond mitigation".

Deepfakes pose a potential threat to the digital forensics process given that video/audio evidence of an individual might be legally admissible. But in reality, the video/audio evidence might be fake. Our law enforcement cybersecurity workforce are not prepared for those big cybersecurity challenges yet. Students have a big learning curve for understanding how deepfake works. Figure 11.1 shows that deepfakes are related to computer vision, GAN, a machine learning algorithm, and other disciplinary. Students have to be guided to master basic concepts before they can follow how deep learning algorithms works in deepfakes. This chapter presents an integration of deepfake leaning modules and a set of deepfake hands-on labs into the cybersecurity curriculum, introducing students to this area while providing them with adequate knowledge and skills that can be used to grasp detection algorithms.

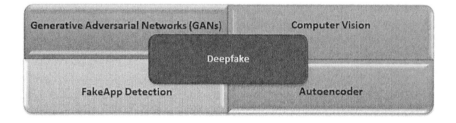

Figure 11.1   Deepfake main components.

This rest of this chapter is organized as follows: Section 11.1 introduces the concept of deepfake. Section 11.2 brings the background of deepfake technology. Section 11.3 describes how the deepfake challenges digital forensics. Section 11.4 introduces several popular deepfake detection/forensic methods with their limitations. Section 11.5 proposed an approach for building an app to detect fake image digital evidence. Conclusions and future work are presented in Section 11.6.

11.2 BACKGROUND

As an irresistible trend of this century, artificial intelligence has become an important power of technology development. It has brought the world with wealth and opportunity, but also some new threats. Deepfake is a rapidly evolving technology that uses machine learning to fabricate images, audio, or video that are very difficult to be detected by humans. The technology has wide medical and entertainment applications. For instance, it is allowing people to get high-quality movies and entertainment effects at a lower cost. However, it also becomes a critical concern for individuals, celebrities, and politicians. The U.S. House of Representatives Intelligence Committee held an open hearing in 2019 to discuss artificial intelligence and consider deepfake as a threat to individuals and national security, because we still lack reliable detection tools to identify deepfaked products. Hany Farid, the image forensics expert who created PhotoDNA, explained, "we're decades away from having forensic technology that [could] conclusively tell a real from a fake" [3].

One Dutch company, DeepTrace, has done an investigation into deepfakes and released a report in 2019 showing that the number of deepfake videos has doubled in the first seven months of 2019. One of the most famous cases that this technique may trigger happened in Gabon 2019, and an attempted coup has sparked by a suspected deepfake video. The president of Gabon Ali Bongo has not been seen in public for a long time because of health problems. People in that country were growing suspicious about the president's well-being. On January 1, the government released the president's customary New Year's address. But the authenticity of the video has widely been questioned. Some people observed that his eyes were barely able to move during the video, so this video may probably be a product of deepfake technology, and the president could have been dead. Others, however, believe that these weird expressions are because the president had suffered a stroke. They consulted a digital forensics expert; however, he said that he could not give a definitive assessment although he thought something was wrong [4]. The reason for this controversy has an obvious relationship to the flow in digital forensics study. When technical experts are unable to authenticate such digital evidence, rumors and conflicts have space to grow.

11.3 DEEPFAKE FORENSICS

As new technology in machine learning and artificial intelligence, deepfake relies on neural networks that analyze large sets of data samples to learn to mimic human facial expressions, mannerisms, voice, and inflections [5]. In the process of neural network training, programmers can fully control the shape of the network by selecting different algorithms, defining how many layers, how many nodes in each layer, and how they are connected, and giving the learning rate and the bias. The process of training the neural network is actually the way we calculate the loss between the value generated by the neural network and the target, and then trying to reduce (optimize) this loss through iterations. The global market for smart machines is expected to exceed 15 billion by 2019, with an average annual growth rate of nearly 20% [6].

Generative adversarial networks, or GANs for short, are the most popular approach for deepfake image generation. The original GAN was proposed by Goodfellow in 2014 [7]. In this algorithm, we will train two models for a two-player game. The generator is responsible for fake images generation. It will generate random or specific images based on algorithmic rules and input the images into the discriminator for identification. While accepting the false images generated by these generators, the discriminator also receives the real images with labels. Then the discriminator is going to determine how similar these false images to the real images and outputs the prediction. Until now, there have been more than 500 variants of GAN. Unlike previous technologies that have been used in forge video, audio, and image, deepfake has advantages on the way of rapid popularization. First, the forgery of video, audio, and image in the past requires different tools and methods. However, if one knows the way how to produce a deepfaked image, one can understand the rest by analogy. Because they all use similar algorithms and knowledge and tools to forgery video, audio, and image.

At the same time, the cost for a person to manipulate deepfake is getting lower. Most machine learning courses are freely available online. For example, YouTube can provide free deep learning video resources from college video courses to YouTube's code case study. There is also a project-learn with Google AI that can offer a slightly more in-depth course from Google offered through Udacity. What's more, most of the algorithms and databases used for deepfake are open source. It reduces the barrier to entry and allows more people to develop the algorithm of deepfake. All of the listed reasons have contributed to a wide application of this technology. Some of these applications will have benign effects on society. And some are likely to be used to harm the country community or individuals. Deepfake technology can manipulate multiple types of activities on video, audio, and images, such as prosthetic body movements, adding and removing objects, realistic fake face photos, and face-swapping. Figure 11.2 shows what we usually do with the deepfake technology.

Digital forensics is the study that has been used to collect criminal analysis evidence in cyberspace. Traditionally, we define digital forensics as dealing with the use of scientifically derived and proven methods toward the preservation, collection, validation, identification, analysis, interpretation, documentation, and presentation of digital evidence derived from digital sources for the purpose of facilitation or furthering the reconstruction of events found to be criminal, or helping to anticipate unauthorized actions shown to be disruptive to planned operations (Digital Forensics Research Workshop). The current investigative process of digital forensics can be divided into four stages. They are preservation-freezing the crime scene, collection-finding related digital information, examination-in-depth systematic search, and analysis-get conclusion. Figure 11.3 shows the four stages of digital forensic processes. The evidence of criminal behavior caused by deepfake technology should belong to the research scope of digital forensics.

As important digital evidence, images have always been considered as a research target for digital forensics. However, existing examination and analysis techniques and tools cannot support the identification of fake images produced by deepfake algorithms.

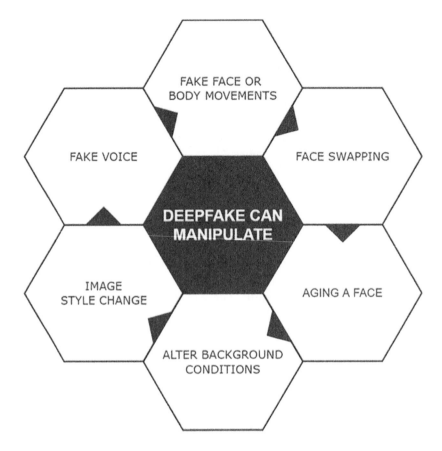

Figure 11.2 Deepfake technology currently enables these forms of manipulation.

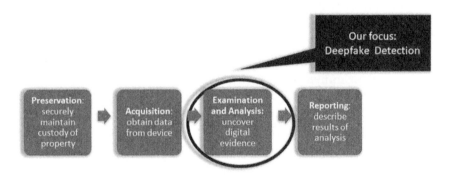

Figure 11.3 Four stages of digital forensic processes.

11.3.1 Limitations in Digital Forensic Processes

Deepfake generation and deepfake forensics will always be a pair of chasing and competing rivals. Although there exist considerable detection/forensic methods, these methods are still not effective in accuracy, efficiency, and coverage scenario, which makes those detection methods easily destroyable by the rapid upgrading of GAN algorithm. So, we still lack reliable tools for deepfake forensics.

The premise behind the current digital forensics process is that all the images are obtained from the real world. The purpose of forensics is to find evidence that criminals modified those images. However, detecting if the images are generated from a deepfake model, is not required in any of the digital forensic stages.

11.3.2 Limitations in Digital Forensic Methods

Existing examination and analysis techniques and tools cannot support the identification of fake images produced by deepfake algorithms. Those methods used for digital forensics are search, event reconstruction, and time analysis. In searching, we use manual browsing or automated searches to collect information. The method of reconstructing past events: such as analysis log, system, and file attribute analysis, is necessary to any digital forensic analysis. The time analysis is to focus on time stamp of any file. It is using time-bounding and dynamic time analysis to verify the authenticity of time stamp. However, the human face image created by deepfake model is a virtual character rather than a partially modified image based on a real person picture. These methods cannot be applied to deepfake detection. In terms of image acquisition, the methods and tools for image acquisition are mainly designed for physical equipment such as the camera. For example, by tracking the design and manufacturing features on each lens, we can find the modifications. By capturing the sensor pattern noise of images, we can correlate it with the RPNU of each device. However, all these methods cannot be used to detect the fake image generated from a training model.

11.3.2.1 Technical Response and Future

The academic and business communities are gradually becoming aware of the shortage of deepfake detection. They are encouraging people to understand deepfake and explore related detection methods through various competitions.

One of the famous competitions is the "deepfake detection challenge", which is founded by Amazon, Microsoft, Facebook, and Partnership on AI. The reward of this challenge is as high as 1 million dollar. The committee is composed of professors in universities such as Cornell University, University of Maryland, and UC Berkeley as committee members and public media, such as the New York Times and XPRIZE. In addition, the Pentagon was taking action to contain damages that arise from this technology. In 2018, a program called MediFor was invested by the DARPA. The program aims to develop technologies to assess the integrity of images and videos.

11.4   RELATED WORK

The boom of GAN algorithms has brought a lot of problems in detecting fake images generated from GAN. However, researchers have also proposed a variety of detection methods for detecting deepfake images generated from GAN. Generally speaking, we can divide the ideas of their detection methods into four categories.

11.4.1   Detecting in Pixel Level

These methods are inspired by the traditional image digital forensics thought, trying to find the statistical difference on RGB channels between the real images and fake images.

Manjunath et al. [8] proposed a method to detect fake images generated from the GAN algorithm by using co-occurrence matrices. This detection method was inherited from the steganalysis, which studies finding digital information hidden in an image, in the traditional image digital forensics. They first compute pixel co-occurrence matrices on the three-color channels and then pass it to a convolutional neural network (CNN) to train a model. By studying the residuals of the high-pass-filtered images and then extracting co-occurrence matrices on these residuals, they can create a feature vector to detect the images generated from the GAN model. In summary, the key point of their method is looking for the statistical deviations between the real images and the fake images. By the way, the co-occurrence matrix is also widely used in the recommendation system. They validated their method by using two datasets – StarGAN and CycleGAN, and both of the results show good accuracy.

McCloskey and Albright [9] noticed two differences between the images generated by the GAN generator and those taken from the camera. First, the weights bias of multi-channel internal representation in the generator is different from the analogous spectral sensitivities in a camera for the generator didn't need to count photons. Therefore, the generator allows negative weights, which the camera never allows. What's more, the spectral response functions in a real camera have limited overlap. However, the generator has no limitation on this. In addition, images taken from a camera usually have saturation or under-exposure regions. However, the GAN images do not have these regions for the normalizations applied in the generator. This finding suggests a straightforward GAN images forensics method. And their experiments also proved their forensics method based on detecting over-exposed pixel frequencies to be very effective.

Li et al. [10] observed that compared to the real images, the deepfake image is more differentiable in chrominance components. First, the disparities between deepfake images and real images show deepfake images are different from the real ones when considering red, green, and blue components together. Besides, deepfake images are different from real images, especially in the chrominance components of color spaces, for example, HSV and YCbCr. Base on the observation, they proposed a detection method that captures features on color images and used statistics to detect the deepfake images and then to evaluate their solution in three detection scenarios: sample-aware, model-aware, and model-unaware. The experimental results show that the proposed features equipped with a binary classifier can effectively differentiate between deepfake images and real images when DNG samples or generative models are available.

Zhao et al. [11] observed that deepfake images are blended by patches from multiple sources with distinct source features (in-camera features and forgery features), and these cues are still preserved after being stitched into deepfake images. So they proposed a patch-wise consistency learning branch and built an inconsistency image generator to provide the pixel-level annotations to the model to compute a pair-wise similarity between patches from different sources.

11.4.2 Subtle Difference Collecting

Zhang et al. [12] proposed the first method of swapped image detection. And they believe this method can directly be used to enhance the security of some existing systems as an authenticity predictor. In their research, they created a dataset with labels on each image to achieve automated face-swapping among a batch of images. Then they are compressing the features of BoW by select numbers of visual words. They used four classifiers (SWM-linear, RF, SVM-RBF, and MLP) to classify the images and record their performance. The results show that this set of BoW feature representations used to describe face features and distinguishable information performs well on different classifiers.

Another solution for detecting forgery in face images is to identify the location of the blending boundary. This solution called Face X-ray was proposed by Li et al. [13]. Li believes that the acquisition process of an image will give each image distinctive marks. Those marks showed a consistent pattern in an image. But the consistency will be destroyed by the face-swapping. These inconsistencies can be considered as a boundary and be detected by their model. Huh et al. [14] proposed a self-supervised method for detecting deepfake images. Their method addresses the problem that detectors usually lack sufficient amounts of deepfake data for training. By using the vast and previously underutilized WXIF metadata building model, they are trying to find out whether different parts of an image are produced by a single imaging pipeline. This model is designed to work in an unsupervised regime, and to flag the "out of ordinary" information. Their experiment shows this method works well in localizing the spliced regions and classifies the spliced image from the authentic image even if the model didn't train with the examples of deepfake images.

Hsu et al. [15] proposed a common fake feature network (CFFN) to distinguish between the deepfake images. They believe the traditional classifier layer on CNN, such as softmax layer, has to rely on the previous layer to feed features, and those features are high-level features. However, the fake features of a fake image can exist not only in the high-level features, but also in the middle-level features. Hence, they design a new CNN structure and capture features from both high-level and middle-level. In this model, they have several dense blocks to capture the representative features of the fake image. In their experiment, they create a training dataset that includes five popular

GAN images to train their model. And use the course-level structure to connect the trained CNN to the last convolutional layer of their detector, so the middle-level features captured by the CNN can be used to detect the fake images.

11.4.3 Modifying the Architecture of CNN

Mo et al. [16] found out in GAN algorithms that both the generator and discriminator need to rely on the convolutional neural network (CNN) model to produce deepfake images. And the previous research reveals that the main difference between fake and real images would be reflected in the residual domain. Therefore, they speculate that they can detect deepfake images by modifying the architecture of the CNN model. In their experiment, they modify the number of layers and activation function and make a high-pass filter for the input images, successfully identifying fake face images with high visual quality from real ones. This method also proves that the statistical artifacts in GAN images can serve as evidence for fake images. Dang et al. [17] proposed a new detection model called CGFace, which is also a model based on CNN. In their five-layer classifier, they input a 64*64 grayscale image and capture the hidden features by using 3 pooling layers, 2 full connection layers, and one flatten layer. Then they test their model by replacing different loss functions and add dropout layers in their model. They finally found that when the softmax was replaced with AdaBoost classifier, the model was shown to perform well on the imbalanced scenario of the dataset. And they test their model with different datasets generated from GAN. The test result shows high accuracy. Marra et al. [18] also gave their deepfake image forensic solution based on the CNN architecture. They focus on image-to-image translation GAN detection and test several different detection methods proposed by the researchers. They create three different scenarios to test 7 different GAN detectors in their experiment. The results show a detector called XceptionNet is the most robust one and behave well even with training–test mismatching. It adopts fully separable filters, and in each layer of this model, it takes 1D depth-wise and 2D point-wise convolution to filter the 3D input feature, which reduced the learning parameters and gave resources to learning the others. Their research also reveals the fact that the compression performed upon image uploading, which is widely used in Twitter and other social networks, can impair the performance of detectors.

11.4.4 Obtaining Fingerprint of GANs

When detecting digital images generated by traditional devices, researchers usually use a method to detect image fingerprints. This is because different cameras will print different PRNU patterns on the photos due to manufacturing imperfections. This pattern can be thought of as the unique fingerprint of an image. Although deepfake images are produced in completely different ways, some researchers insist that the models built by different GAN algorithms will also leave unique fingerprints on images. Marra et al. [19] experimented with this idea and proved that there are unique fingerprints left on each GAN image, which can be used as forensic analysis. Some researchers have put this theory into practice. Wang et al. [20] proposed a detection method called FakeSpotter which spots fake face images by monitoring neuron behaviors. In their paper, the FakeSpotter learns the representation of face by activating neurons to capture subtle features and monitors the layer-by-layer behaviors to find the fake images. They proposed a neuron coverage criteria MNC to capture layer-by-layer neuron activation behaviors. And different from the models that rely on deep neural networks, their model uses a shallow neural network and takes the layer-wise neuron behavior as features rather than the output on the final layer. And the input of the classifier is the general neuron behavior opposed to the traditional ad hoc raw pixels. They test their model with four start-of-the-art GANs, including the famous styleGAN, and the results show the model is highly efficient and robust. Hus et al. [21] proposed a new model called DeepFD (deep forgery discriminator). It was designed to address the issue when the classifier cannot distinguish the images generated from a new variant of GAN. In their solution, by introducing contrastive loss into the neural network, they collect and put fake images generated from 5 different popular GAN algorithms into their training dataset. Then, the first discriminator can learn the jointly discriminative feature from the fake images and some real images. Then, they connect this discriminator with another classifier and train a second classifier to further distinguish the images. Their experiment showed their model has a good identification ability even when they test it with some fake images that were not generated from the GAN algorithms they used for training. For the big GAN family with over 500 variants, their solution innovatively breaks the cycle of the detectors being useless as long as new variants were created.

11.4.5 Deepfake Video Forensic Methods

A novel detection method of deepfake video is to use biological signals to verify the authenticity of the video. Ciftci et al. [22] and Qi et al. [23] used this approach that estimates biological signals in terms of heartbeat, blood flow, or breathing. They may not be visible, but are detectable computationally. Those signals can generate different noises, which can be considered as a projection of the residuals in a known dimension. This gives each model a unique signature to detect. So their solutions can be used for deepfake detection and source model prediction for any given video.

Sun et al. [24] believes that facial geometric information and its dynamic characteristics are efficient and robust in detecting deepfake videos in wild. As such, they proposed a lightweight and easy-to-train model for detecting deepfake videos through temporal modeling on precise geometric features. In order to detect the compressed deepfake videos that are popular on social platforms, Hu et al. [25] proposed a two-stream method. By analyzing the frame level and temporality level of compressed deepfake videos, this method can detect both tempered artifacts and the inconsistency between the frames of compressed deepfake videos. Qian et al. [26] designed the MixBlock framework to learn frequency-aware clues by using the FAD (frequency-aware decomposition) and LFS (local frequency statistics). Thus, the deepfake features can be obtained in the frequency domain.

11.4.6 Datasets

The quality of the datasets is important for model training. Feature representation, reliability, and minimizing skew are three aspects of the quality of datasets. In other words, reducing label errors, features noise, and skewness will be greatly helpful in enhancing the model performance. Currently, we already have some open-source datasets with high quality, and they are very helpful for training models.

DeeperForensics-1.0 [27]: A large-scale dataset with 60,000 videos. The videos are all high-resolution videos with various poses, expressions, and illuminations. Fake videos are generated by an end-to-end face-swapping framework DF-VAR.

CelebFaces Attributes (CelebA) [28]: A large dataset with 202,599 face images of celebrities. Each of the images has 40 attribute annotations.

CelebA-HQ: A high-resolution face image dataset selected from CelebA. The scale of the dataset is 30,000, and the size of each image is 512*512.

Flickr-Faces-HQ Dataset: A dataset crawled from Flickr. It has 70,000 high-quality PNG images. The size of each image is 1,024*1,024. One feature of this dataset is that it varies in age, race, and image background.

UTKFace: A large face dataset with labels. It has over 20,000 images.

Real and Fake Face Detection: A small dataset with 2,000 images.

Wider Face: A large face dataset with 32,203 images.

11.4.7 Software for Deepfake Forensics

Catching deepfakes with AI is something of a cat-and-mouse game. A detector algorithm can be trained to spot deepfakes, but then an algorithm that generates fakes can potentially be trained to evade detection. There are few effective deepfake forensics tools. DARPA currently has two programs devoted to the detection of deep fakes: Media Forensics (MediFor) and Semantic Forensics (SemaFor). MediFor is developing algorithms to automatically assess the integrity of photos and videos and to provide analysts with information about how counterfeit content was generated. (https://crsreports.congress.gov/product/pdf/IF/IF11333)

11.4.8 Challenges

Although the last three years witnessed a growing research interest in deepfake forensics [29], testing methods still cannot keep up with the pace of technological change. The reasons are the following: Deepfake algorithms were updated so fast that the detection methods that addressed the weakness of these algorithms quickly became useless.

In 2018, the deepfake video showed unnatural blinking patterns, which were easily identified by deepfake detectors. Meanwhile, some other deepfake models are struggling with how to produce teeth. But shortly after those detect methods were published in public, weakness was overcome by the improved deepfake algorithms.

Deepfake detection methods are likely to over-fit a dataset that loses accuracy in the others. There are a lot of deepfake detection algorithms that claim the accuracy can be as high as 97%–99%. But this accuracy is tested in a specific database. It is greatly reduced when it is used to test data from other databases or images generated by other algorithms. In other words, these models are over-fitting in this database.

In addition, deepfake makers can develop corresponding methods to attack a certain detection method. For example, adversarial attack is a good solution to interfere with the detection. By adding some subtle noise into the dataset, the image will produce changes that are undetectable to the human eye. However, these adversarial images can trick the detection model into giving an incorrect, but high-confidence output [30].

11.5 APPROACH TO DEEPFAKE FORENSICS

Although the update speed of GAN algorithms is so fast, developing a deepfake image-detecting application that can quickly identify whether the images they upload are deepfaked is very helpful for people who work in the digital forensics field and ordinary users. Here we propose an approach to building an application to quickly detect a deepfake image. As deepfake technology is widely applied in various mobile applications and the growth of the affordable smartphone market makes mobile application development the most active area, our deepfake detection application designed in this solution will serve the users of Android mobile phones.

11.5.1 Application Overview

The application is composed of two parts: the activities on the application used to interact with users. They will gain images from users and return a prediction. Another part is a pre-trained model which can distinguish between the deepfake images and real images. This model is trained using the most popular GAN algorithm by far. It will be placed into the application and will communicate with the frontend by using Android NDK. This detection model tries to addresses the issue when the classifier cannot distinguish the images generated from a new variant of GAN [21]. By introducing contrastive loss into the neural network, the model going to collect and put fake images generated from 5 different popular GAN algorithms into our training dataset. Then, the first discriminator can learn the jointly discriminative feature from the fake images and some real images. Then, by connecting this discriminator with another classifier, a second classifier can be trained to further distinguish the images. When building the training dataset, this app will include the fake images generated by the latest styleGAN and combine them with fake images generated by the other four GAN algorithms to improve the model's performance. For those who want to detect whether a local picture or online picture is created by deepfake technology, this application can quickly help them to analyze. When using this application, users should install and launch this application and then click the submission button to prompt a view for image uploading. If the application didn't report an error toast in the type of the image file, a POST request would be sent to the server from this application. On the server side, a trained detector model will run and send a predicted result to this client application. After receiving feedback from the server, the application will pop up a new activity and showing the prediction to the user. Figure 11.4 shows the use case flow of this application. Figure 1.5 shows the diagram of the proposed application.

11.5.2 Application Design

UI Design: This application will maintain a simple UI design. The app is composed of two activities. The main activity is used to receive pictures uploaded by the users and send a gRPC request to the server. The result activity is designed to show the response from the server. It is composed of two components: a textView to show the prediction and an imageView to show the prediction directly. Figure 11.5 shows the UI design for this application.

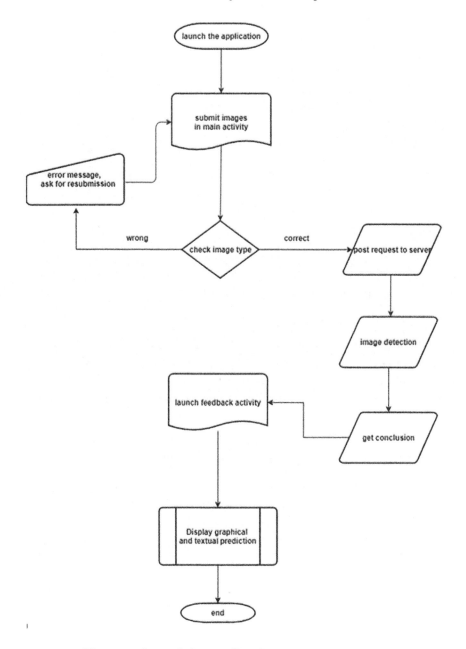

Figure 11.4 Use case flow of the application.

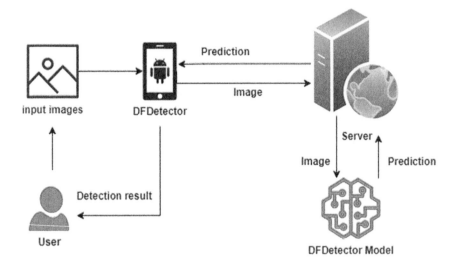

Figure 11.5 Diagram of the proposed application.

Client–Server communication: The communication between the app and the service is mainly done through ServerThread. We will use a ServerThread class that is used to create a server socket with the port of this server. Once the communication has been accepted, a new communication thread will be started (Figure 11.6).

11.5.3 Model Training and Application Deployment

Currently, the detection model for the application will be built based on the solution of DeepFD proposed by Hsu [21]. With a deepfake images dataset generated by the five popular GAN algorithms and a real face image open-source dataset, the model can predict whether an uploaded image is deepfake or not and by which algorithm it was generated. Figure 11.7 shows the training process of the model. The model communicates with app activities through the android SDK and NDK. The other way is to deploy the model in the server, and the user's applications are played as a client to post requests to the server and get responses from the server. In this paper, we will take the second approach to deploy our detection model. Google's TensorFlow-serving is a high-performance open-source library for machine learning model deployment. It can deploy a trained machine learning model

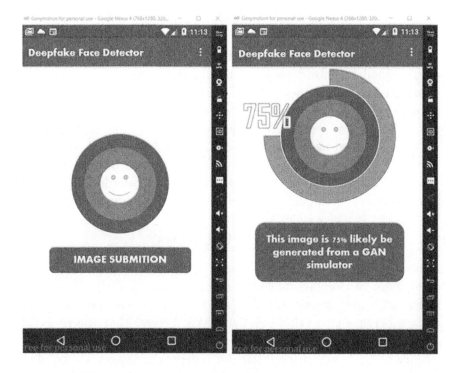

Figure 11.6 UI design for this application.

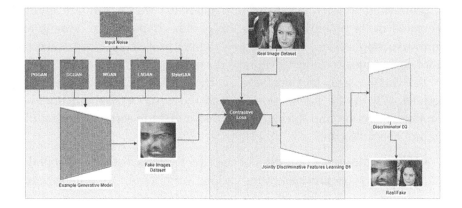

Figure 11.7 The flowchart of the detector model's training process. The discriminator 1 (D1) is used to learn the jointly discriminative features of the fake images dataset and real images dataset. The discriminator 2 (D2) is used to binary-classify the images.

online and accept requests from clients by using gRPC. TensorFlow-serving also adds support for model versioning (for model updates with a rollback option) and multiple models [31]. In this tool, the deepfake detection model will be deployed in the following steps: First, create the SavedModel to export the trained model and use SignatureDef to sign the model. It will create an identity for the model, which is required by the TensorFlow service API. Then create a servable for the model that can be loaded later for inference. This servable will also be fed to a source on the TensorFlow-serving. When the client posts requests to the server, the manager of the TensorFlow-serving will let a loader get the source with the model by identifying the signature of this model.

11.6 CONCLUSIONS AND FUTURE WORK

In this chapter, we have investigated the interactions between the development of deepfake techniques and detection of them in digital forensics. We also described the structure and the associated software that are pertinent to GAN algorithm. We believe that the proposed approach to deepfake forensics is enhanced by the carefully targeted category of GAN algorithms that make deepfake images/videos. This chapter covers the concepts and technology of deepfake forensics. As deep learning technology continues to grow and gain traction, many IT professionals are unaware of how deepfake works, but are highly interested in its potentiality. The aim of this chapter is to develop an innovative application tool that any digital professional can learn to adopt techniques to detect deepfake development.

The main issue of deepfakes is the lack of effective detection methods [32]. As for future work, connected with GAN algorithm and deepfake detection and develop more fast detection software for public use, are the following:

- The continuous evaluation of the effectiveness of various deepfake forensic tools and detecting various variants of GAN algorithm.

- The enhancement of deepfake forensics datasets available online for academic research.

- The development of additional deepfake forensics in the areas of IoT, health care, precision agriculture, precision fishing, public sector, and finance and banking [33].

REFERENCES

[1] Marissa Koopman, Andrea Macarulla Rodriguez, and Zeno Geradts. Detection of deepfake video manipulation. In *The 20th Irish machine vision and image processing conference (IMVIP)*, pp. 133–136, 2018.

[2] J. Schafer. Deepfakes, forensic science and police investigations, pp. 3–9, 2019. https://www.police1.com/technology/articles/deepfakes-forensic-science-and-police-investigations-8PLOqdYGwBp5svYE/.

[3] Danielle K. Citron and Robert Chesney. Deep fakes: A looming crisis for national security, democracy and privacy? *Lawfare*, 2018.

[4] Sarah Cahlan. How misinformation helped spark an attempted coup in gabon, 2020.

[5] Mika Westerlund. The emergence of deepfake technology: A review. *Technology Innovation Management Review*, 9(11), 2019.

[6] Joe Lemley, Shabab Bazrafkan, and Peter Corcoran. Deep learning for consumer devices and services: Pushing the limits for machine learning, artificial intelligence, and computer vision. *IEEE Consumer Electronics Magazine*, 6(2):48–56, 2017.

[7] Ian J. Goodfellow, Jean Pouget-Abadie, Mehdi Mirza, Bing Xu, David Warde-Farley, Sherjil Ozair, Aaron Courville, and Yoshua Bengio. Generative adversarial networks. *arXiv preprint arXiv:1406.2661*, 2014.

[8] Lakshmanan Nataraj, Tajuddin Manhar Mohammed, B.S. Manjunath, Shivkumar Chandrasekaran, Arjuna Flenner, Jawadul H. Bappy, and Amit K. Roy-Chowdhury. Detecting gan generated fake images using co-occurrence matrices. *Electronic Imaging*, 2019(5):532, 2019.

[9] Scott McCloskey and Michael Albright. Detecting gan-generated imagery using color cues. *arXiv preprint arXiv:1812.08247*, 2018.

[10] Haodong Li, Bin Li, Shunquan Tan, and Jiwu Huang. Detection of deep network generated images using disparities in color components. *arXiv preprint arXiv:1808.07276*, 2018.

[11] Tianchen Zhao, Xiang Xu, Mingze Xu, Hui Ding, Yuanjun Xiong, and Wei Xia. Learning to recognize patch-wise consistency for deepfake detection. *arXiv preprint arXiv:2012.09311*, 2020.

[12] Ying Zhang, Lilei Zheng, and Vrizlynn L.L. Thing. Automated face swapping and its detection. In *2017 IEEE 2nd International Conference on Signal and Image Processing (ICSIP)*, pp. 15–19. IEEE, 2017.

[13] Lingzhi Li, Jianmin Bao, Ting Zhang, Hao Yang, Dong Chen, Fang Wen, and Baining Guo. Face X-ray for more general face forgery detection. In *Proceedings of the IEEE/CVF Conference on Computer Vision and Pattern Recognition*, pp. 5001–5010, 2020.

[14] Minyoung Huh, Andrew Liu, Andrew Owens, and Alexei A. Efros. Fighting fake news: Image splice detection via learned self-consistency. In *Proceedings of the European Conference on Computer Vision (ECCV)*, pp. 101–117, 2018.

[15] Chih-Chung Hsu, Yi-Xiu Zhuang, and Chia-Yen Lee. Deep fake image detection based on pairwise learning. *Applied Sciences*, 10(1):370, 2020.

[16] Huaxiao Mo, Bolin Chen, and Weiqi Luo. Fake faces identification via convolutional neural network. In *Proceedings of the 6th ACM Workshop on Information Hiding and Multimedia Security*, pp. 43–47, 2018.

[17] Minh L. Dang, Syed Ibrahim Hassan, Suhyeon Im, Jaecheol Lee, Sujin Lee, and Hyeonjoon Moon. Deep learning based computer generated face identification using convolutional neural network. *Applied Sciences*, 8(12):2610, 2018.

[18] Francesco Marra, Diego Gragnaniello, Davide Cozzolino, and Luisa Verdoliva. Detection of gan-generated fake images over social networks. In *2018 IEEE Conference on Multimedia Information Processing and Retrieval (MIPR)*, pp. 384–389. IEEE, 2018.

[19] Francesco Marra, Diego Gragnaniello, Luisa Verdoliva, and Giovanni Poggi. Do gans leave artificial fingerprints? In *2019 IEEE Conference on Multimedia Information Processing and Retrieval (MIPR)*, pp. 506–511. IEEE, 2019.

[20] Run Wang, Lei Ma, Felix Juefei-Xu, Xiaofei Xie, Jian Wang, and Yang Liu. Fakespotter: A simple baseline for spotting ai-synthesized fake faces. *arXiv preprint arXiv:1909.06122*, 2, 2019.

[21] Chih-Chung Hsu, Chia-Yen Lee, and Yi-Xiu Zhuang. Learning to detect fake face images in the wild. In *2018 International Symposium on Computer, Consumer and Control (IS3C)*, pp. 388–391. IEEE, 2018.

[22] Umur Aybars Ciftci, Ilke Demir, and Lijun Yin. How do the hearts of deep fakes beat? Deep fake source detection via interpreting residuals with biological signals. In *2020 IEEE International Joint Conference on Biometrics (IJCB)*, pp. 1–10. IEEE, 2020.

[23] Hua Qi, Qing Guo, Felix Juefei-Xu, Xiaofei Xie, Lei Ma, Wei Feng, Yang Liu, and Jianjun Zhao. Deeprhythm: Exposing deepfakes with attentional visual heartbeat rhythms. In *Proceedings of the 28th ACM International Conference on Multimedia*, pp. 4318–4327, 2020.

[24] Zekun Sun, Yujie Han, Zeyu Hua, Na Ruan, and Weijia Jia. Improving the efficiency and robustness of deepfakes detection through precise geometric features. *arXiv preprint arXiv:2104.04480*, 2021.

[25] Juan Hu, Xin Liao, Wei Wang, and Zheng Qin. Detecting compressed deepfake videos in social networks using frame-temporality two-stream convolutional network. *IEEE Transactions on Circuits and Systems for Video Technology*, 2021.

[26] Yuyang Qian, Guojun Yin, Lu Sheng, Zixuan Chen, and Jing Shao. Thinking in frequency: Face forgery detection by mining frequency-aware clues. In *European Conference on Computer Vision*, pp. 86–103. Springer, 2020.

[27] Liming Jiang, Ren Li, Wayne Wu, Chen Qian, and Chen Change Loy. Deeperforensics-1.0: A large-scale dataset for real-world face forgery detection. In *Proceedings of the IEEE/CVF Conference on Computer Vision and Pattern Recognition*, pp. 2889–2898, 2020.

[28] Ziwei Liu, Ping Luo, Xiaogang Wang, and Xiaoou Tang. Large-scale celebfaces attributes (celeba) dataset. *Retrieved August*, 15(2018):11, 2018.

[29] Luca Guarnera, Oliver Giudice, Cristina Nastasi, and Sebastiano Battiato. Preliminary forensics analysis of deepfake images. In *2020 AEIT International Annual Conference (AEIT)*, pp. 1–6. IEEE, 2020.

[30] Christian Szegedy, Wojciech Zaremba, Ilya Sutskever, Joan Bruna, Dumitru Erhan, Ian Goodfellow, and Rob Fergus. Intriguing properties of neural networks. *arXiv preprint arXiv:1312.6199*, 2013.

[31] Christopher Olston, Noah Fiedel, Kiril Gorovoy, Jeremiah Harmsen, Li Lao, Fangwei Li, Vinu Rajashekhar, Sukriti Ramesh, and Jordan Soyke. Tensorflow-serving: Flexible, high-performance ml serving. *arXiv preprint arXiv:1712.06139*, 2017.

[32] Thanh Thi Nguyen, Cuong M. Nguyen, Dung Tien Nguyen, Duc Thanh Nguyen, and Saeid Nahavandi. Deep learning for deepfakes creation and detection: A survey. *arXiv preprint arXiv:1909.11573*, 2019.

[33] Arun Ross, Sudipta Banerjee, and Anurag Chowdhury. Security in smart cities: A brief review of digital forensic schemes for biometric data. *Pattern Recognition Letters*, 138:346–354, 2020.

Monitoring HPC Systems against Compromised SSH

Lev Lafayette, Narendra Chinnam, and Timothy Rice

University of Melbourne

CONTENTS

12.1   AN INTRODUCTION TO SSH IN HPC

Internet communication occurs via the transmission of data packets. A packet is defined as a block of data with the necessary addressing information to deliver from one physical node to another, with a packet switching network using the addressing information to switch packets from one physical network to another, towards their final destination, independently of other packets. Under the TCP/IP network stack, data packets are encapsulated in multiple layers. An Ethernet frame has a header and trailer and incorporates an IP datagram. An IP datagram includes an IP header and incorporates a TCP segment. The

TCP segment has a TCP header and incorporates application data. Application data consist of an application header and user data. At the application layer are the protocols used by most user services, such as the Hypertext Transfer Protocol (HTTP), Secure Shell (SSH), File Transfer Protocol (FTP), and Simple Mail Transfer Protocol (SMTP).

Of these application protocols, most transmit the data in plaintext. Using common packet capture and analyser programs (e.g. Wireshark, Kismet, Ettercap, and tcpdump), logging traffic can be intercepted, showing the values of various fields in the packet according to the appropriate specifications. For protocols that transmit information in plaintext and that are used to log in to remote systems (e.g. telnet, rlogin, rsh, rcp, and ftp), this includes the user name and password. For any individual user, this should be considered a serious problem. For high-performance computing (HPC) systems, however, the cost is amplified as such systems usually are provided for research and computational purposes; the account is provided on academic merit with social benefits gained through positive externalities, while the significant cost is borne by the provider.

To avoid inappropriate access to HPC systems, the use of SSH is almost universally applied. SSH was first introduced in 1995 by Tatu Ylönen at the Helsinki University of Technology in Finland. Later that year, the SSH-1 protocol was documented as an Internet Engineering Task Force (IETF) Internet Draft. In 1996, a new, major version of the protocol, SSH 2.0 or SSH-2, that incorporated new algorithms, but was incompatible with SSH-1 was missing some features and was with a more restrictive license. In response, the IETF formed a working group to standardise the protocol releasing the first draft of the SSH-2.0 protocol in 1997, which was eventually fully released in 2006. This included the Diffie–Hellman algorithm for improved security in key exchange and strong integrity checking via message authentication codes and the ability to run multiple shell sessions over a single connection.

At the same time, a number of developers led by Björn Grönvall, desiring a free software version, forked the original 1.2.12 release of the original SSH, the last version released under a free software license, which eventually became OpenSSH by OpenBSD developers, notably Markus Friedl. OpenSSH (also known as OpenBSD SSH) has become the single most popular SSH implementation. Acting as a suite of applications, OpenSSH includes scp ("secure copy", a replacement for rcp), sftp ("secure file transfer protocol", a replacement for ftp, allowing secure copying of files between computers), ssh (secure shell, a replacement for rlogin, rsh, and telnet, to allow shell access to a remote machine), ssh-add and ssh-agent (key-holding utilities that avoid the need to enter passphrases every time they are used), ssh-keygen (a utility to inspect and generate keys that are used for user and host authentication), ssh-keyscan (a utility that scans a list of hosts and collects their public keys), and sshd (the SSH server daemon). Unless specified otherwise, all further examples given in this text assume the use of OpenSSH.

SSH provides authentication of senders and receivers with proof of identity of both parties with server and client authentication, authorisation to provide access control to accounts, and privacy of data and communication via strong encryption, integrity of the same ensuring that they have not been altered through cryptographic integrity checking. Further, SSH provides for forwarding or tunnelling to encrypt other TCP/IP-based sessions. The security advantages of SSH are sufficient that there are strong arguments that computing users should use SSH "everywhere". Such a proposition is no mere fancy; as an adaptable network protocol, SSH can be used not just for remote logins and operations, but also for secure mounting of remote file systems, file transfers, X11 connections, arbitrary port forwarding, UNIX-domain sockets, network tunnelling, web browsing, etc. Typically, of course, the basic means of activity is to use an ssh client to connect a known SSH server, either by specifying the login name as an account or with the −l option. The examples given here and that follow make use of the Spartan HPC system at the University of Melbourne.

```
ssh lev@spartan.hpc.unimelb.edu.au
ssh -l lev spartan.hpc.unimelb.edu.au
```

For users that have multiple accounts, the use of an SSH configuration file, located in ~/.ssh/config, allows for the creation of aliases of user and host names. The file should be readable and writable only by the user and not accessible by others, i.e. chmod 600. Entries in the SSH config file take the form of a stanza block entries of Host and hostname with subsequent SSH options such as the qualified Hostname, the user name, with some globbing options (* for all, ? for a single character, and ! for not). An SSH config file can also be used by related utilities such as scp, sftp, and rsync. Some sample entries to an SSH config file would include the following, in this case using the term "spartan" to represent the user "lev" on the host "spartan.hpc.unimelb.edu.au" and a timeout interval of 120 seconds after which, if no data have been received from the server, ssh will send a null packet through the channel to request a response from the server, to keep the connection alive and avoid a "Broken pipe" error.

```
Host spartan
      Hostname spartan.hpc.unimelb.edu.au
      User lev
Host *
      ServerAliveInterval 120
```

Further, it is common to use passwordless SSH. This is easier for users (as they do not have to use their own memory for complex and multiple passphrases) and the automation of scripts (certainly significantly more preferable than including the password in the script!), and is necessary for some applications. Establishing passwordless SSH, *nix-like systems (e.g. UNIX, Linux, and MacOS X), the use of ssh-keygen is carried out on the client system (in this case, generating a Rivest–Shamir–Adleman public key algorithm public/private key pair). The new public key is appended on the host to the user's authorised keys file located at ~/.ssh/authorized_keys, requiring a final entry of the password, and from that point onwards, the host will trust a system where its public key matches with the client's private key.

```
$ ssh-keygen -t rsa
Generating public/private rsa key pair.
Enter file in which to save the key
 (/home/user/.ssh/id_rsa):
Created directory '/home/user/.ssh'.
Enter passphrase (empty for no passphrase):
Enter same passphrase again:
Your identification has been saved in
 /home/user/.ssh/id_rsa.
Your public key has been saved in
 /home/user/.ssh/id_rsa.pub.
The key fingerprint is:
43:51:43:a1:b5:fc:8b:b7:0a:3a:a9:b1:0f:66:73:a8
 user@localhost
```

```
$ cat .ssh/id_rsa.pub | ssh username@spartan.hpc.unimelb.
  edu.au 'cat >>.ssh/authorized_keys'
```

Depending on the version of SSH being used, the following might also be necessary:

```
Put the public key in .ssh/authorized_keys2
Change the permissions of .ssh to 700
Change the permissions of .ssh/authorized_keys2 to 640
```

For clients using Linux, MacOS X.x, or other UNIX-like systems, this should be sufficient. A number of users, however, use MS-Windows clients. In this case, the process is somewhat more complex, requiring several steps. The following is a recommended procedure from the University of Melbourne.

1) Download additional software called PuTTYgen from https://www.chiark.greenend.org.uk/~sgtatham/putty/latest.html.

2) Launch PuTTYgen tool up. If you are on Windows 7 or higher, right-click on it and select Run as Administrator.

3) Select the parameters; the default value (SSH-2 RSA) is fine.

4) Select Generate.

5) Add the public key to the authorized_keys file in ~/.ssh on Spartan (create it if it doesn't exist). Ensure there are no unexpected line-breaks. Make sure the permissions on the file are 0644.

   chmod 644 ~/.ssh/authorized_keys

6) Back on PuTTYgen, save the private key and public key. Make sure to save public key as .txt, while private key as .ppk.

7) Configure PuTTY to use that newly generated key. Start PuTTY and go to Connection > SSH > Auth and add the location of the private key saved previously.

8) Open PuTTY and log in as usual. If all the steps above have been followed, no password will be required.

The combination of ssh, ssh configs, and ssh key pairs allows a simple command `ssh spartan` to connect, rather than `ssh lev@spartan.hpc.unimelb.edu.au` and having to enter a passphrase. Further, the combination can be applied to other ssh utilities, including rsync (e.g. `rsync -avz --update workfiles spartan:files/`).

12.2   MAN-IN-THE-MIDDLE AND OTHER ATTACKS

It is possible, even with public key authentication, for man-in-the-middle (MITM) attacks to occur. A sender transmitting a message request for a public key to a receiver can have it intercepted by the MITM. The MITM can capture the message, relay the request, and then intercept the return message from the receiver, capturing the receiver's public key. The MITM can then send their key to the original sender, with the sender believing that it is the public key from the receiver. From that point onwards, any transmission that they send to the receiver can be decrypted by the MITM.

Public key systems can use clients and server certificate exchanges from a trusted third party, a certificate authority (CA). As long as the original key to authenticate this CA has not itself the subject of a MITM attack, then the certificates authenticate the connection. In contrast, SSH does not require trust in the third-party authority and does not rely on any external accreditation for authentication. Instead, an SSH server cannot be trusted unless the user's client explicitly authorises its public key on the initial connection. Once established, an attacker simply cannot introduce another public key as belonging to that server. This is the SSH known-host mechanism. When an SSH client and server connect, the server authenticates the client and the client also authenticates the server's host key, to identify itself to clients.

```
$ ssh user@example.com
Host key not found from the list of known hosts.
Are you sure you want to continue connecting (yes/no)?
 [Assume 'yes']
Host 'example.com' added to the list of known hosts.
```

One issue here is that the initial connection must be secure; otherwise, it will be subject to a MITM attack. Usually, this is accepted as a matter of convenience; however, the "trust the SSH connection on first use" approach is rather naive. It would be preferable for the server's public host key to be installed prior to connecting for the first time and a typical approach is for institutions to have pre-installed a set of host keys for systems under their control. Obviously, this does not help for systems outside the control of system administrators, in which case a fallback on systems like X.509 certificates or similar. One particular issue is that when server authentication fails, typically a warning is provided to accept the new host key. Even when the SSH response explicitly states that MITM may be occurring, the tendency for users to act out convenience and accept the new host key is overwhelming.

As an explicit example, it must be mentioned here that earlier versions of SSH, i.e. SSHv1, were susceptible to MITM attacks, as illustrated by the use of dsniff, a suite of network traffic analysis tools written by Dug Song, to the extent that they were able to take over interactive SSH sessions. This was achieved through intercepting the initial connection attempt and inserting an alternative public key. As noted, even when users do have the correct public key for comparison, there is a tendency to accept the alternative key without further consideration. Fortunately, UNIX-like SSH clients are configurable for "strict" host key checking that automatically disallow any connecting where the host key has changed, requiring the user to manually remove the existing key from the known-host file. This certainly should be part of any default or standard operating environment installation; however, it still requires the user to be aware of the potential security risk in removing such a key.

A more contemporary example is SSH-MITM, which is still in active development and specifically targets systems that use password authentication by acting as a proxy server between an SSH client and SSH server. Apart from collecting the plaintext user name and passwords, SSH-MITM can also take over existing sessions. While public key authentication ensures that no confidential data need to be sent to the remote host that could be intercepted by a MITM attack, SSH-MITM is able to request the agent from the client and use it for remote authentication.

Thus, as an alternative to passwords, SSH keys provide the same access as user names and passwords and are extremely convenient; for example, when properly configured, they provide scripting access to accounts. The previous section describes the use of SSH public–private keys from an HPC user's perspective. From a security perspective, it is understood, following the principles of various public key algorithms (e.g. Rivest–Shamir–Adleman (RSA), Elliptic Curve Digital Signature Algorithm (ECDSA), Digital Signature Algorithm (DSA), and Diffie–Hellman key agreement protocol) that an SSH identity uses a pair of keys, one private and one public. The private key is, as the name implies, securely kept in individual hands. An SSH client will invoke it to prove a user's identity to servers. The public key is added to the accounts on SSH servers. In the authentication process, the SSH client issues a request for authentication, the server issues a challenge, and the response from the client is proof of identity through the challenge and the private key, and comparison with the user's public key on the server.

Other attacks against SSH include tools such as BothanSpy and Gyrfalcon, originally revealed by WikiLeaks as plausible tools used by the US government's Central Intelligence Agency to gather user names, passwords, SSH keys, and SSH key passphrases. BothanSpy targets the SSH client program Xshell on the Microsoft Windows operating system to gather user credentials for all active SSH sessions, which are then sent to a CIA-controlled server. In contrast, Gyrfalcon targets the OpenSSH client on various Linux platforms to gather user credentials of active SSH sessions, as well as OpenSSH session traffic. All collected information is stored in an encrypted file for later collection. Both require prior access to the target machine. It can also be assumed that large enough actors with sufficient political backing have compelled or induced manufacturers to include data collection actions on the physical hardware. Discussion of protecting against such attacks is beyond the scope of this review.

12.3 RECENT COMPROMISED SSH CREDENTIALS ON HPC SYSTEMS

In May 2020, there was a series of cyberattacks among multiple HPC centres across Europe via compromised SSH credentials starting on May 11 at the UK's peak academic HPC system at the University of Edinburgh, ARCHER, the UK National Supercomputing Service. A decision was made to disable access to ARCHER. Investigations confirmed that a number of user accounts had been affected, and as a result, a decision was made to disable access until the extent of the issue was determined. Sysadmins warned ARCHER users that their SSH keys may have been compromised as a result of the apparent attack, issuing a recommendation to "change passwords and SSH keys on any other systems which you share your ARCHER credentials with".

Very shortly afterwards, it was understood that this compromise was affecting several supercomputers across Europe and was subject to an investigation by the UK's National Cyber Security Centre (NCSC). In Germany, five HPC systems were shut down on the same day across Baden-Württemberg, Germany, by the bwHPC, which coordinates HPC research projects across that state. These systems included the Hawk supercomputer at the High Performance Computing Center Stuttgart (HLRS) at the University of Stuttgart, the bwUniCluster 2.0 and ForHLR II clusters at the Karlsruhe Institute of Technology (KIT), the bwForCluster JUSTUS chemistry and quantum science supercomputer at the Ulm University, and the bwForCluster BinAC bioinformatics supercomputer at the University of Tübingen. The following day, the Leibniz Supercomputing Center (LRZ), an institute under the Bavarian Academy of Sciences, closed access to its computing cluster, then the Julich Research Centre including the JURECA, JUDAC, and JUWELS HPC systems, and likewise the Taurus HPC system at the Technical University in Dresden, along with the Swiss Center of Scientific Computations (CSCS) in Zurich, Switzerland. Attacks were launched from compromised networks from the University of Krakow, Poland; China Science and Technology Network, PR China; Shanghai Jiao Tong University, PR China; UCLA, the USA; and Stony Brook University, the USA.

Following a rapid investigation, the security team of the European Grid Infrastructure Foundation noted: "A malicious group is currently targeting academic data centers for CPU mining purposes. The attacker is hopping from one victim to another using compromised SSH credentials" (EGI, 2020). The EGI Computer Security and Incident Response Team noted that the compromised hosts were turned into different roles, including XMR Monero cryptocurrency mining hosts (from a hidden XMR binary), XMR-proxy hosts (used for connections to the mining server), SOCKS proxy hosts, and SSH tunnelling hosts, typically to access private IP spaces. Connections to SOCKS proxy hosts were typically carried out by TOR or compromised hosts with malicious activity carried out by a variety of techniques, including the rootkit Linux kernel module Diamorphine.

The recommendations of the European Grid Infrastructure Foundation involved removing the Diamorphine module, which involved multiple steps. The module Diamorphine starts invisible when loaded and requires a signal 63 to a random PID to become visible (signal 64 makes a given user root access). Any files or directories with the MAGIC_PREFIX also become invisible. Following these contents of cron jobs, a collection of files required checking for the hidden XMR mining binary. On the network side, the existing connections (lsoft) and NAT configurations (iptables) required reviewing and decompiling files (ghidra), leading to a privilege escalation as the attacker moved from one victim to another using compromised SSH credentials. The phrase "compromised SSH credentials" does not imply a weakness in SSH as such, but rather practices around SSH key use. As explicitly stated by system engineers, some researchers had been using private SSH keys without passcodes and leaving them in their home directories. These would be used by users to log in from one HPC system to another, as it is not unusual for researchers to have accounts on multiple systems. It is noted that users engaging in such an approach are either unaware of or ignored the principles of keeping a private key private, encrypting private keys, or making use of an SSH agent. Access to the keys could be achieved through inappropriate POSIX permissions, or more usual methods of access (e.g. ignoring policies of sharing accounts), with follow-up escalations. Passphraseless SSH keys are common as they are the default when creating a new key with ssh-keygen and are convenient to use, without needing to set up an ssh agent. Passphraseless SSH is also offered by default as part of many cloud offerings, as a relatively secure way to provide a new user with access to their virtual machines.

12.4 SSH POLICY AND IMPLEMENTATION

At the University of Melbourne, the HPC team took a two-stage approach for dealing with the potential of compromised SSH keys, consisting of policy-based user education and monitoring. There are further recommendations from the system engineers that will come under the section "further research". In terms of user education, recommendations were provided to over three thousand users of the Spartan system to use SSH agent forwarding and the process involved for encrypting private keys. While sub-optimal, agreement was reached to prohibit the storing of unencrypted private keys on the system. In terms of monitoring, considerations of several alternatives were made on how to test for encryption before settling on the ssh-keygen approach, which will be detailed further. It is also recognised that SSH agent forwarding does come with its own security risks when the integrity of a system is not trusted. Forwarded agent channels are independent of any sessions, and closing a session channel does not necessarily imply that forwarded connections are closed. Nevertheless, it is certainly preferable to having private keys on a public system.

In terms of policy, the use of this Spartan service is governed by the University's general regulations for IT resources. This includes responsibility for actions performed under a user ID, unless there is a system reason for a user ID breach. In other words, users are responsible for their ID security and must keep any passwords confidential and not disclose them. Obviously, still as a required statement, the use of systems is restricted by the law as a priority and with additional site-specific policies. For example, there is an absolute prohibition on "creating, transmitting, storing, downloading or possessing illegal material", but also on "the deliberate or reckless creation, transmission, storage, downloading, or display of any objectionable, defamatory, offensive or menacing images, data or other material which may incur legal liability to the University, or any data capable of being resolved into such images or material. An exception can be made in the case of the appropriate use of facilities for properly supervised University work or study purposes, for which a prior written approval must be obtained". Further, there is a prohibition on activities that place "an unreasonable burden" on the systems, including "cryptocurrency miners and similar applications".

In addition to these general University policies, there are specific policies for the use of the Spartan system, albeit the process can be quite informal. Some of these act almost in an object-orientated manner in terms of inheritance and polymorphism. For example, the "unreasonable burden" clause is invoked when users try to run compute jobs on one of the login nodes as HPC architecture means that this does represent a potential bottleneck. Like other HPC centres, one must use SSH to access Spartan. Spartan administrators also strongly recommend against the storing of SSH private keys on the system and prohibit the storing of unencrypted private keys.

As an aside on policy-driven actions, reference is made to the 2015 report of the Computer Security Division of NIST concerning access management with SSH. The report correctly identified that poor SSH access controls constituted a major security risk with the potential of enormous damage to operations, a matter which all system operators should already be aware of. In particular, the report argued that public key authentication is inherently more secure than other methods such as passwords, a matter which we will return to soon. Poorly managed SSH keys can be and have been used by attackers to penetrate IT infrastructure. In particular, the implementation of old or poorly configured SSH systems may allow for unauthorised access, including improper access controls (e.g. readable directories, storing private keys in public accessible directories), keys that have been lost or leaked, unaudited user keys that can be used to create a "backdoor", and most importantly, lack of knowledge and human errors. Institutional administrative procedures in organisations are a particular weakness, where the prospect for employees who have left the organisation or have been transferred may still have keys to systems that they should no longer have access to, or other unnecessary keys (e.g. system keys) remain on a system. A lack of key rotation was identified as a basic requirement for protecting credentials, and private keys without passphrase protection were explicitly identified.

Credit is also given to NIST for their recommendations for IT infrastructure management, which, of course, apply to any HPC centre. This includes stating and implementing clear and unambiguous SSH key management procedures, ensuring secure implementations of SSH, controlling identities and authorised keys, a regular regime of monitoring and auditing with inventory checking, automation, and user education. As a simple example, there should be an explicit statement against the use of the diffie-hellman-group1-sha1 key exchange, which is sufficiently small to be considered breakable. An extremely tight coupling is required between policy and implementation, to the extent that the two must be considered the same. A great number of policies, for example, should be represented as explicit commands in the sshd_config file or equivalent, which the SSH daemon will read for implementation. This will include keyword–argument pairs on whether agent forwarding is allowed, what groups or users are allowed or denied, whether TCP forwarding is allowed, what ciphers are allowed, and whether password authentication is allowed. Importantly, this will also include the location of the system's authorized_keys file, itself a prime candidate for automation through well-known provisioning tools (e.g. Puppet and Ansible).

12.5 SSH USER EDUCATION

User education of these policies by the HPC team at the University of Melbourne is encouraged through official system documentation and irregular system emails and is strongly implemented in the regular introductory training sessions that are conducted for the HPC service, as well for the Research Cloud, where SSH keys are requisite for managing and deploying virtual machines. It is to be noted, for example, that it is not necessary to have a private key on Spartan and indeed the practice is strongly recommended against, with preference given to the public key exchange mechanism described previously. Users are alerted to the fact that when they put their private key on a shared system or server, it means whoever has access to that system may have access to the private key and therefore may be able to impersonate that user. Instead, there is an explicit recommendation on the use of SSH agent forwarding, i.e.

```
$ ssh -A username@spartan.hpc.unimelb.edu.au
[lev@spartan-login1 ~]$ ssh othersystem@example.com
```

A second recommendation and part of user education is encrypting private keys. When keys are initially created, SSH requests the user whether they wish to enter a passphrase; however, this is not enforced and a user may establish their key without any encryption or with a weak and short password, rather than a passphrase with a higher level of entropy. Fortunately, existing private keys can be encrypted with the following command:

```
ssh-keygen -p -f keyfile
```

There is also the need for a strong recommendation to users to keep their SSH clients up to date with security releases. In the course of writing this document, for example, the version of the popular SSH client for MS-Windows systems, PuTTY, had a security flaw revealed on versions less than 0.75 where remote servers could cause a denial-of-service attack, by forcing the PuTTY window to change its title at high speed, forcing many SetWindowTextA or SetWindowTextW calls.

12.6   SSH MONITORING

Following the May 2020 attacks on European HPC systems with compromised HPC keys, system operators at the University of Melbourne explored means to detect user keys with empty passwords. The simple version took the form of using ssh-keygen to test against an SSH key with a random string with the exit status determining whether a private key was encrypted or not. If the key was encrypted, it is almost certain that SSH would respond with: "incorrect passphrase supplied to decrypt private key". The simple form of the script, superior to the initial consideration of running grep for "MII" and "ENCRYPTED" in the keys, was as follows:

```
SSH_ASKPASS=/bin/false ssh-keygen -y -f "${filename}"
 </dev/null 2>/dev/null
```

The complete version of the script will print all the unencrypted file names, even if they are named differently (i.e. other than id_rsa.pub and id_dsa.pub). Of course, it is quickly mentioned that if a malicious user has access to this script and that the permissions on the user's SSH directory has not been set correctly, then they will have access to such encrypted keys. Quite reasonably, however, if such a directory is already open the opportunity for malicious use already exists. The script starts by passing an empty password (-P "") to ssh-keygen because of ssh-keygen option parsing, so that -P will only be accepted if it is coupled with an extra argument. If there is no extra argument, then ssh-keygen will bail out immediately; it won't even try opening the key file to check things out. The script takes the following form:

```
#!/bin/bash
TOPDIR=/home
while read d; do
        if [ ! -e "$TOPDIR/$d/.ssh" ]; then
        continue;
        fi
        cd $TOPDIR/$d/.ssh;
        files=""
```

```
user=""
while read file; do
        ssh-keygen -y -P "" -f $file 2>/dev/null
         >/dev/null;
        if [ $? -eq 0 ]; then
                echo "$TOPDIR/$d/.ssh/$file"
        fi
done < <(grep -rli "begin.*private key" * 2>
/dev/null)
done
```

It is worth noting that the script uses grep -rli to capture those instances when users need to switch between multiple keys and make use of an IdentityFile in their .ssh config or similar. If the keys are in another non-standard directory other than .ssh, parsing the config should also be considered to determine their location, certainly in preference to searching through entire/home or, worse still, shared project directories, recognising that it is legitimate to have authorized_keys or authorized_keys2 in a custom location. System operators must be aware that they should never underestimate the potential for a user to leave an unencrypted private key somewhere on the system that they have access to. Nevertheless, in a more sane sense, an entry will look similar to the following:

```
IdentityFile ~/.ssh/keys/id_ed25519
IdentitiesOnly yes
```

One issue with the script is that it works mainly for rsa/dsa keys and will not work on newer key formats. For example, it will not determine whether the following key has a passphrase or not:

```
-----BEGIN OPENSSH PRIVATE KEY-----
b3BlbnNzaC1rZXktdjEAAAAACmFlczI1Ni1jdHIAAAAGYmNyeXB0AAAAGA
AAABCFnJ+yNBRw6JkUyED823GdAAAAEAAAAAEAAAAzAAAAC3NzaC11ZDI1
NTE5AAAAIFhazP8p7JUmJrSdV34EU6vLP6LDFr6Q2Kyl6nniqHFCAAAAkB
s6oF/4XMOyVGnEOPWqYchfn+OIanG4PPR4WiNOswdyCPtsnnVzkLnLQy+a
QzkAbpsKbnFsR+gCj25MVRdzVedBNv11+eb8R1MPH5apsJJqRLWli4vkQ5
O2TckdxBP8svuxSPImTLOEAtBxjdJN5ehnZ5zEmsjcr9+Y2HqOFCkio29c
yA2R4EvWoGubqgXrAw==
-----END OPENSSH PRIVATE KEY-----
```

A further alternative is a test making direct use of libssh headers. This, however, will require a version of libssh which incorporates the new SSH format, which is atypical for HPC systems which tend to have a degree of stability in the operating system level, even if they make use of diverse versions and compilers on the application level. This was discovered with a test of a local RSA key via OpenSSH 8.4 without a passphrase. The copy of key_audit on Spartan responded that the key was good, but the local key_audit detects that the key has no passphrase locally, libssh was using 0.9.5, but on Spartan HPC, the system libssh was 0.7.1. As we did not want a book chapter entitled "How we put our HPC in the Top500 by Changing to a Rolling Release Distro", alternatives were sought. Of course, invoking a different version of libssh (e.g. through an environment modules approach) provides an alternative solution which can be incorporated into a small C program (key_audit.c, compile with `gcc -o key_audit -lssh key_audit.c`), which elegantly tests validation of an empty passphrase against a given keyfile. At the University of Melbourne, we recommend the use of EasyBuild. The following is the key_audit.c code, plus the EasyBuild script for libssh, and the sample code for such an installation is preceded by the key_audit.c code.

```
easyblock = 'CMakeMake'
name = 'libssh'
version = '0.9.0'
homepage = 'https://www.libssh.org'
description = """Multiplatform C library implementing the
               SSHv2 protocol on client and server side"""
toolchain = {'name': 'GCCcore', 'version': '6.4.0'}
toolchainopts = {'pic': True}
source_urls = ['https://www.libssh.org/files/0.9/']
sources = ['%(name)s-%(version)s.tar.xz']
checksums = ['25303c2995e663cd169fdd902bae88106f48242d7e96
              311d74f812023482c7a5']
osdependencies = [('openssl-devel', 'libssl-dev',
                   'libopenssl-devel')]
builddependencies = [
    ('CMake', '3.12.1'),
    ('binutils', '2.28'),
]
```

```
separate_build_dir = True
sanity_check_paths = {
    'files': ['include/libssh/callbacks.h',
              'include/libssh/legacy.h',
              'include/libssh/libssh.h',
              'include/libssh/libsshpp.hpp',
              'include/libssh/server.h',
              'include/libssh/sftp.h',
              'include/libssh/ssh2.h',
              'lib/libssh.so',
              'lib/libssh.so.4',
              'lib/libssh.so.4.8.1',
              'lib/pkgconfig/libssh.pc'],
    'dirs': ['include/libssh', 'lib/pkgconfig',
             'lib/cmake/libssh'],
}

moduleclass = 'tools'
```

It is a relatively easy process to update the version of libssh to either of the newer versions. The program has been released under a GPL and is available at: https://notabug.org/cryptarch/key_audit

```
#include <stdio.h>
#include <string.h>
#include <libssh/libssh.h>

const char *usage = "Usage: key_audit [-h]
                     /path/to/.ssh/key";

int main(int argc, char **argv) {
    if(argc != 2) {
        fprintf(stderr, "%s\n", usage);
        return 1;
    }
    if(strncmp(argv[1], "-h", 4) == 0) {
        printf("%s\n", usage);
        return 0;
    }
```

```
    ssh_key privkey;
    // This returns 0 if the file does not exist, which is
okay if we regard non-existent keys as secure.
    return ssh_pki_import_privkey_file(argv[1], "",
NULL, NULL, &privkey) ? 0 : 1;
}
```

A simple test against keys without a passphrase illustrates the use:

```
$ key_audit /home/dummy/.ssh/id_ed25519 && echo good
|| echo bad
bad
$ grep -rli 'begin.*private key' /home/*/.ssh/ | while
read k; do key_audit "$k" || printf "%s\n" "$k"; done
/home/dummy/.ssh/id_ed25519
```

For monitoring, such programs are extremely efficient; a test of more than 3,000 user accounts takes <1.5 seconds on a contemporary system. Following this, the use of inotifywait can be applied so that any new insecure keys would be detected immediately instead of waiting for a cron task to initiate. The system can be further strengthened by using SSH key-only logins, rather than allowing for password authentication, or restricting password authentication to VPN logins only with sshd_config and two-factor authentication. Prevention of shared private keys is achieved by checking for duplications in the authorized_keys file. Further, with authorized_keys managed through a repository with version control (e.g. GitHub and GitLab), another layer of protection would exist to prevent multiple users to log in with the same key. Each key would be a separate file named after its own checksum and use an AuthorizedKeysCommand directive.

12.7   CONCLUDING REMARKS AND FURTHER RESEARCH

The security of SSH as a public key system is well recognised by system operators, with few potential security risks when implemented properly. The greatest compromise risk, as illustrated, is primarily due to poor implementation by users, such as sharing passwords and login details, having weak passwords instead of passphrases, using password authentication instead of a paired-key exchange, using private keys on a shared and public system rather than using SSH agent forwarding, and not encrypting private keys. Given the relative lack of knowledge of users compared to system operators, it is highly recommended that a two-pronged approach is used for enhanced SSH security, including user education and implementing processes driven by informed policy.

The phrase "informed policy" is chosen quite deliberately. Managers, for example, are often even less informed than users. For example, one of the authors spoke of a colleague who was forced by their management to install a shared private key on a public server for reasons of convenience despite the oxymoronic situation of something being "shared" and "private". Due to the imbalance in employment power and responsibility, the system operator grudgingly complied: "Technology is dominated by two types of people: those who understand what they do not manage and those who manage what they do not understand" (Archibald Putt, *"Putt's Law and the Successful Technocrat"*, 2006).

This harkens to an SEC Consult study of 2015 of some 4,000 firmware images for embedded devices from some 70 manufacturers, which revealed over 500 keys for SSH and HTTPS, many of them shared between multiple devices from the same vendor or even from different ones. These thousands of images were in use of millions of Internet devices, including routers, modems, IP cameras, and VoIP phones. One wonders whether this situation occurred from a lack of managerial oversight, or because of it. This, of course, should be the subject of further research as it is well outside the scope of this document. However, it will make for a fascinating enquiry to determine to what degree those who manage IT security systems force operators, contrary to their expressed expert considerations, to implement insecure systems, even if this is limited to the HPC or SSH space.

One related subject could also be when management assigns external parties to audit existing security policies, when the auditors themselves are not particularly well versed in the security procedures for HPC or SSH. In the course of this study, this was the experience of operators at the institution in question when a well-known "enterprise" auditing company recommended the use of password logins in preference to key exchange under the guise of security. The authors reiterate the well-known position that passphrase-protected keys are more secure than passphrases, and passphrases are more secure than passwords. Apart from their increased security, they also are more convenient. Key-only logins is certainly an approach that HPC centres should seriously consider.

Assuming that policy preference is based on informed and deliberated technical considerations, further research in this area would involve developing a university-wide API offering public keys for arbitrary ssh logins for various systems on the campus, which is certainly preferable to the inconvenience of multi-factor authentication systems and, naturally enough, the block that they impose for scripted systems administration across multiple systems. Access to systems could also be implemented via a zero trust security framework (e.g. BeyondCorp), which would both protect systems from intruders who are already within a network perimeter, and provide secure access to users who are outside it.

However, multi-factor authentication as it is usually understood is redundant if key pair authentication is in use. Where private keys exist, that already covers the "something you have" authorisation element, and needing to know the right user name to go with a given key covers "something you know". If you think that "something you know" should be a little stronger, recall that personal identification numbers used for identifying yourself to EFTPOS or ATMs are routinely only four digits; the strength of the system comes from coupling the PIN with a physical card, just as user names are coupled with private keys in ssh authentication. Keys can be stored for user accounts, which are used for git clone actions, pull requests, etc.

To address concerns about users sharing private keys with each other, it would be straightforward to use the sshd AuthorizedKeysCommand configuration option to ensure uniqueness of keys. Rather than using an ~/.ssh/authorized_keys file, you could place all public keys in a central repository, one key per file. Name each key after its own checksum to prevent duplicate keys from being added, and have each key owned by whoever first added it. If anyone else tried to add the same key later, it would generate a collision since the filename would be necessarily identical, but the user would be different. Although this system could be managed manually by any HPC admin, it would be trivial to create a web interface, similar to the way keys are added in GitHub or GitLab. The user submits the public key via the web, and a server-side script then creates the file under /etc/ssh/authorized_keys and changes the ownership to match the user. The AuthorizedKeysCommand directive would then be as simple as:

```
#! /bin/bash
[[ $# -gt 0 ]] || exit 1
find /etc/ssh/authorized_keys/ -type f -user "$1"
-exec cat {} +
```

Appropriate permissions and access controls on /etc/ssh/authorized_ keys would make the keys readable to sshd while preventing users from editing the filename or key contents directly.

Of course, all of this would require implementing test cases, along with a substantial change in policy orientation at a large institution as well as the implementation of the necessary infrastructure. However, the overall project is founded on sound principles, and while there would be an initial hurdle of user education, the combination of convenience, reduced costs of implementation and operation, and increased security should make the proposal quite enticing to institutional IT managers who understand the concepts and value.

Overall, SSH is a very well-established and well-developed protocol and suite of utilities in the world of high-performance computing, to the point where it is ubiquitous in such an environment, and an exploration of its features and history as well as basic use from a user perspective has been provided here. It was the particular example of a security breach in European HPC centres in 2020 that led the authors to exploring the possibilities of how to engage in policy, user education, and developing monitoring systems to protect against a similar instance in their own environment with knowledge that is transferable to others. In the course of developing such systems, the possibility for further and wider use of key-based SSH for enhanced security and convenience has also been raised as a future research project. It is hoped that others too will take up such a project with a similar orientation, harkening back to an initial consideration; if SSH is so good, why aren't we using it everywhere? It would seem that only a lack of knowledge and a lack of will.

REFERENCES

[1] Central Intelligence Agency Information Operations Center, BothanSpy v1.0 Tool Documentation, WikiLeaks, July 6, 2017 [FP 2015]. https://wikileaks.org/vault7/#BothanSpy.

[2] Central Intelligence Agency Information Operations Center, Gyr-falcon v2.0 User's Guide, WikiLeaks, July 6, 2017 [FP 2013]. https://wikileaks.org/vault7/#BothanSpy.

[3] Christopher R. Russel, Penetration testing with dsniff, February 18, 2001. http://www.ouah.org/dsniffintr.htm.

[4] Computer Security Division of NIST, "Security of interactive and automated access management using Secure Shell (SSH)", Interagency report 7966 (NISTIR 7966), 2015.

[5] Daniel J. Barrett, Richard E. Silverman, Robert G. Byrnes, *SSH: The Secure Shell (The Definitive Guide)*, 2nd edition. Newton, MA: O'Reilly, 2005.

[6] David Adrian, Karthikeyan Bhargavan, Zakir Durumeric, Pierrick Gaudry, Matthew Green, J. Alex Halderman, Nadia Heninger, Drew Springall, Emmanuel Thomé, Luke Valenta, Benjamin VanderSloot, Eric Wustrow, Santiago Zanella-Béguelin, and Paul Zimmermann, "Imperfect forward secrecy: How Diffie-Hellman fails in practice", *22nd ACM Conference on Computer and Communications Security (CCS'15)*, Denver, CO, October 2015.

[7] EGI Computer Security and Incident Response Team, Attacks on multiple HPC sites, Incident #EGI20200421, Incident #EGI2020512, 2020. https://csirt.egi.eu/attacks-on-multiple-hpc-sites/.

[8] Joe Testa, Timothy Brush, and Manfred Kaiser et al., ssh-mitm, 17 September 2019 [FP May 16, 2017]. https://github.com/jtesta/ssh-mitm.

[9] Lev Lafayette, Greg Sauter, Linh Vu, and Bernard Meade, "Spartan: Performance and flexibility: An HPC-cloud chimera," *Proceedings of the OpenStack Summit*, Barcelona, 2016.

[10] SEC Consult, House of keys: Industry-wide HTTPS certificate and SSH key reuse endangers millions of devices worldwide, November 25, 2015.

[11] Tatu Ylönen, "Announcement: SSH (Secure Shell) remote login program." Usenet comp.security.unix, 12 July 1995. blog.sec-consult.com/2015/11/house-of-keys-industry-wide-https.html.

[12] Vasilios Mavroudis, Andrea Cerulli, and Petr Svenda, Dan Cvrcek, Dusan Klinec, and George Danezis, "A touch of evil: High-assurance cryptographic hardware from untrusted components," *Proceedings of the 2017 ACM SIGSAC Conference on Computer and Communications Security*, Fairfax, VA, 2017.

Index

Note: **Bold** page numbers refer to tables; *italic* page numbers refer to figures.